15th Edition

The Employer's Legal Handbook

Attorney Fred S. Steingold
& Aaron Hotfelder, J.D.

FIFTEENTH EDITION	JULY 2021
Editor	AARON HOTFELDER
Legal Research	JESSICA GILLESPIE & CHRISTOPHER BARTA
Cover Design	SUSAN PUTNEY
Book Design	SUSAN PUTNEY
Proofreading	JOCELYN TRUITT
Index	RICHARD GENOVA
Printing	BANG PRINTING

ISSN 2163-033X (print)
ISSN 2326-7984 (online)

ISBN 978-1-4133-2882-0 (pbk)
ISBN 978-1-4133-2883-7 (ebook)

This book covers only United States law, unless it specifically states otherwise.

Please note

We know that accurate, plain-English legal information can help you solve many of your own legal problems. But this text is not a substitute for personalized advice from a knowledgeable lawyer. If you want the help of a trained professional—and we'll always point out situations in which we think that's a good idea—consult an attorney licensed to practice in your state.

Get Updates and More on Nolo.com

Go to this book's companion page at:

www.nolo.com/back-of-book/EMPL.html

When there's an important change to the law affecting this book, we'll
post updates. You'll also find articles and other related materials.

More Resources
from Nolo.com

Legal Forms, Books, & Software
Hundreds of do-it-yourself products—all written in plain English,
approved, and updated by our in-house legal editors.

Legal Articles
Get informed with thousands of free articles on everyday legal
topics. Our articles are accurate, up to date, and reader friendly.

Find a Lawyer
Want to talk to a lawyer? Use Nolo to find a lawyer who can
help you with your case.

NOLO
LAW for ALL

Acknowledgments

Special thanks to Jessica Gillespie and Chris Barta for their dogged work updating and compiling the 50-state charts that appear at the back of this book. I also owe a huge debt to my coauthor, the late Fred Steingold, who made this book what it is.

Finally, I'd like to thank my wife for her love and support—and for her helpful suggestion that I should read this book to our toddler whenever he can't fall asleep.

—Aaron Hotfelder

About the Authors

Fred S. Steingold practiced law in Ann Arbor, Michigan, until his death in 2017. He represented and advised many small businesses and frequently led seminars on how to start and run a small business. He was the author of several books published by Nolo, including *Legal Guide for Starting & Running a Small Business* and *Legal Forms for Starting & Running a Small Business.*

Aaron Hotfelder is Nolo's employment law editor. He has edited a number of Nolo titles, including *The Manager's Legal Handbook, Working With Independent Contractors,* and *Dealing With Problem Employees.* Prior to joining Nolo, he practiced law at a firm in Columbia, Missouri, and worked as an employment law specialist for a human resources compliance firm. He received his law degree in 2010 from the University of Missouri School of Law.

Table of Contents

All the Law Employers Need to Know

For more than 25 years, *The Employer's Legal Handbook* has been the go-to resource for thousands of employers seeking authoritative answers to workplace questions, quickly and easily. This comprehensive guide, now in its 15th edition, covers, in plain English, all the latest employment law issues you need to know about, including:

- legal guidelines for interviewing, screening, and hiring employees
- best personnel practices—employee files, handbooks, performance reviews, and discipline
- managing remote employees
- wage and hour laws—requirements for overtime, minimum wage, and equal pay
- health care insurance and other employee benefits
- employee taxes and deductions
- workers' compensation and employee health and safety, including issues related to COVID-19
- family and medical leave
- illegal harassment and discrimination, and special issues for workers with disabilities
- guidelines for terminating, laying off, or firing employees
- employee privacy, including policies for Internet and social media use, and
- independent contractors, unions, employment lawyers, and much more.

The Employer's Legal Handbook will help you run an efficient, fair workplace by staying on top of the myriad and frequently changing employment laws. Knowing how employment laws affect your business will help you cut the number of expensive visits or calls you'd otherwise make to a lawyer's office and reduce the risks of costly lawsuits. Your employees will appreciate being treated fairly, and you'll save time, money, and hassles—it's a true win-win.

Get Employment Law Updates on Nolo.com

Statutes and regulations in the area of employment law change regularly. Congress and state legislatures pass new legislation; courts strike down existing laws; and governmental agencies—such as the Department of Labor, the Equal Employment Opportunity Commission, the National Labor Relations Board, and more—write new regulations and issue updated guidance and advisory opinions. It's important for employers to stay up to date on these developments so they understand their rights and obligations.

When there are important changes to the information in this book, we'll post updates online, on a page dedicated to this book:

www.nolo.com/back-of-book/EMPL.html

Hiring

Many state and federal laws—as well as countless court decisions—set out legal protocol for every phase of the employment relationship, including the hiring process. If you've correctly sensed that many workers today are well informed about their legal rights and are willing to fight to enforce them, you may be concerned about making costly mistakes during hiring.

Fortunately, you can steer clear of most of the legal perils of hiring employees by understanding and following these sensible guidelines:

- Avoid illegal discrimination.
- Respect each applicant's privacy rights.
- Don't promise job security unless you mean it.
- Protect against unfair competition.
- Observe the legal rules for hiring young workers and immigrants.

The first part of this chapter discusses these key principles, some of which apply throughout the employment relationship and are discussed elsewhere in this book as well.

The rest of the chapter will explain how to keep legal risks to a minimum as you write job descriptions, advertise for workers, design job applications, interview applicants, check into their backgrounds, and offer them jobs.

> **RELATED TOPIC**
>
> **Hiring independent contractors?** Consult Chapter 12, where you'll find a detailed discussion of the legal and practical issues you'll have to consider.

Legal Guidelines for Hiring Employees

Most large companies maintain human resource departments and in-house lawyers to lead them through the intricacies of employment law. If you run a small or midsized company, however, this is an unaffordable luxury. In either case, the guidelines discussed here should reduce your need for outside legal help when hiring employees.

Avoiding Illegal Discrimination

Federal and state laws prohibit all but the smallest employers from discriminating against an employee or applicant because of race, color, gender, sexual orientation, gender identity, religious beliefs, national origin, disability, age, or genetic information. Also, many states and cities have laws prohibiting employment discrimination based on other criteria, such as marital status or military service.

These antidiscrimination laws—covered in depth in Chapters 8 and 9—apply to all stages of the employment process: preparing job descriptions, writing ads, conducting interviews, deciding whom to hire, setting salaries and job benefits, promoting employees, and disciplining and firing them.

Federal laws apply only to employers who have more than a certain number of employees, which differs for each antidiscrimination law. And many state laws apply to smaller employers who are not covered by the federal laws. To find out whether your business must comply with these laws, see Chapters 8 and 9.

A particular form of discrimination becomes illegal when Congress, a state legislature, or a city council decides that a characteristic—race, for example—bears no legitimate relationship to employment decisions. A law or an ordinance is then passed prohibiting workplace discrimination based on that characteristic, making the characteristic protected. Courts get involved, too, by interpreting and applying antidiscrimination laws and ordinances. Obviously, as an employer, you need to know what types of discrimination are illegal.

At the same time, however, antidiscrimination laws don't dictate whom you must hire. You can exercise discretion based on a wide range of business considerations. You remain free, for example, to hire, promote, discipline, and fire employees and to set their salaries based on their skills, experience, performance, or reliability, or even on your whim. You risk violating antidiscrimination laws only when you treat a person or a group differently for reasons that are based on a protected characteristic.

Some illegal practices are obvious, such as advertising a job for people ages 20 to 30 or paying lower wages to women than men. Other types of discrimination are more subtle, but just as illegal. Employment practices that have a disproportionate and discriminatory impact on protected groups are also barred by antidiscrimination laws. For example, if your primary means of seeking job candidates is through word of mouth and your workforce consists entirely of white men, the word-of-mouth system could constitute illegal discrimination if it results in an applicant pool of mostly white men. The effect of the procedures is what counts, even if you did not intend to discriminate.

To avoid violating antidiscrimination laws at the hiring stage, you should do all of the following:

- Advertise job openings in a variety of places so they come to the attention of a wide pool of applicants.
- Determine which skills, education, and other attributes are truly necessary to perform the job so that you don't impose job requirements that unnecessarily exclude capable applicants.
- Avoid application forms and screening techniques that have an unfair impact on any group of applicants.

Running afoul of antidiscrimination laws can be both time consuming and costly. An unhappy employee or applicant may sue your business. Federal and state agencies also may take legal action against it. And publicity about a violation of antidiscrimination laws can adversely affect your business reputation, driving down revenues. If word gets out that a company has discriminated against female employees, for example, female customers may avoid dealing with the company long after the discriminatory practices have been dropped.

Respecting Applicants' Privacy Rights

As an employer, you likely believe that the more information you have about job applicants, the better your hiring decisions will be. But there's a potential problem in delving too deeply. Your desire to gather information about an applicant may conflict with the applicant's right to privacy or violate federal and state laws.

For example, a number of laws regulate how and when you can request transcripts, credit reports, and other background information. In addition, many states have laws that prohibit you from requesting or requiring the social media account passwords of a job applicant or employee. Laws and court rulings also restrict your right to screen applicants through aptitude tests and drug tests. We discuss those issues more fully below.

You need to be careful, too, about rejecting applicants because of their off-duty, nonwork activities. It's easy to understand why you might want to limit your payroll to people who don't smoke, drink alcohol, or use drugs—even off the job—to hold down health care costs or to keep a harmonious workforce. But, depending on your state, you may not be allowed to dictate such off-the-job behavior. Where legal restrictions are in place, screening out applicants based on off-duty conduct can get you into trouble.

Even if you're in a state where it's legal to reject applicants based on their lifestyles or their conduct away from work, caution is in order. To be on safe legal ground, it's best to avoid rejecting an applicant for lifestyle reasons or off-duty conduct unless you have a convincing business purpose. And, even then, be sure to apply your selection criteria evenhandedly.

Avoiding False Promises of Job Security

If there's no contract for a fixed term of employment, an employee works at the will of the employer and employee. The employer can fire the employee at any time—and the employee is free to quit at any time—for any reason or for no reason at all. That's the basic law, although you can't fire someone for an illegal reason: because of the employee's sexual orientation, for example, or because you prefer to put a younger person in the job.

> **CAUTION**
>
> **The rules are different in Montana.** There, an employee is at will only during the "probationary period": the first six months of the employment relationship, unless the employer specifies a different probationary period while hiring. After the probationary period is over, the employer must have "good cause" to fire the employee, defined as "reasonable job-related grounds for dismissal based on a failure to satisfactorily perform job duties, disruption of the employer's operation, or other legitimate business reason."

The at-will relationship gives you maximum freedom to fire employees, but preserving your legal right to fire at will can be tricky. Courts in many states have held that if employers are not careful about what they tell employees, what they write in employee handbooks, and what they say in documents, letters, and emails, they may lose that right. For example:

- A law firm hires Joan as a receptionist. The managing partner assures her that she will remain employed as long as she does a good job. Eight months later, Joan is fired. She sues the firm. The judge says that the managing partner's assurance created a contract that the firm would fire Joan only for a legitimate business reason. The firm doesn't come up with a good business reason for the firing, so Joan is entitled to damages for breach of contract.

- A restaurant hires Henry as its general manager and gives him an employee handbook. The handbook says that the restaurant can fire an employee only after warnings are given and disciplinary procedures are followed. Later, the restaurant fires Henry without warning and without following the disciplinary steps outlined in the handbook. Henry has a solid basis for suing the restaurant for wrongful discharge.

During the hiring process, don't make promises that you may not be able to honor. It can be difficult to restrain yourself when you're trying hard to entice an attractive candidate to join your workforce. You'll have a natural tendency to say positive things about your business, the candidate, and the future employment relationship. But those upbeat statements can be turned against you if your promises don't come true or if the employee is later fired.

Your best protection is to make sure your application forms, employee handbooks, and offers of employment state that the job is at will and to require the applicant to acknowledge this in writing. This will protect your right to terminate the employment relationship on your own terms, without legal repercussions.

Here's an example of language you may wish to include in your job application form regarding at-will employment.

At-Will Employment. I acknowledge that if hired, I will be an at-will employee, subject to dismissal or discipline without notice or cause, at the discretion of the employer. I also understand that this means I am free to quit my employment at any time, for any reason, without notice. I understand that no representative of the company, other than the president, has authority to change the terms of the at-will relationship and that any such change can occur only in a written contract.

Jno
Initials

Another way to protect yourself is to make sure that you always have a good business-related reason for firing an employee. In legal parlance, this is called firing "for cause." If you fire for cause, the firing will be lawful, even if a court later finds that the employee was not an at-will employee after all.

Prevent Negligent Hiring Claims

The main reason to investigate an applicant's background is to make sure the person will do a good job for you and fit in with your other employees. But sometimes there's an additional, equally powerful reason to conduct a thorough investigation. When you hire someone for a position that may expose customers or others to danger, you must use special care in checking references and other background information.

Legally, you may have a duty to protect your customers, clients, visitors, and members of the general public from injury caused by employees whom you know, or should know, pose a risk of harm to others. In some states, you may also have a duty to protect other employees from an employee whom you know—or should know—is dangerous. If someone gets hurt or has property stolen or damaged by an employee whose background you didn't check carefully, you might be subject to a lawsuit for negligent hiring.

Be especially vigilant when hiring maintenance workers and delivery drivers, whose jobs give them easy access to people's homes.

> **EXAMPLE:** The Village Green, a 200-unit apartment complex, hires Elton as a maintenance worker and gives him a master key. Elton enters an apartment and sexually molests a young girl while the child's parents are running an errand. Had the company checked before hiring Elton, it would have discovered that Elton had just completed a prison term for a sexual offense. The child's parents sue The Village Green for negligent hiring.

Doing a background check can be a delicate matter, because you are also legally required to respect the applicant's privacy. If you hire people for sensitive jobs, you must investigate their backgrounds as thoroughly as possible, without stepping over the line and violating their privacy rights. You can be faulted for not looking into an applicant's criminal convictions, but not for failing to learn about prior arrests that didn't result in convictions, because such arrest records are often protected by privacy laws.

In doing background checks on applicants for sensitive jobs, check for felony convictions. Also, be diligent in contacting all previous employers. Keep a written record of your investigation efforts. Insist that the applicant explain any gaps in employment history. Consider turning over the prehire investigation to professionals who do this for a living. If you choose to follow this route—and can afford it—it can go a long way toward refuting later claims that you failed to use reasonable efforts to learn about the employee's history.

> **CAUTION**
>
> **Strict rules may apply to background checks.** Any time you hire a business—such as a credit bureau or investigative agency—to gather information about applicants (or employees), you must follow the strict guidelines set forth in the Fair Credit Reporting Act or FCRA. (15 U.S.C. §§ 1681 and following.) This federal law requires you to, among other things, get the applicant's consent to the investigation and give the applicant a copy of the investigative report if you decide not to hire the applicant based on its contents.

Protect Against Unfair Competition

Whenever you hire workers, you run the risk that they'll later start a competing business or go to work for a competitor. If so, they may use information or contacts they gained at your workplace to draw away business that otherwise would be yours.

Obviously, you don't need to be too concerned about the employee you hire to flip hamburgers or the clerk you hire to handle dry cleaning orders. But employees who have access to inside information about product pricing or business expansion plans, for example, may pose competitive risks. The same goes for employees who serve valuable and hard-won customers, such as the salesperson who handles your largest accounts.

You can help protect your business from unfair competition by asking new hires to sign agreements not to take or disclose trade secrets and other confidential information. You can also ask select employees to sign covenants not to compete with your business. Such covenants must be carefully written so that a former employee has a reasonable chance to earn a living, however, and they aren't legal in all states.

Trade Secrets

In hiring and working with employees, some business owners need to protect their unique assets from misuse. Some possibly protectable business assets may include, for example:

- a restaurant's recipes for a special salad dressing and a muffin that draw people from miles away
- a heating and cooling company's list of 500 customers for whom it regularly provides maintenance, or
- a computer company's unique process for speedily assembling computer boards.

If they are treated as such, the recipes, the customer list, and the assembly process are all trade secrets. Other examples are an unpatented invention, engineering techniques, cost data, a formula, or a machine. To qualify for trade secret protection, your business information must meet two requirements.

First, you must show that you've taken steps to keep the information secret by, for example:

- keeping it in a secure place such as a locked cabinet or password-protected database
- giving employees access to it on a need-to-know basis only
- informing employees that the information is proprietary, and
- requiring employees to acknowledge in writing that the information is a trade secret.

> **EXAMPLE:** Violet works at Speedy Copy Shop. She has daily access to the list of larger accounts that are regularly billed more than $2,000 per month. Violet quits to open her own competing shop. Before she does, she copies the list of major accounts. One of her first steps in getting her new business going is to try to get their business away from her former employer. Speedy sues Violet for stealing its trade secret. At trial, Speedy shows that it keeps the list in a secure place and permits access only to selected employees who need the information. In light of these precautions, the judge orders Violet not to contact the customers on the list and requires her to compensate Speedy for any profits she has already earned on those accounts.

Second, the information must not be freely available from other sources. Trade secrets lose their protected status if they are published or disclosed to the public. For example, if the recipe for a restaurant's award-winning custard tart can be found in a standard American cookbook or is readily available on the Internet, it's no longer a trade secret. On the other hand, a publication that is brief, temporary, or obscure will not cause a trade secret to lose its protected status. For example, if the restaurant's chef found the recipe in a medieval French cookbook in a provincial museum, translated it, and figured out how to adapt it to currently available ingredients, that is probably obscure enough that the trade secret will still be protected.

In addition to the requirements that a trade secret must be guarded information that is not generally available, judges sometimes look at how valuable the information is to you and your competitors and how much money and effort you spent in developing the trade secret.

Covenants Not to Compete

To prevent employees from competing with you after leaving your workplace, consider having them sign a covenant not to compete (also called a noncompete agreement). In a typical noncompete, the employee agrees not to become an owner or employee of a business that competes with yours for a specific period of time in a specific location.

The best time to secure a covenant not to compete is when you hire an employee. An employee who is already on the payroll may be more reluctant to sign anything. You'll also have less leverage to negotiate the agreement.

CAUTION

Not all states honor noncompete agreements. Noncompete agreements can be difficult—or impossible—to enforce. In California, for example, courts virtually never enforce noncompete agreements, and other states enforce noncompetes only in limited circumstances. Even in the states where they are enforced, it's often hard to overcome a judge's reluctance to interfere with an employee's ability to earn a living. One way around this potential uphill battle is to ask employees instead to sign a nonsolicitation agreement and a nondisclosure agreement. Some courts are more willing to enforce these agreements because they are less restrictive. They can keep ex-employees from using your client or customer lists, luring employees to a competing business, or stealing your trade secrets. If you can get all of these protections, you don't lose much by forgoing a noncompete agreement.

Battles over the legality of these agreements must usually be resolved in court. Judges are reluctant to deprive people of their rights to earn a living, so the key to a legally enforceable covenant not to compete is to make its terms reasonable. In evaluating whether a covenant not to compete is reasonable, focus on these three questions:

- **Is there a legitimate business reason for restricting the future activities of the particular employee?** There probably is if you expect to spend significant time and money training a high-level employee and plan to entrust the employee with sensitive contacts on lucrative accounts. Such an employee could easily—and unfairly—hurt your business by competing with you. This would motivate a judge to find that you have a legitimate business reason for the covenant. On the other hand, if you require a new receptionist or typist to sign a similar covenant, a judge would probably find that you have no valid business purpose for restricting the employee's ability to work elsewhere.
- **Is the covenant reasonably limited in time?** Agreements lasting a year or two are more likely to be upheld than agreements stretching well into the future.
- **Is the covenant reasonably limited as to geographic scope?** A limit spanning several states might not be deemed reasonable, but you may be able to prohibit an employee from competing within your city limits or larger urban area.

EXAMPLE: When Mary hires Sid to be the office manager for her profitable travel agency, she realizes that Sid will have access to major corporate accounts and daily contact with the corporate managers who make travel arrangements. Mary also knows that she'll spend considerable time training Sid and invest more than $4,000 in specialized seminars that she will require Sid to attend. She asks Sid to sign a covenant not to compete in which Sid promises that while working for Mary and for two years afterward, he won't work for or own a travel agency within 50 miles of Mary's agency. After six months, Sid quits and starts a competing agency one mile from Mary's. The judge enforces the covenant not to compete by forbidding Sid from operating his new business and by awarding damages to Mary.

Hiring Young Workers

Federal and state laws restrict your right to hire workers who are younger than 18 years old. These laws limit the type of work for which young people may be hired and the hours they may work. (See Chapter 3 for more information.)

Hiring Immigrants

Federal law prohibits hiring workers not authorized to work in the United States. You and each new employee are required to complete IRS Form I-9, *Employment Eligibility Verification* (discussed below).

Job Descriptions

Write a job description for each position you're seeking to fill. Listing the skills and attributes you're looking for in applicants will make the hiring process more objective. It will also give you ready standards to measure which applicants are most qualified. Current employees can often help you write job descriptions. They know how the business operates and the kind of skills that are needed.

In writing job descriptions, be careful not to violate the laws that prohibit discrimination in employment.

Under federal law, you can't discriminate against applicants on the basis of their race, skin color, gender, sexual orientation, transgender status, religious beliefs, national origin, disability, age (if the applicant is at least 40 years old), pregnancy, or genetic information.

In addition, many states prohibit discrimination based on a variety of other characteristics, including marital status and military veteran status. To learn about laws prohibiting discrimination in employment, see Chapter 8.

Necessary Elements

A well-drafted job description usually contains these components:

- **Qualifications, such as necessary skills, education, experience, and licenses.** Be careful in setting requirements for education and experience. If set too high for the job, your requirements may have an unintended discriminatory effect on groups protected by antidiscrimination laws.
- **Essential job functions.** The federal Americans with Disabilities Act (ADA) has forced employers to take a fresh look at job descriptions and decide what really is the core of each job. (For more on the ADA, see Chapter 9.) To help eliminate unfair discrimination against people with disabilities, the ADA seeks to make sure a person isn't excluded from a job simply because the individual can't perform some marginal duties listed in a job description. For example, suppose your job description for a file clerk includes lifting heavy boxes of office supplies, but the basic functions of the job are to file and retrieve written materials. Employees who work in the mail room usually handle the boxes of office supplies. Someone with an injured back may have a lifting restriction that precludes moving the boxes, but be perfectly able to file and retrieve papers. Lifting the boxes isn't an essential job function and shouldn't be listed as one.
- **Nonessential job functions.** You may wish to specify functions and duties that are desirable but not required for a particular job. That's okay as long as the job description clearly states that these additional functions and duties are not job requirements. Suppose you're seeking a receptionist. If you never or seldom require the receptionist to type, typing isn't an essential function. You could, however, mention typing as a desirable function if you made it clear that it's not required.

RESOURCE
Want help writing job descriptions? Check out *The Job Description Handbook*, by Margie Mader-Clark (Nolo), which provides step-by-step instructions for crafting effective job descriptions.

Permitted Discrimination

Antidiscrimination laws recognize that in certain very limited circumstances, an employer may have a legitimate reason to seek an employee of a particular gender, religion, or ethnicity, even though such a preference would ordinarily be illegal. These are called bona fide occupational qualification (BFOQ) exceptions. Religion, sex, or national origin can be a BFOQ only if it's a reasonably necessary qualification for the normal operation of a business or enterprise. Not surprisingly, courts almost never find that the BFOQ exception applies. Race can never be a BFOQ.

Here are some guidelines.

Religion. Religion can be a job requirement if the job involves religious duties. The U.S. Supreme Court has ruled that the First Amendment gives religious entities the right to decide who will "preach their beliefs, teach their faith, and carry out their mission." This is sometimes referred to as the "ministerial exception" to the usual antidiscrimination rules. Although the usual antidiscrimination rules apply to positions that are not ministerial (such as administrative workers), a religious employer has more freedom in choosing those who will carry and teach its message when it comes to ministerial positions.

National origin. National origin can be a BFOQ, but only very rarely. For example, an American subsidiary of a Japanese company involved in international trade might be allowed to make Japanese nationality a job requirement because of the need for language proficiency and cultural background, but only if the company could show that this restriction is reasonably necessary to do the job. Aside from such a narrow situation, you can't use national origin as a BFOQ.

Gender. About the only time that gender can be a BFOQ is for jobs affecting personal privacy—for example, restroom attendants or security guards who are required to search employees—and acting and modeling work.

Job Advertisements

Even if you write a great job description, you can still get tripped up when summarizing the job in an advertisement, especially if you let someone who's not familiar with the legal guidelines write your ad. Nuances in an ad can be used as evidence of discrimination against applicants of a particular gender, age, or other protected characteristic.

Here are a number of semantic pitfalls to avoid when posting a job.

Don't Use	Use
Salesman	Salesperson
College student	Part-time worker
Handyman	General repair person
Digital native	Tech-savvy
Married couple	Two-person job
Waiter	Server
Young	Energetic
Three to five years' experience	At least three years' experience

Requiring a high school or college degree may be discriminatory in some job categories. You can avoid problems by stating that an applicant must have "a degree or equivalent experience."

The best way to write an ad that meets legal requirements is to keep it short and sweet. Stick to the skills needed and the basic responsibilities the job entails. Some examples:

- "Fifty-unit apartment complex seeks experienced manager with general maintenance skills."
- "Midsized manufacturing company has opening for accountant with tax experience to oversee interstate accounts."
- "Cook trainee position available in new vegetarian restaurant. Flexible hours."

Help wanted ads placed by federal contractors must state that all qualified applicants will receive consideration for employment without regard to race, color, religion, sex, or national origin. Ads often express this with the phrase "An Equal Opportunity Employer" or "EOE."

Some employers who are not federal contractors also use this phrase in their ads; it's a good shorthand way to let potential employees know that you'll give them a fair shake, which can help you attract a more diverse group of applicants.

Job Applications

Develop a standard application form to make it easy to compare the experience and skills of applicants. Limit the form to job-related information that will help you decide who's the best person for the job. Questions like these are fairly standard:

- What is your name, address, and phone number?
- Are you legally entitled to work in the United States?
- What position are you applying for?
- What other positions would you like to be considered for?
- If you are hired, when can you start work?
- What is your educational background, including high school, college, graduate school, and other (including school names, addresses, number of years attended, degree, and major)?
- Describe your employment history, including name, address, and phone number of each employer, supervisor's name, dates of employment, job title and responsibilities, and reason for leaving.
- Do you have any special training or experience relevant to this position?

Avoiding Unlawful Questions

The chart below ("Preemployment Inquiries") outlines the type of information that you can ask for in applications and during job interviews. Follow the chart to comply with federal laws. Adhering to the federal laws might also be sufficient for complying with the laws of your state, but to be sure, check with your state's fair employment office. (You can find charts listing state fair employment laws and offices in the appendix.) Note that in California and several other states, employers can't ask about an applicant's salary history on job applications or at any other point during the hiring process.

In addition to the areas covered in the chart, the ADA prohibits any preemployment questions about a disability. Before you make a job offer, you may ask questions about an applicant's ability to perform specific job functions. You may not, however, inquire about the nature or severity of a disability, ask about medical history or treatment, or require any medical exam. These rules apply to application forms, job interviews, and background or reference checks. See Chapter 9 for more on the ADA.

After you make a conditional job offer and before an applicant starts work, you're free to gather more details. At that point, you can require a medical exam or ask health-related questions, but only if you require this for all candidates who receive conditional offers in the same job category.

Employers may not ask questions that would tend to elicit information about an applicant's disability before a job offer is made. According to the Equal Employment Opportunity Commission (EEOC), the federal agency that enforces workplace discrimination laws, you may not ask questions like these in an interview, on an application form, or in any other context before making a job offer:

- Do you have a disability? Have you ever had a disability?
- Have you ever had or been treated for (followed by a list of conditions and diseases, such as a heart condition, cancer, asthma, diabetes, and so on)?
- How many days were you sick last year?
- Have you ever filed for workers' compensation?
- Have you ever been treated for mental health problems?
- What prescription drugs are you currently taking, if any?
- Are you a drug addict or an alcoholic?

Preemployment Inquiries		
Subject	**Lawful Preemployment Inquiries**	**Unlawful Preemployment Inquiries**
Name	Applicant's full name Have you ever worked for this company under a different name? Is any additional information relative to a different name necessary to check work record? If yes, explain.	Original name of an applicant whose name has been changed by court order or otherwise Applicant's maiden name
Birthplace	None	Birthplace of applicant Birthplace of applicant's parents, spouse, or other close relatives Requirements that applicant submit birth certificate, naturalization, or baptismal record
Age	Are you 18 years old or older? (This question may be asked only for the purpose of determining whether applicants are of legal age for employment.)	How old are you? What is your date of birth?
Religion or creed	None	Inquiry into an applicant's religious denomination, religious affiliations, church, parish, pastor, or religious holidays observed
Race or color	None	Complexion or color of skin Inquiry regarding applicant's race
Photograph	None	Any requirement for a photograph prior to hire
Height	None	Inquiry regarding applicant's height (unless you have a legitimate business reason)
Weight	None	Inquiry regarding applicant's weight (unless you have a legitimate business reason)
Marital status	Is your spouse employed by this employer?	Requirement that an applicant provide any information regarding marital status or children Are you single or married? Do you have any children? Is your spouse employed? What is your spouse's name?

	Preemployment Inquiries (continued)	
Subject	**Lawful Preemployment Inquiries**	**Unlawful Preemployment Inquiries**
Gender	None	Mr., Miss, Mrs., Ms., or an inquiry regarding gender; inquiry as to ability or plans to reproduce or advocacy of any form of birth control
Sexual orientation	None	Inquiry regarding applicant's sexual orientation Do you have a spouse or partner? What is your partner's name?
Transgender status	None	Inquiries into gender identity or gender transition process
Disability	These [provide applicant with list] are the essential functions of the job. How would you perform them?	Inquiries regarding an individual's physical or mental condition that are not directly related to the requirements of a specific job
Citizenship	Are you legally authorized to work in the United States on a full-time basis?	Questions about subjects below are unlawful, but the applicant may be required to reveal some of this information as part of the federal I-9 process: • country of citizenship • whether an applicant is naturalized or a native-born citizen; the date when the applicant acquired citizenship • requirement that an applicant produce naturalization papers or first papers, or • whether applicant's parents or spouse are naturalized or native-born citizens of the United States, and, if so, the date when such parent or spouse acquired citizenship.
National origin	Inquiry into language applicant speaks and writes fluently	Inquiry into applicant's lineage, ancestry, national origin, descent, parentage, or nationality, unless part of the federal I-9 process in determining employment eligibility Nationality of applicant's parents or spouse Inquiry into how applicant acquired ability to read, write, or speak a foreign language
Education	Inquiry into the academic, vocational, or professional education of an applicant and public and private schools attended	

	Preemployment Inquiries (continued)	
Subject	**Lawful Preemployment Inquiries**	**Unlawful Preemployment Inquiries**
Experience	Inquiry into work experience Inquiry into countries applicant has visited	
Arrests	Have you ever been convicted of a crime (depending on state and local law)? Are there any felony charges pending against you?	Inquiry regarding arrests that did not result in conviction (except for law enforcement agencies)
Relatives	Names of applicant's relatives already employed by this company	Address of any relative of applicant, other than address (within the United States) of applicant's father and mother, husband or wife, and minor dependent children
Notice in case of emergency	Name and address of person to be notified in case of accident or emergency	Name and address of nearest relative to be notified in case of accident or emergency
Organizations	Inquiry into the organizations of which an applicant is a member, excluding organizations the name or character of which indicates the race, color, religion, national origin, or ancestry of its members	List all clubs, societies, and lodges to which the applicant belongs

The Legal Effect of Job Applications

A well-written application form can help get the employment relationship started on solid legal footing. Because it's filled out very early in the process, you can use the form to let the applicant know the basic terms and conditions of the job and the workplace. And, because the applicant signs the application, it can be a valuable piece of evidence if a question comes up later about what you actually promised about the job.

You can also use the job application to obtain the employee's consent to a background investigation and reference check. If the applicant consents to your investigation, the applicant will have a tough time later claiming an invasion of privacy. Indeed, if you plan to pull a credit report or hire someone to conduct a background check, you will be legally required to get the applicant's consent first.

Impress on the applicant the need to be honest and accurate in completing the form. Lying or giving incomplete information on an application can be a good legal reason to fire an employee if the correct story later surfaces. So serious is application fraud—or résumé fraud as it's sometimes called—that some courts have allowed employers to use it to justify a firing even if they didn't know of the fraud until the employee was gone.

> **EXAMPLE:** Dolores, age 42, applies for a job as a land surveyor with Progressive Engineering Consultants (PEC). On her application, Dolores states that she has a civil engineering degree from a prestigious college and is licensed by the state. The application form warns that false information will be a cause for immediate discharge. Relying on the application, PEC hires Dolores. Six months later, PEC becomes dissatisfied with Dolores's work and fires her, replacing her with a 30-year-old man. Dolores sues, claiming that the firm discriminated against her based on age and gender. PEC belatedly looks into her application statements and discovers that Dolores has neither the degree nor the license she said she had. Because of Dolores's lies, the judge dismisses her wrongful termination case without getting into the discrimination charges.

Including the following language in an application form can help you establish that you clearly told the applicant about the consequences of lying.

Accuracy. I verify that the statements I have made in this application are true and complete. I understand that if I am hired, any false or incomplete statements in this application will be grounds for immediate discharge.

JMO Initials

Interviews

Before you begin interviewing applicants for a job opening, write down a set of questions focusing on the job duties and the applicant's skills and experience. Some examples include:

- "Tell me about your experience running a mailroom."
- "How much experience did you have making cold calls on your last job?"
- "Explain how you typically go about organizing your workday."
- "Have any of your jobs required strong leadership skills?"

By writing down the questions and sticking to the same format in all interviews for the position, you reduce the risk that a rejected applicant will later complain about unequal treatment. It's also smart to summarize the applicant's answers for your files, but don't get so involved in documenting the interview that you forget to listen closely to the applicant. And don't be so locked in to your list of questions that you don't follow up on something significant that an applicant has said or try to pin down an ambiguous or evasive response.

Interviewing Protocol

Get the interview started by giving the applicant some information about the job: the duties, hours, pay range, benefits, and career opportunities. This will give the applicant a chance to get comfortable before you start in on the questions. Questions about the applicant's work history and experience that may be relevant to the job opening are always appropriate. But don't encourage the employee to divulge the trade secrets of a present or former employer, especially a competitor. That can lead to a lawsuit. And be cautious about an employee who volunteers such information or promises to bring secrets to the new position; such an employee will probably play fast and loose with your own company's secrets, given the chance.

Keep your antennae tuned carefully to the applicant who spouts a litany of complaints against former employers. If you hire that person, your business may well become the next object of the applicant's invective. But watch your step if you learn that the applicant has sued a former employer for discrimination or filed a discrimination charge with the Equal Employment

Opportunity Commission (EEOC). If you refuse to hire the applicant because of the prior proceedings, the EEOC may treat your refusal as a form of illegal retaliation, even though your business wasn't involved in the earlier dispute. See Chapter 8 for more on retaliation claims.

Give applicants plenty of time to answer questions. Make sure they understand your questions; ask them to let you know if something is unclear. Also ask them if they have any questions about your company or the job for which they're applying. Finally, let them know your time frame for getting back to them with a hiring decision so they know what to expect.

RESOURCE

Want additional suggestions on interviewing? See *96 Great Interview Questions to Ask Before You Hire*, by Paul Falcone (AMACOM). In addition, Nolo's *Dealing With Problem Employees*, by Amy DelPo and Lisa Guerin, devotes an entire chapter to the hiring process, including effective interviewing techniques.

Legal Restrictions on Questions

The rules of etiquette once dictated that you avoid discussing sex, religion, or politics in a social setting. While that standard has been relaxed, it still applies to job interviews, along with similar cautions to avoid focusing on an applicant's age, ethnicity, birthplace, or personal finances. In fact, such inquiries are not only bad manners; they may be illegal—plain and simple.

Review the legal restrictions on what you can and can't ask in a job application. (See "Job Applications," above.) The same guidelines and restrictions apply to interviews. As with job applications, the focus of your interviews should be to find the best person for the job based on skill, experience, education, and other relevant qualifications.

To avoid improper inquiries, stay focused on job requirements and company policies. Suppose you're concerned that an applicant with young kids may spend too much time talking with them on the phone. You can't ask: "Do you have children?" or "Who watches the kids when you're at work?" But you can say to the applicant: "We don't allow personal phone calls during work hours.

Do you have a problem with that?" The applicant then knows the ground rules and can let you know if a problem exists. Just be sure you apply your phone policy to all employees.

During an interview, you can ask about the applicant's ability to perform job tasks and about any needed accommodation. Remember, disability discrimination laws prohibit questions about an applicant's disability. Focus on the applicant's ability to do the job, not on the applicant's disability.

> **EXAMPLE:** Zack, who has only one arm, applies at ABC Industries for a job that requires driving. The interviewer avoids asking Zack if or how this disability would affect his driving. Instead, to comply with the law, the interviewer asks: "Do you have a valid driver's license?" and "Can you drive on frequent long distance trips, with or without an accommodation?" The interviewer continues: "At least 80% of the time of this sales job must be spent on the road covering a three-state territory. What is your outside selling experience? What is your accident record?" All are permissible questions.

You can describe or demonstrate the specific job tasks, then ask whether the applicant can perform these tasks with or without an accommodation. If you're interviewing an applicant for a mailroom job, you can say: "The person in this job is responsible for receiving incoming mail and packages, sorting the mail, and taking it in a cart to many offices in two buildings, one block apart. The mail clerk must also receive boxes of supplies weighing up to 50 pounds and place them on storage shelves six feet high. Can you perform these tasks with or without an accommodation?"

You can ask applicants to describe or show how they will perform specific job functions, but only if you require this of everyone applying for a job in this category. For example, a telemarketing firm could require all applicants to demonstrate selling ability by taking a simulated telephone sales test.

Be mindful that some applicants with disabilities will need accommodations to participate in the interview process. For example, you may need to provide an accessible location for an applicant in a wheelchair or a sign interpreter for a deaf person. (See Chapter 9 for an extensive discussion of the disability law requirements.)

Testing

Preemployment testing—which might include skills testing, aptitude testing, honesty testing, medical testing, and drug testing—is most common in larger businesses. But no matter what size your business is, you should know the legal limits on your ability to test applicants.

Skills Tests

Most small businesses—especially new ones—operate on a slim profit margin. This means that your employees must be up to speed from Day One. If you're hiring a data input clerk, you may want to test the applicant for typing speed and accuracy. If you're hiring a person to be a clerk in your bookstore, you may want to test the applicant's knowledge of literature. If you're hiring a driver for a delivery van, a road test would be appropriate. As long as the skills you're testing are genuinely related to the job duties, a skills test is generally legal.

To avoid discriminating against applicants protected by the Americans with Disabilities Act (ADA), be sure your tests measure the actual skills and abilities needed to do a job. (For more on the ADA, see Chapter 9.)

Aptitude and Psychological Tests

Some employers use written tests—usually multiple choice tests—to get additional insight into applicants' abilities. Others attempt to probe the psyche of their applicants.

These tests are going out of fashion and for good reason. A multiple-choice aptitude test may discriminate illegally against members of protected groups, because it really reflects test-taking ability rather than actual job skills. A personality test can be even riskier. Besides its potential for illegal discrimination, such a test may invade an applicant's privacy (by inquiring, for example, into religious beliefs or sexual practices).

If you do decide to use aptitude or personality tests, proceed cautiously. Make sure that the tests have been screened scientifically for validity and that they are correlated to job performance. Review them carefully for any questions that may intrude into the applicant's privacy.

Another concern for employers is the ADA, which lets you give a psychological test or exam to a job applicant only if the test or exam isn't medical. This can be tricky. A psychological test or exam is considered medical if it provides evidence that can help identify a mental disorder or impairment. A test or exam is permissible if it measures only such things as honesty, tastes, and habits. But if it helps identify whether the applicant has excessive anxiety, depression, or a compulsive disorder, it qualifies as a medical test and is illegal if given at the wrong time.

Be aware, too, that the ADA sets special requirements when you test people who have impaired sensory, speaking, or manual skills. Sensory skills include the abilities to hear, to see, and to process information. If applicants wouldn't have to use the impaired skill on the job, you must design your tests so that they don't have to use the impaired skill to take the test.

> **EXAMPLE:** Joe is applying for a position as a food handler, a job that does not require reading. Because of dyslexia, Joe has a very difficult time reading. He should be given an oral rather than a written aptitude test. By contrast, if you were interviewing Joe for a proofreader job—which clearly requires the ability to read without help—a written test would be appropriate and legal.

 RESOURCE

Want more on how to avoid legal problems when using screening tests? Check out the EEOC's guidance on employment tests and selection procedures at www.eeoc.gov/policy/docs/factemployment_procedures.html.

Honesty Tests

Lie detector or polygraph tests—rarely used by small businesses—are virtually outlawed by the federal Employee Polygraph Protection Act. With just a few exceptions, you can't require job applicants to take lie detector tests and you can't inquire about previous tests. The only private employers who can use lie detector tests to screen applicants are businesses that offer armored car, alarm, and guard services or that manufacture, distribute, or dispense pharmaceuticals. Even in those situations, there are restrictions on which applicants can be tested and how the tests must be administered.

About the only time a typical employer can use a lie detector test is to question an employee who is reasonably suspected of being involved in a workplace theft or embezzlement.

You must post a notice of the Employee Polygraph Protection Act where employees and job applicants can readily see it. For a poster containing the required notice, contact the local office of the Wage and Hour Division of the U.S. Department of Labor. (See the appendix for contact details.)

Some employers use written honesty tests to screen job applicants. Because these tests are often inaccurate and can invade an applicant's privacy or have a discriminatory impact, the legality of the tests is doubtful in most states.

Limit honesty tests to situations in which you have a legitimate business reason to be concerned about workers' honesty, such as when hiring workers who will be handling large amounts of cash. Before using a test, ask to see scientific backup establishing the test's accuracy. And, to protect yourself against charges of illegal discrimination, test all applicants for a particular job.

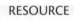

RESOURCE

Want to know more about the Employee Polygraph Protection Act? For detailed information, including whom the law covers, what the law requires and prohibits, tips for compliance, and exceptions to the law, see *The Essential Guide to Federal Employment Laws*, by Lisa Guerin and Sachi Barreiro (Nolo).

Medical Tests

To avoid violating the ADA, don't ask applicants about their medical history or conduct any medical exam before you make a job offer. You can, however, offer a job conditioned on an applicant's passing a medical exam. If you do require such a post-offer exam, you must require exams for all entering employees who will be doing the same job. You can't single out for testing employees who appear to have disabilities.

> **EXAMPLE:** Cornerstone Corporation has openings for construction crane operators. It offers Bill a job conditioned on a medical exam showing he doesn't have a medical condition, such as uncontrolled seizures, which may be risky to other workers. Because Cornerstone requires such exams for all the crane operators it hires, and because the exam screens out only those workers who would not be able to do the job safely, the exam is legal.

If you require medical exams only for people with known disabilities or those who you believe may have a disability, you'll violate the ADA. But the scope of medical exams needn't be identical for all employees. You can give follow-up tests or exams if further information is needed. Suppose, for example, that your restaurant requires all prospective kitchen workers to fill out a questionnaire about exposure to foodborne illnesses. If one person's questionnaire indicates symptoms of typhoid fever, which is a foodborne illness, you can require further tests for that employee to determine whether there is a risk of the employee passing the illness to others.

After making a conditional job offer, you may require a full physical exam and you may ask questions that you couldn't ask at the preemployment stage (for example, questions about previous illnesses, diseases, or medications). You can probe to find out whether the person has the physical or mental qualifications needed to perform the job or to determine whether a person can perform the job without posing a direct threat to the health or safety of others.

If you withdraw a conditional job offer based on results of an exam or inquiry, you must be able to show both of the following:

- Your reasons were job related and consistent with business necessity, or the person was excluded to avoid a direct threat to health and safety.
- No reasonable accommodation could be made or such an accommodation would cause undue hardship. (For more guidance, see Chapter 9.)

To avoid claims that you discriminated against a person with a disability, carefully document all medical inquiries and the responses to them. If you reject a prospective employee, be prepared to show how the medical facts relate to the person's ability to perform the job or reveal a direct threat to health and safety.

EXAMPLE: Kendra's medical exam reveals an impairment that will require her to frequently be away from work for lengthy medical treatment. The job requires daily availability for the next three months. The company doesn't hire Kendra. This is permissible under the ADA because Kendra isn't available to perform the essential functions of the job, and no accommodation is possible.

Drug Tests

You have a legal right to insist on a drug-free workplace, even in states that have decriminalized the use of marijuana. The only problem is that testing to identify drug users might conflict with workers' rights to privacy. The laws on drug testing vary widely from state to state and are changing quickly as legislators and judges struggle to strike a balance between workers' rights and the legitimate needs of businesses. (See "State Drug and Alcohol Testing Laws," in the appendix.) Some state statutes allow you to test employees only in a narrow range of jobs, such as those concerned with safety.

 TIP

Federal contractors must comply with the Drug-Free Workplace Act. The law requires federal contractors and grantees to agree to maintain a drug-free workplace. If your business has a contract with the federal government for $100,000 or more (for something other than goods you're selling to the government), you need to notify employees that they're prohibited from unlawfully making, distributing, possessing, or using controlled substances in your workplace. And you need to set up an awareness program that tells workers about the dangers of drug abuse while at work and lets them know about assistance programs that may be available. For detailed information on these requirements, check out the Drug-Free Workplace Programs page of the Substance Abuse and Mental Health Administration's website, www.samhsa.gov/workplace.

Fortunately, even restrictive states generally allow you much more leeway in screening job applicants than in testing employees who are already on board. If your state permits testing applicants or employees and you plan to do such testing, use the application form to let applicants know of this policy. State law may also require you to give applicants a written policy statement that's separate from the application. When applicants are told up front about drug testing, it's harder for them to later claim that their privacy was violated.

Once an applicant becomes an employee, the rules may be more restrictive. Testing is usually permitted when employees have been in an accident or you've seen them bring illegal drugs to work. Your legal right to test at random and without prior notice is not as clear, in some states.

With any drug testing, treat all individuals consistently, being careful not to single out any one group. And consult with competent drug testing experts to ensure that your test procedures are as accurate as possible. Because the laws of drug testing are in constant flux, talk to a lawyer before administering any tests.

What About Marijuana Testing?

More than two-thirds of the states have legalized the use of marijuana when a doctor prescribes it to treat a medical condition. And more than a dozen states (including California) have decriminalized marijuana for recreational use.

This doesn't necessarily mean that you can't test employees for marijuana use—or fire them for testing positive—however. In some states, employers may fire employees who test positive for marijuana, even if they have a valid prescription for the drug. Other states protect employees from termination in this context, as long as they don't use or possess the drug—and are not impaired—at work. This is one of the most rapidly changing areas of law right now. If you do business in a state that has decriminalized the use of marijuana for medical or recreational use, you should definitely talk to a lawyer before you adopt a drug testing program or fire anyone who tests positive under your existing program.

Recovering addicts are protected from discrimination, but not if they are currently engaged in the illegal use of drugs. The ADA prohibits you from discriminating against people because of their past drug problems. This includes people who no longer use drugs illegally and those who are receiving treatment for drug addiction or have successfully been rehabilitated. However, if an applicant tests positive for drug use, addiction is not a defense. You can make job decisions based on the current use of illegal drugs, even if it is fueled by an underlying addiction.

Alcoholics are also protected from discrimination, whether they are currently using alcohol or not. However, employers can require an alcohol-free workplace and discipline employees if their use of alcohol affects their job performances.

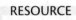 **RESOURCE**

For help developing a drug policy, contact the Center for Substance Abuse Prevention Workplace Helpline. You can also find lots of helpful information on their website at www.samhsa.gov.

Investigations

Because some people give false or incomplete information in their job applications, it's a good idea to do some investigating to verify application information. You might find out, for example, that an applicant doesn't have the work experience or occupational license listed in a job application, or that the applicant didn't really leave the last job voluntarily. What's more, you might learn that the applicant has a history of violent behavior or even a criminal record that would disqualify the applicant from a job that may put members of the public or other employees at risk.

Your need to investigate a job applicant is legitimate. If you go overboard, however, you may violate the job applicant's legal right to privacy. The best way to reduce the risk of an invasion of privacy claim is to do both of the following:

- Seek only the background information you really need to figure out whether the applicant is suited for the job.

- Inform the applicant, in the job application, that you will be requesting information from, for example, schools, credit reporting agencies, former employers, and law enforcement agencies.

As part of the application process, ask the applicant to sign a consent form. Use a separate form rather than making the consent a part of the application. That way, you can easily photocopy the consent and send it to the people from whom you're seeking information.

> **TIP**
>
> **Will your investigation yield relevant information?** It's often a waste of time and effort to acquire and review transcripts and credit reports, although occasionally they're useful. If you're hiring a bookkeeper, for example, experience garnered on the job is much more important than the grades the applicant received in a community college bookkeeping program ten years ago. But if the applicant is fresh out of school and has never held a bookkeeping job, then a transcript may yield some insights. Similarly, if you're hiring a software engineer, information on a credit report would be irrelevant. But if you're hiring a bar manager who will be handling large cash receipts, you might want to find out whether the applicant is in financial trouble.

The Fair Credit Reporting Act

A federal law called the Fair Credit Reporting Act (FCRA) imposes strict rules on the ordering and use of consumer reports, including background checks, credit reports, and other information gathered on applicants for employment. (15 U.S.C. §§ 1681 and following.)

Which Background Checks Are Covered?

The FCRA regulates your ordering and use of any report prepared by a consumer reporting agency (CRA), which is any business that assembles such reports for other businesses. If you order an applicant's credit report from a credit bureau, that is a consumer report covered by the FCRA. So is a report you order from a business about an applicant's driving record or criminal history (though ordering similar information from a governmental agency isn't).

You may be thinking of hiring a CRA, such as a detective agency or professional investigator, to prepare a report based on interviews the CRA conducts with an applicant's friends, neighbors, and associates. This would also constitute a consumer report—and would, therefore, be covered by the FCRA.

Checking an applicant's references may or may not fall under the FCRA. If you or someone within your company does the checking, the FCRA doesn't apply; the statute doesn't cover any information you gather on your own. However, if you use an employment or reference-checking agency—or anyone outside of your company—to do the job, you must comply with the FCRA.

Requirements for Handling Reports

Before you get a consumer report for employment purposes, you must notify the applicant or employee in writing and get that person's written permission to gather the information. This consent must be on a separate, stand-alone document; it may not be part of your employment application form or a general consent form allowing you to check a variety of records. And the agency you ask to prepare the report will require you to certify that you're complying with the federal law and that you won't use the information in the report in violation of federal or state equal employment opportunity laws. These laws—discussed in Chapters 8 and 9—prohibit certain types of discrimination. Special rules apply if your business is in the trucking industry.

After you get the report, special rules apply if you're going to take adverse action against the applicant based on the report. In the hiring process, this is most likely to come up if you decide, based on the information in the report, not to hire the applicant. In this case, you must take the following steps:

Step 1: Before you take adverse action, you must give the applicant or employee a copy of the consumer report and a copy of *A Summary of Your Rights Under the Fair Credit Reporting Act*—a publication prepared by the Federal Trade Commission (FTC). The business that prepared the consumer report will give you the *Summary*, or you can get a copy from the FTC's website at www.ftc.gov.

Step 2: After you take an adverse action, you must notify the applicant or employee that you've taken the action. You can give notice orally, in writing, by email, or by fax. Your adverse action notice must:
  - give the name, address, and phone number of the company (CRA) that supplied the report

- state that the CRA didn't make the decision to take adverse action and can't give specific reasons for it
- say that the applicant or employee has the right to dispute the accuracy or completeness of any information the CRA furnished, and
- say that the applicant or employee can get an additional free consumer report from the CRA upon request within 60 days.

Penalties for Violating the FCRA

You face legal trouble if you don't get an applicant's or employee's permission before requesting a consumer report or if you don't provide the required disclosures about adverse action. The applicant or employee may sue you for damages in federal court. If successful, the person may recover court costs and reasonable attorneys' fees. You can also be ordered to pay punitive damages— damages intended to punish you—for deliberate violations.

Also, federal and state agencies may sue you and obtain civil penalties.

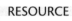

RESOURCE

Want to know more about the FCRA? For detailed information about the FCRA, including whom it covers, what it requires and prohibits, and tips for compliance, see *The Essential Guide to Federal Employment Laws*, by Lisa Guerin and Sachi Barreiro (Nolo).

Information From Former Employers

Some job applicants exaggerate or even lie about their qualifications and experience. The best way to uncover this kind of puffery is to ask some former employers for the inside story.

Former employers are often reluctant to say anything negative for fear that if they speak frankly, they may be hit with a lawsuit for defamation. They're hesitant to do anything more than to verify that the former employee did in fact work there and to give the dates of employment. This can make it hard to get an accurate picture of an applicant's job history. As mentioned, it may be helpful to send the former employer a copy of the applicant's signed consent to a full disclosure of employment information. (See Chapter 10 for suggestions on giving references for former employees when you're the one being asked for information.)

When speaking to former employers, read between the lines. If a former employer is neutral, offers only faint praise, or overpraises a person for one aspect of a job only—"great with numbers" or "always on time"—there's a good chance some negative information is hiding in the wings. Ask former employers: "Would you hire this person back if you could?" The response may be telling. To help put the applicant in perspective, you might ask: "What are this person's greatest strengths and greatest weaknesses?" Since no one is perfect, this may lead to a candid evaluation of the applicant.

If a reference isn't glowing and doesn't address all aspects of the job, check several other references. You may also want to call back the applicant for a more directed interview.

TIP

Former employers may have legal protections. In response to the problem of unhelpful reference checks, many states have passed laws that allow employers to speak more frankly about their former employees. If your state has such a law, don't assume that the former employers you call for reference checks know about it. Telling them about the protection they have under your state's law may allow you to get a fuller picture of a prospective employee. To find out about your state law, contact your state labor department. (See the appendix for contact details.)

School Transcripts

Though on-the-job experience is usually more relevant to employment than an applicant's educational credentials, you may have good reasons for requiring a high school diploma or college degree for some jobs. If so, you may want to see proof that the applicant really received the diploma or degree or took the courses listed in the job application.

If you wish to see these records, ask the applicant to sign a written release acknowledging your right to obtain them. Federal law prohibits schools that receive federal funds from turning over the records without such a release, and many schools won't deliver records to anyone except a former student. This can, of course, complicate your verification, since it creates the possibility of forgery or tampering.

Credit History

Credit information usually isn't relevant to employment, but it might come into play if you hire someone who will handle money. Applicants who can't keep their personal finances in order are probably not a good choice for a job managing your company's finances.

In most other situations, however, a credit check is an unnecessary intrusion into an applicant's private life. What's more, unless you have a good reason for doing a credit check for a particular job, you may run afoul of antidiscrimination laws. According to the EEOC, requiring an applicant to have good credit may subtly discriminate against some minority groups.

Some states have enacted laws barring employers from obtaining credit reports for most job applicants or employees. Typically, the only exceptions are for jobs at banks or similar positions in which credit information is substantially related to the applicant's ability to do the job. Similar laws are under consideration in many more states, and Congress is looking at a national version, called the Equal Employment for All Act.

Assuming that you have a good business reason to order a credit report on a job applicant, be sure to get the applicant's written permission first. This is required by the federal Fair Credit Reporting Act and may also be mandated by state law. And if you decide not to hire the applicant because of something you learn in a credit report, you must notify the applicant. For more information, see "The Fair Credit Reporting Act," above.

Criminal History

Asking an applicant about arrest records or making a hiring decision based on an arrest record can be a subtle form of discrimination that violates state and federal antidiscrimination laws. Many people are arrested and the charges are later dropped or found to be without merit. Asking about arrests can be particularly harmful to black applicants because blacks are arrested at a disproportionately high rate. Very rarely is there a legitimate business reason to reject an applicant simply because of an arrest record.

Convictions are another matter. While it can be unlawful discrimination to automatically exclude every applicant who's ever been convicted of any crime, antidiscrimination laws generally do allow you to inquire about an applicant's conviction record and to reject an applicant because of a conviction that's job related. If you're hiring a delivery truck driver, for example, it wouldn't violate the antidiscrimination laws to reject an applicant based on a conviction for drunk driving.

State laws may specifically prohibit you from asking about arrest records. Some may go even further in restricting your inquiries into an applicant's criminal history. (See "State Laws on Employee Arrest and Conviction Records," in the appendix.) In many states, for example, you can't ask an applicant about juvenile records. In some states, you can't ask about convictions for minor offenses or misdemeanors that go back more than five years if the applicant has had a clean slate since that time.

In recent years, a number of states and cities have passed "ban-the-box" laws and ordinances, which prohibit employers from asking about convictions in employment application forms. You may still ask about convictions during the interview process, but you may not adopt a blanket policy of excluding anyone with a criminal record at the initial application stage. Be aware, however, that in some states you may be required to conduct a criminal records check if a prospective employee will be dealing with vulnerable people, such as children or elderly adults (for example, if the job involves child care or home health care). If your company does this type of work, check with your local police department, state attorney general's office, or state labor department to see if a criminal records check is required.

CAUTION

Expunging the past. Many states have laws that allow individuals to expunge, or seal, their criminal records. When a record is expunged, it is usually not available to anyone other than criminal justice agencies and the courts. If a criminal record has been expunged, an applicant is generally allowed to act and answer questions as if the conviction never happened. In other words, the applicant is legally permitted to deny having a criminal record. Note, however, that most state laws provide for exceptions to an expunged record's unavailability, when the job involves working with children or vulnerable adults.

Driving Records

When a job requires the employee to drive, it's wise to check an applicant's driving record. You usually can obtain driving records for a modest cost from the state authority that issues drivers' licenses. You'll need the applicant's driver's license number to do so.

Using the Internet to Learn About Job Applicants

The Internet can be a rich source of information about someone applying for a job, especially the information an applicant may post on social networking sites, such as Facebook or LinkedIn. The applicant posted this information online for all to see, so you're not invading the applicant's privacy by looking at it.

But there is a potential risk: You may come upon information that you couldn't lawfully request on an application form or during a job interview. Generally, this is information that you can't legally consider in making job decisions. You might, for example, learn an applicant's age, religion, sexual orientation, or marital status. In some cases, you might discover that an applicant is a smoker or drinks alcohol, activities that are legal, even though some employers may not approve of them. (Employers can ban smoking in the workplace, however, and require that employees be sober while at work.)

If your business is big enough, you can arrange for a manager to review and filter the online information for others who make the hiring decisions. The person responsible for filtering would send only legally appropriate information to the decision maker and would not play a role in hiring decisions. This type of separation of duties can help you head off potential problems from a rejected applicant who believes that you violated legal guidelines.

No matter how large or small your business, you should tell potential employees on your application form that you will be searching the Internet—including social networking sites—as part of your prehiring investigation. And keep in mind that a growing number of states prohibit employers from asking applicants and employees to provide their passwords for social media accounts. You are legally allowed to see what an applicant posts for public consumption, but you may not be allowed to require an applicant to show you photos and posts that are privacy protected or restricted for viewing only by social media "friends."

Remember that if you hire a consumer reporting agency to gather this information, you must comply with the Fair Credit Reporting Act, which requires you to get the applicant's written consent. Some states may also require this consent.

Making a Job Offer

Be careful what you say orally and in writing when you make a job offer to any applicant. The positive statements you make to an applicant about long-term opportunities can come back to haunt you if you later fire the person. A judge or jury reviewing the firing may conclude that your glowing statements were actually a contractual promise (for example, that the applicant's job would be secure for years or that you wouldn't fire the applicant without good cause).

To protect yourself from such misunderstandings, you can write an offer letter that includes the following key elements:
- title of the position that you're offering
- date the job begins
- starting salary
- reference to the employee handbook (if you have one)
- job benefits
- disclaimer of oral commitments
- reminder of at-will status, and
- a statement explaining (and limiting) how the at-will relationship can be altered in the future. Many companies require the signed consent of an important company official, like the president.

An example of an offer letter is shown below. Have the employee sign a copy of your letter at the bottom, as suggested in the example. Then put that copy in the employee's file. (See Chapter 2 for more about what you should keep in an employee's personnel file.) That way, you'll have clear proof that the employee received the letter and accepted its terms.

Agreeing to Job Security

Most of the time, a prospective employee won't object to an at-will relationship. Occasionally, however, the best person for the job will insist on some job security. This often happens when the prospective employee is a hot commodity—like an experienced executive—or when the person will have to leave a very secure job or move from far away to take the position.

> **EXAMPLE:** Ron owns a successful wholesale business that buys, processes, and packages organic grain. When his longtime marketing manager retires, Ron advertises throughout a five-state region to find a replacement. After screening a dozen applicants, Ron decides that Natalie, who is doing similar work for another company, is easily the best candidate. The only hitch is that Natalie currently lives about 500 miles from Ron's business, and she is concerned about relocating. To come and work for Ron, she'd need to sell her house and buy a new one. Her two high school kids would have to transfer, leaving behind their best friends. Her husband—an accountant—would need to find a new job. All this would be very disruptive. What if Natalie went to work for Ron and, at the end of two months, was fired? She candidly tells Ron about her worries. Ron wants to allay Natalie's fears.
>
> He knows it's very unlikely that he'd fire her without good cause. After thinking it over, he agrees that if he fires Natalie without cause before she completes three years of work, she'll be entitled to a severance package that includes six months of her salary. This satisfies Natalie. Ron and Natalie shake hands on their deal and then wisely put their agreement in writing.

If you're looking to hire a candidate who seems to have a legitimate need for reasonable job security, you may be willing to work out a similar agreement. Once you do, you can put these terms in your employment letter or in a more formal legal contract. Either way, you'll need to spell out what will constitute sufficient cause for you to fire the employee. Then you'll need to define what happens if you fire the employee *without* cause. Typically, this will involve your business making a significant payment to the employee to ease the pain of moving to a new job. Put another way, you'll be free to fire the employee without cause, but you'll have to pay a price.

It makes sense to have a lawyer help you craft the right wording to capture your agreement, or at least review it before everyone signs it.

Sample Offer Letter

June 10, 20xx

Dear Joe Nolo,

I am pleased to offer you a full-time position with XYZ Company as a tester beginning June 25. Your starting salary will be $1,000 per week.

When you applied, I gave you a copy of our employee handbook. The handbook sets out our current employment policies and describes your job benefits, including medical coverage, paid vacation, and sick leave. It also describes your responsibilities to the company. Each time the handbook is updated, you'll receive a revised copy.

The company's commitments to you and its other employees are stated in the handbook. The company has made no oral commitments to you. No one at the company is authorized to make oral commitments regarding employment, either now or in the future.

While I hope that everything works out here, you are an at-will employee. You have the right to terminate your employment at any time, for any reason, and so does the company. No representative of the company, other than the president, has authority to change the terms of the at-will relationship and any such change can occur only in a written contract.

If this offer of employment is acceptable to you, please sign a copy of this letter and return it to me within ten days. I look forward to having you join our staff.

Sincerely,

Bob Bossman

Supervisor

I accept your offer of employment and acknowledge receiving a copy of your current employee handbook. I understand that my employment is at will and that either you or I can terminate my employment at any time, for any reason or for no reason. No representative of the company has made any oral commitments concerning my employment.

Signature _____ *Joe Nolo* _____

Date __ *June 10, 20xx* _____

Rejecting Applicants

It's courteous to let unsuccessful applicants know that you've hired someone else for the job. You don't, however, owe them an explanation about why they weren't hired. Keep the letter simple and upbeat. If pressed, simply tell them that the person you hired is, in your judgment, better suited to the job.

There's no ideal way to give someone the news that you've offered the job to another person. The least painful way—which also presents the fewest legal difficulties—is to send a short letter (see the sample below) informing the rejected applicant of your decision. Send the letter as soon as you've decided whom you're going to hire or when you've narrowed the field down to a few candidates. Quickly sending your rejection letter will limit the number of post interview calls you get from unsuccessful applicants.

Sample Rejection Letter

June 25, 20xx

Dear Larry Leeds,

Thank you for meeting with me last Thursday to discuss the programmer position with our company. You were among many fine people who applied. I wanted to let you know that we selected another applicant for the position.

It was a pleasure meeting you and I wish you well in your job search.

Sincerely,

Bob Bossman

Supervisor

Some federal and state laws require you to keep a copy of employment applications for at least one year. It's a good idea to keep your rejection letters, along with the applications and other information you gathered during the screening process, for at least that long. Lawsuits by rejected applicants are rare, but you can't predict in advance who might take that step, and you want to have good records showing you acted fairly and legally.

Tax Compliance

Before you hire any employees, you must get an Employer Identification Number (EIN) from the IRS (unless you're a sole proprietor, in which case you can use your own Social Security number). To obtain an EIN, file Form SS-4, *Application for Employer Identification Number.* Some states have similar requirements. (See Chapter 5 for further information.)

Have new employees complete Form W-4, the *Employee's Withholding Allowance Certificate.* This lets you know how many dependents or withholding allowances the employee is claiming and the employee's filing status: single, married, or married but withholding at the higher single rate. Keep the signed form on file. If an employee doesn't complete a Form W-4, you won't know how much income tax to withhold. In that case, you must withhold tax as if the employee were a single person claiming no withholding allowances.

You needn't send the signed Form W-4 to the IRS unless either of the following is true:

- An employee claims more than ten allowances.
- The employee earns more than $200 per week and claims exemption from withholding.

You can find detailed information on your tax obligations as an employer in Chapter 5.

RESOURCE

The IRS has free publications that may be useful in helping establish tax procedures for your business. One is IRS Publication 15, Circular E, *Employer's Tax Guide,* containing withholding tables; it's updated periodically and is mailed automatically to every business that has an Employer Identification Number. Another is IRS Publication 334, *Tax Guide for Small Business,* which covers a wide range of tax issues. You can obtain these and other IRS publications through the agency's website at www.irs.gov.

Immigration Law Requirements

Immigration laws, enforced by U.S. Citizenship and Immigration Services (USCIS), prohibit employers from hiring aliens who don't have government authorization to work in the United States. There are specific procedures you must follow to make sure prospective employees meet these requirements.

You and the new employee must complete Form I-9, *Employment Eligibility Verification*. This one-page form is intended to ensure that the employee can legally work in the United States and has proof of identity.

> **TIP**
>
> **Remote inspection of I-9 documents is temporarily permitted for remote employers.** As a result of the COVID-19 pandemic, the Department of Homeland Security has announced that employers operating remotely can inspect newly hired workers' identity and employment authorization documents remotely rather than in person. When the employer's normal operations resume, employers must conduct an in-person review of employees' I-9 documents within three business days. This measure is temporary and will likely expire when the COVID-19 pandemic has passed. For up-to-date information on the I-9 form, employer requirements, and downloadable copies of the form, go to the website of the USCIS at www.uscis.gov. Click on "I-9 Central" under "Verification" at the bottom of the page.

Employees complete Section 1 of the form, attesting that they are a citizen or national of the United States, a lawful permanent resident alien, or an alien who has authorization to work in the United States. Only people in these three categories are legally allowed to work in the United States. Having "work authorization" usually means possessing an employment authorization card, or "EAD." Exceptions exist, however. For instance, aliens approved for asylum need only a Social Security number in order to work.

Section 2 of the form requires you to review documents—such as a passport, naturalization certificate, or EAD—presented by the employee as proof of both identity and employment eligibility. You must complete

Section 2 within three days of the employee's start date. However, it's a good idea to get this completed right away, to clear up any eligibility problems or complications before the employee starts working. Always make sure you have the most recent version of Form I-9. It will contain an up-to-date list of documents that an employee can use to prove eligibility. You can view and download the latest form at the USCIS website, www.uscis.gov.

You must indicate on Form I-9 which documents you've examined. It's your responsibility to decide whether the employee's documents appear valid. The USCIS advises that you must accept documents that reasonably appear to be genuine and to relate to the person presenting them. To do otherwise could be an unfair immigration-related employment practice and therefore illegal.

You are not required to keep photocopies of the employee's identification and work authorization documents, but you may choose to do so. On one hand, if you have copies of supporting documents and they look genuine, they could cut against a claim that you knowingly hired an unauthorized worker. But, on the other hand, if the documents have glaring errors or look forged, they could be used against you. Whether you keep photocopies depends on a variety of considerations. To get a better idea of which practice is right for your business, you may want to consult with an immigration or employment lawyer.

Whichever practice you end up adopting, make sure to apply it consistently to all employees. And if you do choose to keep copies, it's okay to generate or store them electronically (for example, as PDF documents). However, you must still examine the employee's documents personally (unless the regulations still allow remote inspection due to COVID-19, as discussed above).

Also, hang on to all Form I-9s for at least three years. If the employee stays with your company longer than that, keep the form for at least one year after the employee leaves. USCIS has the right to see your I-9s. You can be fined if you can't produce them.

CAUTION

Are you a federal contractor or subcontractor? If so, you must participate in a federal program called E-Verify. The program allows employers to use a Web-based system to verify an employee's eligibility to work in the United States. If you're not a federal contractor or subcontractor, participation is voluntary. For details, visit www.e-verify.gov. Some states require all employers to use the E-Verify system.

Paperwork Checklist

Here's a list of documents and forms that you should consider each time you hire someone:

☐ **Employment letter.** For a sample, see "Making a Job Offer," above.

☐ **Employee handbook.** If you have a handbook and didn't give it to the employee during the application and interview stages, now is the time to do so. Get a written acknowledgment of receipt and keep it in the employee's file. (For more on employee handbooks, see Chapter 2.)

☐ **Covenant not to compete.** If legally permissible in your state, this is useful if you have employees who could harm your business if they left to work for a competitor or started a business of their own in competition with yours. (For more information, see "Protect Against Unfair Competition," above.)

☐ **Confidentiality agreement.** Use such an agreement if you'll be disclosing trade secrets and other proprietary information to an employee.

☐ **Arbitration agreement.** This will allow you to resolve most disputes with an employee through an informal arbitration process, rather than through court. (For more information, see Chapter 8.)

☐ **IRS Form I-9.** This USCIS-required form is intended to ensure that all of your employees are legally permitted to work in the United States. (See "Immigration Law Requirements," above.)

☐ **IRS Form W-4.** Each employee must complete this form so you can determine how much to withhold from every paycheck for taxes. (See "Tax Compliance," above, and Chapter 5 for details.)

☐ **New hire reporting form.** Within a short time after you hire someone—20 days or less, depending on your state's rules—you must file this form with a designated state agency.

☐ **Employee benefit sign-up.** If your business offers employee benefit programs such as a 401(k) plan, you may have a sign-up procedure so employees can name their dependents and select options.

☐ **IRS Form SS-4 (new employers only).** The IRS requires an Employer Identification Number for all employers except sole proprietorships. (See Chapter 5.)

☐ **Notice of Health Care Coverage.** Under the Affordable Care Act, most employers must give employees written notice of their coverage options. See Chapter 4 for more information.

New Hire Reporting Form

Federal law requires you to report certain identifying information about new and rehired employees to a designated state agency. Under federal law, you have 20 days to provide this information, but some states require you to do it more quickly. The information becomes part of the National Directory of New Hires. It's used primarily to locate parents so that child support orders can be enforced. Government agencies also use the data to prevent improper payment of workers' compensation, unemployment benefits, or public assistance benefits.

Each state has its own form, but all require the following basic information:

- employee's name, address, Social Security number, and date of hire, and
- employer's name, address, and federal Employer Identification Number.

Some states ask for additional information, such as your state unemployment compensation number, the employee's driver's license number, and the employee's date of birth, though providing this information may be optional.

Your state department of labor can tell you how to get the forms and where to send them. (See the appendix for contact information.) ●

Personnel Practices

Y ou can avoid most legal problems in the workplace if you respect employees and treat them well. However, even though you treat workers fairly, there's always a chance that a dispute will get out of hand and an employee will sue your business. Or an unhappy employee may file a complaint with a government agency, alleging that you violated a statute or an administrative regulation. If that happens, you'll have to prove to a judge, jury, arbitrator, or investigator that you met your legal obligations to the employee. That can be harder than you think. Key paperwork may have been lost or never prepared in the first place. And witnesses may have forgotten what happened or have moved on to new jobs, where you might have trouble finding them.

To maintain a solid legal footing, you need a good paper trail. First, you need a good history of an employee's tenure with the company, which you can establish by keeping organized files. Second, you need written policies that establish the company's expectations and communicate those to your employees. Written policies can nip misunderstandings in the bud before they turn into pitched legal battles. They provide a cogent point of reference when you discuss problems with an employee, increasing the likelihood of reaching an amicable resolution. And in the worst-case scenario, these policies can help you defend yourself in a legal proceeding, showing that you treated employees consistently and fairly.

> **CAUTION**
>
> **Actions speak loudly, too.** You must start with sensible and fair policies and apply them with an even hand to all employees. A carefully developed paper trail is important, but if you've violated an employee's rights, the mere fact that you've created good paperwork won't shield you from the legal consequences.

Employee Files

Create a file for each employee, in which you keep important job-related information, including:

- job description
- job application

- offer of employment
- IRS Form W-4
- receipt for employee handbook
- written agreements, such as a confidentiality agreement or arbitration agreement
- periodic performance evaluations
- sign-up forms for employee benefits
- complaints from customers and coworkers
- compliments from customers and coworkers
- awards or citations for excellent performance
- warnings and disciplinary actions, and
- notes on an employee's attendance or tardiness.

Employee files can be a double-edged sword. They provide valuable documentation to support a firing, a demotion, or another action that's adverse to the employee. But the employee, in turn, can point to indiscreet entries and use them against you. It would be a mistake, for example, to include unsubstantiated criticism of an employee in the file or comments about the employee that are unrelated to job performance and qualifications.

Correcting Mistakes

To err is human, but leaving an error uncorrected can turn a mistake into a problem. Knowingly keeping false information on hand increases the risk of a lawsuit for defamation. It can lead people to conclude that you're callous, unfair, or incompetent. An employee is less likely to try to resolve problems with you informally if he or she doesn't see any positive changes as a result, and a judge or jury may likewise have a poor impression of you.

> **EXAMPLE:** Joe doesn't show up for work for a week after his paid vacation has ended. You put a note in his file documenting this. Then you learn that on the last day of his vacation he was in a serious car accident and wound up in intensive care. Put these additional facts in Joe's file. If you don't, Joe will have good reason to be angry with you, and anyone who later looks at the file won't put much stock in anything else they find there.

Confidentiality

Keep employee files locked up, or if you're operating remotely, ensure they are password-protected. Make them available only to people in your company who have a legitimate business need to have access to the files, such as managers, who must make decisions about promotions and discipline. Inform company personnel that the information in the files must remain confidential. While an employee or former employee may have a legal right to see his or her file (see "Access by Employees," below), other people don't, absent a subpoena.

It's a good idea to maintain separate confidential files for each employee's Form I-9, *Employment Eligibility Verification,* as well as photocopies of the documents the employee gives you to comply with the form's requirements. By doing so, you reduce the chances that a supervisor will make an employment decision based on an employee's immigration status (a prohibited practice). Moreover, government agencies are allowed to inspect all your I-9 forms when they visit the workplace, and keeping the forms in a separate file protects your employees' privacy as to the rest of their personal documents.

> **CAUTION**
>
> **Protect employees' Social Security numbers.** As an employer, you'll learn the Social Security number of each employee through a variety of sources such as Form W-4, Form I-9, the new hire reporting form, and employee benefit sign-up forms. (See the Paperwork Checklist at the end of Chapter 1.) It's well known that unscrupulous people use Social Security numbers for identity theft and other scams. To combat such misuse, you should have a privacy policy that protects the confidentiality of employees' Social Security numbers and limits who has access to those numbers. Also, don't put them on badges, parking permits, or lists that you distribute to employees. And check state law: Some states, such as California, make the protection of Social Security numbers a legal requirement.

Medical Information

Special guidelines apply to medical information gathered in the workplace. The federal Americans with Disabilities Act (ADA) imposes very strict rules on how you must handle information obtained from post-offer medical examinations and inquiries, and the Family and Medical Leave Act (FMLA) and Genetic Information Nondiscrimination Act (GINA) impose the same restrictions on records relating to medical leave and genetic information. You must keep the information in medical files separate from nonmedical records, and you must store the medical files in a separate locked cabinet. To further guarantee the confidentiality of medical files, designate a specific person to have access to those files.

These laws allow very limited disclosure of medical information. Under the ADA and FMLA, for example, you may:

- inform supervisors about necessary restrictions on an employee's duties and about necessary accommodations
- inform first aid and safety workers about a disability that may require emergency treatment and about specific procedures that are needed if the workplace must be evacuated
- tell employees of their possible exposure to a COVID-19 case in the workplace without revealing the identity of the individual who has tested positive, and
- provide medical information required by government officials and by insurance companies that require a medical exam for health or life insurance.

Under GINA, there are very few circumstances in which you may disclose genetic information about an employee. If you receive a court order specifically requesting the information or your company is under investigation for GINA compliance, for example, you may disclose this information to the appropriate person. (To find out more about disclosing genetic information under GINA, go to www.eeoc.gov/genetic-information-discrimination.) Otherwise, don't disclose medical information about employees. The best policy is to treat all medical information about all employees as confidential. (For more on the ADA, see Chapter 9, and for more on the FMLA, see Chapter 6.)

Access by Employees

Many states have laws requiring employers to give employees—and former employees—access to their own personnel files. How much access varies from state to state. Typically, if your state allows employees to see their files, you can insist that you or another supervisor be present to make sure nothing is taken, added, or changed. Some state laws allow employees to obtain copies of items in their files, but not necessarily all items. A state law, for example, may limit the employee to copies of documents that the employee has signed, such as a job application. If an employee is entitled to a copy of an item in the file or if you're inclined to let the employee have a copy of any document in the file, you—rather than the employee—should make the copy.

Usually, you won't have to let the employee see sensitive items such as information assembled for a criminal investigation, reference letters, and information that might violate the privacy of other people. In a few states, employees may insert rebuttals if they disagree with information in their personnel files. And some states require employees to request to see their files in writing before employers have to grant access.

For state-by-state rules on this issue, see "State Laws on Access to Personnel Records," in the appendix.

Informing Employees

Generally, the law doesn't require you to voluntarily tell employees what's in their employee files. You need only disclose information when an employee makes an appropriate request under an employee access law. About the only exception is the federal Fair Credit Reporting Act or FCRA (15 U.S.C. §§ 1681 and following), which requires you to tell employees if you're taking adverse action against them because of information in a consumer credit report. (See Chapter 1 for more information about your responsibilities under the FCRA.)

Still, it may be good practice to keep employees informed about what's going into their files. Otherwise, struggling employees may think they're doing fine and be justifiably surprised by a disciplinary action or firing. Admittedly, some employees can get demoralized if they're overwhelmed with negative information about their work, so some discretion is necessary in giving them feedback. But, on the other hand, letting employees know where they stand prevents surprises and can lead to improved performance. And if the employee doesn't shape up and winds up being fired, anyone reviewing the facts—a judge or jury, for example—will be more likely to side with you if you've given the employee fair warning about what was wrong.

> **RESOURCE**
>
> **Information on progressive discipline.** For more information about employee discipline, including how and when to document it, see *The Employee Performance Handbook*, by Margie Mader-Clark and Lisa Guerin (Nolo).

Employee Handbooks

If you have more than a couple of employees, consider creating an employee handbook that clearly explains your employment policies.

Advantages

An employee handbook can be of practical help in running your business. Once you give it to an employee, there can be no dispute over whether you gave the employee a list of paid days off or explained your policies on remote working. It's all there in writing, and everyone is getting the same information.

Beyond the practicalities, a good handbook gives you a bonus: a measure of legal protection if you're challenged by an employee in a court or administrative proceeding. A handbook that contains clear, reasonable policies—such as one stating that sexual harassment won't be tolerated in the workplace—is the critical beginning of your paper trail if problems develop later. It's an objective piece of evidence that shows you've adopted fair and uniform policies and that you've informed your employees of where they stand.

A good handbook should tell your employees how to let you know if they feel unfairly treated or have a workplace problem. This gives you a chance to react before a small misunderstanding erupts into a full-blown legal dispute. As another benefit, a well-written handbook may reduce the anxiety that some employees feel about their jobs. Employees will know what the rules and procedures are and where they can turn if they need to discuss an issue.

Even a small business with only a handful of employees can benefit from an employee handbook. You can produce one quickly and cheaply with *Create Your Own Employee Handbook*, by Lisa Guerin and Amy DelPo (Nolo). The cut-and-paste policies make the task a breeze, and you can pay for just a few hours of an employment lawyer's time to make sure your final product is up to date and complies with state and local laws.

If yours is a very small business, keep your handbook short and sweet at the start. Then, as your business grows, the framework necessary for a more detailed version will be in place. Review your handbook and update it periodically to reflect any changes in the law or your policies.

Don't Increase Your Legal Exposure

Your handbook may be treated as a contract that can actually limit your right to fire employees. To avoid that result, state both of the following in the handbook:

- Employees do not have employment contracts unless they are in writing and signed by the company president.
- Your company reserves the right to terminate employees for reasons not stated in the handbook or for no reason at all, and with or without prior warning or discipline.

Contents

Here are topics to consider covering in an employee handbook.

Introduction. Begin the handbook by describing your company's history and business philosophy. This helps set the tone, which can be friendly and welcoming. Make it clear to employees from the start that the handbook doesn't cover every possible situation.

Hours. State the normal working hours and how overtime pay is authorized for those employees entitled to it. (See Chapter 3 for more about wages and hours.)

Special Policies Related to the COVID-19 Pandemic

Virtually every employer in the United States has had to make major adjustments as a result of the COVID-19 pandemic, from allowing employees to work remotely to requiring employees to wear face coverings in the workplace. While many of these policies were enacted on the fly, employers should amend their employee handbooks to reflect these new rules at the earliest opportunity. Here are a few topics you might want to cover:

Remote work policies. Many employers allowed their employees to work from home to slow the spread of COVID-19, and some of them will continue to offer it after the threat of the virus has passed. It's essential to put your remote working policies in writing to ensure that you and your employees are on the same page. For example, what hours are workers expected to be available during the day, and when are breaks allowed? If you pay your employees hourly, how should they keep track of their time? If you're providing equipment such as laptops or smartphones, will these devices be monitored? What sort of non-business usage—checking personal email or social media sites, for example—is acceptable, if any? What data protection rules do employees need to follow when working from home?

Vaccination requirements. Employers are generally allowed to require employees to receive the COVID-19 vaccination (or other vaccinations) as a condition of employment, as long as they allow for medical and religious exemptions. If you choose to institute a mandatory vaccine policy, you should spell out the specifics in your employee handbook. For example, do employees have to provide proof that they received the vaccine? Do they get time off work—paid or unpaid—for vaccination? How should employees request a medical or religious exemption? Finally, note that mandatory vaccination policies might be illegal in some contexts, including if the work relationship is subject to a collective bargaining agreement, if workers have individual employment contracts that address the topic, or if prohibited by state or local laws.

Special Policies Related to the COVID-19 Pandemic (continued)

Updated health and safety rules. Employers have a legal duty to keep the workplace free of health and safety hazards, which includes protecting workers and customers from the coronavirus. The Occupational Safety and Health Administration (OSHA) has issued guidance for employers on limiting the spread of COVID-19 in the workplace. OSHA recommends that employers undertake a combination of measures including:

- ensuring that workers who have been exposed to COVID-19 are separated from other workers and sent home from work
- instituting mask wearing, social distancing, handwashing, and other good hygiene policies
- improving ventilation and in some cases, installing physical barriers in the workplace, and
- protecting workers who raise COVID-19 safety concerns from retaliation.

Whatever health and safety measures you decide to implement, apply your health and safety rules consistently across all employees and make sure they understand the consequences of not following them.

You can find OSHA's COVID-19 guidance for employers at www.osha.gov/coronavirus/safework. For more information on employee health and the COVID-19 pandemic, see Chapter 7.

Pay and salaries. Be clear about how pay and salaries are set and how they're raised. In very small businesses, this may be little more than a statement that levels of pay are established and adjusted by the company president, taking into consideration past performance, cost of living changes, and the ability of the business to pay. But if you do adopt a more formal procedure based on periodic performance reviews, explain how it works—and whether employees may be eligible for bonuses as well as salary increases.

Benefits. Benefits can be nearly as important to your employees as salary. Employee benefits typically include paid vacations, health benefits, sick pay, and unpaid leaves for extended illness, pregnancy, or family matters. (See Chapter 6 for information on family and medical leave.)

Federal law doesn't require you to provide paid vacation days, so you're free to set the terms under which such benefits are granted. No federal law requires employers to provide paid sick days, but the laws of a handful of states (including California and Massachusetts) and cities do. Before you adopt a sick leave policy, you'll need to check with your state and local labor departments to find out the rules. An employee handbook is the ideal place to inform employees about the rules governing these benefits. Be clear on whether the employee can carry unused sick or vacation days into the next year and what happens to such benefits if an employee quits or gets fired. Some states require employers to compensate employees for unused paid time when they leave; others don't. Check with your state labor department to learn the rule in your state, along with any others relating to vacation or sick leave. (See the appendix for contact information.)

Finally, let employees know what insurance benefits your company provides, such as health care coverage, life insurance, or a 401(k) or another retirement plan. Because these plans often change (and can be complex), it's best to leave the details to official plan documents. In your handbook, simply alert employees to the benefits you provide, and let them know where they can get more information.

Drug and alcohol abuse. Most businesses have a policy prohibiting employees' use of alcohol or illegal drugs in the workplace. In addition, some businesses offer employees help in dealing with abuse of these substances, often through an employee assistance program in which the business pays for professional counseling. Spell out your policies.

Harassment. Remind employees that harassment is illegal and violates your policies. (See Chapter 8 for more on harassment.) Let them know that you won't tolerate unwelcome comments or conduct based on a protected category (such as sex or race) and that you won't retaliate against those who speak up about it in the workplace. Finally, spell out your procedures for handling sexual harassment complaints. Specify how and to whom an employee can submit a complaint. Specify what you will do to investigate any complaints that you receive. Let employees know that you will handle every complaint as confidentially as possible but that you may need to disclose certain information on a need-to-know basis.

Discrimination. Assure employees that your business obeys all laws that prohibit discrimination, including discrimination based on race, color, religion, gender, sexual orientation, gender identity, national origin, age, pregnancy, citizenship, disability, genetic information, or any other protected characteristic. (See Chapter 8 for more on illegal discrimination.)

Attendance. Emphasize the importance of good attendance and showing up on time. Tell employees the types of absences that are excused—such as illness or a family member's death—and explain any requirements for notifying you if the employee won't be coming in or will be late. Clearly explain that piling up a load of unexcused absences or coming to work late too often can be a basis for disciplinary action or even firing.

Discipline. List the kinds of conduct that can get employees in trouble, such as theft, violence, or failing to follow COVID-19 safety protocols. But again, let employees know this isn't an exclusive list and that you always reserve the right to impose harsher discipline, or even terminate employment. (See "Disciplining Employees," below, for more information.)

Grooming and dress rules. If you have a reasonable business purpose for doing so, you can establish on-the-job standards for grooming and dress as a condition of employment. Rules governing employees' appearances may be illegal, however, if they discriminate against a particular group of employees or potential employees. Imposing different dress codes on men and women, for example, is usually not a good idea, although courts have sometimes upheld the practice. Bear in mind that employees may need an exception to your usual workplace dress code or grooming policies for religious reasons. If, for example, an employee wears a hijab (a headscarf) or a yarmulke for religious reasons, you may need to change or allow exceptions to a dress code policy that prohibits employees from wearing any head coverings at work.

If you require your employees to wear a uniform, the federal Fair Labor Standards Act (FLSA) prohibits you from deducting the cost of work-related clothing if doing so would cause the employee's wage to fall below the minimum wage. (For more on the FLSA, see Chapter 3.) And some states require employers to bear the costs of uniforms, including the cost of maintenance if special care is required (such as dry cleaning).

Social media. In your social media policy, you will likely want to prohibit employees from making personal posts during work time or using company equipment. In addition, you should inform employees that company policies prohibiting, for example, harassment, threats, and other misconduct, apply with equal force to their online posts. To comply with Federal Trade Commission rules, you should also let employees know that they must disclose their employment relationship with your company if they use social media to promote the company's services or products (including through online reviews). However, you must make sure that your social media rules don't discourage employees from having online discussions about your company's policies, practices, and working conditions. Federal labor law gives employees the right to discuss workplace issues with each other, whether online or off. And the National Labor Relations Board (NLRB) has been increasingly active in policing employers that adopt policies that might discourage these discussions.

Electronic usage. If you provide computers, cellphones, tablets, email accounts, or other electronic means of communication to employees, advise them not to expect privacy when using these company-issued devices or services. Clearly reserve the right to monitor employee usage. (See Chapter 11 for information on employee privacy.)

Employee safety. State that employee safety is a major concern and that employees are expected to heed the posted safety rules and to call to your attention any potentially dangerous conditions. (See Chapter 7 for more about health and safety.)

Smoking. Many states or cities prohibit workplace smoking. If such regulations exist where your business operates, make sure that your smoking policy follows them. You may have to ban smoking or ensure that smoking areas are segregated entirely from nonsmoking areas or that outdoor smoking areas are not next to building entrances or exits. (See Chapter 7 for more information about smoking in the workplace.)

Complaints. Let employees know what procedures they can follow to resolve complaints. Having a written complaint procedure in your handbook helps shield your business from liability if an employee sues claiming illegal harassment or discrimination.

Sample Employee Handbook Acknowledgment

Please read this handbook carefully. The information in it will acquaint you with company policies and will answer many of your questions. From time to time, these policies may be updated in writing. Copies of these updates will be provided to you.

Please keep in mind that this handbook does not contain all of the information you will need as an employee. You will receive other information through written notices as well as orally.

This handbook is not an employment contract. Unless you have a written employment contract with XYZ Company signed by the president of the company, you are an at-will employee. This means you or the company may terminate our employment relationship at any time, with or without a reason.

In the future, your status as an at-will employee can only be changed through a written contract signed by the president of XYZ Company. No oral statements, promises, or contracts regarding the terms and conditions of your employment are valid.

Receipt and Acknowledgment

I have received a copy of XYZ Company's employee handbook. I have read the above information and I acknowledge that it is a correct statement of my employment status. I understand that this employee handbook is not a contract for employment and does not affect my employment status in any way.

Signature _____

Date _____

Documenting an Employee's Acceptance

Document that employees received the handbook by having each employee sign an acknowledgment form. This form reinforces that the handbook isn't an employment contract, doesn't guarantee continued employment, and doesn't obligate your company to continue current job benefits forever.

Include with your handbook two copies of an acknowledgment such as the one above. Then ask employees to sign both copies to acknowledge that they have received the handbook and are familiar with its terms. Keep one signed copy in the employee's personnel file, and give the employee the other copy. Have each employee sign a similar receipt each time you distribute revisions or updates of your handbook.

Employee Performance Reviews

Most large companies review and evaluate their employees periodically. This is a sound management practice and one that even small companies should consider, especially for new employees.

Benefits of Evaluations

Evaluating employees periodically gives them a chance to improve if they're not performing well. If you later find it necessary to discipline or fire an employee, it won't come as a surprise to the employee.

By putting your evaluations in writing and saving them in the employee's file, you have a credible history of documented problems you can use if an employee claims the termination was for an illegal reason. Legally, you don't have to have a good reason, or any reason, to fire an at-will employee, and you don't have to give notice in advance or afford the employee a chance to improve. However, an employee who is fired may claim that the firing was illegal, for example, because it was based on a prohibited characteristic, such as race or gender. You want to stand ready to rebut any possible claim that you fired an employee for an illegal reason. The best way to do this is to record, in written evaluations and other documents, the legitimate reasons you relied on to fire the employee.

EXAMPLE: Charlotte works at the counter of Parts Plus, an auto parts retailer. Parts Plus fires Charlotte after she's been there for 18 months. She sues, claiming that Parts Plus fired her in retaliation for complaining to a state agency a month before about photos of nude women that were posted in the back room where she had to go to retrieve auto parts for customers. At trial, Parts Plus produces copies of written evaluations from Charlotte's file.

Eight months before the firing, Charlotte's supervisor had written: "You must become more familiar with our inventory of parts for imported cars. Also, you need to make fewer errors on the computer system."

Two months before the firing, the supervisor had written: "You're still having problems with imports. We will arrange for you to attend a computer training seminar at the community college at company expense, but you must improve your performance."

Company records separately show that Charlotte attended only one of the six training sessions and that, two days before the firing, she mixed up orders for three good customers. The upshot: Because of the company's thorough documentation of Charlotte's ongoing problems, Charlotte loses her case against Parts Plus.

Evaluations have two common purposes: to help employees improve performance and to protect employers from wrongful termination claims. To achieve both ends, thoroughly and objectively evaluate each employee at least twice a year. Take the evaluation process seriously, and do a careful, conscientious job. In some states, employees have successfully sued employers who used poor evaluation procedures for "negligent evaluation": failing to review employees' work accurately or giving unfairly poor marks on an appraisal.

The Evaluation Process

To keep the evaluation process as consistent and objective as possible, devise an evaluation form that you can use with all employees in the same job category. (See below for a sample.) The form should focus on how well the employee has performed the various duties of the job.

Fill in the form before you meet with the employee, following these guidelines:

- Give a balanced picture of the employee's strengths and weaknesses.
- Use specific examples of where the employee has met, exceeded, or fallen short of expectations.
- Let the employee know the areas that need improvement. Set objective goals for the employee to meet.
- Where an employee's performance is substantially below par, set a date to meet again with the employee to review progress.
- If the employee's failure to improve may lead to disciplinary measures or discharge, state this clearly in the evaluation.

Leave space on the form for the employee to comment on the evaluation and to acknowledge receiving a copy of it.

Once you've completed the written evaluation, meet with the employee to go over it. If you cringe at confronting an employee with criticism, try the sandwich approach: Say something positive, something negative, then something positive. Remember, too, that employees will find it easier to accept criticism—and try to improve behavior—if you focus on workplace performance and not on the employee's personality.

Whatever your approach, you must tell it like it is. Should you later have legal trouble initiated by a fired employee, a judge or jury won't look at your evaluations in a vacuum. For example, they'll sense that something is wrong if you consistently rate a worker's performance as poor or mediocre but continue to hand out generous raises or perhaps even promotions. The logical conclusion: You didn't take the criticisms in your evaluation report seriously, so you shouldn't expect the employee to take them seriously, either.

It's just as damaging to give an employee glowing praise in report after report—perhaps to make the employee feel good—and then fire the employee for a single infraction. That strikes most people as unfair. And unfair employers often lose court fights, especially in situations where a sympathetic employee appears to have been treated harshly.

CONFIDENTIAL

Employee Performance Evaluation

Employee name _____

Job title _____

Reviewer _____

Review date _____

JOB PERFORMANCE

(In responding, give specific examples of strengths and weaknesses as often as possible.)

General Quality of Work

(Focus on accuracy, attention to detail, originality, timeliness, organization, degree of supervision needed to accomplish tasks.)

_____

_____

Dependability

(Focus on attendance, punctuality, attentiveness, ability to follow instructions, ability to meet deadlines.)

_____

_____

Job Knowledge

(Focus on level of knowledge and skills required to master work required, willingness to take the initiative in tackling new tasks.)

_____

_____

Communication Skills

(Focus on ability to use language effectively, ability to express ideas clearly and grammatically, command of oral and written language, ability to explain concepts to others.)

_____

_____

Employee Performance Evaluation (continued)

Management Ability

(Focus on ability to identify problems, ability to creatively solve problems, ability to plan, assign, and schedule workload, ability to guide an individual or group to complete a task.)

_____

_____

Other Job Requirements

(Focus on specific needs of business or needs for individual improvement: public contact, self-development, quality control, ability to stay within cost guidelines.)

PERFORMANCE SUMMARY

What are the employee's outstanding and strongest points?

_____

_____

What are the employee's shortcomings and weaknesses?

_____

_____

Specific accomplishments and changes since last performance review.

_____

_____

GOALS FOR IMPROVEMENT

What can the employee do to be more effective or make needed improvements?

_____

_____

What additional training or equipment would be helpful?

_____

In what ways could the job be changed to make better use of the employee's skills and abilities?

_____

Employee Performance Evaluation (continued)

EMPLOYEE FEEDBACK

(To be completed by the employee.)

What are your most important accomplishments on the job over the past year?

_____

What are your weakest job performance areas or those most in need of improvement?

_____

What steps could you take to improve?

_____

What can management do to support your efforts to improve?

_____

What are your supervisor's strengths and weaknesses in managing your work?

_____

Other work concerns you would like to discuss.

_____

NEXT REVIEW

Date scheduled for next review _____

Particular areas targeted for improvement:

_____

_____

Employee Signature: _____

Date: _____

Supervisor's Signature: _____

Date: _____

If your system is working, employees with excellent evaluations should not need to be fired for poor performance. And employees with poor performance shouldn't be getting big raises.

> **TIP**
>
> **Once is not enough.** Feedback should be an ongoing process. The written evaluation should be a culmination of the feedback you've given throughout the year. If some or all of your workforce works remotely, consider scheduling a regular one-on-one feedback session with each employee every month or quarter. Your goal is to have no surprises about how an employee is doing. You should keep the employee informed of any problems and take steps to correct them through progressive discipline, discussed in the next section.

Some employers encourage employees to give their own evaluation of how they're doing. Some may also ask employees to rate their supervisors. You'll benefit by making the evaluation process a two-way street. Listen carefully to what the employees say. You'll likely learn a thing or two.

Sample Employee Evaluation Form

The Employee Performance Evaluation form shown above can be adapted to meet your personal style, your workplace, and the type of work that employees perform for your business.

Disciplining Employees

Periodic evaluations can work hand in hand with another management strategy—progressive discipline—to keep employees fairly informed of how they're doing and when their jobs are at risk.

Because losing a job can obviously be painful for an employee, some employers make it a practice to fire problem employees only after the workers have gone through a series of less drastic disciplinary moves. A system of progressive discipline may not be right for all businesses. But if you do see fit to have such a policy in place, it can go a long way toward demonstrating your fairness if you eventually have to fire an employee and the employee sues you.

Among the steps you can build into your program are coaching or counseling, verbal warnings, written warnings, suspension, and, finally, dismissal. A fired employee's potential wrongful termination claim will be weakened if you can show that the employee knew about the problems that eventually led to dismissal but failed to shape up.

If you follow this approach and generally practice a policy of progressive discipline, make it clear to employees that you reserve the right to fire employees at will—especially for serious infractions—and that your policy of progressive discipline is left to your discretion as an employer. (See below for an example of language to include in a disciplinary policy.)

Having a policy of progressive discipline can backfire if you create the impression that every employee transgression will be dealt with in that same way. A fired employee, for example, may claim the right to progressive discipline before being fired.

Obviously, there are times when you may conclude that an employee's conduct is so offensive that decisive action—including immediate discharge—is warranted. To keep an enlightened management policy from turning into a fixed employee right, make it clear that you have the option to dispense with progressive discipline when you choose to do so. (See the sample policy, below, for guidance.)

RESOURCE

Need more information on progressive discipline? For an in-depth discussion, including step-by-step instructions and a sample written policy, see *The Employee Performance Handbook*, by Margie Mader-Clark and Lisa Guerin (Nolo).

Sample Written Progressive Discipline Policy

The following is a sample written progressive discipline policy that you can include in your handbook.

Any employee conduct that, in the opinion of XYZ Company, interferes with or adversely affects our business is sufficient grounds for disciplinary action. This action can range from oral warnings to immediate discharge. Depending on the conduct, it is our general policy to take disciplinary steps in the following order:

- verbal warnings
- written warnings
- suspension, and
- termination.

To decide on the appropriate action, we may consider the seriousness of your conduct, your employment record, your ability to correct the conduct, actions we have taken for similar conduct by other employees, how your action affects customers, and other circumstances.

Some conduct may result in immediate dismissal. Here are examples:

- acting violently or threatening to do so
- theft of company property
- excessive tardiness or absenteeism
- arguing or fighting with customers or coworkers
- using or possessing alcohol or illegal drugs at work
- coming to work under the influence of alcohol or illegal drugs
- failing to carry out reasonable job assignments
- making false statements in a job application
- violating company rules and regulations, and
- unlawful discrimination or harassment.

These are only examples. You may terminate your employment at any time; the company reserves the same right.

Wages and Hours

The main federal law affecting workers' pay is the Fair Labor Standards Act or FLSA. (29 U.S.C. §§ 201 and following.) This law sets out federal requirements for the minimum wage and overtime pay. It also prohibits wage differences based on gender, requires you to pay employees for all the work hours, and sets out the rules regarding the employment of workers younger than 18. This chapter covers your obligations under the FLSA.

Although the FLSA coverage is broad, there are a few instances in which it does not apply:

- If you operate a farm, your workers aren't entitled to full FLSA coverage. (For more information, go to www.dol.gov/whd/regs/compliance/ whdfs12.pdf.)
- If you run a transportation business (such as a trucking company) that's regulated by the federal Motor Carrier Act, there's an overtime pay exemption for workers whose activities affect the safe operation of vehicles, such as certain drivers, drivers' helpers, loaders, and mechanics. (For more information on this exemption, go to www.dol.gov/whd/regs/ compliance/whdfs19.pdf.)

Most states also have their own wage and hour laws. Usually the state law mirrors the FLSA. Some states, however, have more stringent requirements. If you operate your business in one of these states, you must follow the stricter rule. For example, in most instances, California's wage and hour law is more stringent than the FLSA; California employers should therefore follow the California law where it's more stringent. See the appendix to learn the minimum wage requirements in your state. For additional information on the wage and hour rules in your state, contact your state labor department. (See the appendix for contact details.)

Overtime and Minimum Wage Requirements

The FLSA requires you to pay certain employees at least $7.25 per hour and to pay time and a half for any hours more than 40 that those employees work in a workweek. (The Biden administration and many in Congress have announced their support for increasing the minimum wage to as much as $15.00 per hour, phased in over a number of years, but no action has been taken as this book goes to press. Check this book's companion page for updates—the introduction explains how to access it.)

Wage and Hour Laws Don't Cover Independent Contractors

Wage and hour laws cover employees, not independent contractors, so it is important to understand how state and federal laws define each category. Here, we explain the FLSA's definition. To find out about your state law's definition, contact your state labor department. (See the appendix for contact details.)

The FLSA considers workers to be independent contractors if they're economically independent from your business. How can you tell if they are economically independent? Consider the following questions:

- Do you have the right to control how the individual performs the work, as opposed to simply accepting or rejecting a final product? The more you control the way the work is done, the more the worker looks like an employee.
- Does the worker have an opportunity for profit and loss? If the worker bears the economic risk of doing business, then that's a factor in favor of independent contractor status.
- Does the worker have any investment in equipment and facilities? The greater the investment, the more it appears that the worker is an independent contractor.
- Do the worker's services require special skills? The more specialized the skills, the more likely it is that the worker is an independent contractor.
- How permanent is the relationship between you and the worker? A long-term relationship—especially one that lasts for a year or more—is a factor in favor of employee status.
- Are the worker's services an integral part of your business? If so, it's more likely that the worker is an employee. For example, someone who works for a drugstore as a pharmacist would probably be considered to be an integral part of the business.

Independent contractors are covered in more detail in Chapter 12. You can find even more information in *Working With Independent Contractors*, by Stephen Fishman (Nolo).

Those employees who are entitled to the minimum wage and overtime pay are called "nonexempt" employees, because they are not exempt from the requirements. Those who are not entitled to minimum wage or overtime are called "exempt" employees, because they are exempt from the requirements.

In this section, we first examine who is exempt and who isn't:

- **Employees who are always nonexempt.** These employees are always entitled to overtime pay and a minimum wage.
- **Employees who are always exempt.** These employees are never entitled to overtime pay or a minimum wage.
- **Employees who are exempt if they meet certain requirements.** The bulk of workers get classified under the rules described in this section.
- **Employees who are exempt from overtime only.** These employees are still entitled to a minimum wage.

Once you've figured out which employees are exempt and which aren't, we'll cover your duty to pay nonexempt employees a minimum wage or overtime pay.

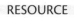 **RESOURCE**

Sometimes, an employee doesn't clearly fall into one of the nonexempt or exempt categories discussed below. If you're unable to tell whether an employee or group of employees is exempt, don't risk getting it wrong. It's better to pay an employment lawyer to figure it out for you than to risk paying fines, back pay, and litigation fees. (See "The Consequences of Bending the Rules," below, for information on what happens if you misclassify an employee.)

Employees Who Are Always Nonexempt

The law sets aside a group of employees who are always nonexempt and therefore always entitled to both overtime pay and a minimum wage, regardless of whether they seem to fall into one of the exempt categories described later in this section. These employees are blue-collar employees and first responders:

- Blue-collar employees are people who perform work involving repetitive operations with their hands, physical skill, and energy. These employees include carpenters, electricians, mechanics, plumbers, ironworkers, craftsmen, operating engineers, longshore workers, construction workers, and laborers (minimally skilled workers such as those who dig trenches or carry lumber or bricks).
- First responders are workers on the front lines of protecting safety and health. As defined by the U.S. Department of Labor (DOL), most first responders are public employees, like police officers and firefighters. But some first responders may work in the private sector as well. These include emergency medical technicians, ambulance personnel, and hazardous materials workers.

If you have employees who are blue-collar workers or first responders, those employees are never exempt, no matter how lofty their title or how much they earn. They're always entitled to a minimum wage and overtime pay.

Employees Who Are Always Exempt

There are a handful of employees who the law says are always exempt and therefore never entitled to overtime or a minimum wage. They are:

- employees of seasonal amusement or recreational businesses, such as a ski resort that's open only during the winter or an amusement park that's open only during the summer
- employees of local newspapers having a circulation of less than 4,000
- newspaper delivery workers
- switchboard operators employed by phone companies that have no more than 750 stations, and
- some farmworkers.

So if you run a small newspaper, for example, or operate a concession stand at a summer amusement park, you don't need to worry about the overtime and minimum wage rules described in this chapter.

Employees Who Are Exempt If They Meet Certain Requirements

The FLSA identifies several categories of employees as being exempt if they meet certain requirements. Those categories are:

- white-collar employees (that is, executive, administrative, and professional employees)
- highly paid employees
- outside sales employees
- computer workers, and
- apprentices.

In the following subsections, we look at each group in more detail.

White-Collar Employees

You do not have to pay overtime or a minimum wage to exempt white-collar employees. To fall into this category, employees must meet all of the following requirements:

- **Earnings requirement.** They must earn at least a set minimum amount per week.
- **Salary basis.** They must receive their minimum earnings on a "salary basis." There's more on this requirement below.
- **Duties.** They must perform certain duties that involve executive, administrative, or professional skill.

Earnings requirement. Currently, employees must earn at least $684 per week ($35,568 per year) to be exempt from overtime and minimum wage requirements.

Salary basis. To pay someone on a salary basis means that you regularly pay that person a preset amount each pay period (such as weekly or biweekly) and that you don't reduce the amount because of variations in the quality or quantity of the employee's work. If you dock an employee's salary for these variations, the employee—and every other employee with that employee's rank and duties—may no longer be exempt. Accordingly, if a salaried employee misses a few hours of work to take care of personal business, you shouldn't reduce his or her salary to make up for that time. The reasoning behind the nonreduction rule is that salaried workers often put in many hours of overtime without getting paid extra for it, so it's unfair to reduce their pay if they miss a few hours now and then. Still, there are times when it's okay to dock a salaried employee's pay without jeopardizing his or her exempt status. To find out more, see "Docking Pay Can Cost You," below.

Duties. To be exempt, the white-collar employee must perform duties that are either executive, administrative, or professional in nature. Let's look at each of these in turn.

Docking Pay Can Cost You

For an employee to fall within the executive, administrative, or professional exemption, the basic rule is that you must pay that employee a full salary for any week in which the employee performs any work, regardless of how many days or hours the employee actually works. You don't, however, have to pay the employee for any workweek in which he or she performs no work. And while docking an employee's salary will generally make an employee (and all other employees with the same rank and duties) nonexempt, in the following situations, you can dock the employee without jeopardizing exempt status:

- when the employee is absent from work for one or more full days for personal reasons other than sickness or disability
- for absences of one or more full days due to sickness or disability if you make the deduction under a plan providing for wage replacement benefits (such as a workers' compensation plan that pays workers for time missed due to a work-related injury or a paid sick leave policy)
- to offset amounts the employee receives as jury or witness fees, or for military pay
- for penalties imposed in good faith for infractions of safety rules of major significance, or
- for unpaid disciplinary suspensions of one or more full days imposed for infractions of workplace conduct rules.

Also, you don't have to pay the full salary in the first or final week of employment if the employee starts or finishes work midweek or for weeks in which an exempt employee takes unpaid leave under the Family and Medical Leave Act.

Executive Employees

Typically, executive employees are people you hire to run your business or one of its departments. They perform high-level management duties such as planning budgets and monitoring legal compliance. They have a lot of autonomy in doing their jobs, and they always have people working under them.

To fit within the executive employee exemption, the employee must:

- have the primary duty of managing a business or one of its departments
- regularly direct the work of at least two or more full-time employees (or their equivalent, such as one full-time employee and two half-time employees), and
- be authorized to hire or fire employees or make recommendations for hiring, firing, and promotions that carry special weight.

Of these requirements, the first is the most vague. After all, what does it mean to "manage"? Fortunately, the U.S. Department of Labor has issued a list of activities that qualify as management duties. An employee who primarily performs any one of these activities will probably meet the management test, but it's better if you can point to two or more:

- interviewing, selecting, and training employees
- deciding how much to pay employees and creating their work schedules
- directing employees' work
- maintaining production or sales records for use in supervision
- appraising employee productivity and efficiency for use in recommending promotions or other changes in status
- handling employee complaints and grievances
- disciplining employees
- planning the work
- determining the techniques to be used
- apportioning work among employees
- determining the type of materials, supplies, machinery, equipment, or tools to be used
- determining the merchandise to be bought, stocked, and sold
- controlling the flow and distribution of materials or merchandise and supplies

- providing for the safety and security of employees or business property
- planning and controlling the budget, or
- monitoring or implementing legal compliance measures.

Let's look at a couple of examples to see these rules at work:

- **This employee fits within the exemption.** Joe works for a mail-order company, where he manages the shipping department. He receives a salary of $750 a week. He directs the work of three employees, whom he can hire or fire. Joe is an exempt executive employee.
- **This employee does not fit within the exemption.** Jerry works for a mail-order company where he is called the "shipping department manager" and receives a salary of $690 a week. Jerry packages orders and gets them ready for UPS to pick up. He also directs the work of two junior employees who are assigned to him, but he doesn't get to hire or fire those coworkers, nor does he have any say about whether they'll be promoted or receive pay increases. Jerry is not an exempt executive employee, even though his title includes the word "manager."

Employees Who Are Also Owners

An employee who owns at least a 20% equity interest in an employing entity (corporation, limited liability company, or partnership)—and is actively engaged in managing the entity—is an exempt executive employee, regardless of whether the employee is salaried or earns a particular amount.

For example, let's say Gina owns 20% of the stock of Pizza Heaven Inc., where she is employed as a pizza maker. Because Gina isn't engaged in managing the business, she isn't an exempt executive, even though she's a part owner of the business. Unless she qualifies under another exemption, she's entitled to a minimum wage and overtime pay.

Gerald, on the other hand, owns a 40% membership interest in Nuts and Bolts LLC and is employed by the company to manage its hardware store. Because Gerald owns at least 20% of the business and is actively engaged in managing it, he's an exempt executive and isn't entitled to overtime or the minimum wage protections.

Administrative Employees

You may have employees who don't supervise any other workers but play important roles in making your business operate efficiently and properly. If these employees make important business decisions and have a fair amount of authority, they may qualify as exempt administrative employees.

To be an exempt administrative employee under the FLSA, a worker must:

- primarily do office or nonmanual work directly related to managing a business or its general business operations, and
- exercise discretion and independent judgment on significant business matters.

These criteria are vague and subjective, and can be frustratingly difficult to apply. Unfortunately, the U.S. Department of Labor provides very little practical information to guide you in real-life situations. Still, it's possible to make some sense of these standards. Let's look at each one.

Work directly related to managing a business or its general business operations. The work must be related to running or servicing a business rather than making things or serving customers. So an employee who works on a production line, sells products in a store, or serves food in a restaurant won't meet this test. By contrast, a worker who prepares budgets or procures supplies or handles advertising and public relations typically will. Here are a couple of examples:

- **This employee does not fit this prong of the test.** Helen works as a barista at a café. Her work isn't directly related to managing the business, so she doesn't meet the first test for being an exempt administrative employee.
- **This employee does fit this prong of the test.** Harold works as an accountant for a chain of coffee houses. Because his work is directly related to managing the business, he may be an exempt administrative employee if he also meets the second test.

The U.S. Department of Labor says that work in the following areas is related to managing a business: tax; finance; accounting; budgeting; auditing; insurance; quality control; purchasing; procurement; advertising; human resources; employee benefits; marketing; research; safety and health; personnel management; labor relations; public relations; government relations; computer network, Internet, and database administration; and legal and regulatory compliance.

Discretion and independent judgment on significant business matters. This is also rather murky territory. The standards are unusually subjective, especially the term "significant business matters." Here are some factors the U.S. Department of Labor looks at in applying this regulation:

- Can the employee formulate and interpret management policies?
- Does the employee carry out major assignments affecting business operations?
- Can the employee commit your business in matters that have significant financial impact?
- Can the employee waive your established policies without prior approval?
- Does the employee provide expert advice to management?
- Does the employee handle and resolve complaints or grievances?

Here are a couple of examples to illustrate how this administrative employee exemption plays out:

- **This employee fits within the exemption.** Irma is the estimator for an electrical contracting firm. She discusses proposed new jobs with customers. She then figures out how much her firm should charge and prepares a written quote. If the customer signs the quote, Irma's company is legally bound to perform the contract at the stated price. Irma also has authority to resolve any disputes with customers. She earns a salary of $1,000 per week. Irma is an exempt administrative employee.
- **This employee does not fit within the exemption.** Irving works as a bookkeeper for an electrical contracting firm. He pays bills as they become due, prepares paychecks, and oversees the firm's bank account. He operates under written guidelines established by the firm's accountant; he can't deviate from the guidelines without prior approval from the firm's accountant or president. Irving earns a salary of $800 a week. He is not an exempt administrative employee. It's true that he does office work directly related to managing the business, but he doesn't exercise independent judgment on significant business matters.

Learned Professionals

Lawyers, accountants, doctors, dentists, engineers, teachers, scientists, architects, and pharmacists are generally exempt employees if their jobs involve using their own judgment and discretion. The same is true of certain health care professionals, such as certified medical technologists, registered nurses, dental hygienists, and physician's assistants. For anyone else who seems like a professional but who doesn't fall into one of these clear-cut cases, consult a lawyer.

Creative Professionals

A creative professional is someone who primarily performs work requiring invention, imagination, originality, or talent in a recognized artistic or creative field. Typical creative professionals include actors, musicians, composers, soloists, graphic artists, writers, cartoonists, essayists, and novelists.

Journalists may qualify if their primary work is creative—for example, contributing a unique interpretation or analysis to the news—but not if they only collect, organize, and record information that's routine or already public.

Job Titles Aren't Everything

Job titles alone don't determine whether someone is an exempt executive, administrative, or professional employee. The actual work relationship is what counts. Some employers try to avoid the minimum wage and overtime requirements by labeling all entry level employees "assistant managers," and then requiring them to work well past the 40-hour workweek with no overtime compensation. The Department of Labor is well aware of such abuses. Employers who mislabel employees to circumvent the law are playing a dangerous game and can wind up paying stiff penalties. (See "The Consequences of Bending the Rules," below, for more about the dangers of violating the FLSA.)

Certain Highly Paid Employees

Most employees who earn big bucks will be exempt because they qualify as executives, administrators, or professionals. Occasionally, however, a high earner can't be neatly pigeonholed into one of these white-collar categories. Such an employee is exempt from overtime if all of the following requirements are met:

- The employee must perform office or nonmanual work.
- The employee must meet a minimum earnings requirement. Currently, the employee's total annual compensation must be at least $107,432, including at least $684 per week paid on a salary or fee basis.
- The employee must regularly perform at least one of the duties of an exempt executive, administrative, or professional employee, as summarized above.

Here are a couple of examples:

- **This person fits within the exemption.** Jack works for a company that makes car accessories. His job is to come up with ideas for new products that have great market potential. To do this, he keeps tabs on what competitors are doing, and he conducts market research. Each month, he presents a written report to management with his recommendations for new products and the reasons why he believes the products will sell well. Because Jack is so good at what he does and has an impressive track record, the company pays him a salary of $1,900 a week ($98,800 a year) plus a year-end bonus of $10,000. Jack is an exempt highly paid employee. He meets the earnings requirement (his total annual compensation exceeds $107,432) and performs at least one duty of an executive or administrator: performing market research and providing expert advice to management.

- **This person does not fit within the exemption.** Joan works for a major natural food market, where she is paid $2,100 a week to inspect farms to make sure that the food the market buys meets her employer's definition of "organic." She applies her employer's standards and doesn't exercise independent judgment. Joan is not an exempt highly paid employee. Although she meets the compensation test (she earns $109,200 annually), her job doesn't require her to perform any of the duties of an executive, administrative, or professional employee.

Outside Sales Employees

Your business may employ salespeople who call on current and potential customers. If so, these employees may be exempt. For an outside sales employee to be exempt, both of the following must be true:

- The employee's primary duty must be making sales or obtaining orders or contracts for services or the use of facilities.
- The employee must regularly work away from your place of business.

Typically, an exempt sales employee makes sales or takes orders at a customer's home or business place. A driver who delivers products—and also sells them—may be exempt as an outside sales employee. The key is whether making sales is a primary duty of the employee. Here are a couple of examples:

- **This person fits within the exemption.** Jessie works for a distributor of medical devices. She regularly visits doctors and hospital administrators in a three-state region to obtain orders for the devices. Jessie is an exempt outside sales employee. Her primary duty is to obtain orders for her employer's products, and she regularly works away from her employer's place of business.
- **This person does not fit within the exemption.** Jamie works for a distributor of medical devices. She spends most of her time in the office responding to phone and email inquiries about her employer's products. Occasionally—about once a month—she visits a customer or two to demonstrate a device, and she may take an order at that time. Jamie is not an exempt outside sales employee. Sales work is only a small part of her job. What's more, she only occasionally works away from her employer's place of business.

Drug company employees who call on doctors are a special case. Sales representatives who are hired to obtain nonbinding commitments from doctors to prescribe their employers' drugs qualify as outside sales employees, even though these reps don't make sales or obtain orders for the drugs.

Employees in Certain Computer-Related Jobs

You don't have to provide a minimum wage or overtime pay to certain computer workers. To qualify for the computer employee exemption, the employee's primary duty must consist of one of the following:

- applying systems analysis techniques and procedures
- designing, developing, documenting, analyzing, creating, testing, or modifying computer systems or programs based on design specs
- designing, developing, documenting, analyzing, creating, testing, or modifying computer programs related to machine operating systems; or
- a combination of the above duties, using the same level of skills.

This exemption applies if you pay the employee an hourly rate of at least $27.63 or at least $684 per week on a salary basis.

Exemptions for certain computer-related jobs don't include employees who make or repair computers and related equipment. The exemption also doesn't include employees who use specialized computer skills but who aren't primarily engaged in computer systems analysis or programming, such as drafters and others skilled in computer-aided design software. (But watch out, because some of these employees—especially engineers—may be exempt as learned professionals.)

Apprentices

An apprentice is a worker who's at least 16 years old and who has signed an agreement with you to learn a skilled trade, such as learning to be an electrician or plumber. Be aware that your state may have a law limiting the number of hours you can hire someone to work as an apprentice. State law may also require you to pay the apprentice a certain percentage of the minimum wage. Check with your state labor department for more information. (See the appendix for contact details.)

The next step after working as an apprentice is to become a journeyman. The FLSA requires that during the time that someone works for you as an apprentice, his or her pay must average at least 50% of what you pay journeymen.

Employees Who Are Exempt From Overtime Only

A number of employees are exempt from the overtime pay requirements only. You must still pay these employees at least the minimum wage. These employees are:

- taxicab drivers
- commissioned employees of retail or service establishments, if the employee's regular rate of pay is more than one and one-half times the minimum wage and if more than half the employee's pay comes from commissions
- employees who sell cars, trucks, trailers, farm implements, boats, or aircraft if they're working for a nonmanufacturing business that sells these items to ultimate buyers
- announcers, news editors, and chief engineers of radio and TV stations located in a town or city that has fewer than 100,000 people (or, in some cases, in a town or city that has fewer than 25,000 people)

- movie theater employees
- home health care companions
- farmworkers (as noted above, workers on some farms are also exempt from the minimum wage requirements), and
- parts clerks and mechanics who service cars, trucks, or farm implements if they're working for a nonmanufacturing business that sells these items to ultimate buyers. Those who work for manufacturers or midlevel distributors aren't exempt, for example, a salesperson who works for a distributor that sells farm implements to retail dealers is entitled to overtime pay.

In addition, employees of hospitals and residential care facilities get special treatment. If you operate this sort of facility, check with the Department of Labor for details.

You can require employees who lack a high school diploma or who haven't finished eighth grade to spend up to ten hours a week in reading and basic skills programs. You must pay these employees their regular wages for time spent in training, but you don't have to pay them at the overtime rate (even if the training is on top of a 40-hour workweek).

Paying a Minimum Wage

You must pay all nonexempt employees (described above) at least the minimum wage, currently $7.25 per hour. Federal law allows you to pay a training wage of $4.25 an hour to employees younger than 20 during their first 90 days on the job. You're not allowed to fire employees just so you can replace them with young workers and pay them the lower training wage.

The law in your state or city may set a minimum wage higher than the federal rate. If so, you must pay your workers the higher rate. But if the federal rate is higher, you must pay that instead. (See "State Minimum Wage Laws for Tipped and Regular Employees," in the appendix.)

Poster Requirements

Federal law requires you to display the federal minimum wage poster, "Employee Rights Under the Fair Labor Standards Act," prominently in the workplace. It's available at the nearest office of the U.S. Department of Labor's Wage and Hour Division, or you can download it from the DOL's website at www.dol.gov. Your state labor department may also be able to provide this poster as well as any poster that may be required by state law. (See the appendix for contact details.)

Paying Overtime

The FLSA requires you to pay nonexempt workers (described earlier in this section) at least one and one-half times their regular rate of pay for all hours worked in excess of 40 in one week. The FLSA doesn't require you to pay an employee at an overtime rate simply because the employee worked more than eight hours in one day, but some states (for example, California and Alaska) do, so be sure to double-check your state's law with your state labor department. (See the appendix for contact details.)

Generally, the FLSA mandates that you calculate and pay overtime by the week. The workweek may begin on any day of the week and any hour that you establish. In applying the minimum wage and overtime pay rules, each workweek stands alone; you can't average two or more workweeks. And you can't manipulate the start of the workweek merely to avoid paying overtime.

RESOURCE

Want to know more about overtime? For extensive information about the federal overtime rules, go to www.dol.gov, then select "Work Hours" from the Topics menu. This will take you to a page with links to in-depth fact sheets, frequently asked questions, and the regulations themselves.

How you compute overtime pay for a particular employee will depend on whether you pay that employee on an hourly rate, piece rate, or salary basis. Piece rate means that you pay the worker based on the number of items produced or assembled by the worker (for example, you might pay a worker a certain amount for each desk lamp assembled).

Hourly rate. If an employee works more than 40 hours during a week, you must pay at least one and one-half times the regular hourly rate for each hour over 40. For example, let's say an employee whose regular rate is $8 an hour works 44 hours in a workweek. You must pay the employee at least $12 for each hour over 40. Pay for the week would be $320 ($8 x 40 hours) for the first 40 hours, plus $48 for the four hours of overtime for a total of $368.

Piece rate. To obtain the regular pay rate for an employee who is paid on a piecework basis, divide the total weekly earnings by the total number of hours worked that week. You must pay the employee the full piecework earnings, plus an additional one-half times this regular rate for each worked hour over 40. For example, let's say an employee who is paid on a piecework basis works 45 hours in a week and earns $405. The regular rate of pay for that week is $405 divided by 45, or $9 an hour. In addition to the straight time pay, you must pay the employee $4.50 (half the regular rate) for each hour over 40, or $22.50. Another way to pay pieceworkers for overtime is to pay one and one-half times the piece rate for each piece produced during the overtime hours. However, you and the employee must agree to this payment arrangement in advance. The piece rate you pay for the first 40 hours must always be enough to give the employee at least the minimum wage for each hour of the regular workweek.

Salary. To obtain the regular rate of pay for an employee paid a salary for a regular or specified number of hours a week, divide the salary by the number of hours for which the salary is compensation. The regular rate cannot be less than the minimum wage required by the FLSA. If a salary isn't paid weekly, you must determine the weekly pay to compute the regular rate and overtime. If, for example, the salary is paid twice a month, multiply by 24 and then divide by 52 weeks to get the weekly equivalent. For example, you pay an employee a salary of $800 twice a month for working a 40-hour week. Multiply $800 by 24 and you get $19,200. Then divide by 52 and you get $369.23. That's the employee's regular rate of pay for a 40-hour week. (If you divide the weekly salary by 40, you'll find that the hourly rate is $9.23.)

You may be wondering if you can pay your employees with compensatory time rather than overtime. The answer is, probably not. The practice of granting hour-for-hour compensatory time—for example, giving a worker six hours time off at some date in the future as compensation for having worked six hours of overtime—isn't usually allowed for private sector employees covered by the FLSA. (The rules are different for public employees.)

Employers and employees are often puzzled when they learn that compensatory time isn't permitted in the private sector, because it seems like a sensible and mutually beneficial way to handle overtime in many situations. So what are the alternatives to simply paying the employee overtime? You may be able to rearrange an employee's schedule during a workweek to ensure that the employee does not work overtime. Under federal law, as long as an employee works no more than 40 hours in a week, the employee has not worked overtime and is not entitled to overtime pay. So, for example, an employee who works four ten-hour days and then has three days off need not be paid overtime. If your state has a daily overtime standard, this may not be possible unless the law explicitly allows you and your employees to agree on an alternative workweek. A daily overtime standard means that workers are entitled to overtime if they work more than a set number of hours in a day, even if they ultimately work fewer than 40 hours in a week. Alaska, California, and Colorado are a few states that have a daily overtime standard.

If an employee is going to work overtime during the week, you can reduce his or her hours the next week to account for the increase in pay. That way, the paycheck will be consistent for each pay period. To make the math come out right, the employee must take an hour and a half off for every hour of overtime worked. For example, if an employee who generally earns $1,200 every two weeks (or $15 an hour) works an extra ten hours during the first week of the pay period, the employee is entitled to $225 in overtime pay: ten hours multiplied by one and a half times the employee's hourly rate, or $22.50. If the employee took 15 hours off in the second week of the pay period, however, the paycheck would remain $1,200. It would include $225 in overtime pay but would be docked $225 (15 hours x $15 an hour) for the time the employee took off.

Some states allow employers to offer compensatory time, but the requirements can get pretty complicated. To find out about your state's rules, contact your state labor department.

Who Wants Overtime?

Some workers love overtime work. It can represent an opportunity to get ahead financially, maybe a chance to buy a house or start a college fund for the kids.

But others don't feel driven to amass as much money as possible from their work. Those who aren't thrilled by overtime may have family responsibilities or may simply place a high value on their private time.

The law allows you to schedule overtime for workers, even if they don't want it, but it may be a more sound management practice to give them some choice in the matter. Otherwise, the workers who don't relish overtime work may feel abused and will drag down morale in the workplace. If you anticipate that you'll be requiring overtime work for certain positions, put that fact in the job description so workers are aware of that likelihood right from the start. Applicants who abhor overtime work can decide to seek work elsewhere.

CAUTION

Private deals can be risky. It's unlikely that a federal or state labor investigator will look into your compensatory time arrangements unless an employee files a complaint. Knowing this, you may be tempted to work out private deals with employees to meet your needs and theirs. This can be dangerous. You never know when an employee may turn sour and look for some legal technicalities to use against you.

Equal Pay Requirements

The Equal Pay Act, which is part of the FLSA, requires you to provide equal pay and benefits to men and women who do the same or equivalent work: work that requires equal skill, effort, and responsibility. Many states have a similar law mandating equal pay between men and women. Job titles aren't decisive in assessing whether two jobs are equal; the work duties are what count. It's illegal, for example, for the owner of a hotel to pay its janitors (primarily men) at a different pay rate than its housekeepers (primarily women) if both are doing essentially the same work.

The federal Equal Employment Opportunity Commission (EEOC) enforces the Equal Pay Act. (See Chapter 8 for a discussion of EEOC enforcement procedures.)

The Equal Pay Act applies to all employees who are not exempt from the minimum wage requirements. It also applies to executive, administrative, and professional employees, and outside salespeople, even though they're otherwise exempt from the FLSA requirements.

The Equal Pay Act allows pay differences based on:

- a seniority system
- a merit system
- a system that pays a worker based on the quantity or quality of what the worker produces, or
- any factor other than the worker's gender (starting salaries, for example, that are based on a worker's experience level).

EXAMPLE: The Ace Tool and Die Company was founded in 1990. The company initially hired 50 male tool and die makers. Many of those men are still working there. Since 2010, the company has expanded and hired 50 more tool and die makers, half of them male and half female. All of the tool and die makers at Ace are doing equal work, but because the company awards raises systematically based on the length of a worker's employment there, many of the older male workers earn substantially more per hour than their female coworkers who are doing equal work. The pay system at Ace Tool and Die doesn't violate the Equal Pay Act, because the pay differences between genders are based on a bona fide seniority system.

In general, two jobs are equal for the purposes of the Equal Pay Act when both require the same levels of skill, effort, and responsibility, and are performed under similar conditions. The jobs do not have to be identical to be equal. There's room for interpretation, but if there are only small differences in the jobs, they should be regarded as equal.

EXAMPLE: At a ceramics company, the major difference between the jobs performed by women and men is a weightlifting restriction: Men are required to lift heavier items than women. The women and men are performing equal work because heavy lifting is only a small part of the job.

How to Pay Employees

The FLSA has rules for how you pay nonexempt employees who are entitled to the minimum wage. The law doesn't mandate any specific system of paying these employees. It does, however, require that you pay them in cash (or something, such as a check, that can be readily converted into cash) or through some other legal forms of compensation (such as food and lodging). Coupons, tokens, or scrip that can be spent only at your store do not count as wages. And, if you grant discounts to these employees, you can't count the discounts toward the minimum wage requirement.

Two common forms of compensation are tips and commissions:

- **Tips.** When an employee routinely earns at least $30 a month in tips, the federal law allows you to pay the employee as little as $2.13 an hour, as long as that amount plus the tips the employee actually earns bring the employee's hourly earnings to the current minimum wage level. If it doesn't, you must pay the employee enough so that the hourly rate plus tips equals at least the minimum wage. If you decide to pay less than the minimum wage (called taking a "tip credit"), you must put the arrangement in writing. (Many states have their own tip credit requirements; some don't allow employers to take a tip credit at all. See "State Minimum Wage Laws for Tipped and Regular Employees," in the appendix, for details.)
- **Commissions.** Commissions that you pay people for sales may take the place of wages for purposes of the FLSA. However, if the commissions divided by hours worked don't equal the minimum wage, you must make up the difference.

EXAMPLE: Julia is a salesperson at Electronics Plus. She's paid a percentage of the dollar volume of the sales she completes. During one slow week, she averaged only $4 in commissions per hour. Under the FLSA, Electronics Plus must pay Julia an additional $3.25 for each hour she worked through the first 40 hours of that week; that will bring her total pay up to the minimum wage level of $7.25 an hour.

The FLSA doesn't require you to pay employees for time off, such as vacation, holidays, or sick days. It may be standard practice for you to pay employees for such time spent away from work, but the FLSA only covers payment for time on the job. (Some states require employers to provide paid sick leave, however.)

Some state laws require paid time off for jury duty and voting, among other things. In addition, laws in some states require you to give employees time off for coronavirus-related reasons; National Guard or other military duty; or to attend a child's school conferences. Most state laws provide that you can't fire or discriminate against an employee for taking such time off. Contact your state labor department for more information about leave laws in your state. (See the appendix for contact details.)

> CAUTION
> **Don't ignore your promises or practices.** If you promise paid vacations, holidays, or sick days in an employee handbook or other written policy, or if you customarily grant such paid time off, you may be legally bound to give those benefits to all employees, regardless of whether your state law or local ordinance requires it.

The FLSA requires only that the pay period be one month or less. State laws often require shorter pay periods, such as every two weeks. If you have a question about pay periods, call your state's labor department. (See the appendix for contact details.)

Calculating Work Hours

Knowing you must pay employees for their work is one thing; understanding exactly which hours count as work and which ones don't can be tricky, particularly when employees are working from home. The FLSA requires you to pay nonexempt employees for any of their time that you control and that benefits you. In general, time on the job doesn't include the time employees spend washing up or changing clothes before or after work, nor does it include meal periods when employees are free from all work duties. The U.S. Supreme Court recently found that the time employees spend waiting in line to pass through a security screening point at the end of their shifts also doesn't count as work time, and therefore doesn't have to be paid. It's legal to round time records off to the nearest five-minute mark on the clock, but not if it results in paying workers for less time than they actually worked. In other words, you can only round up.

The rest of this section describes some common situations that confuse employers as to whether they count as paid work time.

Remote Work

As a result of the coronavirus pandemic, record numbers of employees now work from home. If you have employees who are paid on an hourly basis and working remotely, you must ensure that they're keeping close tabs on their hours worked so they are paid in accordance with the law.

In 2020, the U.S. Department of Labor (DOL) issued guidance to employers on how to track remote employee hours. According to the DOL, employers should establish a system for workers to report all their hours worked, including any unscheduled work time. Employers must then pay employees for all hours worked, whether or not they were requested by the employer. Significantly, an employer isn't obligated to dig into after-hours email records or other IT records to establish whether an employee was working off the clock, as long as a system for reporting unscheduled work time exists.

> **EXAMPLE:** Beverly works from home as a call center agent. Her normal hours are 9 to 5. One day, a longer than usual phone call with a client means that she doesn't stop working until 5:20. Beverly reports this extra time worked to her employer. Her employer is obligated to pay her for these extra 20 minutes, even though Beverly was scheduled to finish work at 5:00.

While employers have an obligation to pay employees for all hours worked —whether scheduled or unscheduled—they should consider adopting policies to limit their employees' ability to work off the clock unless they've received prior approval.

The DOL has released a free Mobile Timesheet app that allows employees to record their work hours and break time using a mobile device. For more information, visit www.dol.gov/general/apps/timesheet.

Commuting Time

You needn't pay employees for the time they spend commuting between their homes and the normal job site; that's not considered on-the-job time.

But you do have to pay for travel time that is actually part of the job. If you run a plumbing repair service, for example, and require workers to stop by your shop to pick up orders, tools, and supplies before going out on calls, their workday begins when they check in at your shop.

Otherwise, just about the only situation in which you must pay workers for commuting time is when they're required to go back and forth from the normal worksite at odd hours in emergency situations.

EXAMPLE: Neil normally works 9 to 5 as a computer technician at Arbor City Computer and is paid hourly. One day, about two hours after Neil gets home, his supervisor calls him to say that some computer equipment is malfunctioning and preventing the late shift employees from doing their work. Neil has to go back to the office immediately to help correct the problem. It takes him half an hour to get there, two hours to fix the problem, and half an hour to drive home again. Arbor City must pay Neil for three hours: two work hours plus the extra hour of commuting time required by the company's emergency.

On-Call Time

You must count as payable time any periods when employees are not actually working but are required to stay on your premises while waiting for a work assignment.

If you require employees to be on call but you don't make them stay on your premises, then two rules generally apply:

- You don't count as payable time the on-call time that employees can control and use for their own enjoyment or benefit.
- You do count as payable time the on-call time over which employees have little or no control and which they can't use for their own enjoyment or benefit.

EXAMPLE 1: Medi-Transit operates a nonemergency ambulance service that transports patients from hospitals to nursing homes. The company hires Ryan to drive an ambulance from 8 to 5, Monday through Friday, and it also requires him to carry a beeper one night a week so he can handle an occasional assignment after normal working hours. Because Ryan is free to pursue personal and social activities during nonworking hours, Medi-Transit doesn't have to pay him for his on-call time.

EXAMPLE 2: AirTec provides mechanical services for small private planes at a local airfield. Joe is an AirTec mechanic. The company requires him to be on call every fourth Saturday. When he's on call, he must stay within a five-minute drive to the airport, keep his cell phone free for calls from the company, and refrain from drinking alcohol. Because Joe isn't free to use his on-call time as he pleases, the company must pay him for the time.

Unless there's an employment contract that states otherwise, you can generally pay a different hourly rate for on-call time than you do for regular work time. But keep in mind that you must pay employees at least the minimum wage.

Sleep Time

If you require an employee to be on duty at the worksite for less than 24 hours at a time, you generally must count as payable any time during which the employee is allowed to sleep in a shift of duty. Similarly, if you require an employee to be at work for 24 hours or more, you also generally must count sleep time as payable work time. But there's a way around this: You and the employee may agree to exclude up to eight hours per day from payable time as sleep and meal periods. However, if conditions are such that the employee can't get at least five hours of sleep during the eight-hour sleep-and-eat period, or if the employee ends up working during that period, then those eight hours revert to payable time.

Lectures, Meetings, and Training Seminars

Generally, if you want a nonexempt employee to attend a lecture, meeting, or training seminar, you'll have to pay for that employee's time, including travel time if the meeting is away from the worksite.

About the only situation in which you don't have to pay for the employee's time is if all of the following are true:

- The employee attends the event outside of regular working hours.
- Attendance is voluntary.
- The instruction session isn't directly related to the employee's job.
- The employee doesn't perform any productive work during the instruction session.

Meal and Rest Breaks

You don't have to pay a covered employee for time spent on an actual meal period. But the employee must be completely relieved from work during that period so that the employee can enjoy a regularly scheduled meal. If, for example, you require employees to remain at their desks during the meal period or to keep an eye on machinery, you must pay for the meal time.

Similarly, you don't have to pay for rest periods or coffee breaks (including for at-home workers) if the employee is truly free from job duties. But, if an employee must listen for the phone or watch for merchandise deliveries during the break, it's not free time and you must pay for it.

Many states have laws requiring employers to provide meal and rest breaks and specifying minimum times that must be allowed. (See "State Meal and Rest Break Laws," in the appendix.) In some states, these breaks must be paid. If your state requires more than the FLSA, then you must follow the stricter state law requirement.

Federal law also requires employers to provide lactation breaks to new mothers. You must provide a nursing mother with reasonable break time and a place to express her breast milk for up to a year after a child's birth. The place must be shielded from view and free from intrusion by coworkers and the public; a restroom doesn't qualify. You don't have to compensate the employee for this break time, however. Smaller businesses—those with fewer than 50 employees—don't have to comply with these requirements if doing so would impose an undue hardship, defined as significant expense or difficulty, considering the employer's size, structure, and resources.

An increasing number of states have similar laws, some of which provide even greater protection for nursing mothers. You can find information on your state's requirements in "State Meal and Rest Break Laws," in the appendix.

Record-Keeping Requirements

The FLSA requires you to keep records of wages and hours for all employees. For nonexempt employees, your records must include:

- the employee's name, address, Social Security number, occupation, and gender
- the employee's birth date if the employee is younger than 19 years old
- the hour and day when each workweek began
- the total hours worked each workday and each workweek
- total daily or weekly earnings
- regular hourly pay rate for any week when overtime was worked
- total overtime pay for the workweek
- deductions from or additions to wages
- total wages paid each pay period, and
- date of payment and pay period covered.

A bit less information is required for employees who are exempt from the minimum wage or overtime pay requirements. Also, you must keep special information for employees to whom you extend lodging or other facilities. You must retain most records for all current employees and for at least three years after an employee stops working for your company.

Your state may impose different or additional requirements. Contact your state labor department for details. (See the appendix for contact information.)

RESOURCE

Want more information on your record-keeping duties? You can view a U.S. Department of Labor fact sheet at www.dol.gov/whd/regs/compliance/whdfs21.pdf.

Child Labor Rules

The FLSA has special rules for younger workers. Those rules are designed to discourage young people from dropping out of school too soon and to protect them from dangerous work, such as mining, demolition and wrecking, logging, and roofing. State laws may impose additional restrictions on hiring young workers, so if you intend to employ workers younger than 18, you should contact your labor department to find out what your state rules are. (See the appendix for contact details.)

The rules are different for youngsters in agricultural and nonagricultural jobs.

Agricultural Jobs

In agricultural work, the following rules apply to younger workers:
- You may hire a worker who is 16 years old or older for any work, hazardous or not, for unlimited hours. (See "Agricultural Occupations Hazardous to Young Workers," below.)
- You may hire a worker who is 14 or 15 years old for any nonhazardous agricultural work outside of school hours.
- You may hire a worker who is 12 or 13 years old for any nonhazardous agricultural work outside of school hours if the child's parents work on the same farm or if you have their written consent.
- You may hire a worker who is younger than 12 years old for non-hazardous work on a farm outside of school hours if the farm isn't covered by minimum wage requirements. You need the written consent of the child's parents.
- You may hire a worker who is ten or 11 years old if you've been granted a waiver by the U.S. Department of Labor to employ the youngster as a hand harvest laborer for no more than eight weeks in any calendar year.
- If you own or operate a farm, you can hire your own children to do any kind of work on the farm, regardless of their ages.

Agricultural work is essentially any work that would be performed on a farm, specifically the following:
- cultivating and tilling the soil
- dairying
- producing, cultivating, growing, and harvesting any agricultural or horticultural commodities

- raising livestock, bees, fur-bearing animals, or poultry, or
- any practices performed by a farmer on a farm as part of farming, such as forestry, lumbering, and preparing items for market.

Agricultural Occupations Hazardous to Young Workers

The U.S. Department of Labor has identified several agricultural occupations that are deemed hazardous for children age 15 and younger, including:

- operating a tractor that has more than 20 horsepower
- working in a yard, pen, or stall occupied by a bull, a stud horse maintained for breeding purposes, or a sow with suckling pigs
- felling timber with a diameter of more than six inches
- working from a ladder or scaffold at a height of more than 20 feet, and
- handling or using blast agents.

For a complete list, go to www.dol.gov. Under Topics, choose "Youth & Labor," then choose "Agricultural Employment." Look for Child Labor Bulletin 102, *Child Labor Requirements in Agricultural Occupations Under the Fair Labor Standards Act* (FLSA), at www.dol.gov/whd/regs/compliance/childlabor102.pdf .

Nonagricultural Jobs

The FLSA sets out a number of restrictions on young workers hired to do nonagricultural jobs:

- You may hire a worker who is 18 years old or older for any job, hazardous or not, for unlimited hours.
- You may hire a worker who is 16 or 17 years old for any nonhazardous job for unlimited hours.
- You may hire a worker who is 14 or 15 years old outside school hours in various nonmanufacturing, nonmining, nonhazardous jobs, but some restrictions apply. The employee can't work more than three hours on a school day, 18 hours in a school week, eight hours on a nonschool day, or 40 hours in a nonschool week. Also, work can't begin before 7 a.m. or end after 7 p.m., except from June 1 through Labor Day, when evening hours are extended to 9 p.m.

Nonagricultural Occupations That Are Hazardous to Young Workers

Under rules of the U.S. Department of Labor, workers younger than 18 cannot perform the following types of jobs:

- manufacturing or storing explosives
- driving a motor vehicle or being an outside helper on a motor vehicle*
- coal or other mining
- logging and sawmilling
- anything involving power-driven woodworking machines**
- anything involving exposure to radioactive substances and to ionizing radiations
- anything involving power-driven hoisting equipment
- anything involving power-driven metal-forming, punching, and shearing machines**
- meatpacking or processing (including anything involving power-driven meat slicing machines)
- anything involving power-driven bakery machines
- anything involving power-driven paper product machines**
- manufacturing brick, tile, and related products
- anything involving power-driven circular saws, band saws, and guillotine shears**
- wrecking, demolition, and shipbreaking operations
- roofing operations,** and
- excavation operations.**

---

* A 17-year-old worker who has a driver's license and no record of any moving violations can drive a car or small truck during daylight hours if the driver has completed an approved driver education course, the car or truck has seat belts, and the driving is only occasional (no more than one-third of the worker's work time any day and no more than 20% of work time in a workweek). Among other rules, the young driver can't tow vehicles, drive a delivery route, or drive beyond a 30-mile radius from your business place.

** There are limited exceptions in these types of jobs for apprentices and students.

For a complete list of nonagricultural occupations deemed hazardous for young workers, and for the special rules that apply to workers who are 14 and 15 years old, go to www.dol.gov/whd/regs/compliance/childlabor101.pdf.

Fourteen years old is the minimum age for most work, but there are a few jobs that workers younger than 14 can perform, including:

- delivering newspapers
- performing in radio, TV, movie, or theatrical productions
- working in a nonfarm business solely owned by the parents, if it's not a manufacturing or hazardous job
- gathering evergreens, and
- making evergreen wreaths.

In addition, there are special rules for young people who cook as part of their jobs. A worker who is 14 or 15 years old can only:

- cook on an electric or gas grill (no open flames)
- warm food in a microwave oven, or
- use a deep-fat fryer that automatically lowers food into the hot oil.

These youngsters can also dispense food from food warmers and steam tables.

Payroll Withholding

Federal law requires you to withhold income taxes and Social Security and Medicare contributions from employees' paychecks. States and municipalities that have income taxes also require withholding, usually under a system that parallels the federal procedures. (See Chapter 5 for more about federal payroll taxes.)

Under federal law, you may also deduct the cost of meals, housing, transportation, loans, debts owed to you, child support and alimony, payroll savings, and insurance premiums. There are exceptions to these rules and limits on how much you can withhold or deduct.

> **CAUTION**
>
> **Rules differ from state to state.** Your state may prohibit some deductions that the federal law allows. In this situation, you must follow your state's law. Before you take any deductions, contact your state labor department to learn your state's rules. (See the appendix for contact information.)

Meals, Housing, and Transportation

Under federal law, you may legally deduct from an employee's paycheck the reasonable cost or fair value of meals, housing, fuel, and transportation to and from work even if these deductions reduce the worker's pay to less than minimum wage. But you must show that you customarily paid these expenses and that all of the following are true:

- They were for the employee's benefit.
- You told the employee in advance about the deductions.
- The employee voluntarily accepted the meals and other accommodations.

Debts Owed to an Employer

Federal law allows employers to deduct money from an employee's paycheck for certain job-related debts. You may, for example, make a deduction for an employee's cash drawer shortage, or to repay you for products or tools the employee has damaged. However, it's illegal to make such a deduction if it would drop a nonexempt employee's pay below the minimum wage.

> **EXAMPLE:** Roadmaster Auto Parts Store hires Bruce at $8 an hour to shelve products. One morning, Bruce drops a box of headlights, shattering all of them. The box of lights has a wholesale value of $80. Bruce agrees that Roadmaster can deduct the $80 from his paycheck. Because Bruce needs to make at least the federal minimum wage of $7.25 per hour, Roadmaster can legally deduct no more than $30 per week (40 hours x $0.75) from Bruce's gross pay to cover the lights. To deduct more would drop Bruce's pay rate of $8 per hour to below the required minimum of $7.25.

This limitation does not apply to money you loan to an employee for personal reasons. Under the FLSA, you can deduct money to repay a wage advancement or loan, even if it drops the employee's paycheck below the minimum wage.

Debts and Wage Garnishments

You may be sent an order from a judge requiring your business to withhold money from an employee's paycheck to satisfy a debt the employee owes to someone else. This order is part of a legal process called wage attachment or wage garnishment. Usually, a judge will issue such an order only after a judgment has been signed stating that the employee actually owes the money. However, such a judgment may not be necessary for garnishments based on an employee's failure to pay student loans, child support, alimony, or taxes.

If you receive a garnishment order, read it carefully. It will specify deadlines you must meet for processing the order. You may have to pay a penalty if you don't comply with the terms and timetables of the garnishment. Procedures vary from state to state, but most likely you'll be required to file a form with the court disclosing how much you owe to the employee for wages. Then you'll be required to send a portion of those wages to the court or, perhaps, to the creditor or creditor's lawyer.

A federal law, the Consumer Credit Protection Act (15 U.S.C. § 1673), prohibits a judgment creditor from taking more than 25% of an employee's net earnings through a wage garnishment. (Some states offer greater protection to the employee.) Usually the papers you receive as part of the garnishment order will explain how much of the employee's earnings you should deduct and where to send the money.

The Consumer Credit Protection Act also prohibits you from firing an employee because of a garnishment order to satisfy a single debt. But if two judgment creditors garnish an employee's wages or one judgment creditor garnishes an employee's wages to pay two different judgments, you're free to fire that employee. Again, some state laws place stricter limits on your right to fire an employee because of garnishments.

Although statutes limit your right to fire employees because of garnishments, you can still fire such employees for a legitimate business reason—or for any reason that isn't illegal, if the employee works at will—as long as you can establish that the firing wasn't based on the garnishments.

Child Support

The federal Family Support Act of 1988 (102 U.S.C. § 2343) requires that new or modified child support orders include an automatic wage withholding order. If you receive a copy of such an order, you must withhold a portion of the employee's pay and send it on to the parent to whom it is owed.

You can't discipline, fire, or refuse to hire people just because their pay is subject to a child support wage withholding order.

Back Taxes

If an employee owes taxes to the federal government and doesn't pay, the Internal Revenue Service (IRS) can grab most—but not all—of the employee's wages. The amount the employee gets to keep is determined by the number of dependents and the size of the standard deduction to which the employee is entitled.

If you receive a wage levy notice from the IRS, don't ignore it. If you go ahead and pay the employee in full, you'll be liable to the IRS for whatever amount you wrongly pay.

Most state and some municipal taxing authorities have similar power to seize a portion of an employee's wages.

The Consequences of Bending the Rules

The Wage and Hour Division of the U.S. Department of Labor enforces the FLSA regulations described in this chapter. Almost always, it is tipped off to investigate a business by an unhappy employee who has complained. Be aware that it's illegal to fire or discriminate against an employee for filing a complaint or participating in a legal proceeding under the FLSA. And many states have similar laws prohibiting such retaliation.

The department can fine you up to $10,000 for violating the FLSA. It can even send you to jail for a second offense if you acted willfully. But fines and jail time are used in only the most blatant cases. More often, you'll be required to pay the employee all unpaid wages, including overtime pay. The real cost comes in the time and expense of being involved in enforcement proceedings, not to mention the damage to employee morale and the animosity that can be created in the workplace.

Beyond the chance of being pursued by the government, there looms the possibility of a private lawsuit. And—especially if yours is a larger company— the private lawsuit may be a class action, with potentially disastrous results for your business. Misclassifying employees as exempt is a common basis for a class action. An employer's exposure to huge verdicts in such lawsuits is so great that many businesses wind up settling. Here are some publicized cases in which it was alleged that the employer incorrectly classified employees as exempt:

- A rental car company settled a class action for close to $8 million.
- A coffeehouse chain settled a class action for $28 million.
- A phone company settled one class action for $35 million and another for $27 million.
- An insurance company settled a class action for $130 million.
- A drugstore chain settled a class action for $11 million.
- An auto club settled a class action for $19.5 million.

Many of these settlement sums included large amounts earmarked for lawyers' fees and litigation costs.

Of course, class actions against small-scale employers are relatively rare, and the verdicts and settlements won't be in the stratospheric range. But even a $100,000 judgment against a small company could be devastating. So before you conclude that certain employees are exempt and, for that reason, are not entitled to overtime pay, make sure you're on solid legal ground. If in doubt, the conservative course is to consult an attorney who specializes in these matters.

Employee Benefits

Employee benefits are such a common part of the workplace terrain today that many assume these benefits are required by law. But, generally, the decision about whether or not to provide such benefits is up to you. There are two main exceptions: Under the federal Affordable Care Act, large employers (those with at least 50 full-time employees or the equivalent in part-time employees) must pay penalties if they don't provide health care coverage to most full-time employees. (In 2017, Congress eliminated the "individual mandate" requiring individuals to carry health insurance or pay a penalty. But it left the employer mandate intact.) And, in Hawaii, businesses must offer health care coverage to virtually all employees and pay at least half of the premiums.

Whether it's required or not, enlightened employers frequently do offer some type of benefit package. Offering benefits can reflect your commitment to keeping a satisfied workforce and help you remain competitive in attracting competent workers.

Federal tax laws allow an employer to deduct the cost of many employee benefits as a business expense, which greatly reduces the financial burden of providing these benefits. Benefits that qualify for favorable tax treatment include health and dental coverage, term life insurance, disability insurance, approved pension plans, educational assistance programs, and dependent care assistance. But if a benefit plan is rigged to favor the owners of a business or employees who receive the highest compensation, the plan may not qualify for a tax deduction.

If you provide health care coverage or pension plans, federal and state laws impose requirements on these plans.

Employees Can Help You Plan

In putting together a benefit program, consider taking a survey of employees or setting up an employee committee to recommend the benefits they'd most like to have. Then, after exploring the options and deciding on the benefits you'll offer, communicate that decision—and the reasons behind it—to the employees.

Perhaps some employee suggestions will be too expensive, impractical, or even impossible to adopt. You may want to reconsider others in the future. Whatever the situation, when employees go to the trouble of making suggestions, let them know that you gave their ideas serious consideration.

RESOURCE

Want details on how the federal tax laws apply to many of the benefits discussed in this chapter? See IRS Publication 15-B, *Employer's Tax Guide to Fringe Benefits*, available at www.irs.gov.

Health Care Coverage

Historically, health care coverage has been the benefit that most employees coveted, because it has been difficult for individuals to find affordable coverage on the open market. These days, the Affordable Care Act makes health insurance available to most Americans. The need for employer-paid coverage may be less urgent as a result. In fact, a growing number of small businesses have stopped paying for coverage. Instead, they opt to give workers a pay boost to help them buy their own insurance.

About 96% of employers have fewer than 50 employees—or, more precisely, fewer than 50 *full-time equivalent* (FTE) employees. If your business is one of those employers, the federal Affordable Care Act will not penalize you for failing to provide health care coverage. Note that you may be free from penalties even if you employ 50 or more people, as long as you don't have 50 FTE employees. Under the federal law, two half-time employees count as one FTE employee in applying the fewer-than-50 threshold. So, for example, a business that employs 18 half-time workers and 40 full-time workers will face no penalties if it decides not to offer coverage because it has only 49 FTE employees.

If your business is in the 96% that has fewer than 50 FTE employees, the Affordable Care Act leaves you free to choose whether to provide health care coverage. But the act also contains an incentive that may affect your business if you have fewer than 25 FTE employees. In that case, your business will qualify for a tax credit of up to 50% of the premiums you pay at the single (employee only) rate. Some conditions apply. To be eligible for the credit, the average yearly wage of your employees must be less than about $56,000 (this figure is adjusted annually for inflation). The insurance must be one of the plans offered through a Small Business Health Options Program (SHOP) marketplace. And, you must pay at least 50% of the insurance premiums. You may claim the credit using IRS Form 8941, *Credit for Small Employer Health Insurance Premiums.* The largest credits go to businesses with fewer than ten FTE employees, whose wages average less than $25,000. For details, visit www.healthcare.gov.

As for the 4% of employers who have 50 or more FTE employees, the Affordable Care Act imposes penalties for failing to provide health care coverage. To avoid penalties, such businesses need to provide coverage to at least 95% of their full-time workers. For a good overview of the Affordable Care Act's requirements for employers, visit www.irs.gov/affordable-care-act/employers.

Whether or not you are large enough to fall within the employer mandate, you still may have to provide your employees with a notice about their health care options, including any benefits you provide and the availability of benefits through the health care marketplace. You can learn more about this notice (and find model notices you can use) at the website of the Employee Benefits Security Administration, www.dol.gov/agencies/ebsa/employers-and-advisers/guidance/technical-releases/13-02.

Shopping for Health Care Coverage

To find affordable health care plans, go to www.healthcare.gov/see-plans/#/small-business. You'll learn what plans are available in your state as part of the Small Business Health Options Program (SHOP) marketplace. These plans are only available to businesses with fewer than 50 FTE employees. If your business has fewer than 25 FTE employees, you must use one of the SHOP plans to qualify for the tax credit discussed above. You can consult an experienced insurance broker to learn what other plans are available in your area if the SHOP marketplace doesn't meet your needs or your business isn't eligible for the tax credit.

CAUTION

Stay up to date on changing health care laws. In recent years, federal health care policy has undergone massive changes, and with a new president and Congress, more could be on the way. To make sure you've got the latest information on your company's obligations and incentives, check for updates on this book's companion page (the introduction explains how to find it) and at www.healthcare.gov.

Types of Coverage

Traditionally, employers who provide health care coverage do so through an indemnity or reimbursement plan that pays the doctor or hospital directly or reimburses the employee for medical expenses already paid.

While traditional coverage allowing employees to seek out their preferred medical provider is still widely used, a growing number of employers today provide coverage through the alternatives of a health maintenance organization (HMO) or a preferred provider organization (PPO).

An HMO is a group of hospitals and doctors who provide specified medical services to employees for a fixed monthly fee. Within the HMO service area, covered employees must use the HMO hospitals and doctors unless it's an emergency or they receive permission to go elsewhere.

A PPO is a network of hospitals and doctors who agree to provide medical care for specified fees. Often the network is put together by an insurance company that also administers the program. Employees usually can choose between using the network's hospitals and doctors or going elsewhere (although an employee may have to pay a higher fee to use doctors or facilities outside of the plan).

Continuing Coverage for Former Employees

A federal law called the Consolidated Omnibus Budget Reconciliation Act, or COBRA (29 U.S.C. § 1162), applies to your business if you have 20 or more employees and you offer a group health care plan. If your business is too small to be covered by COBRA, you may still have to comply with a similar state law. (See "State Health Insurance Continuation Laws" in the appendix.) If COBRA applies to your business, you must offer employees and former employees the option of continuing health care coverage if their coverage is lost or reduced because:

- their employment has been terminated for any reason (except gross misconduct)
- their hours have been reduced, or
- they've become eligible for Medicare.

Members of the employee's family must also be given the opportunity to continue their coverage. "COBRA's Continuing Coverage for Former Employees," below, depicts the circumstances—called "qualifying events"—that trigger an employer's obligation to allow continuing health care coverage under a group plan. How long the benefits must be continued is determined by the qualifying event and by whether the covered employee is disabled. Special rules define a qualifying event if your business is covered by the Family and Medical Leave Act (FMLA) and an employee fails to return to work at the end of an FMLA leave.

Usually, the employee must pay the cost of continuing coverage under COBRA, including your share of the premiums. You can charge up to 102% of the premium cost, using the extra 2% to cover administrative costs. The cost to the employee or the employee's family for continuing coverage must be similar to the cost of covering people still on your payroll.

> **CAUTION**
>
> **COBRA deadlines extended due to COVID-19.** In May 2020, the Department of Labor and the IRS extended a number of COBRA deadlines to give workers additional time to elect COBRA continuation coverage and pay premiums, among other things. The extensions applied to the following:
> - length of special health plan enrollment periods
> - length of election period for COBRA continuation coverage
> - timeframe to provide notice of a qualifying event
> - deadline to make COBRA premium payments
> - deadline to make benefit claims or appeal benefit claims denials, and
> - length of time for plan administrator to provide a COBRA election notice.
>
> The rule essentially stops the clock for purposes of the existing COBRA deadlines during the "outbreak period" of the pandemic. This period is defined as beginning on March 1, 2020 and ending 60 days after the government declares the end of the national emergency (or another date designated by the government). As this book goes to press, the national emergency period is still ongoing. For the most updated information, visit www.dol.gov/agencies/ebsa/laws-and-regulations/laws/cobra.

An employee might also decide to forgo COBRA coverage and instead purchase insurance through the online Health Insurance Marketplace established by the Affordable Care Act. Losing workplace coverage through a qualifying COBRA event gives an employee (and the employee's family) the right to a 60-day special enrollment period under the act. This means they can purchase insurance anytime during the first 60 days after the qualifying event, rather than waiting for the regular open enrollment period to come around (typically, at the end of the calendar year).

COBRA covers HMO and PPO plans in addition to traditional group insurance plans. COBRA also covers all other types of medical benefits, including dental and vision care and plans under which an employer reimburses employees for medical expenses.

If your business is covered by COBRA and has a group health care plan, the plan administrator—the person who handles the plan's paperwork—must give employees and their spouses a written explanation of their COBRA rights when they first become eligible to participate in the plan. A single notice can be sent to an employee and spouse if they live at the same address. Otherwise, the spouse is entitled to a separate notice.

SEE AN EXPERT

Help is available. Small businesses usually find it convenient to let the insurance company serve as the plan administrator and coordinate COBRA notices. The insurance company can provide even more help and information, including a clear explanation of how the plan meets the requirements of COBRA and similar state laws. Any reputable company should be able to provide clear, concise explanatory materials that you can hand out to your employees and, if asked, may send representatives to conduct training seminars and answer employee questions.

COBRA's Continuing Coverage for Former Employees		
Qualifying Event	People Entitled to Continue Coverage	How Long
The employee quits	Employee, spouse, dependents	18 months; 29 months for disabled worker
You fire or lay off the employee for reasons other than gross misconduct	Employee, spouse, dependents	18 months; 29 months for disabled worker
You reduce the employee's hours, causing the employee to lose coverage	Employee, spouse, dependents	18 months; 29 months for disabled worker
The employee dies	Surviving spouse, dependents	36 months
The employee divorces or becomes legally separated	Former spouse, dependents	36 months
The employee goes on Medicare	Spouse, dependents	36 months
The dependent loses coverage through marriage or age	Dependent	36 months

When a qualifying event occurs that gives an employee or family member the right to continue coverage, you must send them a notice listing their rights under COBRA. These beneficiaries have 60 days following the notice to let you know if they want to continue their coverage (unless the exception above applies). If so, the employee or eligible family member sends you the premium each month, and you send it on to the insurance company. If the beneficiaries don't send the payment when due—or within the grace period—you can cut off coverage.

A number of states also have laws giving former employees the right to continue group health care insurance coverage after leaving a job. Depending on the state where you do business, state law may give employees more rights, provide for longer continued coverage, or apply to smaller employers. (See "State Health Insurance Continuation Laws" in the appendix.)

Health Savings Accounts

One way for employers to save money on health coverage for their employees is to provide a plan that has a high deductible. To help employees deal with the high deductibles, consider participating in an employee health savings account (HSA). An HSA is like an IRA, except that the money is for health care costs, not retirement.

Here's how it works. Let's say that you provide a high-deductible health insurance plan for employees. (In 2021, this means a plan with an annual deductible of at least $1,400 for an individual or at least $2,800 for a family. Also, the annual out-of-pocket expenses—deductibles, copayments, and amounts other than premiums—can't exceed $7,000 for individual coverage or $14,000 for family coverage. These figures will be adjusted for inflation each year.) You or the employee can open an HSA, to which you or the employee or both can contribute money. These funds are tax free to the employee if used to pay for:

- medical expenses
- COBRA insurance, or
- Medicare and retiree health insurance premiums (but not Medicare supplement premiums).

If an employee younger than 65 withdraws funds for other purposes, the withdrawn funds are taxable and subject to a 10% penalty. After age 65, such withdrawals are still taxable, but there's no penalty.

In 2021, you and your employees can contribute a total of up to $3,600 for an individual or $7,200 for a family. (Contribution limits will change each year.) For an employee who is 55 years old or older, or who turns 55 by the end of the year, you or the employee can make an additional catch-up contribution of $1,000. (Employees can't make catch-up contributions if they are enrolled in Medicare.) Workers decide how to invest the money.

Money left in an HSA can be rolled over from year to year.

TIP

Small employers: Consider QSEHRAs. Employers with fewer than 50 FTEs that don't provide group health insurance should consider offering qualified small employer health reimbursement accounts (QSEHRAs). A QSEHRA is an employer-funded, tax-free account that an employee can use to pay for health insurance premiums and medical expenses. Only full-time employees who can provide proof of health insurance coverage are eligible for QSEHRAs. In 2021, the maximum amount an employer can contribute to a QSEHRA is $5,300 for employee-only coverage and $10,700 for family coverage. Funds that are left over at the end of each year can roll over if the plan allows it, though the amount of the rollover is subject to legal limits. Unlike a regular health reimbursement account (HRA), a QSEHRA can be offered in conjunction with an HSA, giving employees more opportunities to pay for health care on a pre-tax basis. For more information, visit www.healthcare.gov/glossary/qsehra.

Coverage for Pregnant Women and Older Workers

Federal law imposes some special insurance requirements for pregnant women and older workers.

Women. You must treat women affected by pregnancy and related conditions the same as other employees based on their ability or inability to work. For example, if a woman can't work because she's pregnant, you must provide her with the same health care coverage as you generally provide to employees who become ill or have a disability. (See Chapter 8 for more on the Pregnancy Discrimination Act.) The Family and Medical Leave Act allows workers to take up to 12 weeks a year of unpaid leave connected with childbirth, adoption, and foster placement. (See Chapter 6 for more about family and medical leave.)

Older workers. You must offer workers age 40 and older the same health care coverage you offer to younger workers. And, if your plan requires that all your workers be covered, you can't make older workers pay more to join. But if the insurance isn't mandatory, older workers can be charged more, so long as actuarial charts show their health care costs are higher.

Retirement Plans

Retirement plans provide income to older people when they're no longer part of the workforce. If the plans you offer meet certain IRS guidelines, your contribution to the benefits qualifies as a business expense and is deductible from your company's gross income. We look at a few of your options below. Large businesses may want to look into a defined benefit plan or defined contribution plan, as described below. Small businesses will probably be better off considering a 401(k) plan or an IRA plan; these plans typically cost less and require minimal paperwork. If you are interested in providing retirement benefits to your employees, talk to a benefits specialist to find a plan that will work for you.

Defined Benefit Plans

In a defined benefit plan, you promise to pay an employee a fixed amount of money, usually in monthly increments, after the employee retires. You may base the payments on a formula that combines the number of years the employee has worked and the amount of earnings. You may also choose some other method of setting the timing and amount, such as a fixed monthly sum not tied to length of service or earnings.

To fund a defined benefit plan, employers typically invest money in stocks, bonds, and mutual funds that are expected to grow over the years. You must contribute enough to the plan to pay the promised benefit. Otherwise, you'll have to make up the difference if the plan's investments go bad.

To help protect employees if a business lacks the funds to pay that difference, employers who offer defined benefit plans must generally contribute to the Pension Benefit Guaranty Corporation. For details, visit the agency's website at www.pbgc.gov.

Defined Contribution Plans

In a defined contribution plan, you set up an account for the employee and contribute to it. At retirement, the employee gets whatever is in the account. You don't promise that the employee will receive a specific amount of income after retirement.

You may structure the defined contribution plan as a money purchase pension plan, in which case you'll promise to contribute a specific amount per employee each year, such as five cents for each hour worked. Or you may structure it as a profit sharing plan in which you have the discretion to decide each year how much to contribute, with your contributions allocated to the employees' accounts in a specified way (usually, in proportion to their pay). In either case, the size of the pension check an employee receives each month after retirement will vary according to the interest rate paid on the employee's pension account and other economic factors.

401(k) Plans

A 401(k) plan is an employer-sponsored retirement plan that can be linked with a profit sharing plan. It consists of a retirement account for each employee who participates. An employer can choose whether or not to make contributions and how extensive those contributions will be. You might, for example, choose to contribute only if company profits reach a certain level or to match contributions of only the lower-paid employees.

In 2021, the total amount you and an employee can contribute to all of an employee's defined contribution plans—including a 401(k)—is $58,000 or an amount equal to the employee's annual compensation, whichever is less.

Even if you don't contribute to the 401(k) plan, it still constitutes a valuable benefit to employees, because it helps them save for retirement with tax-deferred dollars. If you set up an employee-funded 401(k) plan, employees can defer the income tax on the money they stash away, which allows their investments to grow faster.

A typical plan, administered by a major mutual fund company, calls for regular payroll deductions from an employee's earnings, in an amount specified by the employee. In 2021, the IRS limits the employee's contribution to $19,500. Employees who are 50 years old or older can also make an additional "catch-up" contribution of $6,500 in 2021.

The employee gets to allocate the account among several different mutual funds and to change the mix from time to time. The funds on the menu run the gamut from conservative to aggressive, so the employee can choose the level of risk. Be aware, however, that it may cost you a few thousand dollars to set up a 401(k) plan for your business. There may also be ongoing expenses for plan administration. (See "Administration Requirements," below.)

TIP

Check out the Roth 401(k). It looks like a mix of the familiar Roth IRA and the traditional 401(k). As with the Roth IRA, contributions are taxable when put into the plan, but when the employee withdraws funds at age 59½ or later, the withdrawals are tax free. The contribution limits are the same as those of the traditional 401(k).

Retirement Benefit Options for Small Businesses

If your business is small, you may want to look into three additional arrangements that may allow you to offer retirement savings options to your employees with limited costs to the business:

- **Payroll deduction IRA.** Your business doesn't contribute cash, but you make it easy for employees to contribute periodically to an Individual Retirement Account (IRA) through payroll deductions. In 2021, an employee can deduct up to $6,000 for the year.
- **SEP IRA.** Under such a plan, your business can make generous, tax-deductible contributions to the IRAs of company employees (including your own, if you're the business owner). In 2021, for example, your business can make tax-deductible contributions of up to 25% of an employee's compensation— but no more than $58,000. Employer contributions are discretionary, and the money is not taxed until the employee starts making withdrawals.
- **SIMPLE IRA.** This option is only available to employers with 100 or fewer employees who each made $5,000 or more in the preceding calendar year. It is funded mainly by employee contributions, though an employer must contribute a matching or nonelective amount. Employer contributions are tax deductible; employee contributions can be made tax free. In 2021, an employee can contribute up to $13,500. An employee age 50 or over can contribute an additional $3,000.

These IRA plans are flexible, require minimal paperwork, and often have lower administrative costs than traditional plans. See your tax adviser for details.

TIP

Special protection for older employees. The Older Workers Benefit Protection Act, an amendment to the Federal Age Discrimination in Employment Act (29 U.S.C. § 621), generally prohibits you from providing reduced benefits to older people in your retirement plan. But the act does allow for some lesser coverage for certain benefits, such as health and disability insurance, if you can show there's a rational cost reason for doing it. For more information, see *The Essential Guide to Federal Employment Laws*, by Lisa Guerin and Sachi Barreiro (Nolo); it includes a chapter explaining the requirements of the Older Workers Benefits Protection Act.

Meeting IRS and ERISA Requirements

When maintaining a retirement plan for your employees, you must comply with two sets of federal laws: the Internal Revenue Code, which sets out the tax law requirements for your plan, and the Employee Retirement Income Security Act (ERISA), which sets out the administrative requirements for your plan. (29 U.S.C. §§ 1001 and following.)

Tax Law Requirements

While you don't have to include all workers in your retirement plan, there are complicated laws that govern whom you can include, whom you can exclude, and for what reasons. In addition, you can't structure the plan to benefit only the top executives or to otherwise discriminate against lower-paid workers.

A retirement plan that passes muster with the IRS is called a qualified plan, which means your contribution qualifies as a tax-deductible business expense. Your contributions won't be taxed as income to employees until they actually receive the benefit.

RESOURCE

Get help from the IRS. For a helpful introduction to these requirements, see IRS Publication 535, *Business Expenses*, available at the IRS website at www.irs.gov.

Administration Requirements

Under ERISA, you'll need to appoint a plan administrator to be responsible for following through on the law's paperwork requirements. This can be a person in your business or an outsider who's associated with the retirement plan. If you have a relatively small business, it may be simpler and cheaper to have an outsider—such as a worker at a bank or mutual fund company—act as plan administrator. It's difficult to develop enough expertise within your business to meet all the legal requirements that affect retirement plans.

The ERISA requirements are heavy on paperwork. There are a number of documents your plan administrator must give to participating employees.

Summary plan description. This is a booklet that describes how your plan operates. Your plan administrator must give employees the summary plan description within 90 days after they begin participating in the plan. Employees are also entitled to plan updates. The description must include the formula for determining an employee's benefits or the contributions that you'll make to the plan. It must also explain any formula for vesting: the point at which the employee's right to retirement benefits becomes locked in and can't be taken away.

Summary annual report. This is a yearly accounting of the plan's financial condition and operations.

Survivor coverage data. This is a statement of how much the plan will pay to the surviving spouse of an employee if the employee dies.

In addition, each year the plan administrator must give participants a detailed, individual statement of the benefits they've earned. And you must annually file with the IRS a Form 5500, which includes a census of employees and participants and is accompanied by summary financial reports.

SEE AN EXPERT

Get help if you can. ERISA is an extremely complicated law that can trip up even the most well-intentioned and savvy employer. Unless you have a large company with an experienced benefits administrator, you'd be wise to hire a professional to help you meet the law's requirements. Often, whatever company administers your plan for you will also take care of ERISA. Talk to your plan administrator to be sure.

Plan Termination Requirements

If you decide to terminate a defined benefit plan—one that promises specific benefits—you must notify covered employees of the approaching termination at least 60 days before the plan ends.

If you decide to reduce the rate of benefit accruals or terminate either a defined benefit plan or a money purchase plan, you must notify covered employees within a reasonable period of time before the amendment takes effect.

> CAUTION
>
> **Former spouses' retirement benefit rights.** In many divorces, an employee's retirement benefits are divided as part of the property settlement. The spouse of an employee may acquire rights under what ERISA calls a qualified domestic relations order (QDRO). When that happens, your company has ERISA obligations to the employee's spouse similar to your obligations to the employee. These include reviewing the court order to see if it meets the requirements for a QDRO, paying out money to the spouse as required by the order, and giving the spouse plan information if benefits aren't paid to the spouse immediately.

Who's In—And Who's Out

You don't have a completely free hand in deciding whom to include in a retirement plan. In general, ERISA requires you to include everyone who:

- is 21 years old or older, and
- has worked for your business for at least a year—1,000 or more hours in the last 12 months.

In an exception to this general rule, you can require employees to be with your company for two years before they will be eligible to participate in the plan. But if you do this, you must also allow an employee's rights to become fully vested as soon as the employee begins participating in the plan.

Other Employee Benefits

Here's a rundown of several other benefit programs that the IRS recognizes as tax-deductible business expenses.

Life Insurance

One of the least expensive benefits you can offer to employees is group term life insurance. This is life insurance that pays off only if the employee dies during the policy term (usually five, ten, or 20 years). You can deduct the premiums you pay for up to $50,000 of group term life insurance for each employee. And employees don't pay tax on the premiums you pay.

If your business doesn't have at least ten full-time employees, you'll need to meet some special requirements to qualify for this tax treatment. For example, you'll have to provide life insurance for all full-time employees, and you can't require physical exams for the coverage. However many employees you have, you can't weight your group term plan in favor of highly paid employees.

Some employers pay for the first $10,000 or so of term life coverage, giving the employee the option of buying additional coverage under the same group plan. This allows employers to offer a growing benefit without having to put out a growing outlay of cash.

In selecting a group insurance policy, look for one that allows terminated employees to switch to an individual policy without having to prove that they are still insurable. Of course, after such a conversion, the former employee becomes responsible for paying the premiums.

Disability Insurance

Consider offering disability insurance to help employees offset lost income if they have a serious injury or illness. You can probably find a group policy under which you pay part of the premium and the employee pays part. Some plans give employees the option of continuing their coverage after they leave your business. They then become responsible for the entire premium.

Your business can take a tax deduction for the premiums it pays, but an employee who receives payments under the insurance policy will owe income tax on those payments. If the employer and employee each pay part of the premium, the employee will owe income tax on part of the payments received.

Cafeteria Plans

Under a cafeteria plan, an employee gets to choose from a menu of benefits such as:

- health insurance
- dental coverage
- vision care
- disability insurance
- group term life insurance
- group legal services
- additional contribution to a 401(k) plan
- additional paid vacation days, and
- cash.

Typically, the employer provides a monthly allowance to be allocated by the employee. If an employee selects benefits that exceed the allowance, the employee pays the additional amount through payroll deductions. If an employee doesn't use the full allowance, the leftover amount is added to the employee's paycheck.

These plans are attractive because they allow employees to tailor their benefits to their particular needs, while giving the employer some control over benefit costs.

Educational Assistance Programs

You may want to pay all or part of the cost of schooling that employees pursue outside working hours. You can set up a written plan with guidelines for the type of continuing education your business will finance, how much you're willing to spend, and the point at which you'll reimburse an employee for tuition.

Under such a plan, you can deduct as a business expense up to $5,250 per year for the educational costs you pay for an employee. These costs are also not included in the employee's taxable income.

A few restrictions apply:

- The education assistance program can't favor highly paid employees or their spouses or dependents.
- No more than 5% of the program's payments during a year can be used to benefit a business's shareholders or owners, or their spouses or dependents.

- You can't offer employees a choice between receiving the educational assistance or other payment that's includable in the employees' gross income.
- Assistance can't be used for courses involving sports, games, or hobbies.

Dependent Care Assistance

The tax law lets your business deduct expenses you pay for assistance to employees who must care for their dependents, a major concern today as more workers have to take care of young children, aging parents, or both.

Your payments qualify for the tax deduction if they enable an employee to care for:

- dependents age 12 or younger for whom the employee can claim a personal exemption
- dependents who are physically or mentally incapable of taking care of themselves, or
- the employee's spouse, if the spouse can't take care of himself or herself.

The amounts you deduct can be for bills you pay or money you reimburse to an employee for:

- at-home child care
- in-home care for elderly or disabled adults who live with the employee
- care at a licensed nursery school or kindergarten, or
- care at a dependent care center that provides day care for more than six people.

You can also provide dependent care assistance at your own on-site facility.

Dependent care payments up to $5,000 a year—or $2,500 a year for a married employee filing a separate tax return—are generally tax free to the employee. For employees with lower household incomes, there's a dependent care tax credit that will be more valuable to them than any dependent care assistance provided by an employer, even though the care the employer provides won't be included in the employee's income for tax purposes. If you offer a dependent care plan, let employees know about tax credit alternatives so they can choose the best option. Because the tax treatment of dependent care assistance is complex, you should consult a tax pro if you plan to offer this benefit.

Adoption Assistance Programs

You can assist employees with adoption expenses. Up to $14,400 (in 2021) of the amount that you pay for an employee's adoption expenses is tax free to the employee, and a deductible expense for your business. Before offering this benefit, you'll need to write up an adoption assistance plan. Your plan must not favor highly paid employees or company owners. For details, see IRS Publication 15-B, *Employer's Tax Guide to Fringe Benefits*.

Benefits That Cost Little or Nothing

In addition to benefits such as health care or retirement savings contributions that cost money, there are other, less tangible benefits that can help you attract and keep good employees. Free or low-cost benefits may include:

- **Good working conditions.** Workers are likely to appreciate a well-lit and ventilated office or shop with a view, and access to a kitchen for preparing lunch.
- **Flexible hours.** This makes it easier for employees to juggle competing time demands, such as caring for children or older parents, or attending classes.
- **Free parking.** Parking on the premises or nearby can save your employees from the daily hassle of finding space on the street, having coins on hand to feed the meter, or paying for space in a public garage.
- **Opportunity to learn new skills and advance.** This can be a powerful incentive for an employee who looks ahead to more lucrative employment. It can help you attract ambitious, motivated employees.
- **Ability to work from home.** Due to COVID-19, telecommuting has never been more popular. It doesn't work for all businesses, but many office-based businesses have learned that their employees can productively work from home at least some of the time. No doubt many employees will expect this perk to continue after the pandemic is over.
- **Supplying beverages and snacks.** This can help make your employees feel comfortable and experience less stress on the job.
- **Membership in a trade or professional organization, or a subscription to a work-related publication.** This will appeal to employees who want to get ahead in the business or professional world.

5

Taxes

As an employer, one of your roles is that of tax collector. The government treats you as an unpaid revenue agent whose job it is to withhold income taxes and Social Security and Medicare taxes from employees' paychecks and pay over those amounts to the IRS. In addition, Uncle Sam requires you to match employees' Social Security and Medicare taxes and to pay a federal unemployment tax (FUTA) based on your payroll. And Uncle Sam's nieces and nephews in state government also look to you to help rake in their dough. You must also account to every employee for the taxes you've withheld and the amounts being sent to the government.

Whether you personally handle employee tax matters or turn them over to someone else—a bookkeeper or an accountant—you must understand at least the fundamentals of the system. If you handle taxes incorrectly, you can be hit with interest and penalties. And you may even be held personally liable if your business fails to transmit employee withholdings to the government. The IRS doggedly pursues its targets, so you don't want to get caught in its clutches.

Handling Employee Taxes

Determine how involved you want to be in handling employee taxes and whether there are tasks you want to delegate to others.

If you want to do it yourself, the IRS puts out some excellent publications to guide you through the process. Relevant IRS publications are noted throughout this chapter. You can get them at the agency's website at www.irs.gov.

A part-time bookkeeper can help compile organized, detailed business records without demanding too much of your time. An accountant can help you set up a plan for your bookkeeper to follow and periodically monitor it to ensure that you meet all tax obligations.

A word of caution about one other possible source of assistance: IRS employees. Most of them are hardworking and well meaning, but their training and supervision are often inadequate. Unfortunately, it's common to receive bad advice in answer to your questions. And if the advice proves to be so inaccurate that it causes you to be assessed interest and penalties, the fact that you got it from an IRS employee won't get you off the hook. In short, it's often cheaper to rely on the advice of an experienced small business accountant than to rely on a free oral opinion from the IRS.

This chapter will help you acquire a good working knowledge of how the tax laws affect you as an employer and how the pieces of the tax system fit together.

CAUTION

Don't forget state and local taxes. This chapter focuses on federal tax law. In addition to being scrupulously mindful of federal payroll taxes, find out whether your state and municipality impose payroll taxes. For example, if your state or city has an income tax, you may be required to withhold taxes from employees' pay much like the federal system, but some states and cities follow different procedures. Contact your state and city treasurers for detailed information.

Employer Identification Numbers

If your business has employees, get an Employer Identification Number (EIN) from the IRS, regardless of whether the business is a sole proprietorship, a partnership, a C corporation, an S corporation, or a limited liability company. Technically, if your business is a sole proprietorship, you can use your personal Social Security number instead of an EIN, but it's still a good business practice to get an EIN to differentiate between personal and business finances.

You'll need an EIN before you file a tax return or make a tax deposit. In some cases, a bank will require you to have an EIN before you open a business account.

How to Apply

The easiest way to get an EIN is to apply online by going to www.irs.gov and clicking on "Apply for an Employer ID Number (EIN)." Applying online allows you to obtain an EIN immediately without having to complete IRS Form SS-4, *Application for Employer Identification Number.*

As an alternative, you can complete Form SS-4 and fax it to the IRS at 855-641-6935. You can also mail the form to the IRS, but you'll face a longer turnaround time. The instructions tell you more about how to submit a completed form. A completed form is shown below.

The form isn't difficult to fill out if you follow the IRS instructions. Here are a few pointers.

Space 1. Insert your official corporate name if you're a corporation. If you're a partnership, use the partnership name shown in your partnership agreement. If you're a sole proprietor, insert your full name.

Space 12. Here you're asked to state the closing month of your business accounting year. Your answer, however, isn't binding. You make your binding election of a fiscal year end on the first federal income tax return that you file for the business.

Sole proprietors, partnerships, S corporations, and personal service corporations are generally required to use a calendar year—that is, a year ending December 31—for tax purposes. Personal service corporations have two basic characteristics:

- The professional employees of the corporation own the stock.
- The corporation performs its services in the fields of health, law, engineering, architecture, accounting, actuarial science, performing arts, or consulting.

To use a tax year other than a calendar year, an S corporation must demonstrate to the IRS that it has a substantial business reason to do so, such as the seasonal nature of the business. Basically, the IRS wants to make sure that permitting you to claim a tax year other than the calendar year won't substantially distort your income.

A regular corporation that's not a personal service corporation has more freedom in choosing a fiscal year. Most small businesses find that, even where there's a choice, the calendar year is the most convenient way to proceed. Sometimes, however, there are tax planning reasons for a business owner to choose a different tax year for the business. See IRS Publication 538, *Accounting Periods and Methods*, for details.

SEE AN EXPERT

An accountant or other experienced tax adviser can help you decide whether you and your corporation can realize a tax advantage by using a fiscal year instead of a calendar year.

Space 13. These numbers can be estimated.

Form **SS-4**	**Application for Employer Identification Number**	OMB No. 1545-0003
(Rev. December 2019)	(For use by employers, corporations, partnerships, trusts, estates, churches, government agencies, Indian tribal entities, certain individuals, and others.)	EIN
Department of the Treasury Internal Revenue Service	▶ Go to *www.irs.gov/FormSS4* for instructions and the latest information. ▶ See separate instructions for each line. ▶ Keep a copy for your records.	

Type or print clearly.

1 Legal name of entity (or individual) for whom the EIN is being requested
 Ted Anderson

2 Trade name of business (if different from name on line 1)
 The Poster Warehouse

3 Executor, administrator, trustee, "care of" name

4a Mailing address (room, apt., suite no. and street, or P.O. box)
 555 Main Street

5a Street address (if different) (Don't enter a P.O. box.)

4b City, state, and ZIP code (if foreign, see instructions)
 Ann Arbor, MI 48104

5b City, state, and ZIP code (if foreign, see instructions)

6 County and state where principal business is located
 Washtenaw County, Michigan

7a Name of responsible party
 Ted Anderson

7b SSN, ITIN, or EIN
 555-55-5555

8a Is this application for a limited liability company (LLC) (or a foreign equivalent)? . . . . ☐ Yes ☑ No

8b If 8a is "Yes," enter the number of LLC members . . . . . . ▶

8c If 8a is "Yes," was the LLC organized in the United States? . . . . ☐ Yes ☐ No

9a **Type of entity** (check only one box). **Caution:** If 8a is "Yes," see the instructions for the correct box to check.
- ☑ Sole proprietor (SSN) 555-55-5555
- ☐ Partnership
- ☐ Corporation (enter form number to be filed) ▶
- ☐ Personal service corporation
- ☐ Church or church-controlled organization
- ☐ Other nonprofit organization (specify) ▶
- ☐ Other (specify) ▶
- ☐ Estate (SSN of decedent)
- ☐ Plan administrator (TIN)
- ☐ Trust (TIN of grantor)
- ☐ Military/National Guard ☐ State/local government
- ☐ Farmers' cooperative ☐ Federal government
- ☐ REMIC ☐ Indian tribal governments/enterprises
- Group Exemption Number (GEN) if any ▶

9b If a corporation, name the state or foreign country (if applicable) where incorporated | State | Foreign country |

10 **Reason for applying** (check only one box)
- ☑ Started new business (specify type) ▶
  sales
- ☐ Hired employees (Check the box and see line 13.)
- ☐ Compliance with IRS withholding regulations
- ☐ Other (specify) ▶
- ☐ Banking purpose (specify purpose) ▶
- ☐ Changed type of organization (specify new type) ▶
- ☐ Purchased going business
- ☐ Created a trust (specify type) ▶
- ☐ Created a pension plan (specify type) ▶

11 Date business started or acquired (month, day, year). See instructions.
 August 1, 20xx

12 Closing month of accounting year December

13 Highest number of employees expected in the next 12 months (enter -0- if none). If no employees expected, skip line 14.

Agricultural	Household	Other
O	O	

14 If you expect your employment tax liability to be $1,000 or less in a full calendar year **and** want to file Form 944 annually instead of Forms 941 quarterly, check here. (Your employment tax liability generally will be $1,000 or less if you expect to pay $5,000 or less in total wages.) If you don't check this box, you must file Form 941 for every quarter. ☐

15 First date wages or annuities were paid (month, day, year). **Note:** If applicant is a withholding agent, enter date income will first be paid to nonresident alien (month, day, year) . . . . ▶ September 1, 20xx

16 Check **one** box that best describes the principal activity of your business.
- ☐ Construction ☐ Rental & leasing ☐ Transportation & warehousing
- ☐ Real estate ☐ Manufacturing ☐ Finance & insurance
- ☐ Health care & social assistance ☐ Wholesale-agent/broker
- ☐ Accommodation & food service ☐ Wholesale-other ☑ Retail
- ☐ Other (specify) ▶

17 Indicate principal line of merchandise sold, specific construction work done, products produced, or services provided.
 sale of posters

18 Has the applicant entity shown on line 1 ever applied for and received an EIN? ☐ Yes ☑ No
 If "Yes," write previous EIN here ▶

Third Party Designee

Complete this section **only** if you want to authorize the named individual to receive the entity's EIN and answer questions about the completion of this form.

Designee's name | Designee's telephone number (include area code)

Address and ZIP code | Designee's fax number (include area code)

Under penalties of perjury, I declare that I have examined this application, and to the best of my knowledge and belief, it is true, correct, and complete. | Applicant's telephone number (include area code) 555-555-5555

Name and title (type or print clearly) ▶ Ted Anderson, Owner

Signature ▶ *Ted Anderson* Date ▶ 7/14/xx | Applicant's fax number (include area code) 555-555-5555

For Privacy Act and Paperwork Reduction Act Notice, see separate instructions. | Cat. No. 16055N | Form **SS-4** (Rev. 12-2019)

Space 18. This question refers to the business, not the owner. Normally, a partnership or corporation has only one EIN. A sole proprietor may have several businesses, each with a separate number.

Use your EIN on all business tax returns, checks, and other documents you send to the IRS. Your state tax authority may also require your EIN on state tax forms.

When to Get a New Number

If your S corporation chooses to change to a regular corporation—or your regular corporation chooses to change to an S corporation—it doesn't need a new EIN; the one you already have is still sufficient. However, you'll need to get a new EIN if any of these changes occur in your business:

- You incorporate your sole proprietorship or partnership.
- Your sole proprietorship takes in partners and begins operating as a partnership.
- Your partnership is taken over by one of the partners and begins operating as a sole proprietorship.
- Your corporation changes to a partnership or to a sole proprietorship.
- You purchase or inherit an existing business that you'll operate as a sole proprietorship.
- You represent an estate that operates a business after the owner's death.
- You terminate an old partnership and begin a new one.

Federal Employment Taxes

There are several types of employment-related taxes the federal government exacts from businesses.

RESOURCE

These taxes are all explained clearly and in great detail in Publication 15, Circular E, *Employer's Tax Guide,* published by the IRS. Updated whenever the tax rates change, Circular E is available at all IRS offices and online at www.irs.gov/publications.

Federal Income Tax Withholding (FIT)

You must withhold income taxes from employees' paychecks based on:
- the employee's filing status (single, married, or married but withholding at the higher single rate)
- the number of dependents (withholding allowances) declared by the employee, and
- the size of the employee's salary.

Each employee should give you a signed Form W-4 stating the withholding allowance. Save these forms in case the IRS wants to see them.

Use the tables in Circular E to figure out how much income tax to withhold.

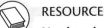

RESOURCE

Need tax help? IRS Publication 334, *Tax Guide for Small Business*, and, if you're just getting started, IRS Publication 583, *Starting a Business and Keeping Records*, are well worth reading. You can download these publications at the IRS website, www.irs.gov.

Working for Yourself: Law & Taxes for Independent Contractors, Freelancers & Gig Workers of All Types, by Stephen Fishman (Nolo), is a comprehensive guide for those starting their own businesses. It includes detailed information on taxes.

Tax Savvy for Small Business: A Complete Tax Strategy Guide, by Frederick Daily (Nolo), is a plain-English guide to business deductions and the tax implications of business decisions.

U.S. Master Tax Guide (Commerce Clearing House) is updated annually and available in law libraries, business school libraries, and the reference departments of major public libraries. It features in-depth explanations of tax complexities.

The Kiplinger Tax Letter, published by the Kiplinger Washington Editors, is a biweekly newsletter that will keep you up to date on what's happening in the tax field. To subscribe, go to store.kiplinger.com.

Social Security Taxes (FICA)

You must withhold the employee's share of the Social Security tax and Medicare tax from the employee's pay. And you must also pay the employer's share.

The amounts to be withheld are listed in the most current edition of Circular E. In 2021, for example, the employee is required to pay 7.65% on the first $142,800 of his or her annual wages—the 6.2% Social Security tax plus the 1.45% Medicare tax. The employer is also required to pay 7.65% on the first $142,800 of the employee's annual wages. There is no Social Security tax on the portion of the employee's annual wages that exceeds $142,800—only Medicare tax; the employer and employee each pay the 1.45% Medicare tax on the excess amount. The rates and the cutoff point for the Social Security tax change annually.

In 2021, there is a Medicare surtax of 0.9% on the wages and self-employment income of high earners. This surtax applies when a single person's earnings exceed $200,000 and when a married couple's earnings exceed $250,000.

On earnings above these amounts, the Medicare tax rate increases to 2.35% (1.45% regular Medicare tax plus 0.9% Medicare surtax). This surtax doesn't affect the employer's share, however. The employer still pays Medicare tax at the 1.45% rate, regardless of how much the employee earns.

Federal Unemployment Taxes (FUTA)

You must report and pay the federal unemployment tax (FUTA); it's not withheld from the employee's pay. In 2021, the FUTA tax rate was 6% of the first $7,000 of the employee's wages for the year. However, employers receive a credit for participating in state unemployment programs. The credit is generally 5.4%, resulting in a net tax rate of only 0.6% (6% minus 5.4%). In other words, employers have to pay only $42 for an employee earning $7,000 a year or more.

Withholding From an Owner's Paycheck

If you own most or all of the stock of a regular corporation, chances are you probably pay yourself a salary, which means that you're an employee as well as an owner. Similarly, if you're an owner and officer of an S corporation and perform substantial services for the company, you're considered an employee for tax purposes.

With either type of corporation, if you receive compensation for your services, you must complete and submit a Form W-4 to the corporation just like any other employee, and the corporation must withhold income, Social Security, and Medicare taxes from your paychecks.

Use IRS Form 940 to report federal unemployment tax. Sole proprietorships and partnerships don't pay the FUTA on the owners' compensation.

Periodic Payments

You must periodically remit to the IRS the income tax you withhold from employee paychecks and the employer's and employees' shares of Social Security and Medicare taxes. The IRS requires you to do this electronically through its Electronic Federal Tax Payment System. For detailed information on using the system, go to www.eftps.gov. How often you must pay is based on the size of your payroll and amounts due. A typical small business makes monthly payments.

In January of each year, you must give each employee a completed Form W-2, *Wage and Tax Statement,* listing the employee's total earnings for the prior year and the amount of employment taxes that you have withheld. The Form W-2 also must state the value of any health care coverage you've provided that's not included in the employee's gross income.

RESOURCE

Get a copy of IRS Publication 509, *Tax Calendars,* **to see when to file returns and make tax payments.** It's available from your local IRS office. You can also obtain it at the IRS website at www.irs.gov. The publication is updated annually.

CAUTION

Deposit taxes on time. Be sure to withhold taxes as required by the tax laws and to deposit those taxes on time. There are substantial penalties if you don't. And if you're an owner of a small business and personally involved in its management, you can be held personally liable for these taxes and the additional penalties, even if the business has the funds to pay them. The IRS has discretion to go after whomever it chooses. If your business suddenly runs into financial trouble, put the withheld taxes at the top of the list for payment. If that means not paying suppliers and others, so be it. The debts of the other creditors can be wiped out in bankruptcy if the business continues to go downhill. Not so with the withheld taxes. You can remain personally liable for these amounts even if the business goes through bankruptcy.

Payroll Taxes Made Easy

If you're overwhelmed by the requirements for calculating payroll taxes and the fine points of when and where to pay them, you can pay a bank or payroll service to do the work for you. A reputable payroll tax outfit that offers a tax notification service will calculate the correct amount due, produce your employees' paychecks and the checks to pay your taxes, and notify you when the taxes are due.

One big advantage of a payroll service over a bank is that it could give you more control over your money. A bank will withhold the amount of the tax from your account when the payroll is done, even though the tax isn't due yet. That means the bank, not you, gets the use of the money in the interim. A payroll service that offers tax notification will prepare the checks and tell you when they must be deposited. Depending on how often you must make payments, that can give you the use of the money for an extra month or more.

At the end of each quarter, the payroll service will produce your quarterly payroll tax returns and tell you how to file them. At the end of the year, the service will also prepare W-2 forms and federal and state transmittal forms.

Payroll services can be cost-effective for even very small businesses. But when you look for one, it pays to shop around. Avoid services that charge setup fees— basically, a fee for putting your information into the computer—or extra fees to prepare W-2 forms or quarterly and annual tax returns.

Federal Self-Employment Taxes

The self-employment tax applies to income you receive from actively working in your business, but not to income you are paid as an employee of that business. Technically, it's not an employment tax, but a first cousin to that tax.

If you're a sole proprietor or a partner, you must pay the federal self-employment tax in addition to regular income tax. The self-employment tax is equal to the employer's and employee's portion of the Social Security and Medicare taxes that you and your employer would pay on your compensation if you received it as an employee.

Computing Your Estimated Taxes

Many taxpayers receive income from sources other than paychecks, such as from investments and royalties. These taxpayers often owe surprising amounts in income taxes on April 15. Sometimes, that's because they had no employer to withhold income tax during the year. Other times, it's because even though there was an employer, the amounts withheld were insufficient to cover the taxpayer's nonemployment income.

As you may know, the IRS doesn't want you to wait until April 15 to pay. Instead, the IRS requires you to pay your taxes in advance in quarterly installments if not enough is being withheld from your salary. These installments are known as estimated taxes. If you don't pay sufficient taxes in advance, you face the burden of paying interest and penalties.

In figuring out what your tax bill will be and whether you need to pay any quarterly installments of estimated taxes, don't overlook the self-employment tax that is added to your regular income tax on your Form 1040 as part of your tax obligation. Make sure your quarterly installments are large enough to cover your self-employment tax as well as your usual income tax.

For more on this subject, see IRS Publication 505, *Tax Withholding and Estimated Tax*, available at the IRS website at www.irs.gov.

Compute this tax each year on Schedule SE, then attach it to your personal Form 1040. Add the self-employment tax to the income tax that you owe. In 2021, for example, the self-employment tax is set at 15.3% on earnings up to $142,800 and 2.9% on earnings over $142,800. Once your earnings reach $200,000 (if your filing status is single) or $250,000 (for married filers), you will have to pay an additional Medicare surtax of 0.9%, for a total tax rate of 3.8%.

If you have income from another job that's subject to withholding—common for people just getting started in business—the income from your other job will reduce the tax base for your self-employment tax.

Federal Tax Deductions for Salaries and Other Expenses

A number of employee-related expenses can be deducted from your business income in computing your federal income tax.

Salaries

You can deduct from your gross income the salaries, wages, and other forms of compensation that you pay to employees for their services, as long as the payments are reasonable. Fortunately, you have broad discretion to decide what's reasonable. Short of a scam—such as paying a huge salary to a spouse or relative who does little or no work—the IRS will almost always accept your notion of what pay is reasonable.

If your business uses the cash method of accounting, you deduct the payments that were actually made during the tax year. For employers using an accrual method of accounting, the rule is different and more complicated. The salaries are deductible for the tax year in which you established your obligation to make the payments, even if you deferred payment to a later time.

Vacation Pay

You can also deduct vacation pay from business income in determining the base for your federal income tax. If you're on a cash basis accounting method, you deduct vacation pay as wages when you pay the employee. If you use an accrual method, you can deduct vacation pay in the year it's earned only if you pay it by the close of your tax year or within two and a half months after the close. If you pay later than this, you deduct it in the year you actually pay it.

Bonuses and Gifts

Many businesses give bonuses to employees to reward them for a job well done or because the company has had a profitable year. You can take a tax deduction for bonuses you pay to employees if they're intended as additional payment for services and not as gifts; most bonuses qualify for deduction. The bonuses are subject to payroll tax withholding.

If your business distributes cash or gift certificates that can be converted to cash, the value of these gifts is considered additional wages or salary regardless of the amount, and it is subject to employment taxes and withholding rules.

Noncash gifts are also generally treated as income to the employee, but not those that are clearly of an advertising nature, such as pens embossed with your company name. Other noncash gifts to employees may also be excluded from the employee's income if they are of nominal value.

> **EXAMPLE:** To promote employee goodwill, Pebblestone Partnership distributes turkeys, hams, and other merchandise of nominal value at holidays. The partnership also gives each employee a check for $200. The value of the turkeys, hams, and other merchandise isn't salaries or wages, but the partnership can deduct the cost of these items as a business expense. The checks can also be deducted but must be treated as income to the employees subject to withholding.

Meals and Lodging

You can deduct at least some of the cost of meals and lodging you provide to employees if these expenses are a reasonable part of doing business. In some cases, the value of the meals or lodging you furnish must be reported as part of the employees' income for tax purposes.

Meals

Normally, you can deduct as a business expense only 50% of the cost of providing meals to employees. However, for 2021 and 2022, a recent change to federal law means you can deduct 100% of the cost of business-related food or beverages provided by a restaurant (including a takeout or delivery meal, business meals with clients, and meals during business travel), as long as the cost is not lavish or extravagant. This change was intended to stimulate the restaurant industry, which has struggled due to the COVID-19 pandemic.

In addition, you can deduct the full cost if any of the following is true:

- You operate a restaurant or catering service and furnish the meals to employees at the worksite.
- You furnish the meals as part of a recreational or social activity, such as a company picnic.

- The value of the meals is included in employees' income. Meals must be included in an employee's income unless the meals are furnished on your premises and for your convenience or consist of food that qualifies as a minimal fringe benefit—coffee, doughnuts, or soft drinks, for example, or the occasional meal you provide to enable an employee to work overtime.

EXAMPLE 1: Carol is a waitress at Sunshine Café. The restaurant provides two meals at no charge during her 7 a.m. to 4 p.m. workday. Sunshine encourages—but doesn't require—Carol to eat breakfast there before starting work. She must eat lunch there. Since Carol works during the normal breakfast and lunch periods, the value of her breakfast and lunch are not treated as income to her. If Sunshine allows Carol to have free meals there on her days off, the value of those meals would be included as income to Carol.

EXAMPLE 2: Frank is a clerk at Omni Department Store, working 9 a.m. to 5 p.m. Omni gives Frank his lunch without charge at a lunch buffet it maintains at the store. This helps Omni limit Frank's lunch break to 30 minutes, a benefit to Omni since its busiest time is during the normal lunch period. If Frank left the store to have lunch, he'd be away much longer than 30 minutes. The value of these meals is not income to Frank.

In addition to the above situations, you can deduct the full cost of the meals you serve on your premises to all employees, as long as more than half of them receive this benefit as a convenience to your business. In the example above, suppose that Omni Department Store were to provide the lunch buffet to 30 of the store's 50 employees as a convenience to the store. Omni could deduct the cost of providing the food to the other 20 employees as well.

Lodging

You can deduct as a business expense the cost of furnishing lodging to employees if it's a reasonable part of doing business. Generally, you must include the value of lodging as part of the employees' income. The value can be excluded, however, if you furnish the lodging on your business premises for your convenience and require the employee to live there to perform the job.

EXAMPLE: Felice is a swimming pool attendant at The Highlands, a resort complex that's 15 miles from town. The Highlands gives Felice the choice of living at the resort free of charge. If Felice chooses to live at The Highlands, the resort must include the value of the lodging in her income. It is not necessary for Felice to live at the resort to properly perform her job duties. It's merely a matter of convenience.

Fringe Benefits

Your business may be able to deduct as a business expense a number of employee fringe benefits, including:

- health and dental insurance
- medical reimbursement plans for items not covered by health insurance
- group term life insurance (limits apply, based on the policy value)
- educational assistance programs
- adoption assistance programs
- qualified employee benefit plans, including profit sharing plans, stock bonus plans, and money purchase pension plans, and
- cafeteria plans that allow employees to choose among two or more benefits consisting of cash and qualified benefits.

(See Chapter 4 for a detailed discussion of employee benefits.)

Be aware that there are restrictions—some of them complex—on deducting these benefits and that deductions may be available to some forms of business and not others. Not only are employee benefits tax deductible by your business, but they also are not taxed to the employee.

But while these benefits sound attractive, there are two serious drawbacks. First, many small businesses—particularly those just starting out—won't have the funds to finance them. Second, the IRS has stringent rules to discourage "top-heavy" plans: those designed to benefit primarily the owners and highly paid employees of a business. If your plan doesn't meet these guidelines, your business won't be able to deduct the cost.

Tax Changes Under the Tax Cuts and Jobs Act

In 2017, Congress passed the Tax Cuts and Jobs Act, which lowered the corporate tax rate to 21 percent; introduced a new and potentially valuable deduction for certain businesses; and eliminated or restricted some existing deductions. Here are a few of the highlights of the law, which took effect in 2018:

- Created the Qualified Business Income Deduction, a tax deduction of up to 20 percent for so-called pass-through businesses, such as S Corporations, partnerships, and sole proprietorships. However, the deduction is not available to most businesses in the fields of health, law, accounting, finance, and similar professional services.
- Disallowed the 50 percent deduction for entertainment expenses.
- Eliminated the employer deduction for the cost of qualified transportation fringe benefits provided to employees, including parking and commuting expenses.
- Limited the ability to deduct business interest expenses.

Consult with an accountant or tax adviser or visit www.irs.gov/tax-reform to learn how your business is affected by the law.

Independent Contractors

Some people you hire will be independent contractors rather than employees. (The differences between these two categories of workers are explained in detail in Chapter 12.) If you do hire someone who meets the IRS tests for an independent contractor, you don't have to withhold income taxes or Social Security taxes from that person's pay, nor are you required to make an employer's contribution to the worker's Social Security fund.

If, however, you pay an independent contractor $600 or more during a calendar year, you must report this to the IRS on Form 1099-NEC. (Prior to the 2020 tax year, you used Form 1099-MISC.)

Ask all independent contractors you hire to complete Form W-9, giving their Social Security numbers or their Employer Identification Numbers (EINs). You'll need this information when you report the payments you made. Because some independent contractors have tried to foil the IRS's attempts to track income, the government has enacted regulations to protect the integrity of the system. If an independent contractor doesn't give you an identification number—Social Security number or EIN—or if the IRS says you were given a wrong number, you may have to withhold from the independent contractor's pay to ensure that taxes aren't evaded.

CAUTION
Be sure workers are properly classified. The IRS believes it has lost large amounts of tax revenues because many employers and workers have improperly agreed to classify the workers as independent contractors rather than employees. In many of these cases, the employer hasn't withheld taxes, and the worker has neglected to report the income and pay tax on it. Given that background, the IRS enforces strict tests for determining who is and who isn't an independent contractor. If you misclassify someone who should have been called an employee, you may be heavily penalized. (To avoid costly problems, see Chapter 12 for a fuller explanation of the IRS criteria.)

Statutory Employees

Statutory employees are a kind of legal hybrid. They tend to be people you might ordinarily think of as independent contractors rather than employees, but they are employees because the law says they are. For statutory employees, your responsibilities for withholding taxes are less extensive than your responsibilities for other employees. You don't withhold income taxes from their pay, but you must withhold Social Security and Medicare taxes and you must make the matching employer's contribution.

The following are statutory employees:

Delivery people. A driver who either distributes meat products, vegetable or fruit products, bakery products, or beverages other than milk, or who picks up or delivers laundry or dry cleaning, if the driver is your agent or is paid on commission.

Insurance salespeople. A full-time life insurance salesperson.

Home workers. A person who works at home on materials that you supply and that must be returned to you or someone you name, if you also furnish specifications for how the work is to be done.

Traveling salespeople. A full-time traveling salesperson, who's not an agent or commission driver, who works on your behalf and turns in orders to you from wholesalers, retailers, contractors, hotels, restaurants, or other similar businesses. The goods sold must be merchandise for resale or supplies used in the buyer's business operation.

There's another twist in the statutory employee story: Not every person who falls into one of the above four categories is treated as a statutory employee. A statutory employee must meet three additional conditions:

- There must be a service contract stating or implying that the person must personally perform the services.
- Someone other than the worker must have invested substantially in the facilities used to perform the services (except for a car or truck).
- The worker must perform the services on a continuing basis.

If these conditions all apply, then you become responsible for withholding the worker's share of Social Security and Medicare taxes and paying the employer's share.

One more wrinkle: You need only pay federal unemployment tax (FUTA) on statutory employees who are delivery people or traveling salespeople.

RESOURCE

Get IRS help on statutory employees. For more information on statutory employees, see IRS Publication 15-A, *Employer's Supplemental Tax Guide*, available at www.irs.gov.

Family and Medical Leave

t's often difficult for working people to deal with family obligations, such as caring for a seriously ill child or parent or attending to the special needs of a newborn or newly adopted child. And, some employees who need time off work to recover from their own serious illnesses worry about being demoted or fired.

To help employees balance the demands of the workplace with personal and family needs, Congress enacted the Family and Medical Leave Act, or FMLA. (29 U.S.C. §§ 2601 and following.) Under the FMLA, if your business has 50 or more employees, you may be required to give an employee up to 12 weeks of unpaid leave for certain family and medical reasons. And the law requires you to return the employee to the same or a similar position when the leave is over, except when it would be prohibitively expensive for you to take back a highly paid employee.

The FMLA also allows certain employees with family members in the military to take leave. As part of their 12-week entitlement, employees may take FMLA leave to handle practical concerns relating to a family member's call to active duty. And, the law grants a 26-week leave entitlement to employees who need time off to care for a family member who is suffering from a serious illness or injury related to his or her military service. These provisions are covered in "Leave for Military Families," below.

This chapter discusses the federal law. Your state might have its own family leave law. To find out more about state law requirements, see "Related Laws," below.

RESOURCE

The FMLA is a complicated law with numerous requirements. To get detailed information about whether it applies to your company, how to administer leave, how the FMLA interacts with other laws, and more, see *The Essential Guide to Family & Medical Leave*, by Lisa Guerin and Deborah C. England (Nolo).

Who Is Covered

The FMLA covers your business if it has had 50 or more employees for 20 or more weeks in the current or preceding year. The count, for FMLA purposes, includes all employees on your payroll whether part time, full time, or already on leave.

An employee in a covered business is eligible for FMLA leave only if the employee works within a 75-mile radius of 50 or more of your employees and has worked for you:

- for at least 12 months (these months do not have to be consecutive), and
- for at least 1,250 hours during the 12 months before the leave.

If you have remote employees who meet the 12 months and 1,250 hours requirements, they are eligible for FMLA leave if they report to a location where 50 employees are present within a 75-mile radius. In other words, a remote employee's worksite is not the home for FMLA purposes—it is the location to which they report.

FMLA Poster Requirements and Remote Employees

If your business is subject to the FMLA, you must display a poster in the workplace titled "Employee Rights Under the Family and Medical Leave Act." It's available at the nearest office of the U.S. Department of Labor's Wage and Hour Division or online at the address below. Your state labor department may also be able to provide this poster, as well as posters describing workplace rights and responsibilities under state law.

If any of your employees work remotely, FMLA regulations allow you to provide the poster to them electronically, for example by posting it on a company intranet site, an external website, or a shared network drive. Simply emailing it to them is not sufficient under the law. Give your employees instructions on how to access the poster and make sure they can view it at all times. Electronic provision is permitted only for remote employees; if you have any on-site workers, you must display the physical poster in a conspicuous location.

You should also inform employees about their rights to FMLA leave in your employee handbook, if you have one. Otherwise, you must give employees written guidance when they request FMLA leave. The easiest way to do this is to print out the FMLA poster at www.dol.gov/whd/regs/compliance/posters/fmlaen.pdf, and give employees a copy.

Reasons for Taking a Leave

If your business is covered, you must grant unpaid leave to an eligible employee to care for a seriously ill parent, child, or spouse, to recover from a serious illness, to bond with a new child, or to handle issues relating to a family member's military service. Generally, the employee is entitled to a total of 12 workweeks of leave during any 12-month period. Some employees may be eligible for up to 26 weeks off; see "Leave for Military Families," below.

> CAUTION
> **Don't retaliate against employees for exercising leave rights.** The FMLA prohibits you from retaliating against an employee who has asked for or taken leave. Retaliation can take many forms. It can be blatant (such as transferring the employee to a job that pays less or is lower status) or more subtle (such as assigning the employee less desirable tasks).

Family Health Problems

An eligible employee may take FMLA leave to care for a spouse, son, daughter, or parent who has a serious health condition.

Defining Serious Health Condition

The FMLA rules for determining who has a serious health condition are complicated. Generally, however, an injury or illness may qualify as a serious health condition if it involves inpatient care: an overnight stay in a hospital or other medical care facility. The person who has been hospitalized is considered to have a serious health condition for as long as the individual can't work, attend school, or perform other normal life activities.

In addition, an injury or illness may qualify as a serious health condition if the patient requires continuing treatment (two or more treatments by a health care provider—or one treatment and an ongoing regimen of care—in a 30-day period) and cannot perform normal activities for more than three consecutive days. A person who needs treatment for pregnancy or prenatal care, a chronic health condition, or a long-term or permanent health condition may also have a serious health condition.

A positive test for COVID-19, by itself, is not considered a serious health condition according to the Department of Labor. However, if an individual has a symptomatic case or complications arise, COVID-19 can qualify as a serious health condition. If in any doubt, employers should treat coronavirus-related absences as FMLA-qualifying events to help minimize the spread of the virus. For more information, visit www.dol.gov/agencies/whd/fmla/pandemic.

State Laws on Family and Medical Leave for Coronavirus-Related Reasons

In March 2020, Congress passed a set of emergency COVID-19 measures that, among other things, temporarily provided paid family and medical leave to employees affected by the pandemic. Although these provisions expired at the end of 2020, many states passed similar laws that will remain in effect in 2021 and perhaps beyond. Depending on the rules in your state, your employees might be entitled to paid leave if they:

- have symptoms or have tested positive for COVID-19
- have been ordered to quarantine by a medical professional or public health body
- need to care for a family member who has COVID-19 or is under quarantine, or
- need to care for a child whose school or childcare provider has closed due to COVID-19.

In addition, as this book goes to press, Congress is weighing whether to allow employers who voluntarily provide leave for the above reasons to claim tax credits to reimburse their costs. For updates, check this book's companion page—the introduction explains how to find it.

To learn whether your state has its own COVID-19 leave laws, visit your state's labor department website. See the appendix for contact information.

Defining Family

An employee is only eligible to take FMLA leave to care for certain family members: the employee's spouse, parent, or child. A spouse is an employee's husband or wife as recognized under state law, which may include common-law spouses in the minority of states that recognize common-law marriage.

An employee's parent can be a biological parent or a person who took the place of a parent when the employee was a child (someone, for example, who took care of and financially supported the child). In-laws aren't considered parents under the FMLA.

An employee's son or daughter can be a biological, adopted, or foster child; a stepchild; or a legal ward. A child whom the employee cares for or financially supports also counts. Children must be younger than 18 or, if age 18 or older, they must be incapable of caring for themselves because of a mental or physical disability.

TIP
State laws may define "family" differently. Many states have family and medical leave laws similar to the FMLA. (See "Related Laws," below, for more information.) These laws may define "family" to include in-laws, domestic partners, and more. So even if the FMLA doesn't apply when an employee asks for time off to care for a family member, make sure to check your state's law, too.

Employee's Health Problems

An eligible employee may take FMLA leave for a serious health condition that makes the employee unable to perform the job.

Birth, Adoption, or Foster Care

An eligible employee may take FMLA leave because of the birth of a child or because a child has been placed with the employee for adoption or foster care. Under the FMLA, foster care is defined as 24-hour care for a child away from parents or guardians, based on a court order or an agreement approved by a state agency.

The period for taking leave based on birth, adoption, or foster care expires one year after the child is born or placed. Men as well as women are eligible for this leave. An expectant mother may begin FMLA leave before the birth of the child for prenatal care or if her condition makes her unable to work. You can require medical documentation of the need for prenatal care or inability to work before you grant a prebirth leave because this is a leave for the employee's serious health condition, not for bonding. Likewise, an employee with a pregnant wife may be eligible for FMLA leave to care for his pregnant spouse before the baby is born, if she needs such care.

Similarly, FMLA leave can begin before actual placement or adoption of a child if an absence from work is necessary. Such an absence may be necessary, for example, if an employee must attend counseling sessions, appear in court, consult with a lawyer or doctor representing the birth parent, or submit to a physical exam.

If both spouses work for your company, you can limit the total number of workweeks taken by both spouses to care for a child to 12 during any 12-month period. However, if the child's parents are not married to one another, each parent is entitled to the full allotment of 12 workweeks of leave. On the other hand, an unmarried employee isn't eligible for FMLA leave to care for a pregnant partner during pregnancy, because he or she doesn't meet the definition of "family member" under the FMLA.

Leave for Military Families

The FMLA also provides leaves to the families of military service members in two cases: when a serviceperson is injured during military service, and when the serviceperson is deployed to active duty. These provisions cover adult children, unlike the other FMLA leave entitlements.

Injury or Illness

Recognizing the strain placed on the families of military servicepeople, the FMLA provides time off for the family members of a member of the armed forces who suffers a serious injury or illness incurred in the line of active duty. This includes a service member with a preexisting injury or illness that was aggravated in the line of duty. It also extends to veterans who were in the military within the past five years and are being treated for a duty-related injury or illness.

The covered family member can take up to 26 weeks of leave during a single 12-month period to care for the service member. (The 26-week cap combines all types of FMLA leave.) For this type of leave only, more family members are covered, including siblings and next of kin.

"Qualifying Exigency"

The FMLA provides that if an employee's spouse, son, daughter, or parent is called to active duty in the military, the employee can take up to 12 weeks of FMLA leave during a 12-month period for a "qualifying exigency." Such events include:

- **Short-notice deployment.** This applies when the service member receives notice of a call-up within seven days of the deployment. The FMLA leave for this purpose is limited to seven calendar days from when the service member receives the notice.
- **Military events.** This allows the family member to attend official ceremonies, programs, or events related to the service member's active duty or call-up.
- **Child care and school activities.** This includes arranging alternative child care, caring for children on an immediate, urgent basis, and attending school meetings.
- **Financial and legal arrangements.** This gives the family member the time to make or update financial or legal plans to address the service member's absence. For example, this can include making a will or trust, or preparing a power of attorney.
- **Counseling.** The employee can take time off to receive counseling.
- **Rest and recuperation.** The employee can take FMLA leave to spend time with the service member who is on short-term R&R during a period of deployment. These leaves are limited to 15 days for each instance of R&R.
- **Postdeployment activities.** This includes arrival ceremonies, reintegration briefings, and other official programs within 90 days after the deployment ends. It also includes leave to address issues arising from the service member's death.
- **Parental care.** The employee can use qualifying exigency leave to arrange alternate care or provide urgent care for a military member's parent, to transfer or admit the parent to a care facility, or to attend meetings with staff at the parent's facility, if the parent is unable to care for himself or herself.
- **Additional activities.** The employee can take FMLA leave for other events related to the service member's deployment, but only if the employer and the employee agree to the timing and length of the leave.

Scheduling Leave

Many times, an employee may request large blocks of time off—days or weeks—under the FMLA. Other times, however, the employee may wish to take off only an hour or two—to attend a follow-up appointment after a surgery, for example—or on an "as needed" basis. You and an employee can agree to flexible work scheduling for the leave time to which employees are entitled under the FMLA. If the employee is taking the leave for his or her own serious health condition, to care for a family member who has a serious health condition, or for qualifying exigency leave, the FMLA requires your company to provide this intermittent leave. However, the company isn't required to provide intermittent leave to employees taking leave to bond with a new child; it can require the employee to take the leave all at once. But it can provide this option, if it wants to.

> **EXAMPLE:** Bill, an employee of Rendex Corporation, normally works Monday through Friday. Bill's wife has given birth to a son. Rendex and Bill agree that he'll use his leave rights in two-day segments by working Monday through Wednesday and staying home on Thursday and Friday.

Alternatively, the leave may be taken by reducing the employee's weekly work hours. Again, you are not required to allow employees on bonding leave to reduce their work schedules, but you must allow employees on leave for a serious medical condition to do so, if a health care provider says a reduced schedule is medically necessary.

> **EXAMPLE 1:** Tim works for Enterprise Associates. His father has a serious health condition requiring radiation treatments each week at a university medical center 100 miles away. Tim needs to drive his dad to treatment every Friday. Enterprise Associates must allow Tim to use unpaid leave time on Fridays.

> **EXAMPLE 2:** Carla, an employee of Cormark Company, adopts a daughter. Cormark and Carla agree that she'll exercise her leave rights by temporarily working from 1 p.m. to 5 p.m. rather than her normal 8 a.m. to 5 p.m. schedule.

Temporary Transfer to Another Job

If it is disruptive to your business to allow a particular employee to have a flexible or reduced work schedule, check to see whether there's another job open that will accommodate the employee's request with less disruption. If so, you can transfer the employee temporarily to the other job. The alternative job must have equivalent pay and benefits. The duties, however, needn't be equivalent as long as it isn't obviously a demotion, which gives the appearance that your company is retaliating against an employee for taking FMLA leave, and could create legal problems.

> **EXAMPLE:** Hilda works for Project Systems Inc. as a manager of ten employees. She is suffering from a major depressive episode which will require psychotherapy three times a week for six months. Project Systems must grant Hilda's request for a reduced leave schedule to permit her to get the necessary treatment. The company also transfers Hilda temporarily to a research position in which her absences will be less disruptive to the company.

Workplace Politics: A Delicate Business

When you temporarily transfer an employee, other employees—especially those who have been eyeing the open job—may feel resentful. This is a delicate situation, and you may be inclined to reduce tensions by informing the other employees about the medical reasons behind the transfer. Restrain yourself. You must respect that person's privacy and could get into legal trouble for disclosing confidential medical information.

Substituting Paid Leave

You're not required to pay for FMLA leave, but if you offer paid time off— vacation, personal, family, or sick leave—as a job benefit, the employee can ask (or you can require the employee) to substitute paid leave for unpaid FMLA leave in most situations.

You or the employee may substitute paid time off for unpaid FMLA leave as long as the reason for leave is covered by your paid leave policy and the employee meets the other requirements of your paid leave program. For example, if your company allows employees to use their sick leave to care for family members who are ill, they may substitute paid sick leave for FMLA leave used to care for a family member with a serious health condition. However, you don't have to allow employees to use sick leave for purposes that aren't covered by your program, such as bonding with a new child.

You may also require employees to follow your usual procedures for paid leave, but you may not deny them unpaid FMLA leave if they don't follow those procedures. An employee's failure to follow company policies for paid leave affects only their right to paid leave, not their rights under the FMLA.

EXAMPLE: Lou works for Star Baking Company. Star's paid time off policies require employees to give at least one week of advance notice before taking vacation time. Lou's mother has emergency surgery, and Lou immediately calls his supervisor and arranges to take three weeks of FMLA leave to care for her. He isn't entitled to use vacation time to get paid for the first week of FMLA leave, because he didn't give notice one week in advance. However, he may use vacation time for the second and third weeks of his leave, after the one-week notice requirement is met.

CAUTION

How much time off is owed. If an employee uses paid leave under circumstances that don't qualify as FMLA leave, the leave won't count against the 12 weeks of FMLA leave to which the employee is entitled. For example, if an employee uses paid sick leave for a condition which isn't a serious health condition as defined in the FMLA, the time off doesn't count against the 12 weeks of unpaid FMLA leave to which the employee may later be entitled.

Creative Solutions for Hard Problems

Family and medical leave laws address only a small part of the issues facing employers and employees in balancing the competing demands of the family and the workplace. To ensure a happy and productive workforce, you may need to work with employees to come up with creative solutions. Consider this list of possibilities from Renee Magid, founder and president of the consulting firm Initiatives Inc.

- flexible career paths
- flexible worktimes for full-time employees
- permanent part-time employment, with benefits
- job sharing
- work-at-home options
- cafeteria-style benefit plans
- education and support programs
- financial assistance with child care, and
- direct child care.

Advance Notice of Leave

Often, an employee can foresee the need for medical or bonding leave. For example, most employees know approximately when a baby will be born or can schedule a nonemergency surgery well in advance. You can require, in these situations, that an employee notify you at least 30 days before the unpaid leave is to begin.

But such advance notice isn't always possible, and the FMLA takes this into account. For example, if a child is born prematurely or an adoption or placement goes through unexpectedly, the employee can give you a shorter notice; the test is what is practical. If an employee doesn't give you 30 days' notice, you are allowed to ask the employee to explain why providing such notice wasn't practicable.

Similarly, where there's a medical emergency involving the employee or a member of the employee's family, it usually won't be practical for the employee to give you any advance notice of the need for leave. In such cases, advance notice isn't required. Where the need for FMLA leave isn't foreseeable, the employee or a family member can notify you either in person or by phone, fax, or email of the circumstances requiring the leave.

If an employee's leave is based on a serious health condition that requires planned medical treatment, you can require the employee to make a reasonable effort to schedule the treatment so that it won't unduly disrupt your business.

Certification

Theoretically, an employee could abuse the system by falsely claiming that the employee or a family member has a serious health condition. The FMLA recognizes this and allows you to require a certificate from the patient's health care provider stating:

- the date the serious health condition started
- the length of time the condition is likely to last
- diagnosis of the condition
- treatment prescribed, and
- whether inpatient treatment is required.

You're free to decide when to ask for a certificate and when not to, but it's best to follow a uniform policy, rather than a selective one. Otherwise, someone who's required to provide a certificate may claim you're discriminating, and you may have trouble justifying why a particular employee was singled out.

The certification requirements for a qualifying exigency caused by an active serviceperson's deployment are a little different. An employer may require the employee to provide a copy of the covered military member's active duty order for each separate call to active duty. The employee may also be required to submit a certification that includes:

- a signed description of the facts supporting the leave request, with supporting available documentation
- the approximate date of the qualifying exigency
- if the request is for a specific time period, the beginning and end dates of that period; or if it is intermittent or a reduced schedule, that schedule, and
- if the exigency involves meeting with a third party, the contact information for that third party and a description of the purpose of the meeting.

There's also a separate certification form for family members who take leave to care for a seriously ill or injured service member.

The U.S. Department of Labor (DOL) has developed certification forms for each type of FMLA leave. To find them, select "Forms" from the Department of Labor's FMLA page, www.dol.gov/WHD/fmla.

Employee's Own Condition

If the employee seeks leave because of the employee's own serious health condition, you can require that the certificate state either that the employee can't perform work of any kind or that the employee can't perform the essential functions of the job. Give the employee or the doctor a list of the job's essential functions.

Family Member's Condition

If the employee seeks leave to care for a family member, you can require that the certificate state that the patient needs help meeting basic medical, hygiene, nutritional, safety, or transportation needs, or that the employee is needed to provide care. The employee must indicate on the certificate what care the employee will provide and how long that care is likely to be required.

Intermittent Leave or Reduced Leave Schedule

If the employee seeks to take intermittent leave or asks for a shortened work schedule, you can require that the certificate state the medical need for or desirability of such leave and how long the situation requiring leave is expected to last.

Unclear or Incomplete Certifications

If you receive a certification that's incomplete or insufficient (that is, some of the spaces on the form are left blank, it isn't signed, or the information provided is vague or not responsive to the form), you must tell the employee in writing and explain what information is necessary to make the certification complete and sufficient. You must give the employee at least seven calendar days to hand in a complete certification.

Even if the certification you receive is complete, you may need to seek clarification or authentication from the employee's health care provider.

For example, you might ask for clarification if you can't read the doctor's handwriting or you don't understand a response on the form. You might ask for authentication if you want the health care provider to verify that the information and signature on the form are accurate. To clarify or authenticate a certification, you must first notify the employee and give him or her seven days to fix it, as you would for an incomplete certification. If the employee is unable to resolve the problem, someone from your company may contact the health care provider directly. Because the law protects the confidentiality of health care information, however, you must follow these rules:

- You may seek only authentication or clarification, as defined above; you may not seek more information than the form requires.
- Only a health care provider, human resources professional, leave administrator, or management official may contact the health care provider. The employee's direct supervisor may not contact the health care provider.
- You must follow the requirements of the Health Insurance Portability and Accountability Act (HIPAA), which, among other things, may require the employee to consent in writing to the conversation.

Second and Third Opinions

If, after receiving a certification, you are not fully convinced the request entitles the employee to FMLA leave, you can require the employee to get an opinion from a second health care provider. This can be someone you designate or approve, but it can't be someone you regularly employ, such as a company doctor. And you, rather than the employee, must pay for the second opinion.

CAUTION
Consider whether it's worth asking for a second opinion. Just because the FMLA allows you to get a second opinion doesn't mean it's a smart thing to do. Often it's not. Think long and hard before getting adversarial with employees over health determinations. If you make an employee jump through hoops to qualify for an unpaid absence, you'll probably wind up with a resentful employee who will never again give you full effort and loyalty. And the fallout from being unnecessarily suspicious about one employee can easily infect the entire workplace.

If you wind up with conflicting opinions, you can require a third opinion from another health care provider who is approved by both you and the employee. This third opinion is binding on both of you.

You may not request second or third opinions for either type of military family leave.

Health Care Providers: What's in a Name?

Generally, a doctor of medicine or osteopathy will sign the employee's medical certificate or render the second or third opinion. But technically, under the FMLA and its regulations, such certificates can be signed by a health care provider. This term includes not only MDs and DOs but others, such as podiatrists, dentists, clinical psychologists, optometrists, physician assistants, nurse practitioners, nurse midwives, clinical social workers, and, for some conditions, chiropractors.

Recertification

You can ask an employee to give you a recertification of a medical condition to support an ongoing leave request. You can require recertifications every six months, or every 30 days, for short-term conditions. You can request recertification more often if any of the following is true:

- The employee requests an extension of leave.
- Circumstances have changed significantly (for example, the duration or nature of the illness becomes different from what was anticipated).
- You receive information casting doubt on the continuing validity of the certification.

Health Benefits

If you have a group health plan for employees, you must maintain coverage for employees who are on FMLA leave. You must keep the coverage at the same level the employees would have if they worked continuously.

In some cases, however, you can require an employee to repay the premiums you paid for this continuing coverage. Generally, you can demand reimbursement if the employee doesn't come back to work after the leave period expires. But you can't demand reimbursement if the employee doesn't return to work in either of the following situations:

- The employee or a family member has suffered continuation, recurrence, or onset of a serious health condition (the kind of thing that would have justified taking the unpaid leave in the first place).
- There are other circumstances beyond the control of the employee. Examples of this include: An employee's spouse is unexpectedly transferred to a job location more than 75 miles from the employee's worksite, a person other than an immediate family member has a serious health condition and the employee is needed to provide care, or the employee is laid off while on leave.

Returning to Work

The FMLA normally gives employees the right to return to their jobs when their leave has been completed.

Job Protection

When an eligible employee returns from taking a leave, your company must restore the employee to the job that the employee held when the leave began or to a similar job—one with equivalent pay, benefits, and other terms of employment. However, an employee has no greater right to reinstatement or other benefits than if the employee had been continuously employed during the FMLA leave period.

> **EXAMPLE:** Anton takes ten weeks of unpaid family leave from his job as a production worker at Smokestack Industries Inc. While he's away, Smokestack eliminates the night shift on which Anton was working and lays off all employees working on that shift. Smokestack would have laid off Anton had he been working instead of taking leave. Smokestack doesn't have to reemploy Anton.

Exemption for Highly Paid Employees

Recognizing that it's difficult for many businesses to carry on in the absence of the customary executives and decision makers, the FMLA lets you decline to take back some highly paid employees after their leave. The exemption applies only if both of the following are true:

- The employee is among the highest paid 10% of the salaried people you employ within 75 miles of the place where the employee works.
- Taking back the employee will cause what the statute calls "substantial and grievous economic injury" to your business.

Unfortunately, the FMLA regulations don't precisely set the level of economic hardship or injury that excuses you from taking back an employee. It's clear that minor inconveniences and costs are not enough to justify cutting off a key employee who's taken a leave. On the other hand, you don't have to show that taking back the employee would threaten the existence of your business.

One test is whether it's feasible to temporarily replace or do without the employee on FMLA leave, or whether you must hire a permanent replacement. If the employee on leave is your company's $125,000-a-year sales manager, you may find that no competent people are willing to take over the job on a short-term basis. Because you need a sales manager, you have no real choice but to hire a permanent replacement. Reinstating the employee on leave to an equivalent job may be much too costly for your business, particularly if you must create a new job to do this. In such a situation, you'd likely be excused from taking back the employee after the leave.

As soon as you determine that substantial economic harm will result if you take back a key employee who has sought a leave under the FMLA, notify the employee in writing. In a letter, explain that your decision is based on your wish to prevent major injury to the business. If the employee then starts or continues the leave, you'll be protected by the FMLA.

Note that if an employee doesn't return to work after you give notice that you intend not to hire the employee back, you must still maintain the employee's health benefits for the full leave period, and you can't recover the cost of health insurance premiums.

Small Necessities Laws

A number of states have enacted so-called small necessities laws to help employees balance their work, personal, and family responsibilities. These laws recognize that employees sometimes need to be away for short periods during a workday—for example, to attend a parent-teacher conference or to take an elderly parent to a doctor's appointment.

Details of these laws vary from state to state, though school-related matters are most often recognized as a valid reason to take some hours of leave time. The California law, for example, applies if you employ 25 or more people at one location. If so, you can't fire or discriminate against an employee for taking up to eight hours of leave a month (maximum of 40 hours a year) to participate in activities at a child's or grandchild's school or day care facility. The employee must give you reasonable notice and can use existing vacation, personal leave, or comp time for this purpose. In some cases, unpaid leave may be available.

You can find information about your state's law in "State Family and Medical Leave Laws," in the appendix; contact your state labor department to find out more about your obligations. If your business is covered by both the FMLA and state law, you'll need to comply with both. Typically, there's not much overlap between the FMLA and the state small necessities law, so the time off allowed for small necessities will be in addition to time off under the FMLA.

Fitness to Work

If an employee has taken leave because of a serious health condition, the FMLA lets you require a medical certification that the employee is able to resume work. You can only impose this requirement if it's part of a policy you uniformly apply to all employees returning from medical leave.

There may be a state law, local ordinance, or union contract that governs the terms under which employees who have taken medical leave can return to work. The FMLA doesn't supersede these other legal controls. You must also comply with the Americans with Disabilities Act (ADA) rule that any physical exam required of an employee returning to work must be job related. (For more on the ADA, see Chapter 9 and "Related Laws," below.)

Related Laws

You must comply with other laws that affect an employee's right to take a leave.

State Family and Medical Leave Laws

Some states have laws guaranteeing some form of family or medical leave. (See "State Family and Medical Leave Laws" in the appendix.) The FMLA doesn't cancel out state law provisions that provide greater family or medical leave rights or that apply to smaller employers than the FMLA does. Leaves granted under a state leave law and the FMLA run simultaneously and are not added together if the leave is covered by both laws.

> **EXAMPLE:** State law where Tess works entitles her to 16 weeks of family and medical leave over two years. Tess takes her 16 weeks of state-permitted leave in one year. This also exhausts her 12 weeks of FMLA leave for that year. In other words, she can't take 16 weeks plus 12 weeks.

Under most state laws, the leave is unpaid. In a few states, however, employees are entitled to receive payments from a state fund while on certain types of leave. Contact your labor department for more information.

Americans with Disabilities Act

An employee with a disability has rights under the ADA as well as the FMLA. (See Chapter 9 for a comprehensive discussion of the ADA.) It requires special attention to coordinate your responsibilities under these two laws.

The FMLA entitles an employee to 12 weeks of leave for a serious health condition, with health benefits maintained during this period. At the end of the FMLA leave, you must reinstate the employee to the same or an equivalent position.

If the employee can't perform the equivalent job because of a disability and the employee has exhausted FMLA leave, the ADA may permit or require you to place the employee in a part-time job, with only the benefits provided to part-time employees. In some cases, you may have to let an employee take unpaid leave beyond the 12 weeks allowed by the FMLA. Under the ADA, such additional leave may be required as a reasonable accommodation to a disabled employee if the additional leave wouldn't impose an undue hardship on your business.

Here are two other variations:

- The ADA may require you to offer an employee a job with a reasonable accommodation, such as the option to work remotely. If the FMLA entitles an employee to unpaid leave, you can't avoid granting the leave by requiring the employee to take an accommodation instead.
- If you require certification that an employee is fit to return to work as permitted by the FMLA under a uniform policy imposed by your business, you must also comply with the ADA requirement that the certification be related to the job.

Paid Sick Leave Laws

More than a dozen states (and the District of Columbia) have passed laws requiring employers to provide employees a minimum amount of paid sick leave. Some local governments have similar laws, applicable to employers doing business within the city or county limits.

Typically, employees who work for covered employers accrue paid sick time at a rate set by the law, which they may use when they are ill. Some of these laws allow employees to use their sick leave right away; others require employees to wait until they have been employed for a set period of time. In some states, employees may use their paid sick leave to care for ill family members, too.

These laws may overlap with the FMLA when an employee who is covered by both laws takes time off for personal illness or to care for a family member who is ill. If the leave is covered by the FMLA and your state sick leave law, you may count it against both leave entitlements—and you must pay your employee for the time off.

EXAMPLE: Jamal has accrued five days of sick leave under his state's paid sick leave law. He takes two days off with a cold. Because a cold doesn't count as a serious health condition under the FMLA, those two days don't reduce his FMLA leave. However, they do count as sick days, for which he uses paid leave. Had Jamal taken two days off while he was nauseated following chemotherapy, that leave would count against both his allotment of FMLA leave (because cancer is a serious health condition) and his paid sick leave.

See "State Family and Medical Leave Laws," in the appendix, for more information about these state laws. You can also find a frequently updated chart of paid sick leave laws at the website of A Better Balance, www. abetterbalance.org.

RESOURCE

Other state and federal laws can also overlap with the FMLA. These include laws prohibiting discrimination, requiring time off in certain situations, or requiring disability or workers' compensation leaves or payments. To learn how these different laws relate to the FMLA, take a look at *The Essential Guide to Family & Medical Leave*, by Lisa Guerin and Deborah C. England (Nolo). You can also check out the Equal Employment Opportunity Commission (EEOC) fact sheet, *The Family and Medical Leave Act, the Americans with Disabilities Act, and Title VII of the Civil Rights Act of 1964*, available online at www.eeoc.gov/policy/docs/fmlaada.html.

Enforcement

An employee who believes his or her rights have been violated may file a complaint against your business with the U.S. Department of Labor or your state labor department, or the employee may file a private lawsuit. If the employee proves your company violated the FMLA, you may have to pay the employee wages, employment benefits, or other compensation, depending on the nature of the violation. You may also have to reimburse the employee for the cost of providing care for a child or an ill family member, up to a sum equal to 12 weeks of wages. And you may be ordered to reinstate or promote the employee, pay penalties and interest, and pay reasonable fees for the employee's lawyer and expert witnesses.

RESOURCE

The U.S. Department of Labor provides online guidance on the legal requirements for family and medical leave. You'll find lots of information and answers to key FMLA questions at www.dol.gov/whd/fmla.

Health and Safety

I f workplace health and safety issues weren't at the forefront of your mind before the COVID-19 crisis, they are now. Employers who have failed to follow government guidelines on COVID-19 have been shamed on social media, seen mass walkouts and protests, and been sued for millions by grieving families. Fortunately, there are a number of relatively low-cost steps you can take to limit the spread of the disease at work (see "COVID-19 Prevention," below).

As an employer, there are many good reasons—in addition to your humane instincts—to keep your workplace free from COVID-19 and other health and safety hazards.

Obviously, healthy workers will be happier and more productive. There will be fewer disruptions to work schedules due to absenteeism. And, health insurance costs may be reduced. Then there are the legal reasons: Federal and state laws and an increasing number of local ordinances require you to take steps to make the workplace safe and healthy.

Workers today are well informed about the link between workplace conditions and health problems. Most know, for example, that secondhand smoke can cause or aggravate respiratory and heart problems and that repetitive motions can lead to carpal tunnel syndrome. And an increasing number of workers will not hesitate to press legal claims against employers who fail to rectify unsafe or unhealthy conditions, especially involving COVID-19.

In addition to health and safety statutes, state law requires your business to provide workers' compensation coverage to pay for medical bills and partial wage loss when an employee is injured in the workplace. By reducing on-the-job injuries and eliminating the workplace causes of disease, you can lower the cost of workers' compensation coverage.

TIP

Get employees involved. In meeting your legal responsibilities for keeping the workplace safe and healthy, don't overlook an obvious resource: your employees. Involve them in identifying safety and health problems and suggesting ways to solve such problems. Organizing a safety committee made up of equal numbers of rank-and-file employees and managers is a good starting point. Consider holding company safety seminars at which you encourage employee suggestions. If employees can voice their safety concerns to you and to other employees who are able to initiate changes, there's less chance that they'll jump the gun and go straight to government authorities to report a complaint. Having such a safety committee can also earn you a break on workers' compensation insurance premiums.

The Occupational Safety and Health Act

In 1970, Congress passed the Occupational Safety and Health Act (the OSH Act), a comprehensive law designed to reduce workplace hazards and improve health and safety programs for workers. (29 U.S.C. §§ 651 to 678.) It broadly requires employers to provide a workplace free of physical dangers and to meet specific health and safety standards. Employers must also provide safety training to employees, inform them about hazardous chemicals, notify government administrators about serious workplace accidents, and keep detailed safety records.

Although there can be heavy penalties for not complying with the OSH Act, such penalties are usually reserved for extreme cases in which workplace conditions are highly dangerous and the employer has ignored warnings about them. If your workplace is inspected—an unlikely event for a typical small business, unless there is an accident—the government will work with you to eliminate hazards.

CAUTION

Don't forget state law! In addition to federal law, you must comply with state law. To learn more about state health and safety laws, see "State OSHA Laws," below.

Covered Employers

Virtually all businesses must comply with the OSH Act, with a few exceptions. The OSH Act won't apply to your workplace if any of the following are true:
- You're self-employed and have no employees.
- Your business is a farm that employs only your immediate family members.
- You're in a business such as mining, which is already regulated by other federal safety laws.

Restroom Access as a Health and Safety Issue

Since 1975, OSHA has had a sanitation standard, which requires workplaces to have a minimum number of toilet facilities, among other things. OSHA has interpreted this standard to also require employers to give employees prompt access to restrooms, without unreasonable restrictions. Preventing employees from using the restroom can lead to serious health concerns, including urinary tract infections and bowel and bladder problems.

Recently, OSHA tackled a more modern bathroom issue: providing safe and appropriate bathroom facilities for transgender employees. OSHA's guidance, "A Guide to Restroom Access for Transgender Workers," offers best practices for ensuring that transgender employees have equal access to restrooms. The guidance advises employers to allow employees to use the restroom that corresponds with their gender identity, which may be different from the gender they were assigned at birth. Transgender employees may then choose the option that feels safest and most appropriate to them. The guidance suggests also that employers provide additional options, such as gender-neutral bathrooms that are either single-occupancy or provide privacy stalls for employees using the facilities. You can find the guidance on OSHA's website at www.osha.gov/Publications/OSHA3795.pdf.

Safety Standards

The OSH Act sets a general standard for all covered businesses. As an employer, you must provide a place of employment that's free from recognized hazards that are causing or are likely to cause death or serious physical harm to employees. Recognized hazards are not clearly defined, which can make it difficult for you to know how to comply with the law. The broad language covers an almost impossibly large range of potential harm, from sharp objects that might cause cuts to radiation exposure.

But there's more. In the OSH Act, Congress created the Occupational Safety and Health Administration—called OSHA—as a unit of the U.S. Department of Labor. Congress authorized this agency to set additional workplace standards, which it has done in great profusion. The specific standards cover a wide range of workplace concerns, including:

- exposure to hazardous chemicals

- first aid and medical treatment
- noise levels
- protective gear, such as goggles, respirators, gloves, work shoes, and ear protectors
- fire protection
- worker training, and
- workplace temperatures and ventilation.

Posting, Reporting, and Record Keeping

You must post a notice called "Job Safety and Health: It's the Law," which is available from the nearest OSHA office. If your business is located in a state that has its own approved OSHA program, you may have to post a state form instead of the national version. Check with your state OSHA office to find out. (See "State OSHA Laws," below, for contact details.)

You must notify OSHA within eight hours after learning that an employee has died from a job-related accident, and within 24 hours after learning that an employee has experienced an eye loss, amputation, or hospitalization because of a workplace accident. Contact the nearest OSHA office to report the location and time of the incident, the number of fatalities or hospitalized employees, the name and phone number of a contact person, and a brief description of the incident. Expect a follow-up investigation.

Unless your business is exempt from OSHA record-keeping requirements (see "Exemption From Record Keeping," below), you must maintain several types of records including:

- **Injury and illness log.** You must keep a log (OSHA Form 300) of all workplace injuries and illnesses, except minor injuries requiring only first aid. This includes COVID-19 deaths and infections that meet certain criteria. (For more information, see www.OSHA.gov/recordkeeping.) Each year, you're required to post the previous year's log by February 1st and display it through the end of April.
- **Medical records.** You must keep up-to-date medical records and records of employee exposure to hazardous substances or harmful physical agents.
- **Training records.** You must keep records of your safety training sessions and make them available for review by employees.
- **Retention.** You must maintain required records for specified periods of time, sometimes as long as 30 years.

RESOURCE

For more information on the OSH Act's provisions, requirements, and enforcement procedures, see *The Essential Guide to Federal Employment Laws,* by Lisa Guerin and Sachi Barreiro (Nolo).

Exemption From Record Keeping

The OSHA requirements for record keeping apply only to businesses with ten or more employees, although state OSHA regulations may impose record-keeping requirements on smaller businesses. In addition, certain low-hazard businesses are exempt from record keeping, including:

- retail trade (except for businesses selling general merchandise, building materials, and garden supplies)
- real estate, insurance, and financial businesses
- service businesses (except for hotels and other lodging places, repair facilities, amusement and recreation facilities, and health services)
- dental offices
- accounting offices, and
- software publishers.

Training

OSHA considers safety training part of your general duty to provide a safe workplace, but individual OSHA rules also impose more specific training requirements, depending on what your business does and what hazards might be present in your workplace. These rules are too extensive to summarize here, but following some commonsense guidelines will help you get started. For example, make sure that all employees know about ways to limit the spread of COVID-19 in the workplace. Also provide training on the materials and equipment with which they'll be working, the known hazards in your business, and how you're controlling those hazards. Pay special attention to the use of chemicals, making sure to train employees in:

- methods of detecting the release of a hazardous chemical in the work area, such as monitoring devices or recognizing the appearance or odor of released chemicals
- physical and health hazards of the chemicals
- measures employees can take to protect themselves from the hazards, including safe work practices, emergency procedures, and protective equipment, and
- details of your labeling system and worksite locations where employees can find chemical safety data. (See "Hazardous Chemicals," below, for more information.)

Don't let employees start a job until they have received instructions in how to do it safely. The exact training you offer will, of course, vary according to the nature of the business. It may be helpful to call in an OSHA consultant to recommend specific training for your workplace.

Don't overlook the need to train existing employees who are moving into new jobs or are starting to use new equipment. And all employees need refresher instruction from time to time, since it's human nature to become complacent and forget the safety rules.

You must maintain records of your safety training efforts and be prepared to show these records to OSHA inspectors.

Inspections

OSHA inspectors can inspect your workplace at any time without advance notice or authorization by a court. Based on what they find there, they can issue citations and impose penalties. However, inspectors are unlikely to make random inspections unless you're in a particularly hazardous business, such as construction. There aren't enough inspectors to go around; OSHA must use its resources prudently.

If you have a workplace with ten or fewer employees and you're in an industry that has a low injury rate, you're exempt from random inspections by federal OSHA officials. State safety and health laws, however, may empower local inspectors to randomly inspect smaller businesses. But if yours is a small insurance agency, retail store, computer repair shop, or similar low-injury business, your chances of receiving a random inspection are remote.

Most small businesses are inspected only if one of the following occurs:
- An employee has complained to OSHA.
- A worker has died from a job-related injury.
- An employee has been hospitalized because of a workplace condition.

As explained above, you're required to report such fatalities and hospitalizations to OSHA.

Even though you may be at low risk of inspection, you're not free to ignore safety and health concerns. You're legally required to take the initiative in identifying and eliminating safety and health problems that can affect employees.

Special Rules for Home Workers

If you allow an employee to do office work at home, OSHA won't inspect the home office and won't hold you liable for conditions there. Office work at a home-based worksite typically consists of such tasks as filing, keyboarding, computer research, reading, and writing. The employee will probably be using office equipment such as a telephone, fax machine, scanner, or copier.

The rules are different for other types of work an employee performs at home. OSHA has found that some types of work in a home setting can be hazardous, such as assembly of electronics, casting lead head jigs for fishing lures, use of unguarded crimping machines, and handling adhesives without protective gloves. If OSHA gets a complaint about non-office work at an employee's home involving a danger to health or safety, OSHA may inspect the home worksite. As an employer, you can be responsible for at-home hazards caused by materials, equipment, or processes that you provide or require the employee to use.

A typical inspection follows a set pattern.

The opening conference. The inspector meets with you and a representative selected by your employees. All of you discuss procedures for the inspection.

The inspector reviews your records on health and safety problems as well as any steps you've taken to monitor workplace conditions such as noise, ventilation, and hazardous chemicals.

The walkaround. The inspector observes the working conditions, looking for signs of health and safety hazards. Are all required signs and notices posted? Are there strong odors in the air? Eye irritants? Dust or fumes? How about noise and temperature levels? Are there signs of spilled or leaking chemicals? These and other problems are noted. The inspector may make measurements of noise levels and take samples of dust and air to be analyzed.

Review of safety and health programs. The inspector checks to make sure that you have qualified people and the right equipment to monitor levels of hazardous materials. The inspector also looks at whether your employees are taking part in training programs on workplace hazards and emergency procedures.

The closing conference. The inspector discusses the safety hazards that have been found and ways to correct the problems. You're given a specific deadline by which you must make the corrections. The inspector documents all violations of OSHA standards and, if a violation is more than a minor one, issues a citation. If you receive an OSHA citation, you must post it near where the violations occurred. This allows employees to get involved in any further enforcement actions by OSHA.

CAUTION

Inspectors can obtain search warrants. OSHA officials can't inspect your place without your consent. If you refuse an inspector entry, the inspector must obtain a search warrant from a judge before coming into your workplace. But, by insisting on a search warrant, you practically ensure that the inspector will go through your place with a fine-tooth comb. Cooperation rather than resistance is usually the wiser course of action. However, if you're nervous about what an inspection may disclose, ask the inspector for an extension of time and seek advice immediately from a lawyer.

Penalties for Violations

Penalties ordered by OSHA depend on the seriousness of the violation. For willful or repeated violations, your company may have to pay thousands of dollars in penalties—the maximum penalty in 2021 is $136,532. And, if a worker has died because you violated OSHA standards, you could even be sent to prison. For less serious violations—problems that are unlikely to cause serious harm or death—the penalty in 2021 may be up to $13,653. OSHA adjusts the maximum penalty amounts each year for inflation.

In assessing penalties, OSHA looks at several factors, including:
- the seriousness of the hazard
- your history of violations
- whether you've made a good faith effort to comply with OSHA standards, and
- the size of your business.

You can challenge an OSHA citation through an appeal process. If the citation is issued by the federal OSHA, you have 15 days to file a notice of contest with the agency. If a state OSHA issues citations in your state, check with that agency to confirm the filing deadline. It makes sense to consult a lawyer before embarking on an appeal.

After you file the notice of contest, an administrative law judge will conduct a hearing, giving you and others concerned a chance to present evidence. If you disagree with the decision of the administrative law judge, there's an additional appeal process within OSHA. Ultimately, you can appeal to a court if you can't reach an acceptable resolution within OSHA. Fortunately, most OSHA disputes are resolved through voluntary settlements.

Workers' Rights

Although workers have many rights under the OSH Act, we discuss only the two most basic ones in this chapter.

First, workers have a right to complain to OSHA about safety or health conditions without being penalized for doing so. Retaliating against employees who have made such complaints is a violation of OSH Act provisions.

Second, in some situations, workers have a right to refuse to work if they think the workplace is unsafe. The legal test is this: Does the worker have a reasonable and good faith belief that there's an immediate risk of serious injury or death? If so, the worker can walk off the job and refuse to work until you've corrected the problem or you've determined, after an investigation, that there's no imminent danger. While you investigate or correct the problem, you can place the worker temporarily in another job at equal pay. It's usually unwise to react by demoting or firing the complaining employee; that can be another violation of the OSH Act if the complaint was made in good faith.

> **EXAMPLE:** Ann works part-time in an office as an administrative assistant. She suffers from chronic kidney disease, which puts her at high risk of developing complications if she catches COVID-19. Despite high levels of COVID-19 in the community, Ann's employer hasn't implemented any of the government-recommended policies, such as mask wearing or social distancing, to limit transmission of the disease. Worried for her health, Ann asks her supervisor, Jane, if she can work from home on a temporary basis. Ann's request is supported by a note from her doctor. Jane refuses, and won't discuss any other workplace accommodations that might be possible for Ann. When Ann decides to stay home from work rather than risk catching COVID-19, Jane fires her. Ann sues for wrongful termination. The court determines that Ann should not have been fired because she reasonably feared an immediate risk of serious illness or death. The company is ordered to compensate Ann for her lost wages and pay punitive damages of more than $80,000.

Getting Help

Your eyes will probably glaze over at the thought of poring over pages of federal regulations on health and safety in the workplace. Fortunately, there are easier ways to learn what you must do to comply with OSHA requirements, and doing your homework will cost you little or nothing.

Safety Code of ABC Inc.

1. All employees of this company must follow these safe practice rules and report all unsafe conditions or practices to a supervisor.

2. Supervisors will require employees to comply with all safety rules.

3. All employees periodically will be given instruction on workplace safety and health.

4. Anyone under the influence of alcohol or drugs will not be allowed on the job while in that condition.

5. No one will be permitted or required to work while his or her ability or alertness is impaired by fatigue or illness.

6. Employees must make sure that all guards and other protective devices are in place and must wear protective equipment and clothing in specified work areas.

7. Horseplay, scuffling, and other acts that may endanger employees are prohibited.

8. Work should be planned to prevent injuries when working with equipment and handling heavy materials. Back injuries are the most frequent and often the most persistent and painful type of workplace injury.

9. Workers must not handle or tamper with electrical equipment, machinery, or air or water lines unless they have received instructions from their supervisors.

10. Report injuries promptly to a supervisor. A first aid kit is located at _____ _____ and a defibrillator is located at _____ .

    Emergency phone numbers are located at _____ _____ .

Adapted from: OSHA *Small Business Handbook*

Worksite Consultations

Each state has an agency (funded mostly by the federal office of OSHA) that offers free, on-site consultations. For information about the agency in your state, go to www.osha.gov/dcsp/smallbusiness/consult.html.

As in a formal OSHA inspection, you and the consultant will tour the workplace together. The consultant will point out safety and health risks and then, at a closing conference, give you practical advice on how to eliminate hazards. The consultant won't issue citations or propose penalties, however. Nor will the consultant provide information about your workplace to the OSHA inspection staff, except in extreme circumstances.

Although OSHA encourages employees to participate in the consultant's walk-through, you're free to exclude employees from the consultation process unless a union contract gives employee representatives the right to take part.

> CAUTION
> **You might be opening the door to enforcement action.** If the consultant finds a serious safety condition—one from which it's reasonably predictable that death or serious harm could result—the consultant will work with you to control or eliminate the hazard within a time period that you jointly determine. If the consultant isn't satisfied with your progress, the consultant may report you to an OSHA official. According to OSHA, however, consultants rarely find conditions that require them to report a business.

Safety Codes

Written safety codes are a good way to let employees know that you take safety seriously. Because each workplace is different, you'll have to make sure that your safety code is tailored to the specific needs of your business.

OSHA has suggested a safety code that you may find useful as a starting point, but you'll undoubtedly need to make changes to make it fit. See "Safety Code of ABC Inc.," above, for an example of how we modified OSHA's code. You can find OSHA's version in the agency's *Small Business Handbook*. (See "Additional Help From OSHA," below.)

> **TIP**
>
> **Defibrillators save lives.** In your written safety code, inform employees of the location of the nearest automatic external defibrillator (AED). These life-saving devices are used to treat individuals who have experienced sudden cardiac arrest, and members of the public can operate them without special training. Many malls, schools, movie theaters, and fitness clubs carry AEDs. If you don't have a defibrillator nearby, consider purchasing one if your company can afford it—they typically cost around $1,000. Asking local business owners for contributions can help defray the cost.

State OSHA Laws

If a state has a health and safety law that meets or exceeds federal OSHA standards, the state can take over enforcement of the standards from federal administrators. This means that all inspections and enforcement actions will be handled by your state OSHA rather than its federal counterpart.

So far, these states have been approved for such enforcement regarding private employers: Alaska, Arizona, California, Hawaii, Indiana, Iowa, Kentucky, Maryland, Michigan, Minnesota, Nevada, New Mexico, North Carolina, Oregon, South Carolina, Tennessee, Utah, Vermont, Virginia, Washington, and Wyoming. Connecticut, Illinois, Maine, New Jersey, and New York also have OSHA-type laws, but they only apply to government employees. You can find an up-to-date list and additional information, at www.osha.gov/dcsp/osp/index.html.

If your business is located in a state that has an OSHA law, contact your state agency for a copy of the safety and health standards that are relevant to your business. State standards may be more strict than federal standards, and the requirements for posting notices may be different.

Hazardous Chemicals

The federal OSHA rules include a section called the Hazard Communication Standard. (29 CFR § 1910.1200.) Many people call this the right-to-know law. Basically, the standard requires you to give information to your employees about the hazardous chemicals they handle.

Many states also have right-to-know laws. If your state has no laws or regulations governing private employers, you must still comply with the federal standards.

These informational requirements vary somewhat from state to state. If your business handles any chemicals, be sure to get a copy of your state's rules. Because most of the state laws are similar to the federal right-to-know rules, this discussion will focus on the federal law. If your state has standards that are more stringent than the federal ones, there are still some unresolved questions about whether you need only comply with the federal standards. Until this legal issue is clearly resolved, it's wisest to follow the stricter standards.

Additional Help From OSHA

For additional help with OSHA rules and regulations, see the *OSHA Small Business Handbook*—OSHA Publication 2209-02R—available at www.osha.gov. It contains self-inspection checklists covering such topics as fire protection, personal protective equipment and clothing, walkways, floor and wall openings, stairs and stairways, elevated surfaces, exit doors, hand tools, and equipment. These checklists can help you and your employees identify potential problems.

You can also find lots of helpful materials on OSHA's website at www.osha.gov. If you want to order the full text of the OSHA regulations, these materials are available from the U.S. Government Printing Office at a small cost or can be found in the Code of Federal Regulations at most law libraries. There are four separate sets of standards:

- General Industry—29 CFR § 1910
- Construction—29 CFR § 1926
- Maritime Employment—29 CFR §§ 1915–1919, and
- Agriculture—29 CFR § 1928.

To understand the right-to-know laws—state or federal—you must first become familiar with the Material Safety Data Sheets (MSDSs) supplied by manufacturers of all hazardous chemicals. They contain a wealth of information, including:

- the physical hazards of the chemical, such as flammability and explosiveness
- health hazards (the symptoms of exposure and the medical conditions that can be made worse by exposure)
- how the chemical enters the body and the limits of safe exposure
- whether the chemical is known to cause cancer
- how to safely handle the chemical
- recommended protection methods, including protective clothing and equipment, and
- first aid and emergency procedures should a chemical be mishandled.

Obviously, if an employee is working with hazardous chemicals, this is essential information. That's why the law requires you to keep the MSDS for each hazardous chemical and make it accessible to employees. You must also keep a list of all the hazardous chemicals used in your business and label all containers. And, you're required to train employees in the safe use of hazardous chemicals.

> **EXAMPLE:** Ace Water Treatment Corporation sells water treatment systems to rural homeowners whose water comes from underground wells. Ace issues demonstration kits to its sales staff so they can demonstrate to potential customers the extent of impurities in the homeowner's water supply. In one test, the salesperson adds a few drops of potassium hydroxide to a sample of the customer's water so that certain impurities will collect at the bottom of the test tube. Potassium hydroxide is a hazardous chemical sometimes known as lye.
>
> The chemical comes from the manufacturer with an MSDS explaining its dangers and how it should be handled (for example, goggles should be used to protect the user's eyes). To comply with the right-to-know law, Ace keeps the MSDS and makes it available to employees. Ace makes sure that all containers are properly labeled and that all employees are thoroughly trained in how to use and handle the chemical. To further protect its employees, Ace issues protective goggles to those who perform water tests using the chemical.

Workers' Compensation

The workers' compensation system provides replacement income and medical expenses to employees who suffer work-related injuries or illnesses. Benefits may also extend to the survivors of workers who are killed on the job.

Workers' compensation is a no-fault system. An injured or ill employee is entitled to receive benefits whether or not the employer provided a safe workplace and whether or not the worker's own carelessness contributed to the injury or illness. But the employer, too, receives some protection, because the employee is limited to certain types of compensation (partial wage replacement and payment of medical bills). The employee can't get paid for pain and suffering or mental anguish. Except in cases where the employer didn't carry workers' comp insurance or the employer's intentional conduct is responsible for the injury, the employee cannot file a private lawsuit. (See "You're Still Liable for Intentional Injuries," below.)

Workers' Compensation for COVID-19?

Are your employees entitled to workers' compensation benefits if they catch COVID-19 at work? The answer is probably not, with some exceptions. Many states have allowed workers in the health care industry and first responders dealing with COVID-19 patients to qualify for workers' comp. But in general, workers who suspect they have contracted COVID-19 at work won't be eligible for workers' compensation. One reason is that workers' compensation only covers injuries and illnesses that occur in the workplace or in connection with work. Given the prevalence of the disease in the community, most workers can't pinpoint where they contracted the disease—whether it occurred at work, at the grocery store, or at home. In a few states, workers might qualify for benefits if they can present strong medical evidence of workplace exposure, or if their employer failed to follow government guidelines of workplace health and safety. But as this book goes to press, most states are disallowing these sorts of claims.

To learn your state's rules on workers' compensation and COVID-19, see your state's labor department website.

To cover the cost of workers' compensation benefits for employees, you'll usually need to pay for insurance, through either a state compensation fund or a private insurance company. While self-insurance is a possibility in some states, the technical requirements usually make this an impractical alternative for a small business.

Coverage Requirements

Although each state has its own workers' compensation statutes, in all states but Texas, if you have employees, you probably need to obtain workers' compensation coverage. (A few states require coverage only if you have more than a handful of employees.) Your state workers' compensation bureau can tell you about any legal requirements you have to inform employees of their rights (generally, you need to display a poster and hand out notices to new hires). Find your state workers' comp agency at the U.S. Department of Labor website at www.dol.gov/owcp/dfec/regs/compliance/wc.htm.

State laws vary as to whether sole proprietors, partners, LLC members, directors, and executive officers can or must be covered by workers' compensation. In some states, a business can choose whether to cover these individuals. If you're in one of these states and you want this coverage—which will give you the same benefits as other workers who are injured—let the insurance company know when you apply for coverage.

In other states, sole proprietors, partners, LLC members, directors, and executive officers are automatically covered, but you might have the option of excluding this coverage. Ask a representative of the state compensation fund or private insurance carrier how to do this when you apply for coverage.

> ⚠ **CAUTION**
>
> **Rejecting coverage can be a mistake.** Workers' compensation coverage isn't mandatory for all private employers in every state. In some states, you might have the option of declining workers' compensation insurance for your workplace. But if you opt not to, you can be sued by an employee who claims to have been injured on the job by your negligence; if you had workers' comp coverage, these types of lawsuits would be barred. Therefore, most wise employers obtain workers' compensation insurance, no matter where their businesses are located.

Arranging for Coverage

Some states allow an employer to self-insure, which typically requires the business to maintain a hefty cash reserve earmarked for workers' compensation claims. Usually, this isn't practical for small businesses. Most small businesses buy insurance through a state fund or from a private insurance carrier. If private insurance is an option in your state, discuss it with the insurance agent or broker who handles the basic insurance policy for your business. Often, you can save money on premiums by coordinating workers' compensation coverage with property damage and public liability insurance. A good agent or broker may also be able to explain the mechanics of a state fund where that's an available option or is required.

In most states that have a state-run workers' compensation fund, you have a choice of buying coverage from the state or from a private insurer. In a handful of states, however, you must purchase from the state fund. Your broker should be able to explain these options to you.

 TIP

Make sure telecommuters are covered. In most situations, an employee who works at home is entitled to the same workers' compensation benefits as any other employee. Make sure your workers' compensation provider knows about any telecommuters on your payroll.

Controlling Costs

Premiums are based on two factors: industry classification and payroll. If your premium is above a certain amount—$10,000 in many states—your actual experience with workers' compensation claims will affect your premiums. Your rate can go up or down, depending on how your claims compare with other businesses in your industry. The number of claims filed by your employees affects your premium more than the dollar value of the claims. If you have a lot of accidents, it's assumed that you have an unsafe workplace and that the insurance company eventually will have to pay out some large claims.

Here are some steps you can take to try to keep your workers' compensation costs down.

Preventing Accidents

Emphasize safety in the workplace. Provide proper equipment, safety devices, and protective clothing. Train and retrain your employees in safe procedures and how to deal with emergencies. Set up a safety committee made up of both managers and workers. Promote employee health by offering wellness and fitness programs.

Buying Coverage Wisely

Seek out a participating plan in which the insurance company pays dividends to its insured employers. It helps to find a solid company with a long history of paying dividends, but dividends are never guaranteed.

Consider being put on a retrospective rating plan (unfortunately, this isn't usually available to many small businesses). In such plans, the insurance company agrees to adjust your premium at the end of the year based on your actual claims experience. If you have a strong safety program, this program can be better for you than a dividend-type program, which generally looks at the insurance company's claims experience, not just the history of your business.

Make sure your business and your employees are properly classified. Don't let the insurance company mistakenly place your business in a class that pays a higher premium because of job hazards. And, since workers are also classified based on the nature of their work, check to see that the insurance company has classified them correctly.

Following Up

Use light-duty or modified work assignments to help workers who have been injured on the job but are allowed back to work on a trial basis.

Monitor claims. If you learn that an employee seems to have recovered but is still accepting workers' compensation benefits, ask for an explanation. If something still seems amiss, notify the insurance company or state fund.

Injuries and Illnesses Covered

As an employer, you needn't dig very deeply into the fine points of workers' compensation law. The state fund or private insurance company that covers your workplace will have its own lawyers resolve legal questions about whether a worker is entitled to compensation for a particular disability and, if so, how much the worker is entitled to receive. When a worker seeks to receive benefits that are questionable, these lawyers will challenge the employee on your behalf.

Still, as a well-informed employer, you may want to learn a bit more about how the system works. While workers' compensation law varies somewhat from state to state, there's enough similarity among the states to justify some general statements.

To be covered by workers' compensation, an employee's injury needn't be caused by a sudden accident such as a fall. Basically, any injury that occurs in connection with work is covered. Many workers, for example, receive compensation for repetitive motion injuries, such as carpal tunnel syndrome, which primarily afflicts the wrists, hands, and forearms. (See "Repetitive Stress Disorder," below, for more about this type of injury.)

In theory, if a worker's injury was intentionally self-inflicted or was caused by substance abuse or by some other nonwork cause (such as a hobby), the injury won't be covered. But, in a disputed case, the worker is still likely to get the benefits by showing that the worker's behavior wasn't the only thing that caused the injury.

Workers may also be compensated for some illnesses and diseases. An illness is likely to be covered by workers' compensation when the nature of the job increases the workers' chances of suffering from that disease. Illnesses that are the gradual result of work conditions—for example, emotional disorders, heart conditions, lung disease, and stress-related digestive problems—increasingly are being covered by workers' compensation.

Finally, there are death benefits. Dependents of workers killed on the job can usually collect workers' compensation benefits.

(!) CAUTION

Don't penalize workers who file claims. In most states, it's a violation of the workers' compensation statute or public policy to discriminate against an employee for filing a workers' compensation claim. This means you can't fire, demote, or take any other negative action against a worker for filing a claim.

You're Still Liable for Intentional Injuries

Although workers' compensation is the employee's exclusive remedy for most work-related injuries or illnesses, there's a major exception: injuries or illnesses caused by the intentional actions of the employer. An employee who can prove that your intentional actions caused an injury or illness can take you to court and seek a full range of damages, including damages for pain and suffering as well as economic losses.

Obviously, if you or a supervisor were to physically assault an employee, that would qualify as an intentional action. But courts sometimes treat other workplace events as intentional, too. Suppose, for example, that, to speed up production, you remove the safety devices from a dangerous machine. An employee is injured using the machine, but you continue to require workers to use the machine in its unsafe condition. You've probably set yourself up for an intentional injury claim, because you can be pretty certain that additional workers will be injured by that machine.

In that situation, injured employees would not be limited to their remedies under your state's workers' compensation law. They would be able to sue you and your business under traditional tort (personal injury) theories. And they could ultimately get more money than they would have under the workers' compensation system.

Benefits Paid

Workers' compensation covers the employee's medical and rehabilitation expenses. It also provides income to the employee to offset a big part of lost wages. Typically, workers receive two-thirds of their average wage, up to a fixed ceiling. But, since these payments are tax free, a worker who receives average wages fares reasonably well.

In most states, workers become eligible for wage-loss replacement benefits as soon as they've lost a few days of work because of an injury covered by workers' compensation. The number of days required to qualify varies by state. Some states allow the payments to be made retroactively to the first day of wage loss if the injury keeps the employee out of work for an extended period.

Workers may receive lump sum benefits if they have a total disability or a permanent partial disability. In some states, there are specific amounts provided for permanent partial disability such as the loss of an eye or a foot.

Independent Contractors

Workers' compensation insurance is required only for employees, not for independent contractors who work for you. (Independent contractors are covered in greater detail in Chapter 12.) Small businesses sometimes buy services from independent contractors to save money on workers' compensation insurance, as well as taxes and other expenses normally associated with employees. That's fine, as long as you correctly label people as independent contractors rather than employees. But if you make a mistake and a person improperly labeled as an independent contractor is injured while doing work for your business, you might have to pay large sums to cover medical bills and lost wages that should have been covered by workers' compensation insurance.

In addition, you can sometimes have a problem with a properly classified independent contractor who hires employees to perform some work for you. If the independent contractor doesn't carry workers' compensation insurance and doesn't have the money to compensate an employee who's injured on the job, the injured worker—in a search for deeper pockets—may sue your business for failing to keep a safe workplace.

TIP
Require proof of insurance. When hiring an independent contractor, ask to see an insurance certificate establishing that the independent contractor's employees are covered by workers' compensation insurance. For good measure, make sure that the independent contractor also has general liability insurance.

How to Implement a Workplace COVID-19 Prevention Program

OSHA recommends that every employer should implement a program designed to limit the spread of COVID-19 in the workplace. Employers should work with their employees at each step to ensure the success of the program. Although the specifics of each program will depend on the type of work performed and the work environment, employers should consider taking the following steps.

1. **Assign a workplace coordinator to handle COVID-19 issues on the employer's behalf.**

2. **Conduct a thorough hazard assessment to identify where and how workers might be exposed to COVID-19 at work.** Be sure to seek input from your workers, as they understand their work conditions better than anyone else.

3. **Identify a combination of measures that will limit the spread of COVID-19 in the workplace.** Examples include improving ventilation, providing masks and other protective equipment, sending home anyone with symptoms, requiring social distancing, performing routine cleaning, installing physical barriers, and more.

4. **Support individuals at higher risk of severe illness.** Consider reasonable modifications for high-risk employees, including older workers and those with preexisting conditions. For example, you might allow them to work from home or move them to a less crowded, better-ventilated part of your workplace.

5. **Encourage open communication with your workers.** Ask your employees to report any COVID-19 symptoms, exposure, and possible workplace hazards without fear of reprisal (see number 12, below).

6. **Educate and train workers on your COVID-19 policies and procedures.** Provide basic facts about COVID-19, including how it is spread and the importance of physical distancing and use of face coverings. Inform them of your COVID-prevention policies and procedures, and track when and how workers have been informed. Make sure workers understand they have a right to a safe work environment and know how to report safety concerns. Emphasize to employees that such reports are encouraged and that they won't experience any form of retaliation for sounding the alarm.

7. **Tell workers who are infected or potentially infected to stay home from work and isolate or quarantine to reduce the risk of COVID-19 transmission.**

How to Implement a Workplace COVID-19 Prevention Program (cont'd)

8. **Minimize the negative impact of quarantine and isolation on workers.** Allow telework when possible. If not possible, allow workers to take paid sick leave. If you don't offer paid sick leave and it's not available under applicable laws, consider offering it on a temporary basis.

9. **Send home workers who show any symptoms.** Workers with COVID-19 symptoms upon arrival—including high temperature, cough, or loss or change to their sense of smell or taste—should be sent home and encouraged to seek medical attention.

10. **Clean and disinfect if people with suspected or confirmed COVID-19 have been in the workplace.** Among other measures, the CDC recommends that you close and perform enhanced cleaning in the areas used by the potentially infected person; open outside doors and windows to increase air circulation; wait at least 24 hours before cleaning; vacuum the space once unoccupied, using a vacuum with a HEPA filter; and provide disposable gloves and other protective equipment to cleaning workers.

11. **Consider implementing a workplace COVID-19 testing program.** This can be arranged through your company's occupational health provider or in consultation with the local or state health department. Inform workers of employer testing requirements, if any, and availability of testing options. Continue to require protective measures such as social distancing and mask wearing even with regular testing, as false negative tests aren't uncommon.

12. **Record and report COVID-19 infections and deaths.** See www.OSHA.gov/recordkeeping for more information on these requirements. Also report outbreaks to health departments as required and support their contact tracing efforts.

13. **Encourage or require employees to get the COVID-19 vaccination.** Give them time off work to do so if required. Provide information and training on the benefits and safety of vaccinations. Require all workers, including those vaccinated, to follow your COVID-prevention policies, as experts believe the vaccine may not entirely prevent transmission of the virus from person to person.

Adapted from OSHA's "Protecting Workers: Guidance on Mitigating and Preventing the Spread of COVID-19 in the Workplace" (www.osha.gov/coronavirus/safework).

COVID-19 Prevention

Under the OSH Act, your business must take precautions to protect employees from COVID-19 infection in the workplace. The exact steps you'll need to take will depend on the nature of the work environment, but might include social distancing policies, regular surface sanitation, plexiglass or other physical barriers, staggered work schedules, and remote work arrangements. The Centers for Disease Control and Prevention (CDC) has issued extensive guidance for employers on how to mitigate the risk of COVID-19 in the workplace. For the most updated information, visit www.cdc.gov/coronavirus/2019-ncov/index.html and select "Workplaces & Businesses."

In addition, OSHA recommends instituting a workplace COVID-19 prevention program to limit the spread of the virus at work (see above).

Tobacco Smoke

A state law or municipal ordinance may limit or prohibit smoking on your business premises. Some laws and ordinances are designed primarily to protect nonsmoking employees from secondhand tobacco smoke. Others seek to protect nonsmoking customers and other visitors as well.

In many states, smoking is prohibited in enclosed workspaces. Some states allow employers to set aside indoor or outdoor areas for smokers, but strict rules apply to make sure that nonsmokers are not affected. These days, some states also regulate electronic cigarettes (e-cigarettes): small, battery-operated devices that allow users to inhale a vapor containing nicotine. Called "vaping" (rather than "smoking"), use of these devices is outlawed along with workplace smoking, in some states and cities. To find out what your state requires and allows, visit www.workplacefairness.org/state-smoking-rights-workplace.

In addition to meeting the requirements of laws and ordinances that limit or prohibit smoking in the workplace, be aware that you may be liable to nonsmoking employees if you don't take appropriate action on their complaints. For example, an employee who develops bronchial asthma from exposure to tobacco smoke may be entitled to workers' compensation benefits. And an employee who has a severe respiratory ailment that's aggravated by tobacco smoke may be entitled under the ADA to a smoke-free workplace.

Although you can prohibit smoking on the job, avoid a policy that prohibits an employee from smoking off the job as well. Such a broad prohibition can invade a worker's privacy and is barred by law in many states.

> **TIP**
>
> **Smokers can use some help.** Recognize that giving up smoking can be difficult. Some experts equate nicotine addiction with a cocaine or heroin habit. To demonstrate your concern, you might offer to pay the cost of an employee's tuition in a stop-smoking program if the smoker successfully kicks the habit.

Drug and Alcohol Abuse

There is no law that prevents you from combating the use of illegal drugs and alcohol in the workplace. There are, however, some limits on your ability to test employees for drug usage.

Legally, you're free to:

- prohibit the use of illegal drugs and alcohol in the workplace
- require that employees not come to work or return from meals or breaks under the influence of alcohol or drugs, and
- require that employees who use alcohol or illegally use drugs meet the same performance standards you impose on other employees.

You needn't tolerate absenteeism, tardiness, poor job performance, or accidents caused by alcohol or illegal drug use.

Most states deny unemployment benefits to workers who are fired for misconduct involving drugs or alcohol. Similarly, most states bar workers' compensation benefits for workers injured in an on-the-job accident caused by a worker's use of drugs or alcohol.

> **TIP**
>
> **Helping those in need.** One enlightened approach—especially if an employee with a drug or alcohol problem has valuable skills—is to offer an assistance program to help the employee deal with the problem. Or you might consider a modified work schedule to permit the person to attend a self-help program.

> ⓘ **CAUTION**
>
> **You can combat only illegal drug use.** Please note that this discussion pertains to your right to address illegal drug use in your workplace. Illegal drug use encompasses both the use of illegal drugs and the improper use of legal, prescription drugs. If an employee is using a prescription drug legally, you are faced with a different set of rules from the ones discussed here. The employee's legal drug use may fall under the protection of the federal Americans with Disabilities Act or the state law equivalent. See Chapter 9 for more information.

Illegal Drug Use

There's nothing wrong with firing an employee or rejecting an applicant who uses, possesses, or distributes drugs illegally. This includes the use of illegal drugs and the illegal use of prescription drugs that are deemed controlled substances under federal drug laws.

> **EXAMPLE:** Starbright Corporation fires Lucy after determining that she takes amphetamines without a doctor's prescription. Amphetamines can be legally prescribed but are classified as controlled substances because of their potential for abuse. If a doctor didn't prescribe amphetamines for Lucy, Starbright would be justified in firing her for illegal use of drugs.

The most reliable way to establish that an employee is using drugs illegally is through a drug test. If you choose to test, however, you must observe legal guidelines.

Federal Laws

There are a few situations in which a private employer is required to test employees for drug use. The U.S. Department of Transportation, for example, requires drug testing of airline pilots and other transportation employees who hold jobs in which drug abuse can affect public safety. And the U.S. Department of Defense requires similar testing by companies that contract with it.

The Drug-Free Workplace Act of 1988 (41 U.S.C. § 701) requires all contractors with the federal government to certify that they will provide a drug-free workplace. To comply, you must do all of the following:

- Inform workers that illegal drug use is prohibited in the workplace.
- Create and maintain a drug awareness program.
- Require employees to notify you of any conviction for drug usage in the workplace, of which you must notify the government.
- Impose remedial measures on employees convicted for using drugs in the workplace.

However, the Drug-Free Workplace Act doesn't require you to test employees.

Discretionary Testing

Preemployment testing is the safest type of testing from a legal standpoint. (Drug testing of job applicants is covered in Chapter 1.) After an employee is hired, testing is more tightly controlled by federal and state laws, as well as court decisions. Because these laws are rapidly changing, be sure to double-check your state law at a nearby library or on the Internet, or through a legal consultation.

If you do decide to test, your primary motive should be to ensure the safety of workers, customers, and members of the general public. You're most likely to withstand a legal challenge if you limit testing of employees to the following three situations:

Safety and security. You can likely require periodic testing of employees whose jobs carry a high risk of injury to people and property, such as heavy equipment operators and workers who handle explosives. Similarly, periodic testing is generally permitted for security workers, including those who transport large sums of cash or guards who carry guns. And you can periodically test employees who routinely work with vulnerable people, such as children, the developmentally disabled, or the elderly.

Accidents. You can likely require testing of an employee who's been involved in an accident, such as a food server who's dumped a carafe of scalding coffee on a customer or a maintenance worker who's drilled through a water pipe. However, in some states, you may conduct post-accident testing only if there is serious injury to person or property, or if there is reasonable suspicion to believe that alcohol or drugs were involved in the accident.

Retesting. You can likely require periodic retesting of an employee who is currently in or has completed a drug rehabilitation program or an employee whom you've given a second chance (for example, one who tested positive for drugs after a personal injury accident but was kept on the job anyway).

Even though you may have a right in these situations to require a drug test as a condition of continued employment, you can't force employees to submit to a test against their will. In most cases, however, you can fire an employee who refuses to be tested. Also, you must follow any state-mandated procedures or requirements for testing.

Avoid a policy of testing all employees. Not all of them will be in a position to cause harm through drug usage. Similarly, avoid a program of random drug testing. If you test all employees, test them randomly, or test without a good reason, you may get sued for invasion of privacy or infliction of emotional harm.

To keep your drug testing program on a solid legal footing, follow all of these guidelines:

- Provide written notice to employees and obtain written consent.
- Use a test lab that's certified by the U.S. Department of Health and Human Services or accredited by the College of American Pathologists.
- Keep the results of drug tests confidential.
- Be consistent in dealing with those who test positive.
- Review your plans with a lawyer—before you implement the program and before you test anyone.

CAUTION

Documentation is essential. Because drug testing is always subject to a legal challenge, it's important to keep good records documenting why and how tests are administered. Request a receipt from employees acknowledging that they have been given a copy of your drug and alcohol policy, or include the policy in your employee handbook and get a receipt for the handbook. Don't give a drug test without having the employee sign a consent form. Keep a record of what tests were performed, what drugs were found, and in what amounts. Finally, document the chain of custody of the tested sample (that is, who had possession of it) so you can show that it wasn't tampered with.

Alcoholism

The law treats alcoholism differently from drug abuse. A person disabled by alcoholism is entitled to the same protection from job discrimination as any other person with a disability.

On the other hand, you're not required to overlook the effects that this disability can have on job performance. Under the Americans with Disabilities Act (ADA), you can discipline, discharge, or deny employment to an alcoholic if the person's job performance or conduct is so badly affected by alcohol usage that the worker isn't qualified to do the job.

> **EXAMPLE:** Don, an alcoholic, is often late for work and sometimes is unable to perform his job. His employer disciplines him because of his tardiness and poor performance. The company holds Don to the same standards as its other employees and disciplines him accordingly. This doesn't violate the ADA.

Neither the ADA nor its regulations define "alcoholic" or "alcoholism." The lack of definitions may have little practical effect, however, because the ADA allows you to judge the employees by their ability to do the job. (For more on the ADA, see Chapter 9.)

Repetitive Stress Disorder

The number of workers suffering from repetitive stress disorder (RSD) is rapidly growing, due in large part to the increased use of computers and mobile devices in workplaces. A familiar form of RSD is carpal tunnel syndrome, which causes swelling inside the tunnel created by bone and ligament in the wrist. This swelling can put pressure on nerves passing through the tunnel, leading, in turn, to pain, tingling, and numbness. Other types of RSD include:
- tendinitis—tears in tissue connecting bones to muscles
- myofascial damage—tenderness and swelling from overworking muscles
- tenosynovitis—irritation of the boundary between the tendon and surrounding sheath, and
- cervical radiculopathy—compression of disks in the neck.

The last disorder often develops in workers who hold a phone on their shoulders while using computers. All of these disorders are painful and can be disabling.

It isn't clear what role OSHA will eventually play in establishing and enforcing ergonomic standards to help stem the rising tide of RSD cases. Currently, OSHA provides voluntary guidelines for specific industries such as grocery stores, nursing homes, and poultry processing plants. In addition, the agency occasionally issues ergonomics-related citations. These citations are issued under general provisions of the OSHA law requiring employers to maintain safe workplaces.

But even though addressing ergonomic issues is largely voluntary, as an enlightened employer you may want to take steps to protect employees from carpal tunnel syndrome and other repetitive stress disorders. You may, for example, change the equipment employees use, train them in improving work techniques, and modify the layout of work stations. Larger employers might consider hiring an ergonomics consultant to help them figure out what changes to make.

Illegal Discrimination

To give workers a fair opportunity to get and keep jobs, Congress and state legislatures have passed laws prohibiting discrimination in the workplace. The main federal law prohibiting workplace discrimination is Title VII of the federal Civil Rights Act of 1964. It outlaws discrimination based on race, color, religion, gender, transgender status, sexual orientation, and national origin. Harassment in the workplace is also prohibited as a type of illegal discrimination. Depending on the state you are in, it might also be illegal to discriminate against workers based on other factors, such as being single, married, or divorced; obesity; marital status; or military service.

Federal laws also bar several other kinds of workplace discrimination:

- **Age.** The Age Discrimination in Employment Act prohibits discrimination against older workers. The Older Workers Benefit Protection Act outlaws discrimination in employee benefit programs based on an employee's age. The protections of both laws apply only to workers who are at least 40 years old. Your state's anti-age-discrimination law might protect people of other ages from discrimination. For example, Minnesota protects people who are 18 years of age or older from age discrimination. To find out about your state's law, see "State Laws Prohibiting Discrimination in Employment" in the appendix.

- **Pregnancy.** The Pregnancy Discrimination Act makes it illegal to discriminate against a woman in any aspect of employment because of pregnancy, childbirth, or related medical conditions.

- **Citizenship.** The Immigration Reform and Control Act prohibits discrimination based on a person's citizenship status.

- **Genetic information.** Federal law prohibits discrimination based on a person's genetic information, such as a genetic predisposition to a certain disease.

- **Pay.** The Equal Pay Act outlaws discrimination in wages on the basis of gender. (See Chapter 3.)

- **Disability.** The Americans with Disabilities Act makes it illegal to discriminate against people because of a disability. (See Chapter 9.)

- **Union membership.** The National Labor Relations Act prohibits discriminating against workers because they do or do not belong to a labor union. (See Chapter 13.)

Workplace Discrimination and the COVID-19 Vaccine

Can you fire, discipline, or take other adverse action against an employee who refuses to get the COVID-19 vaccination? That's the question many employers are asking themselves as they try to create safe and healthy workplaces in the age of COVID-19.

The Equal Employment Opportunity Commission (EEOC), the federal agency that enforces workplace discrimination laws, has stated that employers can institute mandatory vaccination policies as long as they allow for religious exemptions under Title VII of the Civil Rights Act and medical exemptions under the Americans with Disabilities Act (ADA).

Title VII requires that employers must reasonably accommodate their workers' sincerely held religious beliefs unless doing so would cause undue hardship. For example, some members of the Church of Christ, Scientist (known as Christian Scientists) refuse vaccinations and other medical interventions on religious grounds. If a member of this faith seeks an exemption from your mandatory vaccination policy, you will likely have to accommodate it (for example, by allowing remote work) unless doing so would impose a more than minimal burden on your business. Note that an individual's personal skepticism about vaccines in general, or the COVID-19 vaccine in particular, usually won't require an exemption.

People with certain medical conditions (including an allergy to a vaccine component, a history of Guillain-Barré syndrome, or pregnancy) might be unable to receive the COVID-19 vaccine safely. When an employee requests a medical exemption, you may request a physician's note from the employee to support their request. However, be careful to apply this policy uniformly to avoid charges of discrimination. Then, you must engage in the interactive ADA-accommodation process discussed in Chapter 9. In short, you must work with the employee to find a solution—for instance, by allowing remote or flexible work to limit exposure to other employees—unless doing so would cause you significant difficulty or expense.

Given some of the thorny issues surrounding compulsory vaccination policies, it's no surprise that many employers are choosing only to recommend the vaccine, not require it. Some employers are offering incentives to their employees to encourage vaccination. If you go down that route, be sure that your employees who can't get vaccinated for medical or religious reasons can still qualify for the incentive. And don't make the incentive so large that your employees feel pressured or coerced into getting the vaccine.

Workplace Discrimination and the COVID-19 Vaccine (continued)
If you ultimately decide that a mandatory vaccination policy is the only way to create a safe workplace, make sure your managers and supervisors know how to handle requests for accommodations. Also keep in mind that state and local laws can impose additional restrictions. Federal and state agencies are frequently updating their COVID-19 guidance for employers. You can find up-to-date information at www.eeoc.gov/coronavirus or at the website of your state's fair employment agency.

RESOURCE

Want help understanding discrimination laws? You can find lots of helpful information by visiting the website of the Equal Employment Opportunity Commission (EEOC), the federal government agency that administers and enforces antidiscrimination laws, at www.eeoc.gov. The website offers numerous fact sheets, answers to frequently asked questions, guidance on how the EEOC interprets and enforces these laws, and much more.

Title VII of the Civil Rights Act

Title VII (42 U.S.C. §§ 2000 and following), enforced by the U.S. Equal Employment Opportunity Commission (EEOC), is a federal law that addresses many types of workplace discrimination.

Businesses Covered

Title VII applies to your business if you employ 15 or more people, either full time or part time. Most state laws impose similar prohibitions against discrimination and many cover employers with fewer employees.

Discrimination Prohibited

Under Title VII, you can't use race, color, religion, gender, gender identity, sexual orientation, or national origin as the basis for decisions on hirings, promotions, dismissals, pay raises, benefits, work assignments, leaves of absence, or any other aspect of the employment relationship. Title VII applies to everything from help wanted ads to working conditions, performance reviews, and postemployment references.

Obviously, a business that flatly refuses to hire female, black, or Hispanic applicants would be ripe for legal action under Title VII or its state equivalents. Of course, few businesses today would attempt such a flagrant violation of the law. But the mere absence of a discriminatory policy isn't enough to avoid enforcement action.

A business violates Title VII if it treats people differently because of the characteristics protected by law (race, religion, and so on). If a company with 50 employees always passes over its African American employees for managerial positions, there's a good chance the company is discriminating, even though the company hasn't explicitly stated a policy of no African Americans in management. Call it corporate culture. Call it coincidence. But if the end result is that African Americans don't get management jobs, it looks like discrimination in the workplace.

If challenged by an employee or the EEOC, the business should be prepared to show that its promotion decisions have been based on objective criteria and that the more qualified applicant has always gotten the promotion. Without a convincing business reason for the failure to promote any qualified African American managers, the company may be found to have violated Title VII.

Title VII also prohibits employer practices that seem neutral but have a disproportionate impact on a protected group. Such a policy is legal only if there's a valid business reason for its existence. For example, refusing to hire people who don't meet a minimum strength requirement is permissible if it's clearly related to the physical demands of the particular job, such as felling and hauling huge trees. But applying such a requirement to exclude applicants for a job as a cook or receptionist wouldn't pass legal muster. The standard seems neutral on its face but would have a disproportionate impact on women.

There is no legitimate business reason to require a cook or receptionist to meet this requirement, so it would violate Title VII if it ruled out disproportionate numbers of applicants of a particular race or gender. (For more about indirect discrimination, see "Avoiding Illegal Discrimination" in Chapter 1.)

Permissible Discrimination

Under Title VII and other antidiscrimination laws, you have a very limited right to hire on the basis of gender, religion, or national origin if a job has special requirements that make such discrimination necessary. Such a special circumstance is called a bona fide occupational qualification (BFOQ).

EXAMPLE: A religious organization employs counselors who answer telephone inquiries from those interested in becoming members of that religion. The organization can require that the counselors it hires believe in that religion. Being a member of that denomination is a BFOQ.

(For more on BFOQs, see "Permitted Discrimination" in Chapter 1.)

EEOC Enforcement of Title VII

If an employee files a complaint with the EEOC, the EEOC may choose to investigate the claim. If this happens, a staff lawyer or investigator may interview the employee. The interviewer will probably then interview you and possibly some other employees.

The EEOC will likely try to work out a settlement of the complaint through conciliation: an informal process that resolves any legal violation for the employee who filed the complaint (and any employees who are in a similar situation). Terms of the agreement will be set out in a written statement. The agreement will require the complaining employee to give up the right to sue your business, in exchange for your agreement to take the steps outlined in the document.

If the agreement requires you to take some action, such as restoring a demoted employee to an earlier job or holding training sessions to make managers more sensitive to subtle discrimination in the workplace, the EEOC will follow up periodically to make sure you're complying.

If you and the employee who filed the complaint can't reach an agreement, the EEOC will likely give the employee a right-to-sue letter, allowing the employee to sue your business in federal or state court for violating Title VII. Because it has limited resources, in many cases, the EEOC issues this letter without conducting an investigation, so you may not go through this conciliation process first. The letter doesn't mean the EEOC believes the employee's allegations are true. In rare cases that it finds especially egregious or groundbreaking, the EEOC may file a lawsuit against your business on behalf of the employee.

If an employee files a complaint with a state fair employment agency for violation of state antidiscrimination laws, the investigation procedure will be much the same. Likewise, the state agency might issue a letter authorizing the employee to sue, without first conducting an investigation or going through the conciliation process. Most states have a worksharing agreement with the EEOC, by which a complaint filed with the state agency is considered also filed at the EEOC and vice versa. This allows the agencies to avoid duplicating efforts and allows the employee to assert rights under both federal and state laws at the same time.

The Lilly Ledbetter Fair Pay Act

After working for Goodyear Tire & Rubber Co. for many years, Lilly Ledbetter learned that she was being paid a lot less than male employees doing the same work. She sued under Title VII of the Civil Rights Act, claiming she had been discriminated against based on her gender. Her case made its way to the U.S. Supreme Court, where she lost. The Court said that Ledbetter hadn't filed her claim in time, because the discriminatory decisions that resulted in lower pay had taken place many years ago. Ledbetter had argued that each paycheck constituted a "continuing violation" of the law and that she didn't have any way of knowing about the discriminatory act at the time, but the Court didn't agree. (*Ledbetter v. Goodyear Tire and Rubber Co.*, 550 U.S. 618 (2007).)

After the court made its ruling, Congress passed legislation allowing employees in Ledbetter's situation to file a lawsuit. If an employee doesn't know about a discriminatory decision but it continues to affect his or her salary or other benefits, the law today permits the employee to proceed with a suit within 180 days of receiving a paycheck that reflects the disparity.

Consider Arbitrating Discrimination Claims

The Civil Rights Act of 1991 encourages employers to resolve job discrimination disputes through settlement negotiations, mediation, and arbitration. In mediation, a neutral expert—the mediator—helps the employer and employee reach a voluntary resolution of the dispute. In arbitration, a neutral expert—the arbitrator—makes a binding decision that can be enforced in court.

Arbitration is often an excellent way to bring a dispute to a swift conclusion. Employers like arbitration because it's quicker and cheaper than judicial proceedings, and arbitration hearings are conducted in private. Perhaps more importantly, arbitration allows employers to avoid placing their fate in the hands of a jury, whose members might be more inclined to side with the "little guy" than an arbitrator, who is often a former judge or lawyer. As a consequence, employees are often asked, when hired, to sign agreements that specify that they will submit any claims against the company to arbitration, rather than raise them in court.

Over the years, employees have asked courts to set aside arbitration agreements and allow them to file lawsuits that contain discrimination claims. Generally, however, courts have said that these agreements are valid and binding. And in 2018, the U.S. Supreme Court upheld arbitration agreements that forbade class actions. In other words, employers could require workers to arbitrate discrimination and wage claims individually rather than collectively. (*Epic Systems Corp. v. Lewis*, 584 U.S. _____ (2018).) But be aware that even a valid arbitration agreement binds only the employee; it won't prevent a governmental agency from suing an employer to enforce an antidiscrimination law. For example, in a 2002 case (*EEOC v. Waffle House Inc.*, 534 U.S. 279), the U.S. Supreme Court said that even though Eric Baker—a Waffle House employee—had signed a valid arbitration agreement and was therefore unable to sue his former employer in court, the EEOC could sue on his behalf for an alleged violation of his rights under the Americans with Disabilities Act.

For help drafting arbitration provisions that are likely to be legally enforceable, visit www.adr.org/clauses.

TIP

Consider settlement. Never pass up the chance to resolve a complaint through conciliation. A key advantage of conciliation is its confidentiality. Neither the EEOC nor the complaining employee is allowed to make public anything that occurs during conciliation, and they can't use information disclosed there as evidence in a later proceeding without your consent. This is not true of a court case, which is public.

SEE AN EXPERT

Because the stakes can be high in a confrontation over alleged job discrimination, you should consult a lawyer. (See Chapter 14 for guidance on finding an attorney.) If you choose to attend the conciliation conference without legal counsel, you should at least ask a lawyer to review any written agreement before signing it. And, because the antidiscrimination laws are somewhat technical, you'll undoubtedly need assistance from a lawyer in defending a lawsuit in which your business has been accused of employment discrimination.

There are a number of remedies that a court can order if it finds workplace discrimination. You may be ordered to:

- rehire, promote, or reassign the employee to whatever job was lost because of the discrimination
- compensate the employee for salary and benefits lost because of the discrimination (including wages, pension contributions, medical benefits, overtime pay, bonuses, vacation pay, and participation in your profit sharing plan)
- pay damages to compensate the employee for emotional suffering, inconvenience, and mental anguish, and punitive damages to punish your business if you've acted maliciously or recklessly
- change your policies so that similar discrimination won't take place in the future, or
- pay the employee's legal fees and court costs.

> CAUTION
>
> **An employee may have additional recourse.** If the EEOC doesn't issue a right-to-sue letter or file a lawsuit on the employee's behalf, the employee may take other legal action against your business, such as suing in state court for breach of contract or wrongful discharge. The employee may also be able to sue you for violating state antidiscrimination laws.

Retaliation

It's illegal for you to retaliate against an employee for opposing illegal discrimination, for filing a complaint under Title VII, or for cooperating in the investigation of such a complaint. Clearly, you can't retaliate by suspending or firing the employee, but many other responses are also prohibited. You mustn't take any action that would tend to dissuade a reasonable worker from making or supporting a claim of discrimination. For example, if a forklift operator made a discrimination claim, reassigning him or her to duties as a railroad track laborer would be improper because the new duties would be harder and dirtier. This would be true even if the track duties fall within the employee's original job description.

An adverse action is retaliation only if it is done because the employee complained. You are free to take adverse actions against an employee for other reasons, even if that employee has complained about discrimination or some other unlawful workplace situation.

For example:

- If the employee performs poorly on the job, you can give the employee a negative performance evaluation.
- If the employee is habitually late for work, you can discipline the employee for tardiness.
- If the employee brings a gun to work, you can fire the employee.

The problem for employers is that some employees will claim that these adverse actions are retaliation even if they have nothing to do with the employee's complaint.

If you must take an adverse action against an employee who has complained, be prepared to defend that action and to show that you had valid reasons that were unrelated to the complaint. Those reasons should be supported, if possible, by prior warnings to the employee that you have documented and preserved in your files.

EXAMPLE: Nick works for Cool Sweats, a company that sells sportswear online. He files a complaint with the EEOC, complaining that he was passed over for a management position because he is gay. A month later, Cool Sweats suspends Nick without pay for three days for a violation of company rules. Nick asserts that the suspension was in retaliation for filing the Title VII complaint.

Cool Sweats is able to refute this allegation by showing that Nick violated the company rules against charging personal expenses on the company's credit card and using the company van for personal business. These rules are stated in Cool Sweats' employee handbook. Cool Sweats is also able to show that six weeks earlier it warned Nick about similar infractions and that a three-day suspension is consistent with the discipline meted out to other employees for such rule violations.

The U.S. Supreme Court has recently found in favor of employees in most retaliation cases it has considered. There has been one big exception, however. In 2013, the Court held that an employee cannot win a Title VII retaliation case by showing that retaliation was one motivating factor, among others, for the employer's adverse action (for example, firing the employee). Rather, the employee must show that the adverse action would not have happened if not for the retaliatory motive. (*University of Texas Southwestern Medical Center v. Nassar*, 570 U.S. 338.) The Court's endorsement of this more stringent standard has made it harder for employees to win cases based on retaliation.

EXAMPLE: Phil works as an executive assistant for Smith & Stine, a large publishing company. After about a year, Smith & Stine terminates Phil. Smith & Stine tells Phil that it had to make some tough decisions due to downsizing, but that he was one of the more recent hires and wasn't performing as well as they had expected. Phil suspects that he was fired because of a recent complaint that he made to HR about his boss making tasteless jokes and discriminatory remarks about Phil's sexual orientation. To win his retaliation claim, it's not enough for Phil to show that the discrimination complaint played a role in the company's decision to terminate him. Instead, he must show that he would not have been fired if he never made the discrimination complaint. In other words, the company's stated reasons of downsizing and performance issues were not the real reasons for firing him.

Does Résumé Fraud Outweigh Discrimination?

Some employers are fighting back in cases of alleged discrimination by arguing that the employee lied on a job application and shouldn't have been hired in the first place. If an employer wins this argument, the employee's lawsuit may be thrown out or the damages the employee could win may be very limited.

> **EXAMPLE:** Local Transit Inc. hires Lorna to drive a delivery van. In the first few months, Local Transit cites Lorna for infractions for which male drivers were not cited. Then the firm fires Lorna. She sues, claiming sex discrimination. In defending the lawsuit, Local Transit argues that Lorna lied on her job application by claiming she had a perfect driving record, when, in fact, she had two drunk driving convictions. Local Transit claims that had Lorna disclosed the truth about her driving record, the company never would have hired her. Since she isn't entitled to the job, says the company, she can't complain about discrimination. The court rules that Local Transit had a valid reason to fire Lorna.

But employers don't always win based on this defense. One skeptical judge wrote: "A false statement on an employment application is not an insurance policy covering bigotry."

To help lay the groundwork for this type of defense in a discrimination or wrongful discharge case, consider adding the following language to your job application forms in prominent type above the applicant's signature:

"I acknowledge that any misrepresentations or omissions in this application will be grounds for termination."

And make sure to enforce this policy evenhandedly against everyone, not just those employees who have complained or filed lawsuits against you.

Harassment

Title VII doesn't specifically mention illegal harassment. But under federal law, harassment is a form of discrimination.

Sexual Harassment

In 2017, the #MeToo movement gained worldwide media attention and provoked dinner-table discussions in millions of households as reports of widespread sexual assault, abuse, and harassment poured in from Hollywood. In only a short time, that initial wave had caused ripples in virtually every workplace in America, with many employers and HR departments running antiharassment training programs for their employees and strengthening their antiharassment policies.

Federal law has long prohibited sexual harassment in the workplace. In 1980, the U.S. Equal Employment Opportunity Commission (EEOC) issued guidelines stating that harassment in the workplace is a form of sex discrimination prohibited by Title VII. In 1986, the U.S. Supreme Court agreed that harassment on the job is, indeed, a form of sex discrimination, and is therefore illegal. (*Meritor Savings Bank v. Vinson*, 477 U.S. 57.) The Court held that illegal harassment occurs when unwelcome sexual advances, requests for sexual favors, and other verbal or physical conduct of a sexual nature creates a hostile or abusive work environment. In 1993, the Supreme Court made it clear that a harassed employee is entitled to legal relief even without proof that the offending behavior has injured the employee psychologically. (*Harris v. Forklift Systems Inc.*, 510 U.S. 17.)

Most states have additional laws prohibiting sexual discrimination in the workplace. Although the specifics may differ from federal law, these state laws are generally interpreted to include harassment as a type of prohibited discrimination.

If an employer or manager makes unwelcome sexual advances or demands sexual favors in return for job benefits, promotions, or continued employment, that's harassment. But harassment in the workplace can consist of a wide variety of other behaviors, including:
- posting sexually explicit photos that offend employees
- sending sexually suggestive text messages or photos to a coworker
- telling sex-related jokes or jokes that demean people because of their gender
- commenting inappropriately on an employee's appearance
- refusing to call a transgender person by their preferred gender pronouns

- repeatedly requesting dates from a person who clearly isn't interested
- having strippers perform at a company gathering, or
- stating that people of one gender are inferior to people of the other gender or can't perform their jobs as well.

In short, any hostile or offensive behavior in the workplace that has a sexual or gender-based component can constitute harassment.

Although harassment is most often committed by men against women, that's not always the case. There are instances in which women sexually harass men and where people harass others of their own gender. Laws prohibiting harassment offer protection in all of these situations.

Harassment Based on Other Characteristics

Employers and employees alike tend to focus on sexual harassment because it is the type of harassment that is the most notorious. You should know, however, that harassing an individual because of any characteristic protected by state or federal law—for example, race, color, religion, national origin, disability, genetic information, or age—is also considered a form of discrimination and is therefore illegal.

Here are some examples of activities that are not sexual in nature, but can amount to illegal harassment:

- using racially derogatory words or epithets
- making gestures or displaying pictures that would offend a particular racial or ethnic group
- commenting on a person's skin color or other racial or ethnic characteristics
- making disparaging remarks about a person's gender transition
- commenting negatively about a person's religious beliefs (or lack of such beliefs)
- expressing negative stereotypes about an employee's birthplace or ancestry
- making negative comments about a person's age when referring to employees who are 40 years old or older, or
- making derogatory or intimidating remarks about an employee's mental or physical impairment.

Complying With the Law

Generally, your company has a legal duty to take action to stop harassment as soon as management learns about it. If you don't take prompt and effective action to end the harassment once you're aware of it, your company can be held legally liable.

In addition, your company will be liable for harassment committed by its managerial employees if the harassment results in a "tangible employment action": a negative action that changes the harassed employee's job status, like getting fired, reassigned, transferred, or demoted. In these situations, your company is responsible for the actions of its managers and will be legally liable for the employee's damages.

However, in cases of harassment by coworkers or harassment by a manager that doesn't result in negative action against the harassed employee, your company will not be legally responsible as long as both of the following apply:

- You exercised reasonable care to prevent and quickly correct harassment (by adopting a policy prohibiting harassment that includes a complaint procedure and by investigating all complaints of harassment promptly and fairly).
- The employee unreasonably failed to take advantage of the opportunities you offered to correct the harassment (for example, by failing to make a complaint or otherwise make the company aware of the situation).

If you learn of workplace conditions that might create an uncomfortable work environment for some workers—such as the presence of pornographic magazines —take decisive steps to eliminate the offending conditions. An employee may challenge you by asking: "Who's offended by this?" The simple answer: "Me."

You're also required to take corrective action if an employee is being harassed by other people who come into the workplace—clients, patients, customers, suppliers—who are not employees of your business.

> **EXAMPLE:** Stella waits on tables at the lounge at Take Ten Bowling Lanes. One night after winning the league championship, a boisterous team of male bowlers comes into the lounge and begins to harass Stella. The lounge manager quickly sizes up the situation, switches Stella to another table, and compensates her for the tip she missed from the boisterous bowlers. The manager also threatens to expel the rowdies if they continue their behavior. Through this prompt action, Take Ten meets its legal duty to Stella.

Antiharassment Policy

Our company is committed to providing a work environment where all employees can work together comfortably and productively, free from harassment, which is illegal under both state and federal law and will not be tolerated here.

This policy applies to all phases of employment, including but not limited to recruiting, testing, hiring, upgrading, promotion or demotion, transfer, layoff, termination, rates of pay, benefits, and selection for training, travel, or company social events.

This policy applies to the conduct of owners, supervisors, managers, coworkers, clients, vendors, and customers.

Prohibited Behavior

Prohibited harassment includes any offensive or unwelcome conduct—verbal or physical—that is based on a membership in a protected class. It also includes discrimination or discriminatory comments based on a person's race, color, religion, gender, sexual orientation, transgender status, national origin, age, disability, genetic information, or any other characteristic protected by state or federal law. Prohibited harassment also includes unsolicited and unwelcome contact that has sexual overtones. This includes, but is not limited to:

- written contact, such as sexually suggestive or obscene letters, emails, notes, invitations
- verbal contact, such as sexually suggestive or obscene comments, threats, slurs, epithets, jokes about gender-specific traits, sexual propositions
- physical contact, such as intentional touching, pinching, brushing against another's body, impeding or blocking movement, assault, coercing sexual intercourse or contact, and
- visual contact, such as leering or staring at another's body, gesturing, displaying sexually suggestive objects or pictures, cartoons, posters, or magazines.

Harassment also includes continuing to express sexual or social interest after being informed directly that the interest is unwelcome, and using sexual behavior to control, influence, or affect the career, salary, or work environment of another employee.

Antiharassment Policy (continued)

It is impermissible to suggest, threaten, or imply that failure to accept a request for a date or sexual intimacy will affect an employee's job prospects. For example, it is forbidden either to imply or actually withhold support for an appointment, promotion, or change of assignment, or suggest that a poor performance report will be given, because an employee has declined a personal proposition.

Also, offering benefits, such as promotions, favorable performance evaluations, favorable assigned duties or shifts, recommendations, or reclassifications in exchange for sexual favors is forbidden.

Harassment by Nonemployees

In addition, Company will take all reasonable steps to prevent or eliminate harassment by nonemployees—such as customers, clients, and suppliers—who are likely to have workplace contact with our employees.

Monitoring

Company shall take all reasonable steps to see that this policy prohibiting harassment is followed by all employees, supervisors, and others who have contact with our employees. This prevention plan will include training sessions, ongoing monitoring of the worksite, and a confidential employee survey to be conducted and evaluated periodically.

Discipline

Any employee found to have violated this policy shall be subject to appropriate disciplinary action, including warnings, reprimand, or discharge, according to the findings of the complaint investigation.

If an investigation reveals that harassment has occurred, the harasser may also be held legally liable for his or her actions under state or federal antidiscrimination laws or in separate legal actions.

Antiharassment Policy (continued)

Retaliation

Any employee bringing a harassment complaint or assisting in investigating such a complaint will not be adversely affected in terms and conditions of employment or discriminated against or discharged because of the complaint. Complaints of such retaliation will be promptly investigated.

Complaint Procedure and Investigation

Joe Smith is designated as the harassment counselor. All complaints of harassment and retaliation for reporting or participating in an investigation shall be directed to the harassment counselor or to a supervisor of your choice, either in writing or by requesting an individual interview. All complaints shall be handled as confidentially as possible. The harassment counselor will promptly investigate and resolve complaints involving violations of this policy and recommend appropriate action to management.

Training

Company will establish periodic training sessions for all employees concerning their rights to be free from harassment and the legal options available if they are harassed. In addition, training sessions will be held for supervisors and managers, educating them on how to keep the workplace free from harassment and how to handle harassment complaints.

A copy of the policy will be distributed to all employees and posted in areas where all employees will have the opportunity to freely review it. Company welcomes your suggestions for improvements to this policy.

> **TIP**
>
> **Look beyond legal liability.** Avoiding legal liability is just one reason for a business to crack down on harassment. Harassment has a negative impact on employees, causing anxiety and unhappiness. You can't expect high morale and productivity in a workplace in which harassment is tolerated.

Preventing Harassment

Your attitude toward harassment—and the steps you take to prevent it—can help ensure that you won't become the object of a formal complaint. Most potential charges can be handled effectively within the workplace.

Start by adopting a formal policy stating clearly that harassment won't be tolerated. Let employees know who within your business they can complain to if they've been harassed. And provide a backup person to handle the complaint just in case the main person handling complaints is the accused harasser. Distribute a copy of the policy to each employee or put the policy statement in your company's employee handbook.

The sample antiharassment policy shown above can be modified to fit the needs of most workplaces.

Age

An aging population means increasing numbers of older people in the workforce. And there are laws protecting them from discrimination on the job.

The Age Discrimination in Employment Act

The federal Age Discrimination in Employment Act (ADEA) prohibits discrimination against those 40 years old or older. It applies to private businesses with 20 or more employees as well as the federal government. Although the ADEA also protects state government workers, these workers cannot file a lawsuit against the state for age discrimination. Only the EEOC can take action to protect state employees from age discrimination. As is true of Title VII, the ADEA prohibits discrimination in hiring, firing, compensation, and all other aspects of employment.

The ADEA prohibits you from discriminating against older workers in favor of those younger than 40. But also, in dealing with workers who are 40 years old or older, you can't give favorable treatment to younger members of that group.

> **EXAMPLE:** Mary is 53 years old and Wilfred is 43 years old. Both apply for the same job. The employer can't choose Wilfred simply because he's younger, even though both applicants are protected by the ADEA. But the employer is on safe ground if Wilfred is chosen because of his superior skills.

The reverse isn't true, however. Within the group of workers who are 40 years old or older, you are permitted to treat older workers more favorably. You can agree, for example, that, upon retirement, current employees who are at least 50 years old will continue to receive health care coverage. You needn't promise similar future benefits to current employees who are younger than 50.

Some employers believe that it costs more to hire older workers than younger workers. They overlook the possibility that younger workers may be less competent and need more training, making them more expensive. At any rate, a desire to save costs isn't a legitimate reason to discriminate against older workers.

The Older Workers Benefit Protection Act

The federal Older Workers Benefit Protection Act (29 U.S.C. §§ 623 and following) makes it illegal for your business to use an employee's age as the basis for discrimination in benefits. Like the ADEA, this act covers employees who are at least 40 years old. Under this law, you cannot, for example, reduce health or life insurance benefits for older employees, nor can you stop their pensions from accruing if they work past their normal retirement ages. The act also discourages your business from targeting older workers when you cut staff. Some provisions of this law are very difficult for anyone but an experienced benefits administrator to understand. You'll probably have to consult with such an expert if you plan to take action involving a cutback of older workers' benefits.

One relatively clear provision of the law regulates the legal waivers that some employers ask employees to sign in connection with early retirement programs. You might, for example, offer a handsome retirement package to induce an older employee to leave your company voluntarily. As part of the process, you'd ask the employee to sign a waiver—often called a release or covenant not to sue—in which the employee would agree not to take any legal action against your business.

The law sets limits on your use of such waivers as they relate to age discrimination claims under the ADEA:

- You must write the waiver in plain English.
- The waiver can't cover rights or claims that may arise after the worker signs the waiver.
- The waiver must specifically state that the worker is waiving any rights or claims the worker may have under the federal Age Discrimination in Employment Act.
- You must offer the worker something of value—something over and above what you already owe to the worker—in exchange for the waiver.
- You must advise the worker, in writing, to consult with a lawyer before signing the waiver. (Of course, you can't require the worker to hire a lawyer.)
- You must give the employee a fixed period of time in which to decide whether to sign the waiver. That period must be at least 21 days if the waiver has been presented to the employee alone. If you've presented the waiver to a group or class of employees, you must give each worker at least 45 days to decide whether or not to sign. In either case, a worker has seven days after agreeing to such a waiver to revoke the decision.

In addition, if you're making the offer to a group or class of employees as part of an incentive program to encourage early retirement, you must tell each employee in writing and in plain English what class or group of employees is covered by the program, the eligibility requirements for the program, any time limits for accepting the offer, the job titles and ages of all the individuals to whom the offer is being made, and the ages of all the employees in the same job classification or unit who are not eligible for the program.

Because the statute doesn't specify how many employees it takes to constitute a class or group, the most prudent course of action is to provide the information any time you seek a waiver from an employee who's at least 40 years old if you're also offering a retirement incentive package to other employees.

Avoiding Age Discrimination Claims

A few sensible precautions can help you avoid discrimination claims by older workers.

Be aware of remarks that betray a subtle—or not-so-subtle—age bias. A thoughtless comment such as "You can't teach an old dog new tricks" may be used against you if an older employee sues your company. Emphasize to supervisors that your business won't tolerate such unfair comments.

Apply your performance standards evenhandedly to all employees, regardless of their age. Because older people are disproportionately represented on many juries, you want to be able to show that your business deals equally with all employees.

Offer equal training opportunities for employees of all ages. If you're inclined to put more money into training younger workers on the assumption that they'll be with your company longer, forget it. That kind of strategy is a great way to invite an age discrimination lawsuit.

Pregnancy

The federal Pregnancy Discrimination Act (PDA) is an amendment to Title VII. (92 U.S.C. § 2076.) Under the PDA, it's a form of gender discrimination to treat an employee differently because of pregnancy, childbirth, or related medical conditions. If a woman is affected by such a condition, you must treat her the same way that you treat other people in the workforce who are either able or unable to work. You violate the PDA, for example, if you fire a woman whose pregnancy keeps her from working, but you don't fire other workers who are temporarily unable to do the job because of other physical problems. Similarly, if a pregnant worker is able to do the job, you can't lay her off or put her on leave because you think it's in her best interests to stay home.

The PDA requires employers to treat pregnant women with job restrictions like it treats other employees who are temporarily unable to do their jobs. An employer that offers accommodations to all temporarily disabled employees must also offer them to pregnant employees. And, an employer that does not provide such accommodations to any employees need not make an exception only for pregnant employees. But what of employers who accommodate only some temporarily disabled employees—for example, those who are unable to work due to on-the-job injuries?

The Supreme Court answered this question in 2015 in *Young v. United Parcel Service*, 135 S. Ct. 1338. There, the Court found that an employer may treat pregnant employees differently than it treats some employees who are temporarily disabled for other reasons, but only if it has a legitimate, nondiscriminatory reason for doing so.

Some states require employers to provide reasonable accommodations for pregnant employees. State law might require, for example, that an employer provide seating, additional break time, modified job duties or work schedules, light duty, or time off work for employees who need an accommodation due to pregnancy. To find out whether your state has this type of law, contact your state's fair employment practices agency (see www.nolo.com/FEPA for contact information).

Don't Make Assumptions About Employees With Caregiving Responsibilities

Today, many workers have the responsibility of caring for children or elderly family members. In many cases, primary caregivers are female.

The EEOC recognizes that employers sometimes make discriminatory assumptions or decisions about female applicants or employees with caregiving responsibilities. Such gender-based stereotyping is unlawful.

EXAMPLE: Patricia, a recent business school graduate, interviews for a marketing assistant job at a public relations firm. Bob, the interviewer, sees her wedding ring and asks, "How many kids do you have?" Patricia says she has none now, but that she plans to in the future. Bob explains that the job is very demanding, and asks Patricia how she will balance her work with child care responsibilities. She says that she will share those responsibilities with her husband. However, Bob doesn't believe men are reliable caregivers, and decides not to hire Patricia for this reason, explaining to her that being a mother is not compatible with a fast-paced business environment. This decision is unlawful.

For more on this topic, search for "Enforcement Guidance: Unlawful Disparate Treatment of Workers with Caregiving Responsibilities," at www.eeoc.gov.

Note also that the Family and Medical Leave Act allows unpaid leave for childbirth, adoptions, and foster care placements, as well as for an employee's serious health condition, which can include some complications or conditions relating to pregnancy and childbirth. (See Chapter 6 for a discussion of family and medical leave.)

Language, Fluency, and Accent Rules

Requiring that employees speak only English on the job—or that they be fluent in English or speak it without an accent—can be a form of discrimination. The language an employee speaks and the accent an employee uses are often associated with the employee's national origin, a protected trait under federal antidiscrimination laws. However, your business may have valid reasons to require the use of English, or fluency in it. And, in certain jobs, an accent must not interfere with necessary communication.

If your policy is that workers must speak only in English while at work, make sure you didn't adopt the policy for discriminatory reasons. You'll be acting legally if the English-only rule is intended to promote communication and ensure safety in case of an emergency. An English-only rule makes good sense if employees need to work together and some speak only English. It's reasonable, too, to require employees who deal with English-speaking customers to communicate in English. But avoid a rule that forbids workers from ever speaking another language, even during breaks, or to talk to a customer who also speaks that other language. Such a policy is probably too broad to pass legal muster.

Be careful if you're considering a requirement that all employees must be fluent in English. While fluency might be important for workers engaged in customer service, it might not be necessary for warehouse workers. In some circumstances, you can safely require fluency in a language other than English. For example, if your business has many customers who speak only Spanish, you could reasonably require Spanish fluency for workers who will be dealing with those customers.

What about refusing to hire or promote someone who speaks with an accent? If the accent impairs the person's ability to communicate and be understood clearly, you're probably on safe legal ground if the job requires clear communication skills. But if the person can communicate clearly even with the accent, you'll run afoul of antidiscrimination laws by making job decisions based on the accent.

Citizenship

The Immigration Reform and Control Act of 1986 (IRCA), which applies to businesses with four or more employees, makes it illegal to discriminate against workers who are not U.S. citizens or nationals. The law forbids you from discriminating against aliens who have been lawfully admitted to the United States for permanent or temporary residence, and aliens who have applied for temporary residence status.

This can be tricky because, as an employer, you must meet specific legal requirements to avoid hiring immigrants who are not authorized to be in this country or to work, including asking new employees to show you documents verifying their citizenship and their legal ability to be employed in the United States. (See "Legal Guidelines for Hiring Employees," in Chapter 1, for these hiring rules.) In meeting these verification duties, you can't ask to see more or different documents from those required for completion of Form I-9. It's illegal to refuse to honor documents offered by the employee, as long as they appear to be genuine.

Genetic Information

As an employer, you may come into possession of information about an applicant's or employee's genetic makeup. The person may have a genetic predisposition or family history of a disease such as diabetes, heart disease, cancer, or Alzheimer's. This doesn't always mean that someone will develop the disease, just that the risk of getting the disease may be greater than average. Genetic tests that reveal these differences are often useful in finding individualized ways to detect, treat, and prevent disease.

However, the Genetic Information Nondiscrimination Act (GINA) prohibits employers from discriminating on the basis of this genetic information. GINA prohibits employers from requesting or acquiring genetic information from employees or applicants. And, in the small handful of situations in which you might learn such information legally (such as through informal conversation or in a medical certification form for an employee to take FMLA leave), you are required to keep the information strictly confidential.

The law is intended to help ease concerns about discrimination that might keep people from getting genetic testing that could benefit their health. Many states also have laws that prohibit discrimination on the basis of genetic information. (To find the rule in your state, look at "State Laws Prohibiting Discrimination in Employment," in the appendix.)

The nondiscrimination law applies to health care insurers as well, but not to providers of life insurance, disability insurance, or long-term care insurance. For more information on how these laws affect health care insurers, see Chapter 4.

Religion

An increasing number of employees are claiming religious discrimination. In the past, the typical complaint would have been that a person was fired or disciplined or denied a promotion because of practicing a certain faith. But today, claims of religious discrimination tend to be much more subtle and more challenging. An employee might claim, for example, that a supervisor is seeking to impose his or her own religious beliefs on the employee by pressuring the employee to attend prayer sessions or Bible study meetings at work. Or an employee may claim being unfairly deprived of the right to pray at work or to use a company meeting room to discuss the Koran with other employees. Still another employee may claim that wearing a "Stop Abortion" badge with a color photo of a fetus is an exercise of religious rights; other employees may find the badge disturbing, offensive, and a violation of their own rights. Complicating matters is the fact that religion, unlike other protected characteristics, is not inherent: It is based on a belief system, which can change or grow over time, and which varies from person to person.

Unfortunately, the law in this delicate area is unclear. As always, tolerance and common sense are your best guides. If employees complain to you that a coworker is badgering them with religious hectoring, you have a right—if not a duty—to intervene, although you must, of course, use the utmost tact and sensitivity.

The law protects your right to discuss your own religious beliefs with an employee, if you're so inclined, but you can't persist to the point that the employee feels you're being hostile, intimidating, or offensive. So, if an employee objects to your discussion of religious subjects or you even get an inkling that your religious advances are unwelcome, back off. Otherwise, you may find yourself embroiled in a lawsuit or an administrative proceeding.

While you may feel that the best way to resolve these knotty problems is to simply banish religion from the workplace, that's generally not a viable alternative. You're legally required to make a reasonable accommodation to the religious needs of employees. This duty to accommodate is triggered whenever you have reason to believe that an employee needs an accommodation for religious reasons, even if the employee doesn't explicitly request one. In a 2015 Supreme Court case, Abercrombie & Fitch rejected an applicant who wore a hijab (a religious headscarf) to her interview, based on the company's "look policy," which does not allow employees to wear anything on their heads. The company didn't raise the issue with the applicant or talk about accommodations; it simply rejected her application. The Court found that this was discriminatory: Although the applicant didn't ask for an accommodation, the company refused to hire her because it suspected she would need one, which is illegal. (*EEOC v. Abercrombie & Fitch Stores, Inc.*, 135 S. Ct. 2028.)

You don't, however, need to do anything that would cost more than a minimum amount or that would cause more than minimal inconvenience. Allowing workers to use an empty office for voluntary group prayer at lunch-time might be a reasonable accommodation. Letting workers take a limited amount of time off work to attend religious observances might also be a reasonable accommodation. However, it might be better to simply give all employees a few days of personal leave time each year so that religious workers aren't viewed as receiving special privileges.

Recognizing that the issue of religious discrimination is a complicated one for employers, the Equal Employment Opportunity Commission recently released an updated compliance manual that explains how legal protections should be interpreted and applied in cases involving religion. For more information, visit the EEOC's website at www.eeoc.gov/policy/docs/religion.html.

Sexual Orientation and Transgender Status

Title VII doesn't list sexual orientation or gender identity as protected characteristics, like race or religion. However, in 2020 the U.S. Supreme Court ruled in a landmark case, *Bostock v. Clayton County, Georgia* (590 U.S. ___), that discrimination based on sexual orientation—being straight, gay, lesbian, or bisexual—and gender identity are forms of sex discrimination, which is illegal under Title VII. Gender identity refers to the gender with which a person identifies, or a person's gender expression (through clothing, hairstyle, and mannerisms, for example), as opposed to that person's designated gender at birth.

Writing for the Court's six-member majority, Justice Neil Gorsuch noted:

> In our time, few pieces of federal legislation rank in significance with the Civil Rights Act of 1964. There, in Title VII, Congress outlawed discrimination in the workplace on the basis of race, color, religion, sex, or national origin. Today, we must decide whether an employer can fire someone simply for being homosexual or transgender. The answer is clear. An employer who fires an individual for being homosexual or transgender fires that person for traits or actions it would not have questioned in members of a different sex. Sex plays a necessary and undisguisable role in the decision, exactly what Title VII forbids.

The Supreme Court set the stage for this interpretation three decades ago, when it found that an employer was guilty of illegal sex discrimination because it held a female employee to workplace standards based on gender stereotypes. In *Price Waterhouse v. Hopkins*, a woman sued her employer—the famous accounting firm—after she was denied partnership. (*Price Waterhouse*, 490 U.S. 288 (1989).) Among other things, she was told that she was too aggressive; needed to speak, act, and dress in a more feminine manner; and needed "a course in charm school." She won the lawsuit by arguing that these statements were a form of illegal sex discrimination, because she was being penalized for not living up to her employer's notions of how women should act in the workplace.

In light of the Supreme Court's historic ruling in *Bostock*, employers subject to Title VII (those with at least 15 employees) are barred from discriminating against workers on the basis of sexual orientation or gender identity in any aspect of employment, including hiring, promotion, pay and benefits, discipline, and termination. In addition, because harassment is a form of discrimination under federal law, the decision also bans workplace harassment based on sexual orientation or transgender status.

Many states and municipalities ban this sort of discrimination by smaller employers not covered by the federal law. See "State Laws Prohibiting Discrimination in Employment," in the appendix, to learn your state's rules.

State and Local Antidiscrimination Laws

Nearly all state and local laws prohibiting discrimination in employment are echoes of federal antidiscrimination law in that they outlaw discrimination based on race, color, religion, gender, age, and national origin. But state and local laws also tend to go into more detail and may protect employees from discrimination on other bases as well—such as marital status or receipt of government benefits—that aren't covered by federal law. These laws often apply to smaller employers than do the federal laws.

"State Laws Prohibiting Discrimination in Employment," in the appendix, is a state-by-state synopsis of factors that private employers may not use as the basis for any employment decisions. In legal parlance, people who have these characteristics fall into what are called "protected classes."

Keep in mind that this is only a synopsis. Each state has its own way of interpreting who is or is not a member of a protected class. For example, states may differ in how they determine who has a disability. In addition, many of the laws in this chart apply only to employers with a minimum number of employees, often five or more.

For details about your state laws, visit the website of your state's fair employment practices agency (see www.nolo.com/FEPA for contact information). Where no special agency has been designated to enforce antidiscrimination laws, your state's labor department or the closest office of the federal Equal Employment Opportunity Commission should direct you to the agency or person who can give you information about fair employment laws in your state. The chart describes only state laws. Your city or county may have its own set of fair employment ordinances. To learn more about those, contact someone within your local government, such as your county clerk's office. Also, local offices of the Small Business Administration or the Chamber of Commerce can be good sources for information about local laws.

Workers With Disabilities

Some employers are reluctant to hire people who have disabilities. They assume that an applicant with a disability won't be able to handle a particular job. This assumption may be correct for some applicants and some jobs but way off the mark for many others. Not only is it bad business sense to prejudge people with disabilities, but it's also illegal. The federal government and many state governments have laws prohibiting discrimination based on disability. In this chapter, we take a close look at the main federal law. To find out if your state has a disability discrimination law, refer to "State Laws Prohibiting Discrimination in Employment" in the appendix.

The Americans With Disabilities Act

To help eliminate discrimination against people with disabilities, Congress passed the Americans with Disabilities Act, or ADA, in 1990. (42 U.S.C. §§ 1201 and following.) The ADA was significantly amended in 2008 by the ADA Amendments Act (ADAAA). We'll explain those changes throughout this chapter too.

One part of the ADA sets out rules for how businesses must deal with job applicants and employees. That part of the law, known as Title I, is explained in this chapter.

Basically, the ADA states that, in making hiring and employment decisions, it's illegal to discriminate against anyone because of a disability. Some may need an accommodation—special equipment, perhaps, or a simple adjustment in their working conditions—to help them get the job done. If a person is qualified to do the work, or to do it once a reasonable accommodation is made, you must treat that person the same as all other applicants and employees. Although the concept is simple, the ADA requirements can get fairly complicated.

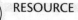 **RESOURCE**

Find much more information on disability discrimination at www.eeoc.gov. There you'll find extensive information about your responsibilities under the ADA and a list of helpful publications you can order. Especially valuable is *The Americans with Disabilities Act: A Primer for Small Business,* which you can download or read online.

The Americans With Disabilities Act (ADA) and COVID-19: FAQs for Employers

Throughout the coronavirus pandemic, many employers have wondered about their ADA obligations when it comes to employees who have or might develop COVID-19. Unfortunately, due to the novel and rapidly changing nature of the pandemic, clear answers aren't always easy to come by. Here's what we know so far:

Question: *Is COVID-19 a disability under the ADA?*

Answer: Probably so, especially for symptomatic cases. That means employers generally have a legal obligation to accommodate individuals who have tested positive or show symptoms of COVID-19, with a few exceptions.

The first exception is that you're not required to provide accommodations if doing so would cause your business to suffer undue hardship. For ADA purposes, that means significant difficulty or expense (see "Undue Hardship," below.)

The second exception is that you're not required to accommodate an employee if doing so would pose a "direct threat" to the health and safety of your workforce. Because the CDC has determined that COVID-19 constitutes a direct threat for ADA purposes, you're generally allowed to (and should) exclude from the workplace anyone with COVID-19 or its symptoms.

Allowing your employees with COVID-19 to work from home is the most straightforward way to accommodate them, but it's not possible for every type of job. If the employee can't work from home, allow them to take FMLA leave, sick days, PTO, or any other leave available until they are no longer contagious.

Question: *If an employee tests positive for COVID-19 and we want to inform our other employees about it, how do we maintain ADA confidentiality?*

Answer: Under the ADA, employers must keep confidential any medical information they learn about their employees, subject to limited exceptions.

In this situation, one option is to ask the person who tested positive to give the names of anyone in the workplace who he or she might have exposed to the virus. Then inform those individuals—and any others who might have been exposed—that a positive COVID-19 case has been identified. Don't reveal the identity of the positive case, although you can specify roughly where the case occurred (for example, on the fifth floor). In small businesses, the person's identity might be easily guessed, but don't confirm it if asked.

The Americans With Disabilities Act (ADA) and COVID-19: FAQs for Employers (continued)

Question: *Can our company require our employees to get a COVID-19 vaccination?*

Answer: Mandatory vaccination policies are generally legal, as long as employers provide exemptions for religious reasons under Title VII of the Civil Rights Act, and for medical reasons under the ADA.

Question: *How do we handle a request for a medical exemption from our mandatory vaccine policy?*

Answer: Provide written notice to employees that exemption requests should be made to their manager or supervisor, for example. To qualify for a medical exemption, the employee must present evidence of a covered disability under the ADA. For example, a person with an allergy to a vaccine component or a compromised immune system would likely qualify. A person with a general skepticism about vaccines, absent any accompanying disability, would not. You are permitted to ask for documentation to support their request—for example, a letter from a health care provider.

Question: *If we decide to require our employees or customers to wear face coverings, how do we handle requests for medical exemptions?*

Answer: Misinformation abounds on this topic. What's clear is that as an employer, you're allowed to require your employees and customers to wear masks to prevent the spread of COVID-19.

If they're unable to wear a mask for medical reasons (rather than simply not wanting to), you must attempt to accommodate them. For example, you might allow your employees to wear face shields instead of masks, or offer your customers curbside pickup. But you're not required to accommodate employees or customers—even if they have a disability—if doing so would put others at risk.

Employers are allowed to ask those claiming exemptions for proof of their eligibility—for example, a note from a medical provider. The widely circulated claim that asking for this sort of evidence is a "HIPAA violation" is bunk. HIPAA covers your health care provider and health insurer, not your employer or grocery store.

Note: Employers should bear in mind that this situation is rapidly evolving, and government guidance could change. For the latest on your ADA obligations when it comes to the COVID-19 pandemic, visit www.eeoc.gov/coronavirus.

Businesses That Are Covered

You're covered by the ADA if you have 15 or more employees working for you for 20 or more weeks during the current or previous calendar year. Part-time employees are counted.

Who Is Protected

To be protected from job discrimination, a person must not only have a disability, but must also be qualified for a particular job.

People With Disabilities

To have a disability under the ADA, a person must either:

- have a physical or mental impairment that substantially limits one or more major life activities
- have a record of being substantially limited, or
- be regarded as having a disability.

Impairments Limiting a Life Activity

When deciding whether an applicant or employee is protected by the ADA, you must first determine whether that person has a disability.

To qualify as an employee with a disability, the employee must have a physical or mental impairment that substantially limits a major life activity. In the past, court cases interpreting the ADA very strictly limited who qualified for protection by narrowly defining what "substantially limits" and "major life activity" mean. It was difficult for an employee to prove a qualifying condition.

However, the ADA Amendments Act (ADAAA), passed in 2008, expanded the definition by more broadly construing what constitutes a "major life activity." According to the ADAAA, major life activities include:

- taking care of oneself
- hearing
- walking
- bending
- learning
- thinking

- performing manual tasks
- eating
- standing
- speaking
- reading
- communicating

- seeing
- sleeping
- lifting
- breathing
- concentrating
- working

Additionally, the ADAAA makes clear that impairments of bodily functions that might limit major life activities also count as disabilities. These include functions of the immune system, normal cell growth, digestion, bowel and bladder functions, or neurological, brain, respiratory, circulatory, endocrine, or reproductive functions.

What constitutes a "substantial limitation" is also being revisited. In the past, courts have interpreted "substantial limitation" to mean that an employee must be very significantly restricted by a disabling condition. If a mitigating measure like a medication or medical device helped the employee do his or her job, the employee was not considered "substantially limited" in a major life activity and thus not disabled.

Now, an employer cannot take mitigating measures into account. So even if a person's disability can be overcome by medications or medical devices, the person may nonetheless be considered a person with a disability. For example, a person whose diabetes is controlled by insulin, or a person whose hearing loss is corrected by a hearing aid, is still entitled to ADA protections. The ADAAA makes an exception for individuals with vision that is corrected by contact lenses or glasses.

Also, the ADAAA interprets the phrase "substantially limited" more broadly than courts have interpreted it in the past. The ADAAA considers a condition that "materially restricts" an individual to be substantially limiting. The EEOC's regulations interpreting the ADAAA state that the term is "not meant to be a demanding standard." A person can be substantially limited in performing a major life activity even if that person is not prevented, or significantly restricted, from performing that activity. These regulations indicate that the condition, manner, and duration of the person's performance of the activity should be examined. If, for example, a person can perform an activity only briefly, only with significant effort, or only by enduring pain, and the general population doesn't face these obstacles when performing the activity, that might constitute a substantial limitation.

Record of Impairment

The ADA also protects people with a history of a disability—cancer or heart disease, for example—whose illnesses are either cured, controlled, or in remission. And it protects people with a history of mental illness.

If a person has a record of disability and you rely on that record to reject that person for a job, that's a violation of the ADA if the person is currently qualified to do the work.

> **EXAMPLE:** Beatrice, who has a learning disability, applies for a job as a secretary-receptionist. Records from a previous employer state that she is developmentally delayed. Still, her résumé shows that she meets all requirements for the secretary-receptionist job. The new employer doesn't interview her because he doesn't want to hire a person who is developmentally delayed. Relying on the records from the prior employer violates the ADA.
>
> In this situation, it's best to determine the applicant's ability through practical tests that measure the skills needed for the job, such as handling phone calls, taking messages, greeting customers, sorting mail, and doing light typing.

Regarded as Impaired

Some job applicants do not have a disability, but employers perceive and treat them as if they do. And, acting on these false perceptions, employers discriminate against these people.

> **EXAMPLE:** Jill is fired because of a false rumor that she has HIV. She has no impairment but is being treated by her employer as if she does. Therefore, her firing falls within the ADA.

In considering whether to hire an applicant or to demote or fire an employee who has a disability, you may be concerned about productivity, safety, insurance, liability, or attendance. Or you may worry that your business will have to spend money to accommodate a disability or that coworkers and customers won't accept the applicant or employee. The best way to avoid problems under the ADA is to get the facts before you act; you must base all employment decisions on legitimate, nondiscriminatory reasons.

ADA Coverage Is Broad

Under the ADA, you can't discriminate against a person with a disability in any aspect of employment, including:

- applications
- interviews
- testing
- hiring
- job assignments
- evaluations
- disciplinary actions
- training
- promotion
- medical exams
- layoffs
- firing
- compensation
- leave, or
- benefits.

In addition, you can't deny a job to someone or discriminate against an employee because that person is related to or associates with a person who has a disability. For example, you can't:

- refuse to hire someone because that person's spouse, child, or other dependent has a disability
- refuse to hire someone because that person's spouse, child, or other dependent has a disability that's not covered by your current health insurance plan or that may cause increased health care costs, or
- fire an employee because that employee has a roommate or close friend who has AIDS, or because the employee does volunteer work for people who have AIDS.

People Who Are Qualified for the Job

To be protected by the ADA, a person must not only have a disability; the person must also be qualified to do a particular job. This emphasizes a key point about the ADA: You don't have to hire or retain anyone who can't do the work. However, you may have to offer an accommodation that will allow the employee to get the job done.

To figure out if a disabled person is qualified for a job in your business, go through these three steps.

Step 1: Define the essential job functions. Make sure you know what skills and abilities the job requires. Employers often create job descriptions to identify exactly what's required to get the job done. (See Chapter 1 to learn how to draft a job description.)

Step 2: Determine whether the person is qualified for the job. Look at the person's education, work experience, training, skills, licenses, certificates, and other job-related requirements, such as good judgment or the ability to work with other people.

> **EXAMPLE:** Trudy, a bookkeeper who has cerebral palsy, applies for a job as a bookkeeping manager. If the company's policy is that all managers must have at least three years of experience working with the company and Trudy has worked there only two years, she's not qualified for a management position. Therefore, she's not protected by the ADA.

Requirements used to screen out candidates must be job related and based on business needs.

Step 3: Determine whether the person can perform the essential functions of the job. When making this determination, consider whether the employee can do the job, with or without a reasonable accommodation from you. (To learn what constitutes a reasonable accommodation, see "Providing Reasonable Accommodations," below.)

The ADA puts a lot of weight on two words: essential functions. The reason is that historically, many people with disabilities who were able to perform the basic tasks necessary for a job were denied employment because they couldn't meet requirements that were marginal at best.

> **EXAMPLE:** The job description for the position of receptionist at a large law firm states that the job may include delivering mail. In fact, the law firm has a mail clerk who typically picks up the mail at the front desk, sorts it, and delivers it. The receptionist has, in the past, filled in and handled this job only when the clerk is sick. Joanne has a mobility impairment and walks with a cane. She is well qualified to answer phones and greet visitors at the front desk, but would find it difficult to walk the halls and drop off mail. Because delivering mail is not an essential function of the receptionist position, Joanne's disability should not disqualify her from getting the job.

If you can write an accurate job description that identifies the essential functions of a job, you'll have an easier time deciding whether people with disabilities—and all other applicants—are qualified for the job. This emphasizes the importance of periodically reviewing your job descriptions to make sure they are current.

Exceptions to Coverage

Certain people and conditions aren't protected by the ADA.

Users of Illegal Drugs

People can't claim they're disabled and entitled to ADA protection because they illegally use drugs. This includes people who use prescription drugs illegally as well as those who use illegal drugs. Applying this part of the ADA becomes tricky, since the law may protect people who have been rehabilitated after drug use or who are in a drug or alcohol rehab program.

Be Alert for Harassment of Workers With Disabilities

Just as you need to spot and crack down on sexual harassment and racial harassment in the workplace, you need to nip in the bud any harassment of disabled workers, whether by supervisors or coworkers. Otherwise, you may get sued for tolerating the bad behavior. Cases against employers have been brought by:

- a hair salon manager with AIDS who claimed that his coworkers had threatened a walkout
- a saleswoman with multiple sclerosis who claimed that her supervisor mimicked and ridiculed her speech and gait, and
- a store manager with a back injury who claimed that his supervisor told him he had to work every minute of his shift and threatened to "ride him until he quit."

Of course, it's out of line to make light of someone else's disability. But, as an employer, you can't depend on employees always exercising good judgment and good manners. You need to make sure that employees know they'll be disciplined or even discharged if they engage in this type of behavior. Make a clear statement to that effect in your employee handbook, and be prepared to take prompt disciplinary action if this objectionable behavior surfaces.

Specified Conditions and Behaviors

The ADA states that the term "disability" doesn't include the following conditions or behaviors:

- transvestism, transsexualism, pedophilia, exhibitionism, voyeurism, gender identity disorders not resulting from physical impairments, or other sexual behavior disorders
- compulsive gambling, kleptomania, or pyromania, or
- psychoactive substance use disorders resulting from current illegal use of drugs.

Physical and Psychological Characteristics

Under the ADA, simple physical characteristics—eye or hair color, left-handedness, or height or weight within a normal range—are not treated as disabilities. Nor are personality traits such as poor judgment or quick temper. Also, environmental, cultural, or economic disadvantages—such as lack of education or a prison record—are not disabilities.

> **EXAMPLE:** Rita can't read because she has dyslexia, a learning disability; Rita has an impairment under the ADA. Sonny can't read because he dropped out of school; his lack of education isn't a legal disability.

You don't have to hire or retain an employee who would pose a direct threat to the health or safety of other employees or to his or her own health or safety. But be careful. You can't deny employment to a person with a disability because of a slightly increased risk. If you turn down an applicant or fire someone you've already employed, you must be prepared to show there is or would be a significant risk and a high probability of substantial harm if that person remained part of the workforce.

> **EXAMPLE:** Carlita has Parkinson's disease, which restricts her manual dexterity. An employer can't assume that Carlita can't work in a lab because she'd pose a risk of breaking bottles that contain dangerous chemicals. The employer must evaluate Carlita's specific abilities and limitations.

Sometimes, you can get rid of or reduce the health or safety risk through a reasonable accommodation (discussed at greater length below). If an employee were to contract tuberculosis, for example, a reasonable accommodation might be to grant the employee a two-week leave of absence. With proper medication, the employee would no longer be contagious at the end of the two-week period.

Psychological behavior is more difficult to evaluate. However, if an employee is violent, aggressive, or destructive—or makes threats—the worker may pose a direct threat to the safety of others. Still, before you make an employment decision based on such behavior, you may want to protect your legal position by asking a psychologist or other mental health professional to evaluate the behavior and the potential for harm.

Providing Reasonable Accommodations

The ADA requires you to accommodate the physical or mental limitations of a qualified applicant or employee who has a disability. However, you're excused from this requirement if making an accommodation would place an undue hardship on your business. (For more on what constitutes undue hardship, see below.)

The idea of a reasonable accommodation is quite simple: You may have to make some changes to help a person with a disability do a job. This can take a number of forms, such as changing the job, the work environment, or an employment practice. But you need not be psychic. Generally, the person with the disability needs to ask you for a reasonable accommodation or at least do something to let you know such an accommodation is needed, as we'll discuss below.

When Accommodations Are Required

You may have to make a reasonable accommodation for any part of the employment process, from completing the application to changing workplace conditions.

Job applications. Someone using a wheelchair may need an accommodation if the hiring office or interview site isn't wheelchair accessible; you may need to move the interview to a place that the applicant can access. A person with bad eyesight may need help filling out an application; you may need to provide the needed assistance at company expense.

Job performance. Someone with poor hearing may need a special telephone that amplifies voices to perform a job. You may need to provide such a telephone at company expense. (See "Improving Accessibility," below.)

Access to benefits. Employees with disabilities must have unrestricted access to lunchrooms, lounges, restrooms, meeting rooms, and other services such as health programs, transportation, and social events. You may need to modify existing facilities or schedules.

Undue Hardship

The ADA doesn't require you to accommodate a disabled applicant or employee if it would place an undue hardship on the business: that is, if it would require significant difficulty or expense. Many legal battles have been waged over this imprecise language.

Whether something is an undue hardship is decided on a case-by-case basis. What's easily managed by a large company may be very difficult for a small or midsized business. The law takes this into account by focusing on your business, not businesses in general. Under EEOC guidelines, several factors are considered in determining whether an accommodation would place an undue hardship on your business.

The net cost of the accommodation. The cost of accommodating an employee may be less than it first appears. You may qualify for a tax credit or deduction, and there are sources of funding to help pay for some accommodations. (See "Financial Assistance," below.)

The size of the business and its financial resources. Obviously, larger and wealthier businesses are better able to put money into accommodations.

The structure of the business. A small facility that's part of a larger company may have access to funds from the home office. If so, the company's total resources become part of the equation.

Ten Tips on Communicating With People Who Have Disabilities

1. When talking with a person who has a disability, speak directly to that person rather than through a companion or sign language interpreter who may be present.

2. When introduced to a person with a disability, it is appropriate to offer to shake hands. People with limited hand use or who wear an artificial limb can usually shake hands. It's perfectly acceptable to greet people by shaking hands with the left hand.

3. When meeting a person who is blind or has partial sight, always identify yourself and others who may be with you. When conversing in a group, remember to identify the person to whom you are speaking.

4. If you offer assistance, wait until the offer is accepted. Then listen to or ask for instructions.

5. Treat adults as adults. Address people who have disabilities by their first names only when extending that same familiarity to all others present. Never patronize people who use wheelchairs by patting them on the head or shoulder.

6. Leaning or hanging on a person's wheelchair is similar to leaning or hanging on a person and is generally considered annoying. The chair is part of the personal body space of the person who uses it.

7. Listen attentively when you're talking with a person who has difficulty speaking. Be patient and wait for the person to finish, rather than correcting or speaking for the person. Never pretend to understand if you are having difficulty doing so. Instead, repeat what you have understood and allow the person to respond. The response will clue you in and guide your understanding.

8. When speaking with a person who uses a wheelchair or crutches, position yourself at eye level in front of the person.

9. To get the attention of a person who is deaf or hard of hearing, tap the person on the shoulder or wave your hand. Look directly at the person and speak clearly, slowly, and expressively to establish if the person can read your lips. For those who do lip-read, be sensitive to their needs by facing the light source. and keeping hands and food away from your mouth when speaking.

10. Relax. Don't be embarrassed if you happen to use accepted, common expressions, such as "See you later" or "Did you hear about this," that seem to relate to the person's disability.

Source: Adapted by Karen Meyer for United Cerebral Palsy Associations, Inc.

The impact of the accommodation on business operations. Even an affordable accommodation might be an undue hardship if it changes the nature of your business.

> **EXAMPLE:** Flo, who has an eyesight problem, applies for a waitress job at Rendezvous Night Club. The club keeps its lights dim to create an intimate setting. Flo requests bright lighting so that she can see to take orders. Rendezvous doesn't have to accommodate her; to do so would seriously affect the nature of the business. If Flo were applying for a bookkeeping position at the same nightclub, and would work in a poorly lit office away from customer areas, the employer could be required to provide brighter lighting as a reasonable accommodation.

Similarly, you wouldn't be required to raise the workplace temperature to accommodate a disabled employee if doing so would make it uncomfortably hot for other employees or customers. That solution would be unduly disruptive. You could be required to provide a small space heater, however.

Deciding What Accommodations Are Needed

Figuring out viable accommodations usually requires cooperation between the employer and the applicant or employee with a disability. In fact, you are legally required to engage in an interactive dialogue with the employee. If a person with a disability asks for an accommodation, chances are excellent that the individual will be able to explain the functional limitations to you. But, if the person isn't articulate or is medically unsophisticated, it may take a letter from a doctor or psychologist to clarify the nature of the problem.

You may have your own creative ideas about an appropriate accommodation, but don't overlook the person with a disability as a good source of ideas. In fact, the EEOC recommends that you consult with the employee or applicant to identify potential accommodations and assess how effective each would be in enabling the person to do the job. Such consultation gets the relationship started on a positive note, as you and the individual are working together to solve a problem. Moreover, this cooperative approach can yield dollars-and-cents benefits to your business; a person with a disability is often able to suggest a cost-effective accommodation that you wouldn't have considered.

> **EXAMPLE:** Tandex Company, a small manufacturer, believes that hiring Chester, a prospective employee who uses a wheelchair, will require it to install a special lower drinking fountain. Chester, however, points out that he can use the existing fountain if Tandex simply provides paper cups next to the fountain.

Sometimes, there are several accommodations that would enable a person with a disability to handle a job. The EEOC recommends that you consider the preference of the disabled person. Still, under the ADA, you're free to make the final choice. For example, you may select an accommodation that's cheaper or easier to provide than the one requested by the employee.

Refusing an accommodation can be costly. So, think twice before you decide to save a few dollars by denying a reasonable accommodation to a worker with a disability.

> **EXAMPLE:** Carol, a computer operator with multiple sclerosis, asked her employer for a covered parking space. Carol's doctor confirmed to the employer that the heat of an uncovered space would worsen her condition. Nevertheless, the employer refused, claiming it had already made a number of accommodations for Carol's illness. When Carol's condition worsened and she became bedridden, she sued. She was awarded $225,000, considerably more than what it would have cost the employer to grant the request for a covered space.

SEE AN EXPERT

Get help identifying reasonable accommodations. The Job Accommodation Network (JAN) is a federally funded service that provides free information and advice on making reasonable accommodations for employees with disabilities. For a telephone consultation, call 800-526-7234. Visit the agency's website at www.askjan.org for more information. You can also seek assistance from the U.S. Equal Employment Opportunity Commission, from state or local vocational rehabilitation agencies, or from state or local organizations representing or providing services to individuals with disabilities.

Improving Accessibility

As an employer, you must make it possible for an individual to apply for a job, which may include moving the interview site. You must also provide access to the job for an employee with a disability. This includes access to a building, to a worksite, to needed equipment, and to all facilities used by the employee. You must provide such access unless it would cause an undue hardship.

The ADA doesn't require you to change existing facilities unless and until a particular applicant or employee with a particular disability needs an accommodation. Then the modifications should meet that individual's work needs. You don't have to make changes to provide access in places or facilities that won't be used by that person.

Here are some workplace alterations you might consider:

- Install a ramp at the entrance to your building.
- Remove raised thresholds.
- Reserve wide parking spaces close to the worksite for people in wheelchairs.
- Provide accessible toilet stalls, sinks, soap, and towels in rest rooms.
- Rearrange office furniture and equipment.
- Make drinking fountains accessible.
- Provide clear paths to copying machines, meeting and training rooms, lunchrooms, and lounges.
- Remove potential hazards from the path of blind people.
- Add flashing lights to alarm bells to alert hearing-impaired people in an emergency.

Other Types of Accommodation

Not all accommodations involve physical changes to the workplace. As the COVID-19 pandemic has shown, a wide variety of jobs are capable of being performed remotely. If you're not able to offer remote work, there are other things you can do to help qualified people with disabilities work effectively. You might, for example, restructure a job by transferring marginal or nonessential functions to another employee. Or you might modify work schedules. You could permit a worker with a mental disability to take off time for twice-a-week visits to a psychiatrist. Or you could assign a fixed shift to a diabetic employee who needs to eat on a regular schedule and take insulin at set times each day, departing from your usual practice of requiring employees to rotate their shifts.

Solutions That Don't Cost a Bundle

As noted earlier, the Job Accommodation Network (JAN) is a free service funded by the federal government. Its consultants can offer practical suggestions for accommodating disabled workers. You can reach JAN by calling 800-526-7234 or logging on to its website at www.askjan.org.

Many examples from JAN and other sources for accommodating people with disabilities are contained in *A Technical Assistance Manual on the Employment Provisions (Title I) of the Americans with Disabilities Act.*

Here are some examples of low-cost accommodations:

- A timer with an indicator light allowed a medical technician who was deaf to perform laboratory tests. *Cost: $27*
- A clerk with limited use of her hands was provided a rotating file holder that enabled her to reach all materials needed for her job. *Cost: $85*
- A groundskeeper who had limited use of one arm was provided a detachable extension arm for a rake. This enabled him to grasp the handle on the extension with his impaired hand and control the rake with his functional arm. *Cost: $20*
- A desk layout was changed from the right to the left side to enable a data entry operator who is visually impaired to perform her job. *Cost: $0*
- A telephone amplifier designed to work with a hearing aid allowed a plant worker to retain his job and avoid being transferred to a lower-paying job. *Cost: $24*

Similarly, a reasonable accommodation might consist of having a flexible leave policy. You don't have to give additional paid leave, but consider allowing employees to use accrued leave or leave without pay to get needed rest or medical treatment. Or, you may decide that it's better to reassign an employee to a different job. But be careful in choosing this option. To avoid discriminating against other employees on the job, it's best to reassign the worker to a position that is vacant and for which the worker is qualified.

Often you can buy equipment—or modify existing equipment—to accommodate an employee. Some examples of equipment and devices that may be used include:

- TDDs (Telecommunication Devices for the Deaf) that enable people with hearing or speech impairments to communicate over the phone
- telephone amplifiers, useful for people with hearing impairments
- software to enlarge print or convert print documents to spoken words for people with vision or reading disabilities
- telephone headsets and adaptive lights for people with cerebral palsy or other manual difficulties, and
- speakerphones, effective for people who are amputees or have other mobility impairments.

Many of these technologies are dramatically more affordable than in years past. And they'll be well worth the cost if they allow you to attract and retain qualified employees.

Workers With Emotional or Mental Impairments

According to the EEOC, about 13% of ADA cases involve workers claiming emotional or psychiatric impairment. This includes workers with anxiety disorders, depression, bipolar disorder, and schizophrenia.

The EEOC has issued guidelines to help you meet your responsibilities to workers and job applicants with these and other mental disabilities.

Covered Disorders

The ADA protects workers who have a mental impairment that limits a major life activity or have a record of such an impairment. The impairment must be more than just a short-term problem. The EEOC offers these examples:

- Jane has had major depression for almost a year. She has been intensely sad and withdrawn and has had problems sleeping and difficulty concentrating. The depth and duration of her problems qualify her for ADA protection.
- Joe, on the other hand, was distressed by his breakup with his girlfriend and, for about a month, sometimes became agitated at work. He sought counseling and his mood improved. He doesn't have a disability under the ADA.

Handling Psychiatric Information

Your job application form must not ask about mental or emotional illness or psychiatric disability, treatment, or hospitalization. You may not ask any disability-related questions before you offer someone a job. You can inquire further if an applicant asks for a reasonable accommodation for the hiring process itself, however.

For example, suppose an applicant for a secretarial job asks to take a typing test in a quiet location instead of a busy reception area "because of a medical condition." You can ask for additional information to verify that the applicant needs a quiet location for the test.

After you offer someone a job, you can require a medical or psychiatric exam, as long as you do the same for all entering employees in that job category.

Be sure to keep medical information confidential. This includes psychiatric information. You can only share this information with supervisors on a need-to-know basis and with first aid and safety workers who may need to deal with emergencies.

Probably the knottiest confidentiality problem is what to tell other employees when you provide time off or other accommodations to a worker with psychiatric problems. In response to coworkers' questions, you can say, for example, that you're "acting for legitimate business reasons" or "acting in compliance with applicable laws," but not much more.

Reasonable Accommodations

Reasonable accommodations vary from case to case. Examples of some accommodations that may reasonably be required for a person with a mental disability include:

- giving the employee time off from work or a modified work schedule
- installing room dividers, partitions, or other soundproofing or visual barriers between workspaces for an employee who has trouble concentrating
- moving an employee away from noisy machinery or lowering the volume or pitch of telephones
- allowing remote work
- providing a job coach
- modifying a workplace policy, and
- adjusting supervisory methods.

The last two points—workplace policies and supervision—provide the most common glitches for employers. A couple of illustrations may help.

EXAMPLE 1: Workplace policies: A store doesn't let its cashiers drink beverages at checkout stations. Cashiers are limited to two 15-minute breaks during an eight-hour shift, in addition to a meal break. Lillian, a cashier, needs to drink water every hour to combat dry mouth, a side effect of psychiatric medicine she takes. To accommodate Lillian, the store should consider changing its policy against drinking beverages at checkout stations or changing its policy limiting cashiers to two 15-minute breaks.

EXAMPLE 2: Supervision: Ted asks for more guidance and feedback because of limitations associated with his psychiatric disability. It's reasonable for Ted's employer to consult with him, his doctor, and his supervisor to work out a plan for adding structure to his job, such as weekly meetings with the supervisor to review long-term projects.

On a related point, you're not expected to make sure that an employee takes medication as prescribed.

Unacceptable Conduct

You remain free to discipline an employee for violating standards of conduct, even if the misconduct resulted from a mental disability. Nothing in the ADA prevents you from maintaining a workplace free of violence or threats of violence or from disciplining a worker who steals or destroys property, for example.

In some cases, strict enforcement of an employer's dress code and courtesy rules can violate the ADA rules, especially if the enforcement isn't necessary from a business standpoint.

EXAMPLE: Arthur, an employee with a psychiatric disability, works in a warehouse loading boxes onto pallets. He has no customer contact and doesn't come into regular contact with other workers. Lately, Arthur has come to work appearing disheveled. His clothes don't fit right and are torn. When coworkers try to engage him in small talk, he turns his back and walks away. When he must talk to a coworker, he's abrupt and rude. The employer's handbook requires employees to have a neat appearance and to be courteous to one another. Arthur claims that his appearance and behavior are the result of a psychiatric disability and that the rules shouldn't be strictly applied to him. The EEOC agrees, based on its conclusion that these rules of conduct are not job related for Arthur's warehouse job. Because Arthur has no customer contact and doesn't come into regular contact with other employees, the standards aren't a business necessity. Therefore, the EEOC reasons, if the employer discharges or disciplines Arthur for not complying the rules, the employer is violating the ADA.

Here are examples of some other situations in which an employer may have to yield to or provide an accommodation for an employee's disruptive conduct if the conduct results from a psychiatric condition:

- A reference librarian with Tourette Syndrome frequently loses her temper, disrupting the library atmosphere by shouting at patrons and coworkers. Her employer may discipline her for violating a rule prohibiting disruptive conduct because the rule is job related and consistent with business necessity. But the employer should grant a request for a leave of absence to seek treatment for her condition, as long as it won't cause an undue hardship.
- An employee with depression is often late because his medicine makes him groggy in the morning. He can be disciplined for his tardiness, but the employer should consider adjusting the work schedule, to allow him to arrive later.

Financial Assistance

There may be financial help available to assist you in complying with the ADA.

Tax Credit for Small Businesses

If your business has gross receipts of $1 million or less for the tax year, or if you have 30 or fewer full-time employees, you can take a tax credit of up to $5,000 a year for accommodations you make to comply with the ADA. You can take this credit for one-half the cost of certain access expenses, including removing physical barriers and providing interpreters or readers. The credit applies to expenses only to the extent that they exceed $250, up to $10,250.

> **EXAMPLE:** ABC Company spends $10,250 to widen doorways to accommodate employees in wheelchairs. The company gets a tax credit of $5,000 (($10,250 − $250) ÷ 2).

To be eligible, you must meet the ADA Accessibility Guidelines. These are available for viewing and downloading at www.access-board.gov, the website maintained by the United States Access Board. The guidelines deal with technical details on accessible design, such as how wide aisles must be to accommodate the needs of people using wheelchairs.

Tax Deduction for Removing Barriers

Any business can deduct up to $15,000 a year for the cost of removing specified architectural and transportation barriers, including steps, narrow doors and inadequate parking spaces, toilet facilities, and vehicles. If your business meets the size and income requirements for the tax credit described above, it can take both the tax credit and the tax deduction. The allowable deduction is equal to the difference between the total expenditures and the amount of the credit claimed. Contact a local IRS office for more details.

> **EXAMPLE:** CompuWay Corporation, a company with gross receipts of $950,000, spends $20,000 to widen its parking spaces and to add wide bathroom stalls that are accessible to workers with disabilities. CompuWay can take the $5,000 tax credit and can deduct the remaining $15,000 of expenditures from its taxable income.

Health and Safety Standards

The ADA doesn't stop you from establishing standards to ensure that your workplace is safe and that your workers are qualified and competent. You're free to set minimum requirements based on education, skills, and work experience, and to specify physical and mental standards needed for job performance, health, and safety. And, you're able to hire the best qualified person for a job. However, the ADA requires that your standards and selection criteria for workers be job related and consistent with real business needs.

⚠ CAUTION

Don't forget the reasonable accommodation rule. If your job standards are job related and consistent with your business needs, you must also consider whether a person with a disability could meet the standards through a reasonable accommodation, such as a modified workstation or special equipment.

You can require, as a job standard, that a person not pose a direct threat to the person's own health and safety or to the health and safety of others in the workplace.

> **EXAMPLE:** Alex applies for a position at Truck Parts Unlimited. The job requires employees to use a forklift truck to move heavy loads through a parts storage facility. Alex is disabled by narcolepsy; he frequently and unexpectedly loses consciousness. The job poses a risk to Alex and other employees working in the building, since they could be seriously injured if Alex were to lose consciousness while operating the fork-lift truck. Because the risk to others can't be reduced by reasonable accommodation, Truck Parts Unlimited may refuse to hire Alex without violating the ADA.

The ADA requirements for exempting job candidates on health or safety grounds are intentionally tough. They are designed to prevent employers from acting on a stereotype or patronizing assumptions about people with disabilities. If you plan to exclude someone from consideration for a particular job on health or safety grounds, be sure you have specific evidence that the employee would create a risk.

Special Rules for Food Handlers

The ADA recognizes that people with certain infectious or communicable diseases may be a direct threat to the health or safety of others if they're handling food. Each year, the U.S. Department of Health and Human Services and its Centers for Disease Control and Prevention update a list of contagious diseases that may be transmitted through food handling, such as hepatitis and salmonella poisoning. The list is short and, in conformance with medical opinion, doesn't include AIDS or the HIV virus.

The list emphasizes that the greatest danger of food-transmitted disease comes from infected animals and contamination in food processing. If someone with a listed disease applies for a food handling job, the usual rules apply: Consider whether there's a reasonable accommodation that would eliminate risks to the health of others. In the case of an employee who becomes infected with one of the diseases on the list, see if you can reassign the person to a job that doesn't require food handling. Be sure that the person is qualified, the job is vacant, and the reassignment wouldn't pose an undue hardship.

Medical Exams

The strict ADA rules that govern medical inquiries and exams during the hiring process are described in Chapter 1. After you hire someone, the rules are even tougher. Any medical exam or medical inquiry about the employee must be job related and justified by business necessity. You may order an exam if you learn of a problem related to job performance or safety, but, again, the exam must be related to job performance. In the case of a physically demanding job, you may order an exam to find out if employees continue to be fit to perform the work.

> **EXAMPLE:** Nelson is a warehouse laborer. He has a back impairment that affects his ability to lift objects. Nelson's employer can require that he be examined by an orthopedic surgeon, but can't require Nelson to submit to an HIV test. Such a test isn't related to either the job or to Nelson's impairment.

You can, however, order a medical exam or make medical inquiries if any of the following is true:
- An employee is having difficulty performing the job effectively.
- An employee becomes disabled.
- The exam is needed for you to make a reasonable accommodation to an employee's disability.
- Exams, screening, or monitoring are required by other laws.

You can also conduct medical exams and tests as part of wellness and health screening programs, but only if they are voluntary.

Enforcement

As explained previously, the EEOC enforces the employment provisions of the ADA. The EEOC sometimes investigates charges of discrimination and attempts to resolve any discrimination it finds. If those attempts don't succeed, the EEOC may sue on its own or—more likely—may issue a right-to-sue letter to the person who filed the charge.

The EEOC has acknowledged that disputes about ADA requirements are often the result of misunderstandings between employers and people with disabilities. It emphasizes that those who have a conflict should try to resolve these disputes through informal negotiation or mediation if possible.

If an ADA case goes through the formal enforcement procedures and your business is found to have discriminated, you may be ordered to take a number of steps, including hiring, reinstating, or promoting the individual; giving back pay or front pay; making reasonable accommodation; or taking other actions. Your company may also have to pay lawyers' fees, expert witness fees, and court costs. What's more, if you're found to have discriminated intentionally, your company may have to pay compensatory and punitive damages. For that reason, consider seeking legal advice before determining that a disabled employee or applicant can't be reasonably accommodated in your workplace.

 RESOURCE
The following sources can provide additional information about the ADA.

Information About Employment Provisions:

Equal Employment Opportunity Commission
www.eeoc.gov and www.eeoc.gov/coronavirus for
COVID-19 information

Information About Public Accommodation Provisions:

U.S. Department of Justice
Civil Rights Division Disability Rights Section—NYA
www.justice.gov/crt/disability-rights-section

The United States Access Board
www.access-board.gov

Termination

M ost employees don't have job security: Absent a written contract, employment is "at will." For the most part, that means you're free to fire the employee for any reason or for no reason at all. On the flip side, the employee can quit at any time, for any reason.

There are some limits, however, on your right to freely fire an at-will employee. As explained below, some of the limits are based on statutes prohibiting things like racial or gender discrimination; other limits are founded on "public policy." In addition, courts sometimes find that an employee has attained job security based on the employer's oral promises or statements in an employee handbook or other document.

And even if it looks like you're on safe legal ground when it becomes necessary to fire an employee, it pays to proceed cautiously. After all, if an employee is fired for no reason or is given a reason that looks like a flimsy excuse, the employee is bound to be suspicious that you're covering something up, maybe even an illegal motive. And juries, composed of people who are mostly employees themselves, are often sympathetic to fired workers. The guidelines in this chapter are designed to help keep you out of court when it's time to let an employee go.

RESOURCE

Want more information on firing employees legally? For a more in-depth discussion of how to fire employees without running afoul of the law or harming your business, see *Dealing With Problem Employees,* by Amy DelPo and Lisa Guerin (Nolo).

Wrongful Discharge Cases

Cases in which a former employee claims that employment was terminated for an improper reason or that an employer bungled the process are known as wrongful discharge or wrongful termination cases. These lawsuits are based on a number of legal theories. You can better avoid being sued for wrongful discharge if you grasp these legal principles.

Because the laws and court decisions of each state vary, not all of the legal theories for wrongful discharge will be available to all former employees. Also, because the law can change, you need to keep up to date on the specific rules in your state.

Statutes

If you discriminate illegally in firing an employee, a statute may give that employee the right to sue you for wrongful discharge. Other statutes prohibit firing an employee for specified reasons, like whistleblowing or complaining about workplace hazards.

You may not fire even an at-will employee for reasons that violate statutory rights granted by Congress, your state legislature, or your local government. Illegal reasons for firing include:

- **Discrimination.** Under federal laws and the laws of many states, you may not fire an employee based on race, color, national origin, sex, sexual orientation, gender identity, religion, disability, age, and so on. (Chapter 8 gives detailed information on discrimination claims; disability discrimination is covered in Chapter 9.)

- **Retaliation for complaining about harassment or discrimination.** The same laws that prohibit discrimination and harassment also protect employees who file complaints. After all, if an employee could be fired for complaining of discrimination, the employer would never be held to account for its potentially illegal behavior.

- **Other types of retaliation.** Many laws intended to protect employees also prohibit retaliation against employees who complain about legal violations. For example, you may not fire an employee who complains of wage and hour violations (covered in Chapter 3), health and safety violations (see Chapter 7), violations of the FMLA (covered in Chapter 6), and more.

- **Whistleblowing.** Many states have passed laws protecting employees who raise certain types of workplace concerns—for example, about food safety, product liability concerns, accounting irregularities, and other potentially dangerous and illegal activities. The purpose of these laws is to encourage employees to come forward with this information, to protect public health and safety.

Court Decisions

Wrongful discharge lawsuits are not always based on statutes. Many courts have awarded wrongful discharge damages to former employees for non-statutory or common law reasons: legal theories that courts have developed when deciding individual cases.

Breach of Contract

Employers sometimes make promises to job applicants to entice them to become employees. And some employers may also dangle inducements in front of current employees to discourage them from leaving. A number of judges have ruled that, if a person relies on such promises, an enforceable contract of employment can be created. An employer may be held liable for wrongful discharge if the employee is fired in violation of that contract.

> **EXAMPLE:** Betty, a diligent worker at AutoTec, is offered a job by a rival employer. She declines the job after AutoTec's president tells her she'll have a job for life at AutoTec if she continues to effectively manage her workload. Three years later, AutoTec fires Betty, even though she has kept up with her work. Betty sues for wrongful discharge, claiming AutoTec violated its employment contract with her by firing her.

Specific promises of job security—either written or oral—are not always necessary for a judge to rule that an employee can't be fired arbitrarily. Some judges have allowed fired employees to collect damages or be reinstated to jobs because the employer created a legitimate expectation that employees wouldn't be fired without good cause. The typical focus in these cases is on implications of job security made by the employer in a written document such as an employee handbook. It, too, may be enforced as a contract. As explained in Chapter 2, you can avoid these claims by including language in your employee handbook that reminds employees that employment is at will, and that the at-will relationship can be modified by written contract signed only by a high level employee (like the president of the company).

> **EXAMPLE:** After six months on the job, Tom is fired from Syspro, a small software house. He sues for wrongful discharge, claiming that Syspro fired him without a good reason even though its employee handbook led him to believe that he'd only be fired for good cause. The judge agrees that it was reasonable for Tom to conclude, after reading the employee handbook, that his job was secure. The court rules that the employer's wording of the handbook constituted an implied contract.

Breach of Good Faith and Fair Dealing

Some wrongful discharge cases are based on the premise that every employment relationship includes an automatic commitment by the employer to deal fairly and in good faith with the employee. Applying this doctrine, judges have held that a discharge was wrongful when an employer has dealt arbitrarily with an employee. Many of these cases have involved longtime employees who were fired as they neared retirement age.

> **EXAMPLE:** Rita has worked for Jones Enterprises for nearly 25 years. The company fires her just three months before her retirement benefits are to become permanent. In a wrongful discharge case against Jones, the judge finds that the company fired Rita to save itself the expense of paying her the full benefit of her retirement program. The judge rules in Rita's favor because the firing breached the implied covenant of good faith and fair dealing.

Violation of Public Policy

Judges sometimes rule that a firing was wrongful because it was against the best interests of the public. Most courts do not allow an employer to fire an employee who was trying to correct an illegal or dangerous business practice, for example.

> **EXAMPLE:** Clifford Robotics, a small company that designs and builds robots for industrial uses, fires Richard, an engineer, because he complained to management twice that workers who had tested positive for COVID-19 were not being allowed to stay home from work. A judge rules that Richard's firing was wrongful because it violated public policy. Workers, the judge notes, should be free to speak up about unsafe practices they find on the job, especially those affecting public health or safety.

Courts have held that it's against public policy to fire a worker for refusing to file phony reports with a state environmental agency, bribe public officials, commit perjury, or engage in industrial espionage. Courts have also held that it is against public policy to fire an employee for refusing to commit an illegal act or for threatening to report an employer's illegal conduct. And it generally violates public policy to fire a worker for exercising a legal right, such as the right to vote or serve on a jury.

Guarding Against Legal Claims

Given the many legal weapons that a disgruntled fired worker can aim at you under the rubric of a wrongful discharge lawsuit, you can understand the danger in blithely relying on your unfettered right to fire any employee. Consider, too, that juries are often sympathetic to fired workers, regarding them as underdogs even in the face of evidence to the contrary.

Having a Valid Reason

The safest approach any time you fire someone is to be sure you have a legitimate business reason, one that you've carefully considered and documented. If challenged on a particular firing, you should be able to show, for example, that the employee did not adequately perform specific job duties or that the employee violated a clearly stated company policy.

> **EXAMPLE:** The Mail Shoppe employs two men and one woman, Virginia, in its packaging department. One Friday afternoon, the owner fires Virginia. She then files a lawsuit claiming she's been discriminated against because of gender. In court, The Mail Shoppe's owner is able to show that Virginia frequently put too little postage on packages and often neglected to insert the bubble wrap as instructed, causing breakage and numerous customer complaints. The owner also shows that three written warnings were given to Virginia over a six-week period. The judge dismisses the gender discrimination complaint.

In addition to bolstering your legal position, using an open and consistent policy for disciplining and firing employees will usually help improve worker morale. It's reassuring to hardworking, competent employees to know that they won't be fired on a whim. They'll also respect you for knowing who's getting the job done and who isn't. And, they'll likely feel relieved when lazy and incompetent workers are let go.

Safely Handling Layoffs

Usually, you're free to lay off or terminate employees because business conditions require a reduction in the workforce. But, don't leave your business open to claims that the layoffs were really a pretext for getting rid of employees for illegal reasons. If your layoff primarily affects black workers, for example, someone may well question your motives. So if you need to reduce your workforce, be sensitive to how your actions may be perceived. Spread the pain around; don't let the burden of a reduction in force fall on just one group of employees.

If you're a larger employer, you must comply with the Worker Adjustment and Retraining Notification Act, or WARN. (29 U.S.C. §§ 2101 and following.) The law covers your business if either of the following is true:

- You have 100 or more full-time employees.
- You have 100 or more employees whose total work amounts to 4,000 or more hours a week, not counting overtime hours.

To comply with WARN, you must notify employees if you plan to:

- close an employment site, causing 50 or more full-time employees at the site to lose their jobs
- lay off at least one-third—but not fewer than 50—of the full-time employees at a site, or
- lay off 500 or more employees at one site.

In those situations, you must notify each employee—or the employee's union representative—in writing 60 days before you close the site or lay off the employees. You must also send written notice to the state's dislocated worker unit and the chief elected officer of the municipality where the closing or layoff will take place. There are a number of exceptions to WARN. For example, you needn't give a full 60 days' notice if a closing or layoff is caused by unforeseen business circumstances or a natural disaster.

If you fail to give the required notice, your employees can sue you for back pay and benefits. You may also have to pay penalties if you don't give timely notice to the local government.

A handful of states have passed their own layoff notice laws. These laws apply to employers with fewer than 100 employees, who would not be covered by the federal WARN law. Check with your state's labor department or consult an employment lawyer for more information.

RESOURCE

WARN and the COVID-19 pandemic. To learn more about how the WARN Act applies to layoffs made as a result of the COVID-19 pandemic, go to www.dol.gov/agencies/eta/layoffs/warn. For more general information for employers about WARN, visit www.dol.gov/sites/dolgov/files/ETA/Layoff/pdfs/_EmployerWARN2003.pdf. And detailed information on WARN's requirements and prohibitions—and a complete list of the exceptions to WARN—can be found in *The Essential Guide to Federal Employment Laws*, by Lisa Guerin and Sachi Barreiro (Nolo).

Guidelines for Firing Employees

Even though your motives for firing someone may be completely honorable and legitimate, you still run a legal risk that the employee may decide to go to court, regardless of your actions. But there are several steps you can take to greatly reduce the chances of a former employee suing your business and being awarded a judgment against you.

Contractual Commitments

Before you fire an employee, check into whether you, or anyone else in the company, made an oral or written contractual commitment that may limit your right to fire. Consider the following:

- Is there a written or oral contract or document (including a hiring letter) that promises the employee a job for a fixed period of time?
- When you hired the employee, did you make any statements about job security?
- Have you assured the employee that you'd fire him or her only for good cause?
- Have you listed causes for termination—in a contract, employee handbook, or elsewhere—in a way that limits you to those specified causes?
- Does your employee handbook or other written policy or memo make any promises about job security?

Your answers to these questions will help you identify whether you've limited your ability to fire the individual. Even if you are positive that you have never given the employee any assurances of job security—either oral or written—you should still proceed with caution, especially when dealing with an employee who has been with your business for a number of years. Some courts have held that a long employment relationship can imply assurances of job security, which can be evidence of an implied employment contract that limits your ability to fire the employee. If an employee has been working for you only for a few months—or even for a year—you probably don't have to worry about this issue. If the employee has been with your business for, say, ten years, however, you should be careful. If you don't have a really good reason for firing the employee, consider consulting a lawyer before taking action.

Employment contracts can be a two-way street. While they may limit your right to fire an employee, the flip side is that they usually spell out the employee's obligations to your business. If employees aren't performing well, chances are that they are in breach of the contract, giving you the legal right to terminate the relationship. Because the interpretation of contract terms can involve legal subtleties, consider having a brief conference with a lawyer before firing an employee who has a written contract.

Say What You Mean and Mean What You Say

The words you use in hiring someone and in writing an employee handbook can create a contractual commitment unintentionally. To prevent this, your employee handbook and similar documents should reserve your right to terminate employees at your discretion. While you may also wish to list some specific types of conduct that will result in termination, such as dishonesty or excessive absenteeism, those shouldn't be stated in a way that implies they are the *only* reasons to end the relationship. Also, your handbook and other communications with employees should not make any promises about long-term job security. If they do, it's time for a rewrite.

Lawful Reasons for Firing

To head off the possibility that an employee may try to base a wrongful termination action on alleged illegal conduct or motives in your workplace, be prepared to show the real—legitimate—reason for the firing.

Reasons that may support a firing include:

- performing poorly on the job
- refusing to follow instructions
- unexcused absences
- being tardy habitually
- possessing a weapon at work
- violating company rules
- being dishonest
- endangering health and safety
- engaging in criminal activity
- using alcohol or drugs at work
- behaving violently at work
- gambling at work, or
- disclosing company trade secrets to outsiders.

A Firing Is Sometimes Implied

Usually, it's clear when an employee has been fired. That's because the employer typically informs the employee of that fact in no uncertain terms. But sometimes, if an employer's conduct is so extreme that it makes it virtually impossible for the employee to continue on the job, the employer's conduct may be treated as being equal to a formal firing. In legal jargon, this is called a "constructive discharge."

This can occur, for example, where an employer has:

- created an abusive or hostile environment
- insisted that an employee put in excessive overtime
- subjected the employee to intolerable working conditions
- refused to create a COVID-safe workplace
- offered the employee a "quit or be fired" ultimatum
- substantially changed the employee's job duties, or
- harassed the employee.

The legal consequences of a constructive discharge are exactly the same as an actual discharge: If the employee can show that working conditions really were intolerable, the employee will be able to seek damages for being wrongfully discharged under any of the legal theories discussed above.

Depending on the nature of your business, you may have other legitimate reasons to fire employees as well. Whatever your reasons, it's absolutely essential that you treat your employees evenhandedly. That is, if you regularly let some employees engage in prohibited conduct, you'll be on shaky legal ground if you fire others for the same reason.

> **EXAMPLE:** Andrew, a black attendant, is a half-hour late for work three days in a row. His employer, a medical clinic, fires him. In suing for wrongful discharge based on illegal discrimination, Andrew shows that two white attendants had been similarly tardy in recent weeks but received only a verbal warning to shape up. Even though excessive tardiness is a valid business reason for firing someone, the jury awards damages to Andrew because it looked like he was being singled out due to his race.

Independent Review

Avoid giving an employee's direct supervisor the sole authority to hire and fire. The supervisor may be too close to the situation to make an objective decision. Because firing is such a drastic and traumatic step—and has such potentially serious legal consequences—consider conducting an independent review within your business before anyone is fired. Although this may not be practical in small companies, you should use this procedure if it's feasible.

Any independent review should verify all of the following:
- The firing wouldn't violate antidiscrimination or other statutes.
- The firing wouldn't be a breach of contract, including oral assurances of job security or statements made in an employee handbook.
- Your company has given the employee adequate and documented warnings, except if the misconduct clearly warrants immediate firing.
- You have followed your stated personnel practices.
- You have followed the same procedures in similar situations involving other employees.

Investigating Complaints Against Workers

You may learn of misconduct that requires you to discipline or fire an employee from a complaint by a coworker, a manager, or even a customer or another outsider. This is particularly likely with complaints of sexual harassment or dishonesty.

Investigating the facts can be tricky. The law doesn't require you to learn the truth with absolutely certainty. But, to protect yourself legally, your safest course is to investigate complaints quickly, thoroughly, fairly, and as confidentially as is possible under the circumstances, before you discipline or fire an employee.

RESOURCE

Want more information on investigations? For a detailed discussion of investigating employee complaints, including step-by-step instructions and sample forms, see *The Essential Guide to Workplace Investigations,* by Lisa Guerin (Nolo).

The Investigation

Privately interview each witness and the accused employee. Listen carefully and take good notes. Don't show any bias for or against the accused. Further investigate any evidence that surfaces, such as a claim that another employee is aware of facts that will shed light on the complaint. Have good reasons for whatever conclusions you reach. If you follow reasonable procedures and reach a reasonable result, you can't be faulted legally, even if another person may have reached a different conclusion.

After an employee files a complaint, it's a good idea to keep the complaining employee informed about the general steps you're taking to investigate. The complaining employee needs to know that you're taking the matter seriously. But that doesn't mean the employee is entitled to know all the details of what you find out. If you give out information too freely, you could easily step on the toes (and violate the privacy rights) of other employees.

Hiring Investigators

If you have qualms about your ability to investigate a complaint, consider hiring an experienced employment consultant or someone else who knows the ropes. Far better to lay out some cash to do it right than risk the consequences of a clumsy investigation. For example, if there's an issue of employee dishonesty or criminal conduct, look into companies that specialize in corporate security.

Similarly, if someone charges sexual harassment because a manager has displayed offensive cartoons or photos in a work area, consider hiring a consultant experienced in sexual harassment issues to review your entire workplace and recommend a course of action. Bringing in an outsider may also help to defuse tensions between workers, especially if anyone involved in the incident doubts the company's ability to be impartial.

Locating a Good Investigator

When you suspect an employee of dishonesty or criminal conduct, a private investigator may help sort out the facts. The job of interviewing witnesses, analyzing documents, watching for misconduct, and preserving evidence isn't easy. The investigator must follow procedures that respect the accused employee's legal rights. If a court later finds that you trampled an employee's due process rights during an investigation, your business may have to pay for that violation.

It's crucial to find an investigator who's experienced in conducting internal investigations for businesses. There are many people who have recently hung out their shingles as consultants but don't really have training or experience.

This is sensitive work, and the stakes are high. No matter where you find names of possible investigators—from Internet searches, management newsletters, trade associations, or other businesspeople—ask for references. Look for positive feedback from at least two or three other businesses before you hire an investigator.

> CAUTION
> **If your lawyer investigates, another lawyer should litigate.** You may choose to have an experienced employment lawyer conduct a workplace investigation, but be careful if you do. Although the information you share with your attorney is usually confidential and doesn't have to be disclosed in a lawsuit, this may not be true if the attorney acted as the investigator, as opposed to just giving you legal advice. To be safe, if you do decide to have an attorney conduct the investigation, it's probably best not to use someone you want to represent you in a lawsuit. You don't want your confidential communications disclosed in court.

Alternatives to Firing

Sometimes, firing a troublesome employee is the best course of action. You owe it to your business—and to your diligent, conscientious employees—to get rid of a troublemaker who can't be turned around. But, occasionally, there are good alternatives to firing a worker, which can help you avoid the risk of a wrongful discharge lawsuit while at the same time providing the spared employee with a chance to improve.

One possibility is to redesign the employee's job to eliminate the problem areas. Or you may assign the employee to another job. For example, an employee who has a tendency to quarrel with customers, but is otherwise organized and efficient, might do an excellent job working alone in the warehouse. Of course, you must be careful not to unload work unfairly on other employees.

If yours is a slightly larger business, and there's a personality clash between an employee and a supervisor, you may be able to assign the employee to a different supervisor. Where the conflict is between two employees, neither of whom is a supervisor, you may be able to assign them to separate work areas. If a personal problem is at the root of an otherwise good employee's difficulties, you might offer to pay for at least a limited amount of counseling or offer the employee a leave of absence to get help with the problem.

Sometimes you and an employee can come to an understanding that the working relationship isn't a good fit for either of you and that the employee is expected to move elsewhere in the near future. Allowing the employee to look for a new job during regular working hours may be one rational way to handle such a situation.

If you decide to pursue an alternative to firing, keep in mind that it doesn't offer full protection against a lawsuit. If the employee can characterize a change of duties as a demotion, for example, the employee may still sue the company. For that reason, it's still important to make sure identified problems, and the solutions, are well documented.

The Firing Process

Where possible, give employees ongoing feedback about job performance, conduct formal job evaluations once or twice a year, and impose progressive discipline. Ideally, a firing shouldn't come suddenly or as a surprise.

> **RESOURCE**
>
> **Want more information on improving employee performance through discipline?** See *The Employee Performance Handbook*, by Margie Mader-Clark and Lisa Guerin (Nolo).

When you've reached the point where firing an employee is the best or only option, you must mind some legal restrictions as you carry out the firing.

> **TIP**
>
> **Speedy action is sometimes appropriate.** There can be situations in which moving quickly to fire someone—without a warning—may be the best course. For example, if your delivery truck driver is convicted of drunk driving, it makes sense to get rid of the driver immediately. Similarly, you shouldn't feel it necessary to give advance warning to a bookkeeper who has embezzled money from your company. In general, use your judgment and err on the side of giving an employee a chance to correct a problem. But, in extreme circumstances, especially those involving illegal conduct or the risk of harm to others, don't hesitate to act quickly.

Severance Packages

Many employers and employees wrongly believe that every fired employee is legally entitled to severance pay. The truth is that you have to give severance only if you have promised the employee that you would. Such a promise might be made in a contract with the employee, through a written policy in your employee handbook, or through a clearly established pattern of conduct in which you have given severance to other employees in similar circumstances. Even if the law does not require you to pay severance, however, you may wish to offer severance pay and other benefits to help cushion the impact of a firing (and alleviate ill will).

If you're inclined to offer a severance package, it makes sense to be more generous with longtime employees than with those who have been with you just a year or two. For a short-term employee—someone who's worked for you for two years, for example—you might offer one month's pay. For an employee who's been on your payroll for 15 years, it might be reasonable to offer four to six months of salary.

You can be creative in putting together a severance package. The benefits you may wish to consider include:

- severance pay
- continuation of employee benefits, such as payment of health insurance premiums for a limited time
- a favorable letter of reference if your normal policy is to give only a former employee's position and term of employment
- releasing the employee from special obligations (such as a covenant not to compete)
- allowing the employee to keep any advance of expense funds or commissions that otherwise would be repayable to your business
- allowing the employee to keep the computer, cellphone, or tools that you provided
- agreeing not to contest the employee's right to unemployment compensation
- characterizing the separation as a voluntary resignation or layoff
- paying for outplacement services, or
- promising to pay an employee's moving expenses, up to a stated limit.

Also, consider paying the employee for unused vacation time that the employee would otherwise lose. Unless state law requires you to pay out unused vacation time, you are free to adopt a policy whereby departing employees forfeit any unused vacation days. (To see the law in your state, check out "State Laws That Control Final Paychecks," in the appendix.)

> **EXAMPLE:** Alpine Ski Shop pays its employees for two weeks of vacation time each year but states in its employee handbook: "You must take your vacation during June, July, or August and while you are on Alpine's payroll. Vacation time not used during that period will be forfeited unless you secure prior approval." Employee Kurt takes one week of his vacation in July and doesn't ask for permission to take the second week later. In October, Alpine fires Kurt because of an attitude problem. As part of a severance package, Alpine pays Kurt for the unused week of vacation time.

CAUTION

Paying for vacation time might be mandatory. In some states, the law doesn't allow an employer to set a policy forcing employees to forfeit unused vacation time once it has accrued. In such states, the accrued vacation time is treated as wages and must be included in an employee's final paycheck. Check with your state department of labor to learn how much latitude you have regarding payment for vacation time. (See the appendix for how to find contact details.)

Preparing the Paperwork

Before you fire an employee, prepare a letter describing the severance package you intend to offer. And, if you want the employee to waive possible legal claims against your business to qualify for the severance benefits, consider preparing a severance agreement as well.

Termination Letter

To soften the shock of a firing, you may wish to present the employee with a letter (such as the one below) during the termination meeting.

Use such a letter if you're not requiring the employee to sign a release waiving possible legal claims against your business to qualify for the severance package.

Release of Claims

You may wish to provide a severance package to a terminating employee only if the employee agrees to waive all potential legal claims. For a release to be enforceable, you must offer the employee something of value—for example, the severance package—in exchange for the employee's giving up possible claims against your business.

CAUTION

If the law already requires you to pay severance (for example, because you have already promised it to the employee through a written contract), then you must give something to the employee beyond what the severance package requires in exchange for the employee's signing the release.

Also, give the employee a reasonable time—two or three weeks, for example—to decide whether to accept your severance package and sign the severance agreement containing a release of claims. A coerced release is legally worthless.

Special rules apply if the employee is releasing claims under the Age Discrimination in Employment Act (ADEA). If you present a release to an individual employee who's 40 years old or older, you must give the employee a fixed period of time in which to decide whether to sign the waiver. That period must be at least 21 days if the waiver has been presented to the employee alone. If you've presented the waiver to a group or class of employees, you must give each worker at least 45 days to decide whether to sign. In either case, a worker has seven days after agreeing to such a waiver to revoke the decision. For that reason, you should wait to release the severance check until the revocation period has passed. (See Chapter 8 for details.)

If you plan to ask the employee for a release, talk to a lawyer. Your state law may dictate the language you use, claims you can ask the employee to give up, and other details of the release. A release that doesn't meet these requirements won't stand up in court. An attorney can help you draft a release form that will meet your needs.

Sample Termination Letter— No Release Required

June 10, 20xx

Dear Joe Jones,

Your employment with XYZ Company is being terminated at 5 p.m. on July 1, 20xx.

You will receive a paycheck that includes earned wages and your accrued vacation time. In addition, you will receive the following severance benefits:

1. Four weeks of additional pay at your regular salary.
2. Payment of your health insurance premiums for six months (or until you begin work at a new job, if that occurs sooner).
3. You will be allowed to keep the $500 advanced to you for job-related expenses.
4. The Company will not contest your right to receive unemployment compensation.

I wish you well in your further endeavors.

Lars Ingram
President, XYZ Company

Return of Property

In planning for the termination meeting, make a list of all company property that has been given to the employee. Be prepared to get these items back from the employee either at the meeting or within a reasonable time afterward. Items to think about include:

- automobiles or other vehicles
- laptops, tablets, and cellphones
- confidential manuals and other documents
- keys, key fobs, credit cards, uniforms, ID badges, and
- parking permits.

Don't overlook any expense account funds you advanced to the employee.

The Termination Meeting

Call the employee into a private office or meeting room and announce your decision. Be honest and direct in stating your reasons for ending the employment. If you've given the employee ongoing feedback, the firing shouldn't come as a complete shock. Make it clear that this is a final decision and that you're not going to change your mind. Go over any severance package the employee will receive, and explain the severance agreement if you require one to be signed.

Then give the employee a reasonable chance to vent about the discharge. Just listen and don't argue. Don't insult or abuse the employee even if the employee expresses anger and disappointment. Typically, this will fade with time. Unless the employee is likely to be a menace in the workplace, allow the rest of the day—but no longer—to clear out belongings and say goodbye to coworkers.

Heading Off Trouble

As noted, there are many ways to fortify your legal position so that an employee will be less likely to succeed in a claim against you for wrongful discharge. Some additional practical steps can help you keep the good will of an employee who's being terminated, making it less likely that you'll be sued in the first place.

Offering a Chance to Resign

Permitting the employee to resign gives the employee the opportunity to save face. This, in turn, may make the employee less bitter about the termination and less hostile to your business. Be aware, however, that if you give the employee a stark choice between resigning and being fired, it's probably not legally considered a voluntary termination. The employee likely will be eligible for unemployment compensation benefits. (See below for more about this issue.) And a forced resignation may be treated the same as a firing if the employee does decide to sue for wrongful discharge.

Common Sense Can Help Avert Violence

You may have zeroed in on scary newspaper headlines about disgruntled former employees who open fire on former employers. Although the actual incidence of such violence is quite low, it pays to be prudent.

Violence following a firing is most apt to occur in a workplace where there are high levels of stress, autocratic and unpredictable managers, poor communication, and employees who feel powerless.

Be especially careful if you're firing an employee for performing poorly, a charge that may be emotionally loaded. Some workers who are fired without warning can go over the edge because they feel there was nothing they could do to control the situation. In giving feedback before a firing, let the employee know if performance is below par. Focus on the specific ways job performance falls short of the mark. Warn the employee about the possibility of losing the job if you don't see improvement.

At a termination meeting with a potentially volatile employee, confine your discussion to the specific behavior about which the employee was warned. Never attack the employee personally. Remind the employee that you had given fair warning and an ample opportunity to change work habits.

Let the fired employee know that you won't be discussing the reasons for the firing with the rest of the workers. This will help preserve the employee's self-esteem, making violence less likely.

Troubled employees often exhibit behavioral clues that you shouldn't ignore: high absenteeism, known substance abuse, chronic tardiness, fascination with weapons, and harassing and threatening others. If you're about to fire someone who appears to have a potential for violence, consider consulting first with a psychologist who specializes in workplace issues.

Offering a Favorable Reference

If you would be willing to give a former employee a positive reference, say so. Knowing that there will be a favorable recommendation can help temper a worker's ire over a termination. Obviously, such a reference isn't always possible. But, quite often, an employee who wasn't a good fit at your business could do well elsewhere, and you won't have a difficult time emphasizing the employee's good qualities.

When prospective employers call, follow through and accentuate the positive. Keep in touch with the former employee by phone and by sending copies of any letters in which you state positive things. (For more on references, see "Deciding What to Say," below).

Help Finding a New Job

You may be able to inform an employee of openings elsewhere that would be better suited to the employee's skills and personality. Or, if it's a longtime employee to whom you feel a lot of loyalty, you may even consider footing the bill to have a personnel agency assist the employee in finding another job.

Final Paychecks

Most states have laws specifying when you must give a final paycheck to a terminated employee, which range from immediately (at the time of termination) to the next regular payday. Most of these laws set different deadlines for employees who have quit and those who have been fired. (See "State Laws That Control Final Paychecks," in the appendix.) If you don't give a final paycheck on time, you may have to pay damages to the employee and perhaps a penalty to the employee or state as well.

Note that, in many states, the law requires that the final paycheck include accrued vacation pay and anything else owed to an employee who's covered by the law. If you have additional questions about final paychecks, contact the wage and hour division of your state's labor department to double-check your state law. (See the appendix to find contact details.)

Continuing Health Insurance

If you have 20 or more employees and you offer a group health insurance plan, a federal law called the Consolidated Omnibus Budget Reconciliation Act (COBRA) requires you to offer former employees the option of continuing their coverage for some time after their employment ends. Your state may also have a health insurance continuation law. (See Chapter 4 for more about continuing health care coverage.)

Unemployment Compensation

Unemployment benefits were a vital lifeline to the tens of millions left unemployed during the COVID-19 pandemic, when changes to federal and state laws extended and expanded benefits. (See your state labor department's website for current information on unemployment benefits and the coronavirus pandemic; check the appendix to find contact information.) In normal times, unemployment benefits are usually limited to employees who are terminated because of cutbacks or because they are not a good fit for a job. Employees who are fired for serious misconduct—stealing or selling drugs in the workplace, for example—or who voluntarily leave a job without good cause are not entitled to unemployment payments.

Applying these categories to a particular termination isn't always easy. For example, suppose you and an employee get into an argument and the employee leaves shortly afterward. If the employee has quit, benefits are not legally due. If the employee was fired, however, the employee is entitled to unemployment benefits absent truly bad conduct. It's sometimes difficult to discern whether a termination is a quitting or a firing.

The Claims Process

Although the details of unemployment compensation vary in each state, some general principles apply in most cases. As a private employer, you contribute a relatively small amount to an unemployment insurance fund in your state. Your rate is normally based on the size of your payroll and the amount of unemployment benefits paid from your account. Employers with smaller payrolls and low levels of unemployment claims will, over time, pay less in unemployment taxes.

An unemployment claim typically proceeds through a number of steps:

Filing the Claim

The former employee files a claim with the state unemployment program. You receive written notice of the claim and can file a written objection. Typically, you'll have seven to ten days to object. If you want to file an objection, don't miss this deadline, or you may waive your right to do so.

Eligibility Determined

The state agency makes an initial determination of whether the former employee is eligible to get unemployment benefits. Usually there's no hearing at this stage.

Referee's Hearing

You or the former employee can appeal the initial eligibility decision and request a hearing before a referee: a hearing officer who is on the staff of the state agency. Normally conducted by telephone or in a private room at the unemployment office, this airing of the situation is the most important step in the process. At the hearing, you and the former employee each have your say. In addition, you're entitled to have a lawyer there and to present witnesses and any relevant written records, such as employee evaluations or warning letters.

Before the hearing, ask to see the agency's complete file on the claim. This will give you a chance to be prepared to refute inaccurate statements. Bring all pertinent employment records to the hearing. Also, line up witnesses who can give firsthand testimony about why the former employee was guilty of misconduct, quit voluntarily, or is otherwise ineligible for benefits. If your hearing is by phone, ask the agency how to submit documents and present witness testimony.

It may be too expensive to hire a lawyer to handle an unemployment compensation hearing. In some states, you have the alternative of hiring an experienced nonlawyer specialist to oppose claims, at a fraction of what lawyers charge. A clerk in the referee's office may know of someone who performs these services in your area. But since the procedures in the hearing are designed to be simple and nontechnical, you probably won't need any hired help.

CAUTION

The referee's ruling can seriously affect subsequent lawsuits against the employer. The referee's decision sometimes influences what happens in a related civil lawsuit. For example, if the referee rules that the employee quit because of sexual harassment, that ruling may be decisive in a later harassment lawsuit that the employee brings against your business. Consult a lawyer if you anticipate that complicated legal issues—such as sexual harassment, illegal discrimination, or retaliation—may surface at the hearing.

Administrative Appeal

Either side can appeal the referee's decision to an administrative agency, sometimes called a board of review. This appeal usually is based solely on the testimony and documents recorded at the referee's hearing, although some states allow the review board to hear additional evidence. While the review board is free to draw its own conclusions from the evidence and overrule the referee, it usually goes along with the referee's ruling.

Judicial Appeal

Either side can appeal to the state court system, but this is rare. Typically, a court will overturn the agency's decision only if the decision is contrary to law or isn't supported by substantial evidence.

RESOURCE

Need to know more about unemployment? For more information, see *Controlling Unemployment Insurance Costs: An Employer's Guide*, published by the National Foundation for Unemployment Compensation and Workers Compensation, available online at www.uwcstrategy.org. Although the book recommends taking a more aggressive stance in fighting claims than may be prudent, it also contains lots of useful information.

Saving Money

In theory, you'll save money if you recognize and successfully oppose questionable claims. But this isn't always true, for several reasons. First, lots of claims you think are questionable probably will be allowed under unemployment compensation laws, which are deliberately lenient to give unemployed workers a transitional source of income. Unless there's strong evidence that the employee pilfered from the company or engaged in other fairly extreme conduct, the employee will usually win in a claims contest.

Second, fighting a claim can be time consuming, emotionally draining, and costly for you, especially when balanced against the fact that a few unemployment claims spread over several years are unlikely to greatly increase your insurance rate. Third, fighting an unemployment claim will guarantee an angry former employee who is far more likely to file a lawsuit or try to harm you or your business in some other way. Of course, this might happen anyway. But your challenge to the employee's right to receive unemployment benefits may be the last straw that prompts the former employee to strike back.

Balance the benefits of saving on unemployment taxes against the trouble it takes to fight the claim and the risk of inviting a lawsuit against your business.

In addition to challenging questionable claims, there are other ways you may be able to reduce the costs of unemployment benefits.

Double-check the information your state unemployment agency uses to compute your tax rates and to compute benefits paid to former employees. Make sure the agency's records don't indicate that your business has had more claims filed against it than it really did have. Clerical errors can be costly.

Also, keep in mind that a former employee may be eligible for benefits at first but later become ineligible. For example, three weeks after being fired, a claimant may decide to return to school full time, meaning that the claimant is unavailable to take a new job. Or you may hear that the employee is working for another business but being paid under the table so as to keep getting unemployment benefits. If you learn any such information, notify the state agency promptly.

Protecting Your Business Information

Some employees have access to sensitive business information or trade secrets. When these employees leave—either because they quit or because you've fired them—you may be concerned that they'll use this information to their personal advantages. For example, a former employee may open a business that competes with yours or go to work for a competitor.

Chapter 1 discusses how you may be able to protect yourself by asking certain employees to sign covenants not to compete and agreements not to divulge or use trade secrets. This section explains what to do if a former employee begins to compete unfairly with your business in violation of such a covenant or agreement.

Enforcing Noncompete Agreements

You might assume it would be difficult to learn whether a former employee is competing with you. However, many businesses are fairly public, which makes it difficult for a former employee to hide. Also, there's a good chance that you'll be contacted by your loyal customers if they are approached by the former employee. The lure of a lower price offered by the former employee often isn't enough to win over a customer who suspects the former employee of cheating you.

If the former employee's conduct violates a valid noncompete agreement, you may choose to remind the individual about the terms of the agreement in a letter. You may also be able to contact a competitor if the former employee is using the information on the competitor's behalf.

If that doesn't work, you can seek a court order (called an injunction) to put a legal stop to the unfair activities. You'll probably need to hire a lawyer to help. In some cases, you may want to go straight to court, especially if your company will suffer immediate damage from the employee's conduct, or you don't want to give the employee advance notice that you're going to be bringing a lawsuit.

Fortunately, the procedures for getting a ruling from a judge in this situation are fairly fast and efficient. Your lawyer will likely ask the judge assigned to your case to set an early hearing to decide whether to issue a preliminary injunction: an order that prohibits the former employee from unfairly competing with you while the case is pending. A judge who's convinced that the threat of damage to your business is great may even grant a temporary restraining order forbidding the former employee from taking any action until the initial hearing can be held.

A restraining order or an injunction is a powerful legal weapon. An individual who violates such an order can be found in contempt of court. The punishment for contempt is a fine, imprisonment, or both.

Weighing Your Chances of Success

Whether a judge will enforce a covenant not to compete is always an iffy question. The legal system puts a high value on a person's right to earn a living. In California, noncompetes are illegal in all but the most limited circumstances. Elsewhere, covenants not to compete won't be enforced if they're found to be unreasonable. A covenant may be held unreasonable if it covers too wide a geographic area or lasts for too long.

> **EXAMPLE:** Walt—a veterinarian who operates three animal hospitals in Anderson County—hires Fred, another veterinarian, to work for him. Fred signs an employment contract that states that, for three years after his employment ends, he won't practice veterinary medicine within 15 miles of any veterinary practice operated by Walt. Together, the three prohibited areas embrace nearly all of Anderson County, plus parts of several adjoining counties. The contract also states that Fred will pay $30,000 in damages if he violates the covenant.
>
> Fred quits his job and begins a mobile veterinary practice in Anderson County, bringing his work within the restricted areas. Walt sues Fred for $30,000, but he's out of luck: Because the covenant is so broad, the court won't enforce it.

A covenant may also be held unreasonable if the information revealed to the worker isn't all that sensitive.

> **EXAMPLE:** Image Supplies Inc., a printing supply company in Chicago, hires John as a salesman. John signs a covenant stating that, for one year after his job ends, he won't compete with Image Supplies within 100 miles of Image Supplies' headquarters. John resigns and goes to work for a competitor in the Chicago area.
>
> Image Supplies seeks an injunction—a court order prohibiting John from working for the competitor—because John has the names and locations of its customers and the prices charged to each customer. The court refuses to grant an injunction. It holds that Image Supplies has no protectable business interest in the information that John has. The names of firms in the printing business are easily found in the phone book and trade publications, and anyone can learn about prices by asking the customer.

Judges are more likely to enforce restrictive covenants against high-level managers who truly are given inside information. Such former employees are in a position to do real harm.

Protecting Trade Secrets

A trade secret is information that gives you a competitive advantage because it isn't generally known and can't be readily learned by other people who could benefit from it. It can be a formula, pattern, compilation, program, device, method, technique, or other process that you've made reasonable efforts to keep secret.

A judge may order the employee not to use a trade secret even if the employee didn't sign a secrecy agreement. However, you must show that what the employee took truly meets the definition. This usually involves establishing two things: that the information was not readily obtainable elsewhere and that you took precautions to keep it secret. For example, if you developed a unique plant fertilizer that you manufacture and distribute, you should be able to establish that you created the fertilizer through extensive trial and error and then made sure that employees learned the formula on a strict need-to-know basis.

Similarly, if you put together a valuable customer list that includes your customers' buying history and buying habits, you should be able to show that you painstakingly built up the list over several years and that you allowed only a limited number of employees to see it.

Handling Postemployment Inquiries

One of your knottiest dilemmas after an employee quits or has been fired is deciding what to tell other businesses that inquire about the former employee. You may be tugged in several directions:

- You want to tell the truth—good, bad, or neutral—about the former worker.
- You may want to help the former worker find another job.
- You may fear that if you do say anything negative, you'll be sued for libel or slander.
- You may feel that the best way to head off possible lawsuits or complaints by angry employees is to help them find new jobs.
- You don't want to overpraise a marginal employee and risk the anger of the new employer.

The law doesn't require you to completely clam up about a former employee. If you follow some basic legal guidelines, you can disclose significant information about the former employee without risking a lawsuit.

Legal Requirements

The key to protecting yourself is to stick to the facts and act in good faith. When you go beyond the facts or are motivated by a desire to harm the former employee or cover up the truth, you can find yourself in deep trouble.

Former employees who feel maligned can sue for defamation (called slander if the statements were spoken or libel if they were written). To win a defamation case, a former employee must prove that you gave out false information, and that the information harmed the employee's reputation. If you can prove that the information you gave out was true, the defamation lawsuit will be dismissed.

Employers in most states are entitled to limited protection in defamation cases, even if the information they provide is false. This is based on a legal doctrine called qualified privilege. To receive the benefit of this protection, you must show all of the following:

- You made the statement in good faith.
- You and the person to whom you disclosed the information shared a common interest.
- You limited your statement to this common interest.

The law recognizes that a former employer and a prospective employer share a common interest in the attributes of an employee. To get the protection of the qualified privilege, your main task is to stick to facts that you've reasonably investigated and to lay aside your personal feelings about the former employee.

If you can establish that you're protected by the qualified privilege, the only way a former employee can succeed in a defamation lawsuit is to prove that you knew the information was false but you passed it on anyway, or that you acted recklessly in sorting out the facts.

Deciding What to Say

A practical policy—and one that gives you a high degree of legal protection—is to simply not discuss an employee with prospective employers if you can't say something positive. Just tell the person inquiring that it's not your policy to comment on former workers.

Be Careful Within Your Business

Usually, when a former employee sues for defamation, it's because the old employer has gone overboard in giving information to a prospective employer. But you can also get in trouble if you're not discreet in what you say about the former employee within your own company.

To help avoid liability, follow a few commonsense policies.

- Disclose the reasons for a firing strictly on a need-to-know basis (for example, to an employee who handles unemployment compensation claims for your business).
- Avoid discussing firings at meetings and employee gatherings. Limit announcements to something noncommittal: "Bob has left the company as of last Friday. His position is being filled by Rita."
- Be sure your personnel files reflect fairness, objectivity, and good faith. A former employee who sues you will certainly subpoena employment records. These must be free of unprovable gossip, or your whole case may be jeopardized.

Where an employee's record is truly mixed, it's sometimes possible to accent the positive while you try to put negative information into a halfway favorable, or at least less negative, perspective.

> **EXAMPLE:** Madeline, a copywriter for your ad agency, started working for you right out of college. She was a creative writer with lots of clever ideas but never really figured out how to manage the production details for the mail order catalogs that are the bread and butter of your business. After a year, you concluded that this was just not a good fit and you reluctantly gave Madeline 60 days to find a slot elsewhere—hopefully with an agency looking for the dazzling, witty prose that was Madeline's forte.

Possible approach to inquiries: Emphasize that Madeline is full of creative energy and enthusiasm, but sometimes doesn't do well tracking mundane details. Suggest that Madeline would do best in a spot where creative writing and initiative are required, and where new and clever ideas are needed.

However, if an employee has committed very serious misconduct, you must include that information in your reference. Remember, you're not under any obligation to give a reference. But, if you choose to offer more than simple confirmation that the employee worked for you, you must include any information you have that the employee might harm someone. If, for example, an employee threatened or committed violence or otherwise put others in danger, you must reveal those facts. If you provide a detailed reference but don't include this type of information, and the employee causes harm at the new job, you could be liable for damages. Not every state follows this rule, but there seems to be a growing trend toward holding former employers responsible for misleading prospective employers about a dangerous employee.

> **EXAMPLE:** Brad was fired from his job as a nurse for stealing medication, taking opioid painkillers at work, and putting patients at risk. Despite the reason for his termination, his employer gave him a positive reference, recommending him highly and stating that he would be an asset to any nursing facility. The reference didn't mention his drug abuse. At his new job, Brad failed to respond to a patient who had a stroke; Brad's slow response caused the patient to suffer more serious complications. The patient's family sued the facility, which turned around and sued the former employer for misrepresenting Brad's employment there.

It also pays to watch your tongue in informal settings. Don't let down your guard at trade meetings or other places where you're chatting socially with others. If a fired employee was with your business for a while, a supplier or customer may ask, "Where's John these days?" If you reply in a vindictive way, describing all your grievances that led you to fire John, word will likely spread. And John may wind up being blackballed in your field or town. This can lead to legal complications for you and your business.

Employee Privacy

There may be times when you'd like to monitor an employee's activities, look at material on an employee's computer, or even search an employee's desk or belongings. You may, for example, want to see if an employee is conducting personal business on company time, harassing other employees through email messages, stealing from your business, or packing a gun. The problem is that the employee may view your efforts as needlessly intrusive and an invasion of privacy. In some cases, the law will support the employee's position.

It's hard to predict where a particular judge will draw the line between your right to control your workplace and your employees' right to privacy. But, fortunately, legislators and judges recognize an employer's legitimate business interests. Although there are legal pitfalls to be avoided, your hands aren't completely tied. If you're sensitive to the legal nuances, you can take appropriate actions to maintain a safe and productive workplace.

This chapter focuses on several key privacy issues, including the following:

- Do you have a right to check on the websites employees are visiting?
- How far can you go in monitoring an employee's on-the-job communications, such as phone conversations and email, when the employee is working on-site or remotely?
- What are the legal limits on your use of cameras, recorders, and computer productivity software?
- When can you safely search an employee's possessions or work area?
- Can you dictate what employees can and cannot do on their own time?

As you'll see, you can go a long way toward avoiding worker resentment and legal entanglements by observing two key principles. First, make sure that you do only what's necessary for your business purposes; an employer who tracks employees out of mere curiosity or an obsessive desire to exercise control is skating on thin ice. Second, do your best to reduce employees' expectations of privacy in the workplace. Judges who are called on to decide whether an employee's privacy was invaded will weigh your legitimate interests against the employee's reasonable expectations of privacy. If you let employees know in advance that your company reserves the right to read email messages sent on company equipment, for example, then it will be harder for them to later argue that they had a reasonable expectation of email privacy.

Overcoming an employee's privacy expectations may not be all that hard. For starters, you can notify employees if you plan to monitor their activities. And it makes sense to tell them why you're taking such actions and what the consequences are. For example, you might notify employees that your company monitors employee Internet use, including the sites remote employees visit using the company's equipment. Many judges say that an employee who receives such notice no longer has a reasonable expectation of privacy in the activities described in the notice. Often, a worker who has received such notice and continues on the job is found to have given implied consent to the employer's monitoring activities. You can give notice in many ways, such as memos, posters, and an employee handbook.

Privacy Issues Discussed Elsewhere in This Book

- For information on respecting the privacy rights of job applicants—including during job interviews; when using job applications; when using aptitude, psychological, and other types of tests; and when investigating an applicant's credit history, employment history, school records, and other background areas—see Chapter 1.
- For information on the requirements of confidentiality when handling employee files, see Chapter 2.
- To learn about the limitations on your right to impose grooming and clothing rules, see Chapter 2.
- To learn about your obligation to keep information about medical leaves and temporary transfers confidential, see Chapter 6.
- To learn about your right to limit smoking in the workplace, see Chapter 7.
- To learn how much you can say about why you fired an employee, see Chapter 10.

To build an even stronger defense, you can get each employee's express consent. You can provide a written statement for employees to sign, acknowledging your policies and practices and consenting to your monitoring. Another method is to include your policies and practices in an employee handbook and then require the employee to sign a receipt acknowledging that the employee has received the handbook and consents to the policies and practices described there. With express written consent, you don't have the potential problem of proving in court that the employee did receive notice of your monitoring activities.

Be aware, however, that notice and consent will only go so far. Some states have outlawed specific practices, such as using video cameras in restrooms and changing areas. In these situations—and others where most people would agree that monitoring would be offensive—you won't be able to overcome an employee's reasonable expectation of privacy even if you obtain consent.

Monitoring Employees at Work

In general, keeping tabs on what employees are doing at work is a legitimate interest for an employer. For one thing, it gives you an objective way to evaluate job performance. For another, it helps you detect theft, thwart disclosure of confidential information, prevent discrimination and harassment, and ensure that employees are not misusing company equipment.

As a result, the law gives you considerable latitude to monitor employees, but not a completely free hand. Employees retain some claim to workplace privacy. The following guidelines will help you avoid legal problems.

Internet Use

If your business provides computers for employees to use in their work—whether the employee is working on-site or remotely—you may worry about whether employees are using the computers as you intend. When employees are quietly tapping away at the keyboard or intently scrutinizing the screen, are they really conducting business? Maybe, maybe not. For all you know, employees may be shopping online, viewing pornography, buying or selling stock, checking the latest sports scores, or playing computer games. You may not mind if employees' nonbusiness use of the computer is limited and doesn't interfere with job performance. But you'll understandably be disturbed if employees are whiling away big chunks of time on personal matters or inappropriate sites.

You can buy inexpensive software that enables you to check on the websites that employees are visiting. If you decide to install Web-tracking software, you'll want to head off potential claims by employees that they reasonably expected privacy in their computer use. Accordingly, it's prudent to take the following precautions:

- Adopt a policy saying that employees are to use your computers only for business matters during their work hours.
- Inform employees of this policy and also tell them that you're installing software that will show what websites they're visiting.
- Let them know that they can be disciplined or fired for using your computers for personal matters during their work hours.
- Have employees acknowledge in writing that they've received notice of your policy and of the fact that you use Web-tracking software.

EXAMPLE: Inco Corporation hires Allen and provides a computer for him to use at work. At Inco's request, Allen acknowledges in writing that he's aware of the company's policy that he's to use the computer for business matters only, and that he mustn't use it for "improper, derogatory, defamatory, obscene, or other inappropriate purposes." He also acknowledges that Inco may monitor his computer usage and may discipline or fire him for improper use. Inco fires Allen after discovering that he's used the computer to visit pornographic sites. Allen has no legal basis to complain that Inco has invaded his privacy. His notice of Inco's policy, combined with his written consent to that policy, defeats any claim by Allen that he had a reasonable expectation of privacy concerning his computer use.

Even if you don't install Web-tracking software, you may still want to have a policy prohibiting using the Internet for inappropriate purposes (such as visiting pornographic sites) or install Web-filtering software to block access to certain websites.

Mobile Devices Pose Additional Privacy Questions

It's tempting to allow—or even encourage—employees to use their own personal smartphones, tablets, or laptops to conduct business. Not only can employees be productive away from the workplace, your company will also save the hassle and expense of purchasing devices for them.

But there are plenty of drawbacks to consider to this type of BYOD ("bring your own device") policy. To start, there are the usual concerns you'll have with any mobile device: What are the consequences to your business if the device gets lost or stolen? Will competitors gain access to confidential information? Will the device make it easier for outsiders to hack into your business accounts? Will malware bring down your computer system?

Beyond these first-tier concerns, additional concerns apply as a result of your legitimate desire to have access to the business information stored on the employee's device. Remember, these devices will certainly contain not only business information, but personal information as well—private emails, social media links, text messages, medical records, and photographs, among other things. This creates the risk that your access to business files may expose you to the employee's personal information.

The courts and legislatures have not yet fully addressed the privacy issues when employees use their own mobile devices. This is an emerging area of employment law. If you want employees to use devices as part of their work, you can play it safe by buying the devices for them. You can require that they use the devices for work-related matters only. This will eliminate some of the privacy concerns.

But suppose you want to avoid that expense, and you're comfortable with employees using their own devices. The best solution for now is to establish a clear written policy. Let employees know that if they do job-related work on their devices, you may need access to the devices and that personal information may be revealed in the process. With such a policy, it will no longer be reasonable for the employees to expect full privacy for the information on their mobile devices.

Another concern is reimbursement of expenses. In some states, if an employer requires or allows its employees to use their own personal devices for work, the employer must reimburse them for business related expenses. For example, an employer may be required to pay for cellphone expenses incurred by employees in sending work emails or making work calls.

In addition to monitoring employee Internet use, you may want to check on how productive employees are in using your business computers. Here again, software can be useful. You can buy a program that monitors an employee's keystrokes. To be on the safe side legally, let employees know what you are doing beforehand.

Phone Calls

There are a number of good business reasons for monitoring employee phone calls. For example, you may want to ensure that employees are providing good service to customers and clients. Or you may want to discourage excessive personal use of your phones while employees should be working. Also, you may want to make sure that employees aren't violating the law or your business policies by engaging in harassment or discrimination. Additionally, monitoring phone calls can help you detect the disclosure of trade secrets and other confidential information. If you decide to monitor phone calls, you must follow some legal rules.

Under two federal laws—the Omnibus Crime Control and Safe Streets Act of 1968 and the Electronic Communications Privacy Act (ECPA)—you can monitor phones calls if either of the following is true:

- Your monitoring is in the ordinary course of your business.
- You have the employee's consent.

CAUTION
Your right to monitor voicemail is unsettled. The federal statute is silent on voicemail messages, and the courts haven't ruled definitively on the matter. The safe course is to deal with voicemail messages and phone calls in a single monitoring policy and to obtain employees' written consent to monitor.

This section discusses federal law requirements. Your state's law might also add a twist. Check with your state labor department for more information. (See the appendix to find contact details.)

Keeping an Eye on Remote Employees

With more employees than ever working from home due to COVID-19, employers are trying to figure out the best ways to track their remote employees' performance while still respecting their privacy. Many employers have turned to productivity and monitoring apps and software—Time Doctor, Hubstaff, and DeskTime are a few examples—with features such as:

- logging keystrokes
- taking screenshots at regular intervals
- recording Internet activity, and
- monitoring computer idle time.

Unsurprisingly, these digital tools tend to be unpopular among employees, who often view them as an invasion of privacy. Still, as an employer, you're generally on solid legal ground if you decide to monitor your remote workers' activity, as long as you've provided their equipment and obtained their consent to monitor. Whether installing such a program is worth the inevitable hit to employee morale is a decision for each employer to make, but the tools are out there.

Some states impose additional restrictions on employers, so consider checking with an employment lawyer in your area before instituting a digital monitoring program.

Ordinary Course of Business

Though federal law authorizes you to monitor phone calls in the ordinary course of business, it doesn't say what that is. And, courts have done little to fill in the blanks. That being said, it is clear that this applies if employees use your phones as an inextricable part of your business and if you listen in to make sure the employees are serving your customers well. For example, if you have a telemarketing operation or if a primary component of your business is to sell goods or services by phone, monitoring will likely be allowed.

It will also apply if you want to check up on an employee who you think is giving trade secrets to a competitor or using the phone to make personal calls.

In addition, one court has ruled that a burglar and fire alarm company could monitor all calls, based on industry practice and insurance rules.

No matter what, however, ordinary course of business applies only to business calls. If you happen to monitor a personal call, you must stop listening as soon as you determine that it is personal.

Consent

The second way to monitor phone calls is to obtain employee consent. An employee's consent can be either implied or express. If you notify employees that you'll be monitoring their phone calls, they've given their implied consent if they continue to use the phone. You can give this notice in an employee handbook or through prominent posters in the work area.

Although implied consent is legally sufficient to permit monitoring under the federal law, you may have trouble later on proving that you actually gave the notice. For that reason, you'll make your life easier by getting each employee's written consent. Have employees acknowledge in writing that they know you'll be monitoring their phone calls when they use business phones, and that they consent to such monitoring.

Several states impose additional requirements on monitoring phone calls. Primarily, they require the consent of both parties to the call, typically by a beep that both parties can hear or a message notifying both parties of the monitoring. To find the rule in your state, you'll need to research your state's statutes and utilities commission rules or check with a lawyer.

Email

When it comes to email, courts have almost uniformly found that employers have a right to monitor, as long as they have a clear policy reserving the right to do so. Such a policy is a good idea for many reasons: Even if you don't particularly want (or feel you need) to read employee email, there may come a day when you need to. If you learn an employee has sent threats to a coworker, divulged trade secrets to a competitor electronically, or sent racist or sexual images on company equipment, you will need to see those messages.

Some companies don't want employees to use the company's email system for personal messages of any kind. After all, the equipment (and bandwidth) belongs to the company, and sending personal messages wastes work time and might create liability. So, why not just ban personal use altogether?

Perhaps the biggest reason is that a ban on personal use of company email is likely to be violated fairly often. The truth is, most of us have sent the occasional personal email on company equipment. And, if you have a policy that doesn't reflect reality, you can get into trouble when you try to enforce it. The employee you crack down on will be able to point to many other employees who were not punished for the same behavior. This type of inconsistency leads to confusion, poor morale, and even potential discrimination claims, if the employee who got disciplined believes you had biased motives for being selective. The bottom line is that a policy prohibiting all personal use of email is not a great idea. Instead, consider limiting personal use to occasional messages sent during nonwork hours.

Monitoring Performance and Workplace Behavior

You may have a legitimate business reason to install video cameras in the workplace. For example, you may want to discourage theft from a cash register, or you may want to ensure the safety of employees and customers. You're generally free to use video cameras for such purposes, though it's always a good idea to notify employees that this is your policy. An employee who continues to work for you after getting such a notice has given implied consent to the video monitoring. Some states forbid the use of electronic surveillance in areas such as restrooms, locker rooms, or lounges, so, to be safe, don't monitor areas where most people would find it highly offensive to be watched.

Monitoring conversations through microphones—either separately or in connection with video cameras—falls under the same rules as apply to phone conversations. You should have employees' consent before you listen in on their conversations. Notifying them in advance will suffice to establish implied consent. Having them sign an express consent is even better, because you don't have to prove that employees received notice.

Searches

Sometimes you may feel a need to search an employee's property or work space. The reasons vary, but the most common is to investigate actual or potential wrongdoing. You may, for example, want to look for evidence of theft or illegal drug use or the presence of a weapon. Although such motives are understandable, they may conflict with an employee's right to privacy.

Most employees would regard their own personal property—including their lunch boxes, briefcases, purses, and vehicles—as private. And many employees expect that some of the property you provide for their use—for example, a desk, an office, or a locker—will be private. If you want to be able to search such property without risking severe legal consequences, you must do your best to eliminate the expectation of privacy.

Consider taking the following precautions:

- Adopt a written policy that lets employees know which of the company's property—and which of their own—may be subject to searches.
- Specifically address workplace facilities—such as desks, lockers, and cabinets—that employees might expect to be private. And, if you anticipate more extensive searches, also address such items as handbags, briefcases, and parcels.
- Make sure that employees are well informed of your policy. (Ideally, you'd like employees to sign an acknowledgment that they've received a copy of the policy and agree to be bound by it.) When you let employees know that you may be searching certain property, it's hard for them to later contend that they reasonably expected privacy.
- If you give an employee a key to a desk or locker but retain a master key, make sure the employee knows. Without that knowledge, the employee may have a higher expectation of privacy. If you allow employees to use their own locks, require them to give you the combination or a duplicate key.
- Apply your search policy consistently to all employees.
- Limit any searches, if you can, to company-owned property; try not to search the employees' personal property.
- Have a good business reason for any search you conduct (for example, to look for stolen property or controlled substances).

> ⚠ CAUTION
>
> **Avoid searching employees themselves.** The legal stakes are much higher if you get up close and personal by, for example, searching clothing that an employee is wearing or conducting pat-downs or strip searches of the employees themselves. If you feel that such searches are needed, call the police and let them handle the problem. Otherwise, the employee may later sue you not only for invasion of privacy but also for a number of other torts, including assault, battery, false arrest, false imprisonment, and intentional infliction of mental distress.

Off-Duty Activities

In some situations, employers may want to discipline—or even fire— employees for their off-duty activities. You can see why such a practice might meet with employee resistance: Why should you have a right to dictate what employees may do on their own time? However, certain employee activities may affect your business. For example, an employee might want to work for a competitor on the weekends, which could put your company's confidential information at risk and call the employee's loyalty into question.

A number of states have off-duty conduct laws that limit an employer's right to make business decisions (including decisions to discipline or fire an employee) based on what employees do on their own time. In some states, these laws are limited to an employee's use of legal products; generally, these laws are intended to protect employees who smoke or otherwise use tobacco products. Some states have broader laws about off-duty conduct. However, many states that have these laws also recognize that an employer may have a legitimate interest in an employee's off-duty conduct.

Consider what happened when Delta Air Lines fired Mike, a baggage handler, for writing a letter to the *Denver Post* criticizing Delta's cost-cutting program. Mike sued Delta, claiming his job was protected by Colorado's off-duty conduct statute. The judge said Mike's right to off-the-job privacy had to be balanced against Delta's business needs. The judge went on to say that the Colorado statute didn't allow employees to strike indiscriminate public blows against the business reputation of their employer. Mike's case was thrown out. (*Marsh v. Delta Air Lines, Inc.*, 952 F.Supp. 1458 (1997).)

The legal activities law in New York specifies four types of off-duty activities that an employer can't act on:

- political activities, such as fundraising or running for office
- legal use of consumable products, which seems intended to cover cigarettes, alcohol, and prescription drugs
- legal recreational activities, or
- union activities.

The New York law does, however, permit an employer to restrict moonlighting and activities that create a conflict of interest. And an employee isn't protected if an off-duty activity—such as drinking alcohol—leads to poor performance on the job. An employer can still fire someone who comes to work intoxicated.

As you can see, even in the states that have lawful activity laws, you have some discretion in deciding whether to fire or discipline someone for off-duty conduct. And, in the other states, you have virtually a free hand. For example:

- A Kentucky court said it was okay for an employer to fire a worker for attending law school at night.
- A Pennsylvania court said an employer could lawfully fire an employee for looking for work elsewhere.
- A Florida court said a doctor was free to fire an employee who took her daughter to another doctor.

But even though you can use your power as an employer to regulate what an employee does on his or her own time, think long and hard before you do so. If you attempt to restrict employees away from work, you run the risk of employee resentment. This often translates into a reduced work effort.

The following guidelines should protect you from potential liability and perhaps even from worker resentment:

- Let employees know in advance what kinds of off-duty conduct will get them into trouble.
- Apply your rules in an even-handed way to all employees.
- Don't apply your off-duty rules in a way that violates—or appears to violate—the antidiscrimination laws. For example, don't fire someone for conduct that may look like it has a religious, racial, or gender component.

- Don't use off-duty rules as a subterfuge for engaging in illegal discrimination.
- If possible, warn an employee before you resort to discipline or firing for off-duty conduct.

RESOURCE

Want more information on employee privacy? For comprehensive research on this subject, consult *Privacy in Employment Law*, by Matthew Finkin (Bloomberg BNA), and check the website of the Privacy Rights Clearinghouse at www.privacyrights.org. You can also find a lot of free information on privacy in the workplace on Nolo's website at www.nolo.com.

Prohibitions Against Smoking

As explained in Chapter 7, you can—and are sometimes required to—prohibit smoking in the workplace or otherwise protect nonsmokers from secondhand smoke. Off-duty smoking is another matter. More than half the states have laws that prohibit you from requiring an employee to abstain from smoking away from work. In the states that don't have such laws, you're free to prohibit off-premises smoking. But is it a good idea? Generally not. Trying to impose a smoking ban outside the workplace would be hard to police and would alienate employees who are smokers. True, smokers do increase health care costs and have a higher rate of absenteeism. But you might be better off using a carrot rather than a stick to deal with the problem. As suggested in Chapter 7, you might offer to pay the cost of a smoking cessation program for any employee who succeeds in giving up the habit.

Independent Contractors

Many businesses hire independent contractors rather than employees to perform at least some work. Typically—but not always—independent contractors have special skills that you need to call upon only sporadically. Common examples are a lawyer or an accountant, a painter, plumber, or carpenter who works on your office space, or a computer consultant who installs specialized software at your store and teaches your employees how to use it.

There are often advantages to such an arrangement, but there can be a downside, too. If you misclassify a worker as an independent contractor rather than as an employee, you face potentially serious legal problems, particularly when it comes to taxes. The IRS prefers to have a worker classified as an employee rather than as an independent contractor if there's any doubt about the worker's status.

> **RESOURCE**
> **Get detailed help with contract issues.** *Working With Independent Contractors,* by Stephen Fishman (Nolo), provides clear and comprehensive guidance that will help you avoid a collision with the IRS or another government agency over how you classify a worker.

Comparing Employees and Independent Contractors

Sometimes, your company has needs that can be filled equally well by an employee or an independent contractor.

In choosing which route to take, there are several factors worth considering.

Tax Obligations

Employee. You must make the employer's contribution for the worker's Social Security and Medicare taxes. You're also responsible for withholding federal and state income taxes and the worker's share of Social Security and Medicare taxes, and for keeping records and reporting on these items to the federal and state governments. Each year, you must send the employee a Form W-2 showing how much the employee earned and how much you withheld.

Independent contractor. When you hire an independent contractor, you're not required to withhold taxes from the amount you pay the worker, and you don't have to pay any portion of the worker's Social Security and Medicare taxes. Your only tax responsibility is to complete a Form 1099-NEC at the end of the year if you paid the independent contractor $600 or more during the year. (This replaced Form 1099-MISC starting with the 2020 tax year.) You must send copies of this form to both the IRS and the contractor.

Workers' Compensation

Employee. You must carry workers' compensation insurance for an employee. The workers' compensation system provides replacement income and pays medical expenses to employees who are injured or become ill as a result of their jobs.

Independent contractor. Generally, an employer does not pay for workers' compensation for an independent contractor.

Penalties Lurk If You Misclassify a Worker

If you weigh both possibilities and conclude it's in your company's best interests to hire and classify a worker as an independent contractor rather than an employee, fine. But make sure the worker really qualifies for this status under government rules. If you classify a worker as an independent contractor when the worker should have been treated as an employee, you can be required to pay:

- the employer's and employee's share of Social Security and Medicare contributions
- income tax that should have been withheld from the employee's wages, and
- federal unemployment tax.

You may also be liable for the employee's state income taxes that should have been withheld, as well as unemployment compensation taxes. And, if the worker is injured on the job, you may have to pay for failing to cover the worker under your company's workers' compensation policy.

Unemployment Compensation

Employee. You must contribute to an unemployment insurance fund in your state and pay a federal unemployment tax. An employee who is laid off or fired for a reason other than serious misconduct is entitled to unemployment benefits from the state fund.

    Independent contractor. Generally, an employer does not make contributions to a state unemployment fund or pay the federal unemployment tax for an independent contractor. (Note, however, that contractors were temporarily eligible for unemployment benefits during the COVID-19 crisis. Check with your state's labor department for the latest information on unemployment eligibility.)

Job Benefits

Employee. An employer often provides job benefits for an employee, such as paid vacations, sick leave and holidays, health insurance, and a retirement plan.

    Independent contractor. Independent contractors are paid only for the work they do. They are responsible for paying for their own health insurance and retirement savings plan.

Workspace

Employee. An employer provides workspace and equipment for an employee. The employer pays for rent, maintenance, property insurance, and utilities, as well as for tools, computers, furniture, and vehicles, depending on the type of business. If the employer allows employees to work from home, the employer might provide laptops, monitors, phones, or other equipment, or an allowance to purchase such equipment.

    Independent contractor. An independent contractor usually—but not always—works away from your place of business and provides his or her own equipment.

Firing the Worker

Employee. If you become unhappy with an employee's work and you don't see improvement, you will likely have to fire the worker. This can be a traumatic and legally hazardous course of action.

Independent contractor. An independent contractor is usually hired for a set assignment to be completed by a fixed deadline. If the independent contractor isn't satisfactory, you can simply turn to another independent contractor for future work. Typically, you will use a written contract for longer projects or ongoing work which will state how and when the relationship can be terminated.

Cost

Employee. The hourly rate you pay an employee may be relatively low, but the true cost also includes the money you pay for taxes, insurance, job benefits, workspace, and equipment.

Independent contractor. The hourly rate of an independent contractor may be relatively high, because the worker must earn enough to cover business expenses and taxes.

Governmental Regulations

Employee. An employer is subject to a wide range of governmental regulations intended to protect employees, including laws dealing with wages and hours (see Chapter 3), employee benefits (see Chapter 4), family and medical leave (see Chapter 6), workplace health and safety (see Chapter 7), and illegal discrimination (see Chapters 8 and 9).

Independent contractor. A company's relationship with an independent contractor—if the worker has been properly classified as such—is subject to fewer legal restrictions. For example, you needn't pay an independent contractor time-and-a-half for overtime hours, and you're not responsible for monitoring health and safety conditions at an independent contractor's own home, shop, or office.

Liability for Worker's Actions

Employee. An employer generally is legally liable for injuries or property damage caused by an employee's negligence. If, for example, an employee carelessly injures a customer while at work or damages someone's property, the employer can be held responsible.

Independent contractor. If you hire an independent contractor, your company generally won't be liable for the negligence of that person. Be aware, however, that in some situations your company may be liable for the actions of an independent contractor, especially if the worker was acting as your agent.

Liability for Injury to Worker

Employee. An employer is responsible for medical treatment if an employee is hurt on the job and for paying money to partially cover the employee's lost wages. This is generally handled through workers' compensation insurance. These payments are required whether or not your company was at fault for the employee's injuries.

Independent contractor. An independent contractor who is injured because of some dangerous situation at your business premises can recover medical bills and lost income from your business, as well as money for pain and suffering. But first, the independent contractor must show that you were negligent. You're not liable for injuries the independent contractor receives elsewhere while working for you unless you had control over those premises.

Worker's Preferences

Employee. A worker may prefer to be an employee because that status promises a steady, predictable salary, paid vacations, medical care, and other job benefits at the employer's expense, along with freedom from worry about the paperwork and record keeping required of people who are in business for themselves. What's more, an employee usually doesn't have to invest in tools and equipment.

Independent contractor. A worker may prefer to be an independent contractor to have greater control over working hours and conditions and to maintain the freedom to work for several businesses. Workers may also see benefits in being treated as independent contractors because they're able to deduct their business expenses from their gross incomes, including money spent on cars, home offices, and even some meals and travel.

Employer's Preferences

Employee. An employer may prefer to hire a worker as an employee because the business has that worker's undivided loyalty and the employer can better control the worker's hours and methods of doing the job.

   Independent contractor. An employer may prefer to hire a worker as an independent contractor because it allows more flexibility to adjust to fluctuating needs. For example, if an employer anticipates a two-month crunch on a project, farming out the extra work to an independent contractor may involve less workplace disruption than hiring an employee, providing workspace, and then laying off the employee once the project is complete.

The IRS Rules

To determine whether someone is an employee or an independent contractor, the IRS looks at the degree of control you have over the worker. If you control—or can control—not only what is to be done but also how it's done, the worker is an employee.

> **CAUTION**
>
> **Other tests may apply.** The IRS tests for independent contractor status are emphasized here because the IRS is the agency with which you're most likely to have a problem. Be aware, however, that in dealing with other agencies and laws, slightly different tests may be used. For example, a different test is used to determine if a person is an independent contractor under the Fair Labor Standards Act. And other tests may apply under state laws dealing with workers' compensation insurance and unemployment compensation.

The IRS doesn't care what label you apply to a worker. You can designate someone as a partner, coventurer, agent, or independent contractor. But, if the person legally qualifies as an employee, the IRS insists that you withhold income taxes and the employee's share of Social Security and Medicare contributions and pay the employer's share of those contributions.

In deciding whether a person is an employee or an independent contractor, the IRS used to rely on a list of 20 factors cobbled together from various court decisions. The IRS failed, however, to spell out what weight it accorded to any one factor, which led to inconsistent rulings and considerable confusion.

Because a worker's status often remained unclear after applying the traditional test, it was easy for the IRS to classify the worker as an employee. The IRS prefers employee status because it assumes the government stands to collect more tax revenue if a worker is classified as an employee rather than as an independent contractor.

Although the IRS hasn't formally repealed the 20-factor test, it decidedly moved away from that test in 1996, when it published the worker classification training materials it now uses for training IRS examiners. For employers trying to figure out where they stand on independent contractor issues, the training materials are a vast improvement over the old 20-factor test. The training materials provide welcome guidance on the weight given to various factors.

RESOURCE

Get help from the IRS. For more information on the IRS rule for classifying workers, see IRS Publication 15-A, *Employer's Supplemental Tax Guide.*

To determine whether a worker should be classified as an employee rather than as an independent contractor, IRS examiners are instructed to look primarily at three categories:

- **Behavioral control.** Do you have the right to direct or control how the worker performs specific tasks?
- **Financial control.** Do you have the right to direct or control how the business aspects of the worker's activities are conducted?
- **The relationship.** How do you and the worker perceive your relationship? The following sections discuss these categories in more detail.

Behavioral Control

The type of instruction or training you give a worker helps show the extent to which you retain the right to control the worker's method of getting the job done. IRS examiners may check on other types of behavioral control as well.

Instruction

The IRS recognizes that you'll probably impose some form of direction on all workers, whether they're independent contractors or employees. For example, you might require that the job be performed within a specified time period. The big question is how far you go in telling the worker how the job should be done, rather than just indicating the end result. Giving a worker autonomy in making decisions is evidence that you're not controlling the worker's behavior.

> **EXAMPLE:** Star Brite Manufacturing Company hires Lou Ann as a management consultant for its sales department. She is to ensure that the department is fully staffed and that sales brochures are stocked and available. She is also to review all sales contracts. Star Brite requires Lou Ann to get prior approval before she hires or fires anyone in the sales department, purchases additional sales materials, or accepts any sales contract.
>
> The IRS views the requirement of prior approval as evidence that Star Brite controls Lou Ann's behavior in the performance of her services. If Star Brite were not to require these prior approvals but were to leave matters to Lou Ann's discretion, this would be evidence of her autonomy in doing the work and therefore consistent with independent contractor status.

The IRS distinguishes between telling a worker what is to be done and how it is to be done. A worker can be an independent contractor even though you indicate what the job entails; after all, you are hiring the contractor to do a particular job for your company.

> **EXAMPLE:** Jim is an independent truck driver. Young Industries Inc. calls him to make a delivery run from the Gulf Coast to the Texas Panhandle. Jim accepts the job and agrees to pick up the cargo the next morning. Upon arriving at the warehouse, Jim is given an address to which to deliver the cargo and is advised that the delivery must be completed within two days. The IRS treats this as a direction of what is be done—not how it is to be done—and therefore consistent with independent contractor status. Jim is still free to choose his route, plan his driving time, and perhaps perform other work along the way.

On the other hand, if you give too much instruction on how the work is to be done, you may have to classify the worker as an employee.

EXAMPLE: Tess, a truck driver, does local deliveries for Zancor. She reports to Zancor's warehouse each morning. The warehouse manager tells Tess what deliveries have to be made, how to load the cargo in the truck, what route to take, and the order in which the cargo is to be delivered. This is instruction on how the work is to be performed, consistent with employee status in the eyes of the IRS.

Training

If you provide periodic or ongoing training to a worker, it's usually strong evidence of an employer-employee relationship. That's not true, however, of training that merely informs a worker about your policies, a new product line, or applicable governmental regulations. Similarly, the IRS won't imply an employer-employee relationship from programs a worker attends voluntarily and without compensation.

Suggestions

Mere suggestions to a worker don't constitute control over the worker's behavior. So, suggesting that a worker avoid Main Street because of traffic congestion is consistent with the worker's status as an independent contractor.

Business Identification

In the past, requiring workers to identify themselves with your business was evidence of employment status. For example, if you required workers to wear a uniform bearing your company's name or to paint your logo on their truck, that would have been an indication that the workers were employees.

Today, the IRS recognizes that safety concerns play into these types of rules: People often want reassurance about who's coming to their homes or workplaces. If there's a valid security reason for requiring a uniform or logo, the requirement is now a neutral factor in analyzing whether an employment relationship exists.

Financial Control

The IRS looks at whether your business has the right to direct or control the economic aspects of the worker's activities.

Significant Investment

Although it's not necessary for a worker to buy or rent costly equipment to be considered an independent contractor, evidence of such an investment does help establish independent contractor status. There are no precise dollar guidelines on what constitutes a significant investment.

There can be a significant investment even if you're selling or leasing the equipment to the worker, but the worker must pay the full market value or full rental value. Otherwise, the evidence may be insufficient to establish a significant investment.

> **EXAMPLE:** Cal operates a backhoe for Yorba Distributing Company. He leases the backhoe from Yorba at less than its fair rental value and can turn it in at any time without liability for further payments. Yorba pays for liability insurance and regular maintenance on the backhoe. Although Cal is paying something to rent the backhoe, the facts here don't establish that he's made a significant investment.

Business Expenses

The extent to which a worker chooses to incur expenses and be responsible for them can affect the worker's potential to make a profit or sustain a loss. A worker's unreimbursed business expenses can be evidence that the worker has the right to control the financial side of business operations, which shows independent contractor status.

But there are limits to this principle. If the unreimbursed expenses are minor, this isn't evidence of an independent contractor relationship. The same is true of heavier expenses that are customarily borne by an employee in a particular line of business, such as an auto mechanic's tools.

Advertising and Visibility

An independent contractor is generally free to seek out other business opportunities. The fact that a worker advertises or maintains a visible business location to attract new clients is evidence that the worker is an independent contractor. On the other hand, neither advertising nor having a visible business location is a requirement for independent contractor status. A worker with special skills who gets jobs through word of mouth can qualify as an independent contractor.

In addition, the IRS recognizes that a person who has negotiated a long-term contract may find advertising unnecessary and may even be unavailable to work for others for the duration of the contract. That will not affect the person's status as an independent contractor. Other independent contractors may find that a visible business location doesn't produce enough business to justify the expense.

In short, the IRS treats the absence of advertising or a visible business location as well as the temporary inability to work for others as neutral factors.

> **EXAMPLE 1:** Unicorn Ventures engages Cindy to mow the lawn weekly and trim the hedges yearly at Unicorn's headquarters. Cindy advertises in the yellow pages that she does landscaping. The advertising indicates that Cindy is available to perform services to the relevant market. This is evidence that she is an independent contractor.

> **EXAMPLE 2:** Cindy negotiates a long-term contract with Unicorn to maintain all of Unicorn's business locations. Cindy decides to drop her yellow pages advertising, although she continues to be available to other businesses. The lack of advertising doesn't automatically change her independent contractor status.

Method of Payment

A worker who's paid hourly, weekly, or by another unit of time is guaranteed a return for labor. This is generally evidence of an employer-employee relationship, even when a commission is also paid. However, in some fields, such as law, it's typical to pay independent contractors on an hourly basis, so the hourly payment can be a neutral factor.

Paying a worker a flat fee for a particular project is generally evidence of an independent contractor relationship, especially if the worker incurs expenses in performing the job. When you pay the worker—daily, weekly, or monthly—isn't relevant.

A person who's paid solely on a commission basis can be either an independent contractor or an employee. The worker's status may depend on the ability to realize a profit or incur a loss in performing services.

Profit or Loss

A worker's ability to earn a profit or incur a loss is probably the strongest evidence that the worker controls the business aspects of the work. The four economic factors discussed above all relate to the worker's potential for profit or loss. A key question is whether the worker can make decisions that affect the worker's bottom line. These might, for example, be decisions involving ordering inventory, investing money, hiring other workers, or purchasing or leasing equipment.

A worker's ability to decide whether to work longer hours to earn more money or to work fewer hours and take less money is a neutral factor.

The Relationship

The IRS considers how you and the worker view your relationship. Your perceptions and those of the worker may suggest what the two of you intend regarding the all-important issue of control.

Written Contract

If you have a written contract with a worker, the IRS will focus on its substance, not on labels. Calling the worker an independent contractor isn't enough. The more important clauses are those dealing with the method of compensation, payment of expenses, and, most crucial, the rights and obligations of you and the worker regarding how work is to be performed.

Form W-2

Filing a Form W-2 usually indicates that the worker is an employee. However, the IRS may find independent contractor status anyway, depending on the economic realities of the relationship.

Incorporation

If a worker has formed a corporation and you hire the corporation to do the work, the IRS will almost always treat the worker as an employee of the worker's own corporation, not as an employee of your business.

Employee Benefits

Providing a worker with benefits traditionally associated with employee status can be evidence that the worker is an employee. If you give the worker paid vacation days, paid sick days, health insurance, life or disability insurance, or a pension, that's some evidence of employee status. The evidence of employee status is strongest if you provide benefits under a tax-qualified retirement plan, a 403(b) annuity, or a cafeteria plan.

If you exclude a worker from a benefit plan because you don't consider the worker to be an employee, that's relevant but not conclusive evidence that the worker is an independent contractor.

Discharge or Termination

The IRS may look at the conditions under which you or the worker can terminate the working relationship. It's clear, however, that the IRS regards this as a complicated legal question and doesn't usually treat it as a decisive factor in deciding whether a worker has been properly classified.

Permanency

If you and the worker arranged for work to be done with the expectation that the relationship would continue indefinitely rather than for a specific project or period, that's generally evidence that the two of you intended to create an employment relationship. However, this requires more than simply setting up a long-term relationship, which is consistent with either employee or independent contractor status. The IRS recognizes that your relationship with an independent contractor may be long term because that's what your work agreement requires or because you renew the agreement regularly due to superior service, competitive prices, or lack of competition.

For these reasons, if a relationship is long term but the worker has a clearly defined role (for example, cleaning your windows regularly or providing specialized computer training as needed), the IRS disregards this as a factor in looking at the worker's status. The IRS also treats the temporary nature of a relationship as a neutral factor.

Regular Business Activity

The IRS may look at whether the services performed by a worker are a key aspect of your company's regular business. This can be a bit subtle.

The mere fact that a service is desirable, necessary, or even essential to your business doesn't mean that the service provider is an employee. If you have an appliance store, for example, you need workers to install electricity and plumbing in your building. This work can be done equally well by employees or independent contractors. The IRS examiner focuses on the fact that the work of the electricians and plumbers isn't part of your regular business.

By contrast, the work of an attorney or legal assistant is part of the regular business of a law firm. It's likely that a law firm will direct or control the work of a lawyer or legal assistant it hires, since the firm's name will go on documents the worker produces. In this situation, the IRS will probe for further facts showing the firm's right to direct and control the worker.

Sidestep IRS Problems by Contracting With Business Entities

If you want to hire someone as an independent contractor but you're not convinced that the worker will pass IRS muster as an independent contractor, the easiest solution is to require the worker to form a corporation or an LLC.

One-person corporations and LLCs are simple to create. After the worker forms the entity, your business signs a contract with the corporation or LLC in which the worker's entity agrees to provide the needed services. You pay the worker's corporation or LLC as specified in the contract. The worker receives a paycheck— and possibly bonuses as well—from the worker's entity, which is the employer.

The IRS will recognize this arrangement except in cases of clear abuse, and independent contractor status will no longer be an issue.

Facts of Lesser Importance

In addition to the three primary categories of evidence listed above, the IRS looks at other facts, but gives them less weight.

Part-Time or Full-Time Work

Whether a worker performs services on a full-time or part-time basis is a neutral fact. The same is true whether a worker performs services for one business or several.

Seeking a Safe Harbor

Despite the strict IRS rules, a business that wrongly classifies a worker as an independent contractor may escape the usual harsh consequences in some circumstances.

In theory, at least, you're protected by the safe harbor language of the tax law if you had a reasonable basis for classifying a worker as an independent contractor. For example:

- You relied on court rulings, IRS rulings, or advice given to you by the IRS.
- You were audited by the IRS and weren't assessed employment taxes for workers holding jobs similar to the one held by the misclassified worker.
- You followed a long-standing and recognized practice of your industry.

But theory is one thing and the real-world experience of challenging the IRS is another. If you seek the protection of the safe harbor provisions, the IRS won't give up without a fight.

Place of Work

Whether work is performed on your premises or somewhere you select often has no bearing on worker status. Usually it's only relevant as part of the IRS inquiry into your right to control how the work is to be done.

In many cases, services can only be performed at one location. To repair a leaky pipe, for example, a plumber must go to the site where the pipe is located. Similarly, a camera operator must shoot a commercial where the director and actors are located. These requirements aren't evidence of the right to direct and control how the work is to be performed.

Sometimes, work can be performed at many different locations. Off-site work can be consistent with either independent contractor or employee status. If a worker has an outside office or business location, this can be evidence of an independent contractor relationship. However, the IRS gets into this as part of its examination of the worker's investment, unreimbursed expenses, or opportunity for profit or loss.

Hours of Work

The IRS generally considers hours of work when it looks at the extent of the instructions you give the worker. As with work location, some work, by its nature, must be performed at a specific time; the photographer must shoot the commercial at the time scheduled for the director and actors to be present.

Flexible work hours are not given much importance by the IRS, as they can be consistent with either employee or independent contractor status.

Workers Automatically Classified as Employees

In most situations, the status of a worker is determined by the factors already explained. Certain workers, however, fall into special categories, and the usual IRS criteria don't apply to them. For example, the federal tax law says that certain workers are automatically employees—in legal lingo, statutory employees—including the following:

- **Delivery drivers.** Drivers who deliver meat, vegetables, fruit, bakery products, or beverages other than milk, or who pick up and deliver laundry or dry cleaning. These drivers are employees if they're legally agents of a company and are paid on a commission. (An agent is someone who's authorized to act on another's behalf.)

    > **EXAMPLE:** Rachel, a bread truck driver, sells on commission to a customer route for Barry's Bakery and no other bakeries; under the federal law, she's a statutory employee of the bakery. But Allen, a restaurant supply distributor who buys bread from Barry's Bakery at wholesale prices and resells it at a profit, is neither an agent nor a statutory employee of Barry's Bakery.

- **Insurance agents.** Insurance sales agents whose main job is selling life insurance, annuity contracts, or both, primarily for one life insurance company.
- **Home workers.** People who work at home according to a company's specifications on materials or goods that are supplied by a company and must be returned to that company or to someone the company designates.

- **Business-to-business salespeople.** People whose main job is to sell for a company and turn in orders to that company from wholesalers, retailers, contractors, hotels, restaurants, or other business establishments. The goods sold must be merchandise for resale or supplies for use in the buyer's business, rather than goods bought for home consumption.

Federal tax law also provides that licensed real estate agents and door-to-door salespeople are generally treated as nonemployees or exempt employees, but they may be treated as employees for the purpose of liability and workers' compensation.

State Laws

The IRS method for differentiating between employees and independent contractors is similar to the standards followed in many states for state taxes and unemployment compensation, but there can be some differences. For example, in deciding whether a worker is an employee for purposes of workers' compensation coverage or unemployment compensation benefits, a state may use a simple economic reality test or the ABC Test (see below).

If you plan to hire independent contractors, check first with the labor department in your state to see what rules are in effect. (See the appendix for contact details.)

The Risks of Misclassification

There are at least four ways that the IRS can learn about your hiring and classification practices. First, the IRS may look into the affairs of an independent contractor who hasn't been paying income taxes. Second, disgruntled employees may complain to the IRS if they think independent contractors are getting favored treatment. Third, during tax audits, the IRS routinely checks to see if workers have been misclassified as independent contractors. Fourth, the worker you treated as an independent contractor may claim to have been misclassified by seeking benefits or rights available only to employees. For example, the worker might file a claim for unemployment insurance, file a lawsuit claiming unpaid wages or overtime, or file Form 8919, *Uncollected Social Security and Medicare Tax on Wages,* asserting that workers who perform similar services for you under similar control are classified as employees.

Strict ABC Test on the Rise

A growing number of states, including California, have adopted the more stringent ABC test to determine whether a worker is an employee or independent contractor for purposes of state taxes, wage and hour laws, unemployment benefits, workers' compensation, and more. The ABC test makes it much harder for employers to classify their workers as contractors.

Under this test, the worker must meet all three of the following factors to be classified as an independent contractor:

A. The worker is free from the direction and control of the hiring entity with respect to how the work is performed, both under the terms of the contract and in fact.

B. The worker performs work that is outside the hiring party's usual course of business.

C. The worker is customarily engaged in an independently established trade, occupation, or business of the same nature as the work performed.

The first prong of the test effectively mirrors the direction and control test used by the IRS. Under the second prong, the worker must be doing a type of work that is different from what the hiring entity normally performs. For example, if an accounting firm hires an electrician to fix an electrical fault, this factor is satisfied—but not if the firm tries to hire an accountant as a contractor. The third prong focuses on whether the worker is engaged in an independent trade or occupation. In our example, the electrician is a tradesperson performing electrical work, so this part of the test would clearly be satisfied.

Some states have exempted certain industries from this test, only apply certain parts of the test, or only use it for limited purposes.

It's possible that some federal agencies could adopt this test in the months or years ahead. Keep an eye on this book's online companion page for updates—the introduction explains how to find it. For more information on how and where the ABC Test applies, see *Working With Independent Contractors*, by Steve Fishman (Nolo).

The IRS presumes that a worker is an employee unless proven otherwise. If the IRS questions the status of a worker, it's up to you to prove that the worker is an independent contractor rather than an employee.

If the IRS determines that an employee was misclassified, the cost to your business will be heavy. You'll be responsible for paying the employee's Social Security tax, federal income tax, and federal unemployment insurance for up to three years. In addition, the IRS can add penalties and interest to the tally you must pay.

State government officials are also interested in businesses that misclassify employees as independent contractors. A state employment office may audit your business to see if there's been any misclassification. The audit can be the result of a spot check by the state employment office or a request by an independent contractor for unemployment or workers' compensation benefits. You may wind up owing money to a state unemployment insurance fund.

The IRS isn't the only federal agency looking for misclassification. The U.S. Department of Labor (DOL) is also looking over your shoulder. The DOL's interest in misclassification is that it denies workers a range of benefits and protections, from minimum wage and overtime pay to family and medical leave and protection from discrimination. The DOL has indicated that it plans to step up enforcement in this area, too. State tax agencies and state labor departments may be interested in misclassification issues for the same reasons.

Hiring Independent Contractors

There are several things you can do to help establish that a worker is properly classified as an independent contractor right from the start of the relationship.

Sign a contract spelling out the worker's responsibilities and how payment is to be determined for each job. (See sample contract, below.) The contract should allow the independent contractor to hire assistants and provide that the contractor will carry insurance, including workers' compensation. In addition to helping satisfy the federal or state government that a worker is truly an independent contractor, a good written contract will reduce disputes with the

State Laws on Employee Arrest and Conviction Records (continued)

Kansas

Kan. Stat. Ann. §§ 12-4516; 22-4710

Rules for employers: Cannot require an employee to inspect or challenge a criminal record in order to obtain a copy of the record to qualify for employment, but may require an applicant to sign a release to allow employer to obtain record to determine fitness for employment. Employers can require access to criminal records for specific businesses. Employer is not liable for making hiring or contracting decision based on applicant's criminal record, as long as it reasonably bears on applicant's trustworthiness or the safety or well-being of customers or other employees.

Rights of employees and applicants: Need not disclose expunged records on employment application except for sensitive positions enumerated in Kan. Stat. § 12-4516(2)(A)-(K).

Agency guidelines for preemployment inquiries: Kansas Human Rights Commission, "Guidelines on Equal Employment Practices: Preventing Discrimination in Hiring," at www.khrc.net/hiring.html.

Kentucky

Ky. Rev. Stat. Ann. §§ 431.073, 431.076

Rights of employees and applicants: Need not disclose expunged records on employment application.

Louisiana

La. Rev. Stat. Ann. § 37:2950

Rights of employees and applicants: Prior conviction cannot be used as a sole basis to deny an occupational or professional license, unless conviction directly relates to the license being sought and the reasons for denial are stated explicitly, in writing.

Special situations: Protection does not apply to medical, engineering and architecture, or funeral and embalming licenses, among others listed in the statute.

Maine

Me. Rev. Stat. Ann. tit. 5, § 5301

Rights of employees and applicants: A conviction is not an automatic bar to obtaining an occupational or professional license. Only convictions that directly relate to the profession or occupation, that include dishonesty or false statements, that are subject to imprisonment for more than one year, or that involve sexual misconduct on the part of a licensee may be considered.

Agency guidelines for preemployment inquiries: The Maine Human Rights Commission, "Pre-Employment Inquiry Guide," at www.maine.gov/mhrc/guidance/pre-employment_inquiry_guide.htm, suggests that asking about arrests is an improper race-based question, but that it is okay to ask about a conviction if related to the job.

Maryland

Md. Code Ann. Crim. Proc. §§ 10-109, 10-301, 10-306; Md. Regs. Code § 09.01.10.02

Rules for employers: May not inquire about criminal charges that have been expunged or criminal records that have been shielded under the Maryland Second Chance Act. May not use a refusal to disclose information as sole basis for not hiring an applicant.

State Laws on Employee Arrest and Conviction Records (continued)

Rights of employees and applicants: Need not refer to or give any information about an expunged charge or shielded record. A professional or occupational license may not be refused or revoked simply because of a conviction; agency must consider the nature of the crime and its relation to the occupation or profession; the conviction's relevance to the applicant's fitness and qualifications; when conviction occurred and other convictions, if any; and the applicant's behavior before and after conviction.

Agency guidelines for preemployment inquiries: DLLR's Office of Fair Practices, "Guidelines for Pre-Employment Inquiries Technical Assistance Guide," at www.dllr. maryland.gov/oeope/preemp.shtml.

Massachusetts

Mass. Gen. Laws ch. 6, § 171A; ch. 151B, § 4; ch. 276, § 100A; Mass. Regs. Code tit. 804, § 3.02

Rules for employers: Unless federal or state law disqualifies applicants with certain convictions from holding position, may not ask about criminal record information of any kind on initial written application. If job application has a question about prior arrests or convictions, it must include a formulated statement (that appears in the statute) that states that an applicant with a sealed or expunged record is entitled to answer, "No record." May not ask about arrests that did not result in conviction. May not ask about first-time convictions for drunkenness, simple assault, speeding, minor traffic violations, affray, or disturbing the peace; may not ask about misdemeanor convictions 3 or more years old unless

applicant has another conviction within the last 3 years.

Rights of employees and applicants: If criminal record is sealed may answer, "No record" to any inquiry about past arrests or convictions.

Special situations: Employer must give applicant a copy of criminal record before asking about it. Employer must give applicant a copy of record after making adverse job decision (if it didn't already provide the record). Additional rules apply to employers that conduct five or more criminal background checks per year.

Agency guidelines for preemployment inquiries: Massachusetts Commission Against Discrimination, "Employment Discrimination on the Basis of Criminal Record," at www.mass.gov/mcad/ resources/employers-businesses/emp-fact-sheet-discrim-criminal-record-gen.html.

Michigan

Mich. Comp. Laws § 37.2205a

Rules for employers: May not request information on any misdemeanor arrests or charges that did not result in conviction. May ask about felony arrests and misdemeanor or felony convictions.

Rights of employees and applicants: Employees or applicants are not making a false statement if they fail to disclose information they have a civil right to withhold.

Agency guidelines for preemployment inquiries: Michigan Department of Civil Rights, "Pre-Employment Inquiry Guide," at www.michigan.gov/documents/mdcr/ Preemploymentguide62012_388403_7.pdf.

State Laws on Employee Arrest and Conviction Records (continued)

Minnesota

Minn. Stat. Ann. §§ 181.981, 364.01 to 364.03

Rules for employers: Employers may not ask, consider, or require applicants to disclose criminal record or history until selected for an interview or, if there is no interview, until a conditional offer of employment is made. However, employer may notify applicants that particular criminal records will disqualify applicants from holding particular jobs.

Rights of employees and applicants: No one can be disqualified from pursuing or practicing an occupation that requires a license, unless the crime directly relates to the occupation. Agency may consider the nature and seriousness of the crime and its relation to the applicant's fitness for the occupation. Even if the crime does relate to the occupation, a person who provides evidence of rehabilitation and present fitness cannot be disqualified.

Special situations: Employee's criminal record is not admissible in any civil lawsuit against the employer based on the employee's actions if: the lawsuit is based on the employer's compliance with the state's "ban the box" law; the employee's record was sealed or pardoned prior to the actions; the employee's record consists only of arrests or charges that did not lead to conviction; or the employee's job duties did not create any greater risk of harm than being employed in general or interacting with the public outside of work.

Agency guidelines for preemployment inquiries: Minnesota Department of Human Rights, "Criminal Background" at http://mn.gov/mdhr/employers/criminal-background.

Mississippi

Miss. Code Ann. § 99-19-71

Rules for employers: Employer may ask applicant if expunction order has been issued regarding the applicant.

Rights of employees and applicants: Applicant need not disclose expunged arrest or conviction when responding to inquiries.

Missouri

Mo. Rev. Stat. § 314.200

Rights of employees and applicants: No one may be denied a license for a profession or occupation primarily on the basis that a prior conviction negates the person's good moral character, if the applicant has been released from incarceration by pardon, parole, or otherwise, or the applicant is on probation with no evidence of violations. The conviction may be considered, but the licensing board must also consider the crime's relation to the license, the date of conviction, the applicant's conduct since the conviction, and other evidence of the applicant's character.

Montana

Mont. Admin. Rule 24.9.1406

Rules for employers: Employer should not ask questions about arrests at any point in the hiring process. Employers may ask about convictions, however.

State Laws on Employee Arrest and Conviction Records (continued)

Nebraska

Neb. Rev. Stat. § 29-3523

Rules for employers: May not obtain access to information regarding arrests after one year if no charges are filed by prosecutor decision; after two years if no charges are filed as a result of completed diversion; or after three years if charges were filed but were dismissed by the court. May not ask about sealed records in an employment application.

Rights of employees and applicants: As to sealed records, employee may respond as if the offense never occurred.

Nevada

Nev. Rev. Stat. §§ 176A.850, 179A.100(3), 179.285, 179.301

Rules for employers: Unless applicant consents, employer may obtain only records of convictions or incidents for which the applicant or employee is currently within the criminal justice system, including parole or probation.

Rights of employees and applicants: Employees may not be required to disclose sealed convictions, or convictions for which they were honorably discharged from probation (except to a gaming establishment or state employer).

Agency guidelines for preemployment inquiries: Nevada Equal Rights Commission, "Guide to Pre-Employment," at http://detr.state.nv.us/Nerc_pages/premployment_guide.htm.

New Hampshire

N.H. Rev. Stat. Ann. § 651:5(X)

Rules for employers: May ask about a previous criminal record only if question substantially follows this wording, "Have you ever been arrested for or convicted of a crime that has not been annulled by a court?"

New Jersey

N.J. Stat. Ann. §§ 5:5-34.1, 5:12-89, 5:12-91, 34:6B-11 to 34:6B-19

Rules for employers: Employers with 15 or more employees may not publish a job advertisement that states that applicants who have been arrested or convicted will not be considered for the position. These employers also may not ask applicants about criminal history until after an interview has been conducted. These employers also may not refuse to hire an applicant based on a criminal record that has been expunged or erased through executive pardon.

Special situations: There are specific rules for casino employees, longshoremen and related occupations, horse racing, and other gaming industry jobs.

New Mexico

Criminal Offender Employment Act, N.M. Stat. Ann. §§ 28-2-1 through 28-2-4

Rules for employers: Employers may not ask about an applicant's arrest or conviction record on the employment application but may consider conviction after reviewing and discussing the application with the applicant.

Special situations: For a license, permit, or other authority to engage in any regulated trade, business, or profession, a regulating agency may consider felony and

State Laws on Employee Arrest and Conviction Records (continued)

convictions for misdemeanors involving moral turpitude. Such convictions cannot be an automatic bar to authority to practice in the regulated field, but may be disqualifying if they relate directly to the profession, the agency determines after investigation that the applicant isn't sufficiently rehabilitated to warrant the public's trust, or the field is teaching or child care (for certain offenses).

New York

N.Y. Correct. Law §§ 750 to 754; N.Y. Exec. Law § 296 (15), (16)

Rules for employers: It is unlawful discrimination to ask about any arrests or charges that did not result in conviction, unless they are currently pending. Employers also may not ask about sealed convictions or youthful offender adjudications. Employers with ten or more employees may not deny employment based on a conviction unless it relates directly to the job or would be an "unreasonable" risk to property or to public or individual safety. Employer must consider eight factors listed in statute. If employer considers these factors and makes a reasonable, good-faith decision to hire or retain employee, there's a rebuttable presumption that evidence of the employee's criminal history should be excluded in any subsequent lawsuit for negligent hiring or retention.

Rights of employees and applicants: Upon request, applicant must be given, within 30 days, a written statement of the reasons why employment was denied.

Agency guidelines for preemployment inquiries: New York State Human Rights Law (NYSHRL) prohibits employers from discriminating on the basis of criminal conviction history. Entities that are not direct employers may also be liable, however only for aiding and abetting a violation of the NYSHRL.

Griffin v. Sirva, Inc., No. 35, 54 N.Y.S.3d 360, 2017 N.Y. Slip Op. 03557, 2017 WL 1712423, (N.Y., May 04, 2017).

North Carolina

N.C. Gen. Stat. § 15A-146

Rules for employers: May not ask applicants about expunged arrests, charges, or convictions.

Rights of employees and applicants: Person whose arrest or charge was expunged may omit expunged entries in response to questions.

Special situations: Licensing board may not automatically deny professional or occupational license to applicant based on criminal history. If board is authorized to deny license based on crime of fraud or moral turpitude, must consider: level and seriousness of crime; when crime occurred; age of applicant when crime occurred; circumstances of crime; relationship between crime and profession or occupation; prison, parole, rehabilitation, and employment records since crime was committed; any subsequent criminal activity; and affidavits and other documents, including character references.

State Laws on Employee Arrest and Conviction Records (continued)

North Dakota

N.D. Cent. Code § 12-60-16.6

Rules for employers: May obtain records of arrests (adults only) occurring in the past three years or of convictions, provided the information has not been purged or sealed.

Agency guidelines for preemployment inquiries: North Dakota Department of Labor, "Employment Applications and Interviews," www.nd.gov/labor/publications/docs/employment.pdf.

Ohio

Ohio Rev. Code Ann. §§ 2151.357, 2953.33, 2953.55

Rules for employers: May inquire only into convictions or bail forfeitures that have not been sealed, unless question has a direct and substantial relationship to job.

Rights of employees and applicants: May not be asked about arrest records that are sealed; may respond to inquiry as though arrest did not occur.

Oklahoma

Okla. Stat. Ann. tit. 22, § 19(F)

Rules for employers: May not inquire into any criminal record that has been expunged.

Rights of employees and applicants: If record is expunged, may state that no criminal action ever occurred. May not be denied employment for refusing to disclose sealed criminal record information.

Oregon

Or. Rev. Stat. Ann. §§ 181A.230, 181A.240, and 181A.245, 659A.030, 659A.360

Rules for employers: Employer may not ask about criminal convictions on an employment application. Employer may ask about criminal convictions only after an initial interview or after a conditional offer of employment has been made.

Employer may request information from state police department about convictions and arrests in the past year that have not resulted in dismissal or acquittal. Before making request, employer must notify employee or applicant; when submitting request, must tell department when and how person was notified. May not discriminate against an applicant or current employee on the basis of an expunged juvenile record unless there is a "bona fide occupational qualification."

Rights of employees and applicants: Before State Police Department releases any criminal record information, it must notify employee or applicant and provide a copy of all information that will be sent to employer. Notice must include protections under federal civil rights law and the procedure for challenging information in the record. Record may not be released until 14 days after notice is sent.

Pennsylvania

18 Pa. Cons. Stat. § 9125

Rules for employers: May consider felony and misdemeanor convictions only if they relate to person's suitability for the job.

Rights of employees and applicants: Must be informed in writing if refusal to hire is based on criminal record information.

State Laws on Employee Arrest and Conviction Records (continued)

Rhode Island

R.I. Gen. Laws §§ 12-1.3-4, 13-8.2-1 through 8, 28-5-7(7)

Rules for employers: It is unlawful to include on an application form or to ask as part of an interview if the applicant has ever been arrested or charged with any crime. Application form may not include questions about arrests, charges, or convictions, except questions about convictions for specific offenses that would legally disqualify the applicant for the position under federal or state law, or would preclude bonding (if bonding is required for the position). May ask about convictions during the first interview or later.

Rights of employees and applicants: Do not have to disclose any conviction that has been expunged. As to sealed records for arrests due to mistaken identity, employee may respond as if the offense never occurred.

Special situations: Those convicted of crimes may apply to the parole board for a Certificate of Recovery and Re-Entry, stating that the holder has achieved certain rehabilitation goals. Parole board will consider applications for a certificate one year or more after conviction of a misdemeanor, or three years or more after conviction of a nonviolent felony. Although the purpose of this certificate is to assist the holder in reentering society, employers are not liable for denying employment based on prior conviction(s), even if the applicant holds a certificate.

Agency guidelines for preemployment inquiries: Rhode Island Commission for Human Rights, "Pre-Employment Inquiries Guidelines," at www.richr.state.ri.us/pei.pdf.

South Carolina

S.C. Code Ann. § 40-1-140

Rights of employees and applicants: Person may not be denied authorization to practice, pursue, or engage in regulated profession or occupation based on prior conviction, unless it relates directly to the profession or occupation or the applicant is found unfit or unsuitable based on all available information, including the prior conviction.

South Dakota

Agency guidelines for preemployment inquiries: South Dakota Division of Human Rights, "Pre-Employment Inquiry Guide," at www.sdra.org/dwnld/preemplo.htm suggests that an employer shouldn't ask or check into arrests or convictions if they are not substantially related to the job.

Texas

Tex. Crim. Proc. Code Ann. § 55.03; Tex. Fam. Code Ann. § 58.261

Rights of employees and applicants: Employee may deny the occurrence of any arrest that has been expunged. An employee whose juvenile records have been sealed is not required to disclose in a job application that the employee was the subject of a juvenile court proceeding.

State Laws on Employee Arrest and Conviction Records (continued)

Vermont

13 Vt. Stat. Ann. §§ 7606 to 7607; 21 Vt. Stat. Ann. § 495j

Rules for employers: May not ask about criminal history on an employment application, except for specific offenses that would disqualify the applicant for the position under state or federal law. Employer may ask about criminal history during an interview or once the applicant has been deemed qualified for the position.

Rights of employees and applicants: Need not disclose arrests or convictions that have been expunged or sealed.

Virginia

Va. Code Ann. § 19.2-392.4

Rules for employers: May not require an applicant to disclose information about any arrest or criminal charge that has been expunged.

Rights of employees and applicants: Need not refer to any expunged charges if asked about criminal record.

Washington

Wash. Rev. Code Ann. §§ 49.94.010, 9.96.060(3), 9.96A.020, 43.43.815; Wash. Admin. Code § 162-12-140

Rules for employers: An employer may not ask about, seek, or consider an applicant's criminal history until after it has determined that the applicant is "otherwise qualified" for the job. At a minimum, the employer must first determine that the applicant meets the basic criteria of the job. After that, employers may seek out criminal history, subject to the limitations below.

An employer that obtains a conviction record must notify the applicant within 30 days of receiving it and must allow the employee to examine it. And, according to the Human Rights Commission, employers with eight or more employees must consider certain information before rejecting an applicant based on criminal history. With respect to arrest records, these employers must ask whether the charges are still pending, have been dismissed, or led to conviction that would adversely affect job performance and whether the arrest occurred in the last ten years. These employers may make an employment decision based on a conviction record, but only if the conviction or the applicant's release from prison occurred within the last ten years and the crime reasonably relates to the job duties.

Rights of employees and applicants: If a conviction record is cleared or vacated, may answer questions as though the conviction never occurred. A person convicted of a felony cannot be refused an occupational license unless the conviction is less than ten years old and the felony relates specifically to the occupation or business.

Agency guidelines for preemployment inquiries: Washington Human Rights Commission, "Preemployment inquiry guide," at http://apps.leg.wa.gov/WAC/default. aspx?cite=162-12.

West Virginia

W. Va. Code § 49-4-723

Rules for employers: Employers may not discriminate on the basis of juvenile criminal records that have been expunged.

State Laws on Employee Arrest and Conviction Records (continued)

Agency guidelines for preemployment inquiries: West Virginia Bureau of Employment Programs, "Pre-employment Inquiries Technical Assistance Guide," at www.wvcommerce.org/App_Media/assets/pdf/workforce/WFWV_Afirmative_Action_Pre-employment_Inquiries.pdf. The state's website says that employers can only make inquiries about convictions directly related to the job.

Wisconsin

Wis. Stat. §§ 111.31 and 111.335

Rules for employers: It is a violation of state civil rights law to discriminate against an employee on the basis of a prior arrest or conviction record. Arrest records: May not ask about arrests unless there are pending charges. May not reject applicant unless pending charges are substantially related to the job or would preclude required bonding. Convictions: May not ask about convictions unless charges substantially relate to job or would preclude required bonding.

Special situations: Employers are entitled to obtain complete criminal record information for positions that require bonding and for burglar alarm installers.

Agency guidelines for preemployment inquiries: Wisconsin Department of Workforce Development, Equal Rights Division, Civil Rights Bureau, "Fair Hiring & Avoiding Loaded Interview Questions," at dwd.wisconsin.gov/er/civil_rights/discrimination/avoiding_discriminatory_interview_questions.htm.

Wyoming

Wyo. Stat. Ann. § 7-13-1401

Rights of employees and applicants: If an arrest or charge has been expunged, may respond to questions as if arrest or charge never occurred.

State Laws on Access to Personnel Records

This chart deals with only those states that authorize access to personnel files. Generally, an employee is allowed to see evaluations, performance reviews, and other documents that determine a promotion, bonus, or raise; access usually does not include letters of reference, test results, or records of a criminal or workplace violation investigation. Under other state laws, employees may have access to their medical records and records of exposure to hazardous substances; these laws are not included in this chart.

Alaska

Alaska Stat. § 23.10.430

Employers affected: All.

Employee access to records: Employee or former employee may view and copy personnel files.

Conditions for viewing records: Employee may view records during regular business hours under reasonable rules.

Copying records: Employee pays (if employer requests).

California

Cal. Lab. Code §§ 432,1198.5

Employers affected: All employers subject to wage and hour laws.

Employee access to records: Employee or former employee has right to inspect personnel records relating to performance or to a grievance proceeding, within 30 days of making a written request for records. Employer may redact the names of any nonmanagerial employees. Employer need not comply with more than one request per year from a former employee. If employee files a lawsuit against employer that relates to a personnel matter, the right to review personnel records ceases while the suit is pending.

Written request required: Yes. If employee makes an oral request, the employer must supply a form to make a written request.

Conditions for viewing records: Employee may view personnel file at reasonable times, during break or nonwork hours. If records are kept offsite or employer does not make them available at the workplace, then employee must be allowed to view them at the storage location without loss of pay. If former employee was terminated for reasons relating to harassment or workplace violence, employer may provide copy of records or make them available offsite.

Copying records: Employee or former employee also has a right to a copy of personnel records, at the employee's cost, within 30 days of making a written request.

Colorado

Colo. Rev. Stat. § 8-2-129

Employers affected: All.

Employee access to records: Upon request, current employee may inspect personnel file at least once per year. Former employee may inspect personnel file once after termination of employment.

Conditions for viewing records: Employer must make personnel file available at its place of business at a time convenient to employee and employer. Employer may have a designated representative present at the time of inspection.

Copying records: Employee or former employee may request a copy of the

State Laws on Access to Personnel Records (continued)

personnel file. Employer can require the employee to pay reasonable copying costs.

Connecticut
Conn. Gen. Stat. §§ 31-128a to 31-128h

Employers affected: All.

Employee access to records: Employee has right to inspect personnel files within seven business days after making a request, but not more than twice a year. Former employee has right to inspect personnel files within ten business days after making a request.

Written request required: Yes.

Conditions for viewing records: Employee may view records during regular business hours in a location at or near worksite. Employer may require that files be viewed in the presence of designated official.

Copying records: Employer must provide copies within seven days (current employee) or ten days (former employee) after receiving employee's written request; request must identify the materials employee wants copied. Employer may charge a fee that is based on the cost of supplying documents. Employee is entitled to a copy of any disciplinary action against the employee within one business day after it is imposed; employer must immediately provide terminated employee with a copy of the termination notice.

Employee's right to insert rebuttal: If employee disagrees with information in personnel file and cannot reach an agreement with employer to remove or correct it, employee may submit an explanatory written statement (a "rebuttal"). Rebuttal must be maintained as part of the file. Employer must inform employee of the right to submit a rebuttal in evaluation, discipline, or termination paperwork.

Delaware
Del. Code tit. 19, §§ 730 to 735

Employers affected: All.

Employee access to records: Current employee, employee who is laid off with reemployment rights, or employee on leave of absence may inspect personnel record; employee's agent is not entitled to have access to records. Unless there is reasonable cause, employer may limit access to once a year.

Written request required: At employer's discretion. Employer may require employee to file a form and indicate either the purpose of the review or what parts of the record employee wants to inspect.

Conditions for viewing records: Records may be viewed during employer's regular business hours. Employer may require that employees view files on their own time and may also require that files be viewed on the premises and in the presence of a designated official.

Copying records: Employer is not required to permit employee to copy records. Employee may take notes.

Employee's right to insert rebuttal: If employee disagrees with information in personnel file and cannot reach an agreement with employer to remove or correct it, employee may submit an explanatory written statement (a "rebuttal"). Rebuttal must be maintained as part of the personnel file.

State Laws on Access to Personnel Records (continued)

Illinois

820 Ill. Comp. Stat. §§ 40/1 to 40/12

Employers affected: Employers with five or more employees.

Employee access to records: Current employee, or former employee terminated within the past year, is permitted to inspect records twice a year at reasonable intervals, unless a collective bargaining agreement provides otherwise. An employee involved in a current grievance may designate a representative of the union or collective bargaining unit, or other agent, to inspect personnel records that may be relevant to resolving the grievance. Employer must make records available within seven working days after employee makes request (if employer cannot meet deadline, may be allowed an additional seven days).

Written request required: At employer's discretion. Employer may require use of a form.

Conditions for viewing records: Records may be viewed during normal business hours at or near worksite or, at employer's discretion, during nonworking hours at a different location if more convenient for employee.

Copying records: After reviewing records, employee may get a copy. Employer may charge only actual cost of duplication. If employee is unable to view files at worksite, employer, upon receipt of a written request, must mail employee a copy.

Employee's right to insert rebuttal: If employee disagrees with any information in the personnel file and cannot reach an agreement with employer to remove or correct it, employee may submit an explanatory written statement (a "rebuttal"). Rebuttal must remain in file with no additional comment by employer.

Iowa

Iowa Code §§ 91A.2, 91B.1

Employers affected: All employers with salaried employees or commissioned salespeople.

Employee access to records: Employee may have access to personnel file at time agreed upon by employer and employee.

Conditions for viewing records: Employer's representative may be present.

Copying records: Employer may charge copying fee for each page that is equivalent to a commercial copying service fee.

Maine

Me. Rev. Stat. tit. 26, § 631

Employers affected: All.

Employee access to records: Within ten days of submitting request, employee, former employee, or authorized representative may view and copy personnel files.

Written request required: Yes.

Conditions for viewing records: Employee may view records during normal business hours at the location where the files are kept, unless employer, at own discretion, arranges a time and place more convenient for employee. If files are in electronic or any other nonprint format, employer must provide equipment for viewing and copying.

State Laws on Access to Personnel Records (continued)

Copying records: Employee entitled to one free copy of personnel file during each calendar year, including any material added to file during that year. Employee must pay for any additional copies.

Massachusetts

Mass. Gen. Laws ch. 149, § 52C

Employers affected: All.

Employee access to records: Employee or former employee must have opportunity to review personnel files within five business days of submitting request, but not more than twice a calendar year. (Law does not apply to tenured or tenure-track employees in private colleges and universities.) Employer must notify an employee within ten days of placing in the employee's personnel record any information to the extent that the information is, has been, or may be used, to negatively affect the employee's qualification for employment, promotion, transfer, additional compensation, or the possibility that the employee will be subject to disciplinary action. (This notification does not count toward employee's two allotted opportunities to view personnel file.)

Written request required: Yes.

Conditions for viewing records: Employee may view records at workplace during normal business hours.

Copying records: Employee must be given a copy of record within five business days of submitting a written request.

Employee's right to insert rebuttal: If employee disagrees with any information in personnel record and cannot reach an agreement with employer to remove or correct it, employee may submit an explanatory written statement (a "rebuttal"). Rebuttal becomes a part of the personnel file.

Michigan

Mich. Comp. Laws §§ 423.501 to 423.505

Employers affected: Employers with four or more employees.

Employee access to records: Current or former employee is entitled to review personnel records at reasonable intervals, generally not more than twice a year, unless a collective bargaining agreement provides otherwise.

Written request required: Yes. Request must describe the record employee wants to review.

Conditions for viewing records: Employee may view records during normal office hours either at or reasonably near the worksite. If these hours would require employee to take time off work, employer must provide another reasonable time for review.

Copying records: After reviewing files, employee may get a copy; employer may charge only actual cost of duplication. If employee is unable to view files at the worksite, employer, upon receipt of a written request, must mail employee a copy.

Employee's right to insert rebuttal: If employee disagrees with any information in personnel record and cannot reach an agreement with employer to remove or correct it, employee may submit a written statement explaining his or her position. Statement may be no longer than five 8½" by 11" pages.

State Laws on Access to Personnel Records (continued)

Minnesota

Minn. Stat. §§ 181.960 to 181.966

Employers affected: Employers with 20 or more employees.

Employee access to records: Current employee may review files once per six-month period; former employee may have access to records once only during the first year after termination. Employer must comply with written request within seven working days (14 working days if personnel records kept out of state). Employer may not retaliate against an employee who asserts rights under these laws.

Written request required: Yes.

Conditions for viewing records: Current employee may view records during employer's normal business hours at worksite or a nearby location; does not have to take place during employee's working hours. Employer or employer's representative may be present.

Copying records: Employer must provide copy free of charge. Current employee must first review record and then submit written request for copies. Former employee must submit written request; providing former employee with a copy fulfills employer's obligation to allow access to records.

Employee's right to insert rebuttal: If employee disputes specific information in the personnel record, and cannot reach an agreement with employer to remove or revise it, employee may submit a written statement identifying the disputed information and explaining his or her position. Statement may be no longer than five pages and must be kept with personnel record as long as it is maintained.

Nevada

Nev. Rev. Stat. § 613.075

Employers affected: All.

Employee access to records: An employee who has worked at least 60 days, and a former employee, within 60 days of termination, must be given a reasonable opportunity to inspect personnel records.

Conditions for viewing records: Employee may view records during employer's normal business hours.

Copying records: Employer may charge only actual cost of providing access and copies.

Employee's right to insert rebuttal: Employee may submit a reasonable written explanation in direct response to any entry in personnel record. Statement must be of reasonable length; employer may specify the format; employer must maintain statement in personnel records.

New Hampshire

N.H. Rev. Stat. § 275:56

Employers affected: All.

Employee access to records: Employer must provide employees with a reasonable opportunity to inspect records.

Copying records: Employer may charge a fee reasonably related to cost of supplying copies.

Employee's right to insert rebuttal: If employee disagrees with any of the information in personnel record and

State Laws on Access to Personnel Records (continued)

cannot reach an agreement with the employer to remove or correct it, employee may submit an explanatory written statement along with supporting evidence. Statement must be maintained as part of personnel file.

Oregon
Or. Rev. Stat. § 652.750
Employers affected: All.

Employee access to records: Within 45 days after receipt of request, employer must provide employee a reasonable opportunity to inspect payroll records and personnel records used to determine qualifications for employment, promotion, or additional compensation, termination, or other disciplinary action.

Conditions for viewing records: Employee may view records at worksite or place of work assignment.

Copying records: Within 45 days after receipt of request, employer must provide a certified copy of requested record to current or former employee (if request made within 60 days of termination). If employee makes request after 60 days from termination, employer shall provide a certified copy of requested records if employer has records at time of the request. May charge amount reasonably calculated to recover actual cost of providing copy.

Pennsylvania
43 Pa. Cons. Stat. §§ 1321 to 1324
Employers affected: All.

Employee access to records: Employer must allow employee to inspect personnel record at reasonable times. (Employee's agent, or employee who is laid off with reemployment rights or on leave of absence, must also be given access.) Unless there is reasonable cause, employer may limit review to once a year by employee and once a year by employee's agent.

Written request required: At employer's discretion. Employer may require the use of a form as well as a written indication of the parts of the record employee wants to inspect or the purpose of the inspection. For employee's agent: Employee must provide signed authorization designating agent; must be for a specific date and indicate the reason for the inspection or the parts of the record the agent is authorized to inspect.

Conditions for viewing records: Employee may view records during regular business hours at the office where records are maintained, when there is enough time for employee to complete the review. Employer may require that employee or agent view records on their own time and may also require that inspection take place on the premises and in the presence of employer's designated official.

Copying records: Employer not obligated to permit copying. Employee may take notes.

Employee's right to insert rebuttal: The Bureau of Labor Standards, after a petition and hearing, may allow employee to place a counterstatement in the personnel file, if employee claims that the file contains an error.

State Laws on Access to Personnel Records (continued)

Rhode Island

R.I. Gen. Laws § 28-6.4-1

Employers affected: All.

Employee access to records: Employer must permit employee to inspect personnel file when given at least seven days' advance notice (excluding weekends and holidays). Employer may limit access to no more than three times a year.

Written request required: Yes.

Conditions for viewing records: Employee may view records at any reasonable time other than employee's work hours. Inspection must take place in presence of employer or employer's representative.

Copying records: Employee may not make copies or remove files from place of inspection. Employer may charge a fee reasonably related to cost of supplying copies.

Virginia

VA Code § 8.01-413.1

Employers affected: All.

Employee access to records: Employer must furnish, within 30 days of written request, a copy of all records or papers in any format referencing employees dates of employment, wages, job description, job title, and injuries sustained during the course of employment.

Written request required: Yes.

Copying records: Employer may charge a reasonable fee for copying records or supplying electronic records.

Washington

Wash. Rev. Code §§ 49.12.240-49.12.260

Employers affected: All.

Employee access to records: Employee may have access to personnel records at least once a year within a reasonable time after making a request.

Employee's right to insert rebuttal: Employee may petition annually that employer review all information in employee's personnel file. If there is any irrelevant or incorrect information in the file, employer must remove it. If employee does not agree with employer's review, employee may request to have a statement of rebuttal or correction placed in file. Former employee has right of rebuttal for two years after termination.

Wisconsin

Wis. Stat. § 103.13

Employers affected: All employers that maintain personnel records.

Employee access to records: Employee and former employee must be allowed to inspect personnel records within seven working days of making request. Access is permitted twice per calendar year unless a collective bargaining agreement provides otherwise. Employee involved in a current grievance may designate a representative of the union or collective bargaining unit, or other agent, to inspect records that may be relevant to resolving the grievance.

Written request required: At employer's discretion.

State Laws on Access to Personnel Records (continued)

Conditions for viewing records: Employee may view records during normal working hours at a location reasonably near worksite. If this would require employee to take time off work, employer may provide another reasonable time and place for review.

Copying records: Employee's right of inspection includes the right to make or receive copies. If employer provides copies, may charge only actual cost of reproduction.

Employee's right to insert rebuttal: If employee disagrees with any information in the personnel record and cannot come to an agreement with the employer to remove or correct it, employee may submit an explanatory written statement. Employer must attach the statement to the disputed portion of the personnel record.

State Minimum Wage Laws for Tipped and Regular Employees

The chart below gives the basic state minimum wage laws. Depending on the occupation, the size of the employer's business, or the conditions of employment, the minimum wage may vary from the one listed here. Minimum wage rates in a number of states change from year to year; to be sure of your state's current minimum, contact your state department of labor or check its website, where most states have posted the minimum wage requirements. Also, some local governments have enacted ordinances that set a higher minimum wage; contact your city or county government for more information.

"Maximum Tip Credit" is the highest amount of tips that an employer can subtract from the employee's hourly wage. The employee's total wages minus the tip credit cannot be less than the state minimum wage. If an employee's tips exceed the maximum tip credit, the employee gets to keep the extra amount.

"Minimum Cash Wage" is the lowest hourly wage that an employer can pay a tipped employee.

State and Statute	Notes	Basic Minimum Hourly Rate (*=tied to federal rate)	Maximum Tip Credit	Minimum Cash Wage for Tipped Employee	Minimum Tips to Qualify as a Tipped Employee (monthly unless noted otherwise)
United States 29 U.S.C. §§ 203,206	This is the current federal minimum wage	$7.25	$5.12	$2.13	More than $30
Alabama	No minimum wage law				
Alaska Alaska Stat. § 23.10.065	Adjusts annually for inflation, posted at http://labor.alaska.gov/lss/whact.htm	$10.34	No tip credit	10.34	N/A
Arizona Ariz. Rev. Stat. § 23-363	Adjusts annually for inflation, posted at www.azica.gov/labor-minimum-wage-main-page; does not apply to small businesses (those with gross revenue of less than $500,000 that are exempt from federal minimum wage laws)	$12.15	$3.00	$9.15	

State Minimum Wage Laws for Tipped and Regular Employees (continued)

State and Statute	Notes	Basic Minimum Hourly Rate (*=tied to federal rate)	Maximum Tip Credit	Minimum Cash Wage for Tipped Employee	Minimum Tips to Qualify as a Tipped Employee (monthly unless noted otherwise)
Arkansas *Ark. Code §§ 11-4-210, 11-4-212*	Applies to employers with 4 or more employees	$11	$8.37 (increases as minimum wage increases)	$2.63	More than $20
California *Cal. Lab. Code § 1182.12*		Employers with 25 or fewer employees: $13 ($14 on January 1, 2022; $15 on January 1, 2023); employers with 26 or more employees: $14 ($15 on January 1, 2022)	No tip credit	Same as for non-tipped employees	N/A
Colorado *Colo. Const. 18 § 15; 7 Colo. Code Regs. § 1103-1:3*	Adjusted annually for inflation, posted at www.coworkforce.com	$12.32	$3.02	$9.30	More than $30
Connecticut *Conn. Gen. Stat. §§ 31-58(j), 31-60; Conn. Admin. Code § 31-61-E2*		$12 ($13 on August 1, 2021; $14 on July 1, 2022)	$5.62 for wait staff in hotel and restaurant industries; $3.77 for bartenders (increases as minimum wage increases)	$6.38 for wait staff in hotel and restaurant industries; $8.23 for bartenders	$10 per week (full-time employees); $2 per day (part-time employees)

State Minimum Wage Laws for Tipped and Regular Employees (continued)

State and Statute	Notes	Basic Minimum Hourly Rate (*=tied to federal rate)	Maximum Tip Credit	Minimum Cash Wage for Tipped Employee	Minimum Tips to Qualify as a Tipped Employee (monthly unless noted otherwise)
Delaware *Del. Code tit. 19, § 902(a)*		$9.25	$7.02 (increases as minimum wage increases)	$2.23	More than $30
District of Columbia *D.C. Code § 32-1003*	Adjusted for inflation annually beginning in 2021	$15	$10 (increases as minimum wage increases)	$5	Not specified
Florida *Fla. Const., X § 24; Fla. Stat. § 448.110*		$8.65 ($10 on September 30, 2021; $11 on September 30 2022; $12 on September 30, 2023; $13 on September 30, 2024; $14 on September 30, 2025; $15 on September 30, 2026; annual increases beginning September 30, 2026, in proportion to inflation)	$3.02	$5.63 (increases as minimum wage increases)	More than $30

State Minimum Wage Laws for Tipped and Regular Employees (continued)

State and Statute	Notes	Basic Minimum Hourly Rate (*=tied to federal rate)	Maximum Tip Credit	Minimum Cash Wage for Tipped Employee	Minimum Tips to Qualify as a Tipped Employee (monthly unless noted otherwise)
Georgia *Ga. Code § 3 4-4-3*	Applies to employers with 6 or more employees and more than $40,000 per year in sales	$5.15 if not covered by Federal Regulations, otherwise Federal Minimum Wage	Minimum wage does not apply to tipped employees	N/A	N/A
Hawaii *Haw. Rev. Stat. §§ 387-1–387-2*		$10.10	75¢ in 2016 and beyond, but only if the employee makes at least $7 more than minimum wage with tips	$9.35	More than $20
Idaho *Idaho Code §§ 44-1502, 44-1503*		$7.25	$3.90	$3.35	More than $30
Illinois *820 Ill. Comp. Stat. § 105/4; Ill. Admin. Code tit. 56, § 210.110*	Applies to employers with 4 or more employees (and all employers with respect to domestic workers)	$11 ($12 on January 1, 2022; $13 on January 1, 2023)	40%	$6.60 ($7.20 on January 1, 2022; $7.80 on January 1, 2023)	At least $20
Indiana *Ind. Code § 22-2-2-4*	Applies to employers with 2 or more employees	$7.25*	$5.12	$2.13	Not specified

State Minimum Wage Laws for Tipped and Regular Employees (continued)

State and Statute	Notes	Basic Minimum Hourly Rate (*=tied to federal rate)	Maximum Tip Credit	Minimum Cash Wage for Tipped Employee	Minimum Tips to Qualify as a Tipped Employee (monthly unless noted otherwise)
Iowa Iowa Code § 91D.1		$7.25	40%	$4.35	At least $30
Kansas Kan. Stat. § 44-1203	Applies to employers not covered by the FLSA	$7.25	$5.12	$2.13	Not specified
Kentucky Ky. Rev. Stat. § 337.275		$7.25*	$5.12	$2.13	More than $30
Louisiana	No minimum wage law				
Maine Me. Rev. Stat. tit. 26, §§ 663(8), 664	Indexed annual increases begin on January 1, 2021	$12.15	50%	$6.08	More than $30
Maryland Md. Code Lab. & Empl. §§ 3-413, 3-419		Employers with 14 or fewer employees: $11.60 ($12.20 on January 1, 2022; $12.80 on January 1, 2023). Employers with 15 or more employees: $11.75 ($12.50 on January 1, 2022; $13.25 on January 1, 2023)	Employers with 14 or fewer employees: $7.97. Employers with 15 or more employees: $8.12 (increases as minimum wage increases)	$3.63	More than $30

State Minimum Wage Laws for Tipped and Regular Employees (continued)

State and Statute	Notes	Basic Minimum Hourly Rate (*=tied to federal rate)	Maximum Tip Credit	Minimum Cash Wage for Tipped Employee	Minimum Tips to Qualify as a Tipped Employee (monthly unless noted otherwise)
Massachusetts *Mass. Gen. Laws ch. 151, §§ 1, 7; Mass. Code Regs. tit. 454, § 27.03*		$13.50 ($14.25 on January 1, 2022; $15 on January 1, 2023)	$7.95 ($8.10 on January 1, 2022; $8.25 on January 1, 2023)	$5.55 ($6.15 on January 1, 2022; $6.75 on January 1, 2023).	More than $20
Michigan *Mich. Comp. Laws §§ 408.931 and following*	Applies to employers with 2 or more employees; minimum wage increases take effect only if unemployment rate for preceding year is below 8.5%	$9.65 ($9.87 on January 1, 2022; $10.10 on January 1, 2023)	62% of the regular minimum wage	38% of the regular minimum wage	Not specified
Minnesota *Minn. Stat. § 177.24*	Indexed annual increases posted at www.dli.mn.gov/ business/employment-practices/minimum-wage-minnesota	$10.08 for large employers; $8.21 for small employers (businesses with annual gross volume of sales of less than $500,000)	No tip credit	Same as for non-tipped employees	N/A
Mississippi	No minimum wage law				
Missouri *Mo. Rev. Stat. §§ 290.502, 290.512*	Adjusted annually according to cost of living	$10.30 ($11.15 on January 1, 2022; $12 on January 1, 2023)	50% of the minimum wage	$5.15 (increases as minimum wage increases)	Not specified

State Minimum Wage Laws for Tipped and Regular Employees (continued)

State and Statute	Notes	Basic Minimum Hourly Rate (*=tied to federal rate)	Maximum Tip Credit	Minimum Cash Wage for Tipped Employee	Minimum Tips to Qualify as a Tipped Employee (monthly unless noted otherwise)
Montana *Mont. Code §§ 39-3-404, 39-3-409; Mont. Admin. R. 24.16.1508 and following*	Adjusted annually; posted at http://erd. dli.mt.gov/labor-standards/wage-and-hour-payment-act/minimum-wage-history	$8.75 ($4 for businesses with gross annual sales of $110,000 or less)	No tip credit	$8.75	N/A
Nebraska *Neb. Rev. Stat. § 48-1203*	Applies to employers with 4 or more employees	$9	$6.87	$2.13	Not specified
Nevada *Nev. Rev. Stat. §§ 608.100, 608.160, 608.250; Nev. Admin. Code § 608.100; Nev. Const. art. 15, § 16*	Adjusted annually, posted at labor.nv.gov	$8.75 if employer provides health benefits; $9.75 if no health benefits provided	No tip credit	$8.75 if employer provides health benefits; $9.75 if no health benefits provided	N/A
New Hampshire *N.H. Rev. Stat. § 279:21*		$7.25*	55%	45%	More than $30
New Jersey *N.J. Stat. § 34:11-56a4*	Adjusted annually based on consumer price index; posted at http://lwd.dol.state. nj.us/labor	$12*	$7.87 (increases as minimum wage increases)	$4.13 (suggested, not required)	Not specified

State Minimum Wage Laws for Tipped and Regular Employees (continued)

State and Statute	Notes	Basic Minimum Hourly Rate (*=tied to federal rate)	Maximum Tip Credit	Minimum Cash Wage for Tipped Employee	Minimum Tips to Qualify as a Tipped Employee (monthly unless noted otherwise)
New Mexico *N.M. Stat. § 50-4-22*		$10.50 ($11.50 on January 1, 2022; $12 on January 1, 2023)	$7.95 ($8.70 on January 1, 2022; $9 on January 1, 2023)	$2.55 ($2.80 on January 1, 2022; $3 on January 1, 2023)	More than $30
New York *N.Y. Lab. Law § 652*	Beginning January 1, 2021, the rate will be adjusted annually for inflation until it reaches $15 an hour.	$12.50	Depends on occupation; see www.labor.ny.gov/legal/counsel/pdf/tips-frequently-asked-questions.pdf	Depends on occupation	Depends on occupation
North Carolina *N.C. Gen. Stat. §§ 95-25.2(14), 95-25.3*		$7.25	$5.12	$2.13	More than $20
North Dakota *N.D. Cent. Code § 34-06-22; N.D. Admin. Code 46-02-07-01– 46-02-07-03*		$7.25	33% of minimum wage	$4.86	More than $30
Ohio *Ohio Rev. Code § 4111.02; Ohio Const. art. II, § 34a*	Adjusted annually, posted at www.com.ohio.gov/dico	$8.80 ($7.25 for employers with gross income under $323,000)	50%	$4.40	More than $30

State Minimum Wage Laws for Tipped and Regular Employees (continued)

State and Statute	Notes	Basic Minimum Hourly Rate (*=tied to federal rate)	Maximum Tip Credit	Minimum Cash Wage for Tipped Employee	Minimum Tips to Qualify as a Tipped Employee (monthly unless noted otherwise)
Oklahoma *Okla. Stat. tit. 40, §§ 197.2, 197.4, 197.16*	Applies to employers that are not covered by the FLSA and that have more than 10 full-time employees or more than $100,000 in gross annual sales	$7.25	50% of minimum wage for tips, food, and lodging combined	$3.63	Not specified
Oregon *Or. Rev. Stat. §§ 653.025, 653.035(3)*	Beginning July 1, 2023, the rate will be adjusted annually for inflation; posted at www.boli.state.or.us	$12.75 ($13.50 on July 1, 2022)	No tip credit	$12.75 ($13.50 on July 1, 2022)	N/A
Pennsylvania *43 Pa. Cons. Stat. §§ 333.103, 333.104; 34 Pa. Code §§ 231.1, 231.101*		$7.25*	$4.42	$2.83	More than $30
Rhode Island *R.I. Gen. Laws §§ 28-12-3, 28-12-5*		$11.50	$7.61	$3.89	Not specified
South Carolina	No minimum wage law				
South Dakota *S.D. Codified Laws §§ 60-11-3–60-11-3.2*	Adjusted annually based on cost of living; posted at http://dlr.sd.gov/employment_laws/minimum_wage.aspx	$9.45	50%	$4.73	More than $35
Tennessee	No minimum wage law				

State Minimum Wage Laws for Tipped and Regular Employees (continued)

State and Statute	Notes	Basic Minimum Hourly Rate (*=tied to federal rate)	Maximum Tip Credit	Minimum Cash Wage for Tipped Employee	Minimum Tips to Qualify as a Tipped Employee (monthly unless noted otherwise)
Texas *Tex. Lab. Code §§ 62.051, 62.052*		$7.25	$5.12	$2.13	More than $20
Utah *Utah Code § 34-40-102; Utah Admin. Code 610-1*		$7.25	$5.12	$2.13	More than $30
Vermont *Vt. Stat. tit. 21, § 384(a)*	Applies to employers with 2 or more employees; annual indexing began January 1, 2019, posted at www.vtlmi.info	$11.75	50% for employees of hotels, motels, restaurants, and tourist places	$5.88 (increases as minimum wage increases)	More than $120
Virginia *Va. Code §§ 40.1-28.9, 28.10*	Applies to employees not covered by FLSA	$9.50 ($11 on January 1, 2022; $12 on January 1, 2023)	Tips actually received	Minimum wage less tips actually received	Not specified
Washington *Wash. Rev. Code § 49.46.020; Wash. Admin. Code § 296-126-022*	Adjusted annually; posted at www.lni.wa.gov	$13.69	No tip credit	$13.69	N/A
West Virginia *W. Va. Code §§ 21-5C-1, 21-5C-2, 21-5C-4*	Applies to employers with 6 or more employees at one location who are not covered by the FLSA	$8.75	70% of minimum wage	$2.62 (increases as minimum wage increases)	Not specified

State Minimum Wage Laws for Tipped and Regular Employees (continued)

State and Statute	Notes	Basic Minimum Hourly Rate (*=tied to federal rate)	Maximum Tip Credit	Minimum Cash Wage for Tipped Employee	Minimum Tips to Qualify as a Tipped Employee (monthly unless noted otherwise)
Wisconsin Wis. Admin. Code DWD § 272.03		$7.25	$4.92	$2.33	Not specified
Wyoming Wyo. Stat. § 27-4-202		$5.15 if federal regulations do not apply	$3.02	$2.13	More than $30

State Meal and Rest Break Laws

Note: Any state not listed in this chart does not have any applicable laws or regulations on rest and meal breaks for workers employed in the private sector. Many states also exclude professional, administrative, and executive employees from these rules.

Other exceptions may apply. For example, many states have special break rules for specific occupations or industries, which are beyond the scope of this chart. Check the statute or check with your state department of labor if you need more information.

Alabama
Ala. Code § 25-8-38

Applies to: Employers with minor employees.

Breast-feeding: No employment-specific laws. However, breast-feeding is allowed in any public or private location where the mother's presence is authorized.

Special Laws for Minors: Employees aged 14 and 15 may not work more than five continuous hours without a meal or rest break of at least 30 minutes.

Alaska
Alaska Stat. § 23.10.350

Applies to: Employers with minor employees.

Special Laws for Minors: Minors (under 18) must receive unpaid break of at least 30 minutes when scheduled to work six hours or more or after working for five consecutive hours.

Arizona

Breast-feeding: No employment-specific laws. However, breast-feeding is allowed in any public place or place of public accommodation where the mother is lawfully present.

Arkansas
Ark. Code § 11-5-116

Applies to: All employers.

Breast-feeding: Reasonable unpaid breaks to express breast milk; if possible, break time to run concurrently with other breaks.

California
Cal. Lab. Code §§ 512, 1030; Cal. Code Regs. tit. 8, §§ 11010–11170

Applies to: Employers in most industries.

Exceptions: Motion picture and other occupations. See wage orders, Cal. Code Regs. tit. 8, §§ 11010 to 11160, for additional exceptions.

Meal Break: 30 minutes, unpaid, after five hours, except employer and employee can agree to waive meal period if employee works 6 hours or less. Second 30-minute unpaid meal period when employee works more than ten hours a day, except employer and employee can agree to waive the second meal period if the employee works 12 hours or less and took the first meal period. On-duty paid meal period permitted when nature of work prevents relief from all duties and parties agree in writing.

State Meal and Rest Break Laws (continued)

Rest Break: Paid ten-minute rest period for each four hours worked or major fraction thereof; as practicable, in the middle of the work period. Not required for employees whose total daily work time is less than three and a half hours.

Breast-feeding: Reasonable unpaid breaks to express breast milk; if possible, break time to run concurrently with other breaks. Employer must make reasonable efforts to provide a private location, other than a bathroom, for the employee to express milk.

Colorado

Colo. Rev. Stat. §§ 8-13.5-101–8-13.5-104. Colo. Code Regs. tit. 7 §§ 1103-1:1–1:5

Applies to: Retail and service, food and beverage, commercial support service, and health and medical industries.

Exceptions: Numerous exceptions are listed in the regulation.

Meal Break: 30 minutes, unpaid, after five hours of work, to the extent practical at least one hour after the start and one hour before the end of the shift. On-duty paid meal period permitted when nature of work prevents break from all duties.

Rest Break: Paid ten-minute rest period for each four hours or major fraction worked; if practical, in the middle of the work period.

Breast-feeding: Reasonable unpaid time and private space to express breast milk for up to two years after child's birth.

Connecticut

Conn. Gen. Stat. §§ 31-40w, 31-51ii

Applies to: All employers, except as noted.

Exceptions: Employers that pay for rest breaks as described below, those with a written agreement providing other break rules, and those granted an exemption for reasons listed in statute.

Meal Break: 30 minutes, unpaid, after first two hours of work and before last two hours for employees who work seven-and-a-half or more consecutive hours.

Rest Break: As alternative to meal break, a total of 30 minutes paid in each seven and a half hour work period.

Breast-feeding: Employee may use meal or rest breaks for breast-feeding or expressing breast milk. Reasonable efforts to provide private space.

Delaware

Del. Code tit. 19, §§ 707, 710-711

Applies to: All employers, except as noted.

Exceptions: Employers with alternative written agreement and those granted exemptions specified in statute. Law does not apply to teachers.

Meal Break: 30 minutes, unpaid, after first two hours and before the last two hours, for employees who work seven and a half consecutive hours or more.

Breast-feeding: Reasonable accommodations for limitations of a person related to pregnancy, childbirth, or a related condition may include break time and appropriate facilities for expressing breast milk, unless accommodation imposes an undue hardship.

State Meal and Rest Break Laws (continued)

District of Columbia

D.C. Code §§ 2-1402.82, 32-1231.01 - 32-1231.03

Applies to: All employers.

Breast-feeding: Reasonable unpaid time to express breast milk; runs concurrently with other paid or unpaid breaks provided by employer. Employer must make reasonable efforts to provide a private, sanitary location (other than a toilet stall) for expressing breast milk. Employer must provide reasonable accommodations to nursing mothers, unless it would cause an undue hardship.

Florida

Fla. Stat. § 450.081

Applies to: Employers with minor employees.

Breast-feeding: No employment-specific laws. However, breast-feeding is allowed in any public or private location where the mother's presence is authorized.

Special Laws for Minors: Minors aged 17 and younger may not work more than four continuous hours without a meal break of at least 30 minutes.

Georgia

Ga. Code § 34-1-6

Applies to: All employers.

Breast-feeding: Reasonable unpaid break time to express breast milk. Employer is not required to provide break time if unduly disruptive to workplace operations. Breast-feeding is allowed in any public or private location where the mother's presence is authorized.

Hawaii

Haw. Rev. Stat. §§ 378-2, 378-91 - 378-93, 390-2

Applies to: All employers.

Breast-feeding: Reasonable break time to express milk for nursing child for one year after birth each time the employee has a need to express breast milk, in a location, other than a bathroom, that is sanitary, shielded from view and free from intrusion. Employers with fewer than 20 employees exempt if requirements impose undue hardship.

Special Laws for Minors: Minor employees aged 14 or 15 may not work more than five consecutive hours without uninterrupted break of at least 30 minutes.

Illinois

820 Ill. Comp. Stat. §§ 140/3, 140/3.1, 260/10, 260/15

Applies to: All employers.

Exceptions: Employees whose meal periods are established by collective bargaining agreement. Employees who monitor individuals with developmental disabilities or mental illness, or both, and who are required to be on call during an entire eight-hour work period; these employees must be allowed to eat a meal while working.

Meal Break: 20 minutes, no later than five hours after the beginning of the shift, for employees who work seven and a half or more continuous hours. Hotel room attendants are entitled to a 30-minute meal break if they work at least seven hours.

State Meal and Rest Break Laws (continued)

Rest Break: In addition to meal break, hotel room attendants must receive two paid 15-minute rest breaks, if they work at least seven hours.

Breast-feeding: Employers with 5 or more employees must provide reasonable paid break time (can be concurrent with other break time) to express breast milk and reasonable efforts to provide a room or other location, other than a toilet stall, where an employee can express her milk in privacy for up to one year after the child's birth.

Indiana

Ind. Code §§ 22-2-14-1, 22-2-14-2

Applies to: Employers with 25 or more employees.

Breast-feeding: Employer must make reasonable efforts to provide a private space, other than a restroom, for an employee to express breast milk.

Iowa

Iowa Code § 92.7

Applies to: Employers with minor employees.

Breast-feeding: No employment-specific laws. However, breast-feeding is allowed in any public or private location where the mother's presence is authorized.

Special Laws for Minors: Minors under age 16 who work five hours or more in a day must receive a break of at least 30 minutes.

Kansas

Kan. Admin. Reg. 49-30-3

Applies to: Employees not covered under FLSA.

Meal Break: Not required, but if less than 30 minutes is given, break must be paid.

Breast-feeding: No employment-specific laws. However, breast-feeding is allowed in any public or private location where the mother's presence is authorized.

Kentucky

Ky. Rev. Stat. §§ 337.355, 337.365, 344.030, 344.040; 803 Ky. Admin. Regs. 1:065

Applies to: All employers, except as noted.

Exceptions: Written agreement providing different meal period; employers subject to Federal Railway Labor Act.

Meal Break: Reasonable off-duty period close to the middle of the shift; cannot be required to take it before the third or after the fifth hour of work. Coffee breaks and snack time do not count toward the meal break.

Rest Break: Paid ten-minute rest period for each four-hour work period. Rest period must be in addition to regularly scheduled meal period.

Breast-feeding: Employers with 15 or more employees must make reasonable accommodation for nursing mothers and employees with pregnancy- or childbirth-related conditions, unless doing so would cause undue hardship. Accommodation may include more frequent or longer breaks and a private space other than a bathroom to express breast milk.

State Meal and Rest Break Laws (continued)

Louisiana

La. Rev. Stat. § 23:213

Applies to: Employers with minor employees.

Breast-feeding: No employment-specific laws. However, breast-feeding is allowed in any public or private location where the mother's presence is authorized.

Special Laws for Minors: Minors may not work more than five hours without a 30-minute break.

Maine

Me. Rev. Stat. tit. 26, §§ 601, 604

Applies to: All employers, except those with fewer than three employees on duty who are able to take frequent breaks during the workday.

Exceptions: Collective bargaining or other written agreement between employer and employee may provide for different breaks.

Meal and Rest Break: 30 minutes after six consecutive hours of work, except in cases of emergency. Time may be unpaid if employee is completely relieved of duty.

Breast-feeding: Adequate unpaid time to express breast milk, or employee may use rest or meal time, for up to three years following childbirth.

Maryland

Md. Code Lab. & Empl. §§ 3-210, 3-710

Applies to: Retail establishments with 50 or more retail employees, minors.

Exceptions: Employees who work in an office or who work at a single location with five or fewer employees are not covered.

Meal Break: 30 minutes, after six consecutive hours of work.

Rest Break: 15 minutes, when working four to six consecutive hours. (This may be waived if the employee works less than six hours). Employees working eight or more consecutive hours must receive a 15-minute break for every additional four consecutive hours after a meal break.

Breast-feeding: No employment-specific laws. However, breast-feeding is allowed in any public or private location where the mother's presence is authorized.

Special Laws for Minors: Minors (under 18) may not work more than five hours without a break of at least 30 minutes. (Requirement applies to all employers with minor employees.)

Massachusetts

Mass. Gen. Laws ch. 149, §§ 100, 101; ch. 151B, § 4

Applies to: All employers, except as noted.

Exceptions: Excludes iron works, glass works, paper mills, letterpresses, print works, and bleaching or dyeing works. Attorney general may exempt businesses that require continuous operation if it won't affect worker safety. Collective bargaining agreement may also provide for different breaks.

Meal Break: 30 minutes, if work is for more than six hours.

Breast-feeding: Employers must make reasonable accommodation for nursing mothers and employees with pregnancy-related conditions, unless doing so would

State Meal and Rest Break Laws (continued)

cause undue hardship. Accommodation may include more frequent or longer breaks and a private non-bathroom space for expressing breast milk.

Michigan
Mich. Comp. Laws § 409.112

Applies to: Employers with minor employees.

Special Laws for Minors: Minors (under 18) may not work more than five consecutive hours without a break of at least 30 minutes.

Minnesota
Minn. Stat. §§ 177.253, 177.254, 181.939

Applies to: All employers.

Exceptions: Excludes certain agricultural and seasonal employees. A collective bargaining agreement may provide for different rest and meal breaks.

Meal Break: Sufficient unpaid time for employees who work eight consecutive hours or more.

Rest Break: Paid adequate rest period within each four consecutive hours of work to utilize nearest convenient restroom.

Breast-feeding: Reasonable unpaid break time to express milk. Employer must make reasonable efforts to provide a private room, other than a bathroom, for expressing breast milk.

Mississippi
Miss. Code § 71-1-55

Breast-feeding: Employee may use meal or rest break for expressing breast milk.

Missouri

Breast-feeding: No employment-specific laws. However, breast-feeding is allowed in any public or private location where the mother's presence is authorized.

Montana

Breast-feeding: No private employment-specific laws. However, breast-feeding is allowed in any public or private location where the mother's presence is authorized.

Nebraska
Neb. Rev. Stat. §§ 48-212, 48-1102

Applies to: Meal break provisions: assembly plant, workshop, or mechanical establishment. Breast-feeding provisions: employers with 15 or more employees.

Exceptions: Other written agreement between employer and employees.

Meal Break: 30 minutes off premises for each eight-hour shift.

Breast-feeding: Employer with 15 or more employees must provide reasonable accommodation to nursing mothers, unless it would cause an undue hardship. Accommodation may include breaks and an appropriate location for breast-feeding or expressing breast milk.

Nevada
Nev. Rev. Stat. §§ 608.019, 608.0193

Applies to: Employers of two or more employees.

Exceptions: Employees covered by collective bargaining agreement; exemptions for business necessity.

State Meal and Rest Break Laws (continued)

Meal Break: 30 minutes for eight continuous hours of work.

Rest Break: Paid ten-minute rest period for each four hours or major fraction worked; as practicable, in middle of the work period. Not required for employees whose total daily work time is less than three and a half hours.

Breast-feeding: Employer must provide reasonable break time with or without compensation to express breast milk as needed; and a place, other than a bathroom, reasonably free from dirt or pollution, protected from the view of others, and free from intrusion by others. Employer with less than 50 employees exempt if requirements constitute undue hardship. Certain licensed contractors are not required to comply with regard to employees who work at a construction job site located at least three miles from the employers regular place of business. If employer believes complying will cause an undue hardship, the employer and employee must engage in a timely, good faith and interactive process to determine an effective, reasonable accommodation. If the parties cannot reach an agreement, the employer can require the employee to accept the reasonable alternative selected by the employer, subject to the employee's right to appeal the decision to the appropriate authorities.

New Hampshire
N.H. Rev. Stat. § 275:30-a
Applies to: All employers.

Meal Break: 30 minutes after five consecutive hours, unless the employer allows the employee to eat while working and it is feasible for the employee to do so.

Breast-feeding: No employment-specific laws. However, restricting or limiting the right of a mother to breast-feed her child is discriminatory.

New Jersey
N.J. Stat.§ 10:5-12, 34:2-21.4
Applies to: All employers.

Breast-feeding: Employer must provide reasonable break time and a suitable private location, other than a toilet stall, unless it would cause undue hardship on the employer.

Special Laws for Minors: Minors (under 18) may not work more than five consecutive hours without a break of at least 30 minutes.

New Mexico
N.M. Stat. § 28-20-2
Breast-feeding: Flexible unpaid breaks to use breast pump in the workplace. Employer must provide a private space, other than a bathroom, for expressing breast milk.

New York
N.Y. Lab. Law §§ 162, 206-c
Applies to: Factories, workshops, manufacturing facilities, mercantile (retail and wholesale) establishments.

Meal Break: Factory employees, 60 minutes between 11 a.m. and 2 p.m.; mercantile employees, 30 minutes between 11 a.m.

State Meal and Rest Break Laws (continued)

and 2 p.m. If a shift starts before 11 a.m. and ends after 7 p.m., every employee gets an additional 20 minutes between 5 p.m. and 7 p.m. If a shift starts between 1 p.m. and 6 a.m., a factory employee gets 60 minutes, and a mercantile employee gets 45 minutes, in the middle of the shift. Labor commissioner may permit a shorter meal break; the permit must be in writing and posted conspicuously in the main entrance of the workplace.

Breast-feeding: Reasonable unpaid break time to express breast milk for up to three years after child's birth. Employers must make reasonable efforts to provide a private room or other location for expressing breast milk.

North Carolina

N.C. Gen. Stat. § 95-25.5

Applies to: Employers with minor employees.

Breast-feeding: No employment-specific laws. However, breast-feeding is allowed in any public or private location where the mother's presence is authorized.

Special Laws for Minors: Minors under age 16 may not work more than five consecutive hours without a 30-minute break.

North Dakota

N.D. Admin. Code § 46-02-07-02; N.D. Cent. Code § 23-12-17

Applies to: Applicable when two or more employees are on duty.

Exceptions: Waiver by employee or other provision in collective bargaining agreement.

Meal Break: 30 minutes for each shift over five hours; unpaid if employee is completely relieved of duties.

Breast-feeding: Breast-feeding is allowed in any public or private location where the mother's presence is authorized. Employers may use the designation "infant friendly" by adopting voluntary workplace breast-feeding policies.

Ohio

Ohio Rev. Code § 4109.07

Applies to: Employers with minor employees.

Special Laws for Minors: Minors (under 18) may not work more than five consecutive hours without a break of at least 30 minutes.

Oklahoma

Okla. Stat. tit. 40, §§ 75, 435

Breast-feeding: Reasonable unpaid breaks to breast-feed or express breast milk. Breaks run concurrently with other breaks already provided to the employee, if possible. Employers may make reasonable efforts to provide a private room, other than a toilet stall, for expressing milk or breast-feeding. Employers are not required to provide breaks if it would cause undue hardship.

Special Laws for Minors: Minors under age 16 must receive a one-hour cumulative rest period for every eight consecutive hours of work; may not work more than five consecutive hours without a 30-minute break.

State Meal and Rest Break Laws (continued)

Oregon

Or. Rev. Stat. 653.077; Or. Admin. R. §§ 839-020-0050, 839-020-0051

Applies to: All employers except as noted.

Exceptions: Agricultural workers and employees covered by a collective bargaining agreement.

Meal Break: 30 minutes for employees who work at least six hours, unpaid if relieved of all duties; paid time to eat if employee cannot be relieved of duty; a shorter paid break (but no less than 20 minutes), if employer can show that it is industry practice or custom. If shift of seven hours or less, meal break must occur between hours two and five; if shift longer than seven hours, meal break must be between hours three and six.

Rest Break: Paid 10-minute rest period (15 for minors) for each four hours or major fraction worked; if practical, in the middle of the work period. Rest period must be in addition to usual meal break and taken separately; can't be added to meal period or deducted from beginning or end of shift to reduce length of total work period. Rest period is not required for certain solo adult employees serving the public, although they must be allowed to use restroom.

Breast-feeding: Employer must provide a reasonable rest period each time an employee needs to express milk, for up to 18 months after child's birth. If possible, breaks should run concurrently with other breaks already provided to the employee. Employers must make reasonable efforts to provide a private location, other than a bathroom, for expressing milk. Employers

with ten or fewer employees are not required to provide breaks if it would cause undue hardship.

Pennsylvania

43 Pa. Cons. Stat.§§ 40.3, 107

Exceptions: Female employees.

Meal Break: No females may work more than five continuous hours without a break of at least 30 minutes.

Breast-feeding: No employment-specific laws. However, breast-feeding is allowed in any public or private location where the mother's presence is authorized.

Special Laws for Minors: Minors (under 18) may not work more than five consecutive hours without a break of at least 30 minutes.

Rhode Island

R.I. Gen. Laws §§ 28-3-8, 28-3-14, 28-5-7.4

Applies to: Meal break provisions: Employers with five or more employees. Breast-feeding provisions: Employers with four or more employees.

Exceptions: Employers of health care facility or employers with fewer than three employees on any shift.

Meal Break: 20 minutes, unpaid, within a six-hour shift or 30 minutes, unpaid, within an eight-hour shift.

Breast-feeding: Reasonable unpaid break time to breast-feed infant or express breast milk. Employers with four or more employees must provide reasonable accommodations to nursing mothers, which may include break time and private space for expressing breast milk, other than a restroom.

State Meal and Rest Break Laws (continued)

South Carolina

S.C. Code § 41-1-130

Breast-feeding: Employer must provide reasonable unpaid break time or allow employee to use paid break or meal time to express breast milk. Employer must make reasonable effort to provide private location other than toilet stall.

South Dakota

Breast-feeding: No employment-specific laws. However, breast-feeding is allowed in any public or private location where the mother's presence is authorized if the mother is in compliance with all other laws.

Tennessee

Tenn. Code §§ 50-1-305, 50-2-103(h), 50-5-115

Applies to: Employers with five or more employees, and/or minor employees.

Meal Break: 30 minutes unpaid for employees scheduled to work six consecutive hours or more, unless workplace environment provides ample opportunity for appropriate meal break. Tipped employees who work in food or beverage service may waive right to meal break if employee requests waiver, knowingly and voluntarily, in writing, and employer consents. Employer may not coerce employee into waiving right to meal break. Employer must post waiver policy that includes a form stating the employee's right to a break, how long the waiver will last, and how the employee or employer may rescind the waiver.

Breast-feeding: Reasonable unpaid break time to express breast milk. Breaks should run concurrently with any breaks already provided to the employee, if possible.

Employers must make reasonable efforts to provide a private room, other than a toilet stall, for expressing breast milk. Employers are not required to provide breaks if it would unduly disrupt business operations.

Special Laws for Minors: Minors must receive 30-minute break period when scheduled to work six consecutive hours.

Texas

Tex. Gov't Code § 619.005

Breast-feeding: Public employees only. However, breast-feeding and expressing breast milk is allowed in any public or private location where the mother's presence is authorized. Employers voluntarily implementing policies supporting worksite breastfeeding may designate themselves "mother-friendly."

Utah

Utah Code § 34A-5-106, Utah Admin. Code § R610-2-3

Applies to: Employers with 15 or more employees, and/or minor employees.

Breast-feeding: Employer must provide reasonable accommodations related to breast-feeding unless employer demonstrates accommodations create an undue hardship on employer.

Special Laws for Minors: No later than five hours after start of workday, minors (under 18) must receive meal period of at least 30 minutes (paid if employee not relieved of all work duties). Minors must also receive 10-minute rest break for each four-hour period of work, no later than after three hours of consecutive work.

State Meal and Rest Break Laws (continued)

Vermont

Vt. Stat. tit. 21, §§ 304, 305

Applies to: All employers.

Meal Break: Employees must be given a "reasonable opportunity" to eat and use toilet facilities during work periods.

Rest Break: Employees must be given reasonable opportunities to eat and use toilet facilities during work periods.

Breast-feeding: Reasonable time to express breast milk for up to three years after the child's birth. Breaks can be paid or unpaid. Employer must make reasonable efforts to provide a private location (other than a bathroom stall) for expressing breast milk. Employer not required to provide breaks or a private space if it would substantially disrupt its operations.

Virginia

Va. Code §§ 2.2-1147.1, 40.1-80.1

Breast-feeding: Breast-feeding is allowed in any public or private location where the mother's presence is authorized. Employers with 5 or more employees must make reasonable accommodations for pregnancy or related medical conditions.

Special Laws for Minors: Minors may not work more than five continuous hours without a lunch break of at least 30 minutes.

Washington

Wash. Rev. Code § 43.10.005; Wash. Admin. Code §§ 296-125-0285, 296-125-0287, 296-131-020

Applies to: All employers except as noted.

Exceptions: Newspaper vendor or carrier, domestic or casual labor around private residence, sheltered workshop; separate provisions for agricultural labor.

Meal Break: 30-minute break, if work period is more than five consecutive hours, not less than two hours or more than five hours from beginning of shift. This time is paid if employee is on duty or is required to be at a site for employer's benefit. Employees who work three or more hours longer than regular workday are entitled to an additional half hour, before or during overtime. Agricultural employees: 30 minutes if working more than five hours; additional 30 minutes if working 11 or more hours in a day.

Rest Break: Paid ten-minute rest break for each four-hour work period, scheduled as near as possible to midpoint of each work period. Employee cannot be required to work more than three hours without a rest break. Scheduled rest breaks not required where nature of work allows employee to take intermittent rest breaks equivalent to required standard.

Breast-feeding: Employers with 15 or more employees must provide reasonable break time whenever employee has a need to express breast milk, for up to two years after child's birth. Employer must provide a private location, other than a bathroom, to express breast milk. If no such location exists at the worksite, employer must work with employee to identify a convenient location and work schedule to meet employees needs.

State Meal and Rest Break Laws (continued)

Special Laws for Minors: Minors age 16 or 17 may not work more than five consecutive hours without a meal break of at least 30 minutes; must also receive 10-minute rest break for each four hours worked, at least every three hours. Minors age 14 or 15 may not work more than four consecutive hours without 30-minute meal break; must also receive at least 10-minute rest break for every two hours of work.

West Virginia
W. Va. Code §§ 21-3-10a, 21-6-7

Applies to: All employers.

Meal Break: At least 20-minute break for each six consecutive hours worked, unless employees are allowed to take breaks as needed or to eat lunch while working.

Rest Break: Rest breaks of 20 minutes or less must be counted as paid work time.

Special Laws for Minors: Minors under age 16 may not work more than five continuous hours without lunch break of at least 30 minute..

Wisconsin
Wis. Stat. §§ 103.68, 103.935; Wis. Admin. Code § DWD 274.02

Applies to: All employers.

Meal Break: For most workers, 30-minute meal period is recommended but not required. Meal period should be close to usual meal time or near middle of shift. Shifts of more than six hours without a meal break should be avoided. If employee is not free to leave the workplace or relieved of all duties for at least 30 minutes, meal period is considered paid time.

For migrant workers employed exclusively in agricultural labor, 30-minute meal period required after six continuous hours of work, unless the shift can be completed in an additional hour.

Rest Break: For migrant workers not employed exclusively in agricultural labor, rest period of at least ten minutes within each five hours of continuous employment.

Breast-feeding: No employment-specific laws. However, breast-feeding is allowed in any public or private location where the mother's presence is authorized.

Special Laws for Minors: Minors may not work more than six consecutive hours without meal break of at least 30 minutes.

State Health Insurance Continuation Laws

Alabama
Ala. Code § 27-55-3(a)(4)

Special Situations: 18 months for subjects of domestic abuse who have lost coverage they had under abuser's insurance and who do not qualify for COBRA.

Arizona
Ariz. Rev. Stat. §§ 20-1377, 20-1408, 20-2330

Employers affected: All employers that offer group disability insurance. Under § 20-2330, employers that offer group health insurance and have one to 19 employees.

Eligible employees: Employees covered under an employer's health benefits plan for at least three months before a qualifying event.

Length of coverage for employee: 18 months.

Length of coverage for dependents: 18 months, plus an additional 11 months for dependents with disabilities.

Insurer must either continue coverage for dependents or convert to individual policy upon death or divorce of covered employee. Coverage must be the same unless the insured chooses a lesser plan.

Qualifying event: Death of an employee; change in marital status; any other reason stated in policy (other than failure to pay premium).

Under § 20-2330, voluntary or involuntary termination of employment other than for gross misconduct; reduction of hours required to qualify for coverage under group plan; divorce or separation; employee's death or eligibility for Medicare; dependent child ceases to qualify as dependent under group plan; retired employees or their spouses or dependent children lose coverage within a year before or after employer files for bankruptcy.

Time employer has to notify employee: No provisions for employer. Insurance policy must include notice of conversion privilege. Clerk of court must provide notice to anyone filing for divorce that dependent spouse is entitled to convert health insurance coverage.

Under § 20-2330, 30 days after the qualifying event.

Time employee has to apply: 31 days after termination of existing coverage.

Under § 20-2330, 60 days after date of employer's notice.

Arkansas
Ark. Code §§ 23-86-114-23-86-116

Employers affected: All employers that offer group health insurance.

Eligible employees: Employees continuously insured for previous three months.

Length of coverage for employee: 120 days.

Length of coverage for dependents: 120 days.

Qualifying event: Termination of employment; change in insured's marital status. Employer may—but is not required to—continue benefits on death of employee.

Time employee has to apply: Ten days.

State Health Insurance Continuation Laws (continued)

California

Cal. Health & Safety Code §§ 1366.20-1366.29, 1373.6, 1373.621; Cal. Ins. Code §§ 10128.50-10128.59

Employers affected: Employers that offer group health insurance and have two to 19 employees.

Eligible employees: All covered employees are eligible.

Length of coverage for employee: 36 months.

Length of coverage for dependents: 36 months.

Qualifying event: Termination of employment; reduction in hours; death of employee; change in marital status; loss of dependent status; covered employee's eligibility for Medicare (for dependents only).

Time employer has to notify employee: 14 days.

Time employee has to apply: 60 days.

Special situations: Employee who is at least 60 years old and has worked for employer for previous five years may continue benefits for self and spouse beyond COBRA or Cal-COBRA limits (also applies to COBRA employers). Employee who began receiving COBRA coverage on or after January 1, 2003, and whose COBRA coverage is for less than 36 months may use Cal-COBRA to bring total coverage up to 36 months.

Colorado

Colo. Rev. Stat. § 10-16-108

Employers affected: All employers that offer group health insurance.

Eligible employees: Employees continuously insured for previous six months.

Length of coverage for employee: 18 months.

Length of coverage for dependents: 18 months.

Qualifying event: Termination of employment; reduction in hours; death of employee; change in marital status.

Time employer has to notify employee: Within 10 days (by postmark or employee's signature on notice) after termination of employment.

Time employee has to apply: 30 days after termination; 60 days if employer fails to give notice.

Connecticut

Conn. Gen. Stat. §§ 38a-512a, 31-51n, 31-51o

Employers affected: All employers that offer group health insurance.

Eligible employees: All covered employees are eligible.

Length of coverage for employee: 30 months.

Length of coverage for dependents: 30 months; 36 months in case of employee's death, divorce, or loss of dependent status.

Qualifying event: Layoff; reduction in hours; termination of employment; death of employee; change in marital status; loss of dependent status.

Special situations: When facility closes or relocates, employers with 100 or more employees must pay for insurance for employee and dependents for 120 days or

State Health Insurance Continuation Laws (continued)

until employee is eligible for other group coverage, whichever comes first (does not affect employee's right to conventional continuation coverage, which begins when 120-day period ends).

Delaware
18 Del. Code § 3571F

Employers affected: Employers that offer group health insurance and have one to 19 employees.

Eligible employees: Employees continuously insured for previous three months.

Length of coverage for employee: Nine months.

Length of coverage for dependents: Nine months.

Qualifying event: Employee's death; termination of employment; divorce or legal separation; employee's eligibility for Medicare; loss of dependent status.

Time employer has to notify employee: Within 30 days of the qualifying event.

Time employee has to apply: 30 days.

District of Columbia
D.C. Code §§ 32-731 to 32-732

Employers affected: Employers with fewer than 20 employees.

Eligible employees: All covered employees are eligible.

Length of coverage for employee: Three months.

Length of coverage for dependents: Three months.

Qualifying event: Any reason employee or dependent becomes ineligible for coverage, except employee's termination for gross misconduct.

Time employer has to notify employee: Within 15 days of termination of coverage.

Time employee has to apply: 45 days after termination of coverage.

Florida
Fla. Stat. § 627.6692

Employers affected: Employers with fewer than 20 employees.

Eligible employees: Full-time (25 or more hours per week) employees covered by employer's health insurance plan.

Length of coverage for employee: 18 months.

Length of coverage for dependents: 18 months.

Qualifying event: Termination of employment (other than for gross misconduct); reduction in hours; employee's death; change in marital status; employee's eligibility for Medicare; loss of dependent status; loss of coverage within one year of employer's bankruptcy.

Time employer has to notify employee: Carrier notifies within 14 days of learning of qualifying event (beneficiary has 63 days to notify carrier of qualifying event).

Time employee has to apply: 30 days from receipt of carrier's notice.

State Health Insurance Continuation Laws (continued)

Georgia

Ga. Code §§ 33-24-21.1-33-24-21.2

Employers affected: All employers that offer group health insurance.

Eligible employees: Employees continuously insured for previous six months.

Length of coverage for employee: Three months plus any part of the month remaining at termination.

Length of coverage for dependents: Three months plus any part of the month remaining at termination.

Qualifying event: Termination of employment (except for cause).

Special situations: Employee, spouse, or former spouse who is 60 years old and who has been covered for previous six months may continue coverage until eligible for Medicare. (Applies to companies with more than 20 employees; does not apply when employee quits for reasons other than health.)

Hawaii

Haw. Rev. Stat. §§ 393-11, 393-15

Employers affected: All employers required to offer health insurance (those paying a regular employee a monthly wage at least 86.67 times state hourly minimum—about $876).

Length of coverage for employee: If employee is hospitalized or prevented from working by sickness, employer must pay insurance premiums for three months or for as long as employer continues to pay wages, whichever is longer.

Qualifying event: Employee is hospitalized or prevented by sickness from working.

Idaho

Idaho Code § 41-2213

Employers affected: All employers that offer group disability insurance.

Eligible employees: Employees or dependents who are totally disabled at the time the policy ends. (Applies to policies that provide benefits for loss of time during periods of hospitalization, benefits for hospital or medical expenses, or benefits for dismemberment.)

Length of coverage for employee: Must provide a reasonable extension of coverage (in the case of medical and hospital expenses, a reasonable extension is at least 12 months).

Length of coverage for dependents: Must provide a reasonable extension of coverage (in the case of medical and hospital expenses, a reasonable extension is at least 12 months).

Illinois

215 Ill. Comp. Stat. §§ 5/367e, 5/367.2, 5/367.2-5

Employers affected: All employers that offer group health insurance.

Eligible employees: Employees continuously insured for previous three months.

Length of coverage for employee: 12 months.

Length of coverage for dependents: Upon death or divorce, two years' coverage for spouse under 55 and eligible dependents who were on employee's plan. A dependent child who has reached plan age limit or who was not already covered by plan, is also entitled to two years' continuation coverage.

State Health Insurance Continuation Laws (continued)

Qualifying event: Termination of employment; reduction in hours; death of employee; divorce.

Time employer has to notify employee: Ten days.

Time employee has to apply: 30 days after termination or reduction in hours or receiving notice from employer, whichever is later, but not more than 60 days from termination or reduction in hours.

Iowa
Iowa Code §§ 509B.1-509B.5

Employers affected: All employers that offer group health insurance.

Eligible employees: Employees continuously insured for previous three months.

Length of coverage for employee: Nine months.

Length of coverage for dependents: Nine months.

Qualifying event: Any reason employee or dependent becomes ineligible for coverage.

Time employer has to notify employee: Ten days after termination of coverage.

Time employee has to apply: Ten days after termination of coverage or receiving notice from employer, whichever is later, but not more than 31 days from termination of coverage.

Kansas
Kan. Stat. § 40-2209(i)

Employers affected: All employers that offer group health insurance.

Eligible employees: Employees continuously insured for previous three months.

Length of coverage for employee: 18 months.

Length of coverage for dependents: 18 months.

Qualifying event: Any reason employee or dependent becomes ineligible for coverage.

Time employer has to notify employee: Reasonable notice.

Time employee has to apply: 31 days after termination of coverage.

Kentucky
Ky. Rev. Stat. § 304.18-110

Employers affected: All employers that offer group health insurance.

Eligible employees: Employees continuously insured for previous three months.

Length of coverage for employee: 18 months.

Length of coverage for dependents: 18 months.

Qualifying event: Any reason employee or dependent becomes ineligible for coverage.

Time employer has to notify employee: Employer must notify insurer as soon as employee's coverage ends; insurer then notifies employee.

Time employee has to apply: 31 days from receipt of insurer's notice, but not more than 90 days after termination of group coverage.

Louisiana
La. Rev. Stat. §§ 22:1045, 22:1046

Employers affected: All employers that offer group health insurance and have fewer than 20 employees.

State Health Insurance Continuation Laws (continued)

Eligible employees: Employees continuously insured for previous three months.

Length of coverage for employee: 12 months.

Length of coverage for dependents: 12 months.

Qualifying event: Termination of employment; death of insured; divorce.

Time employee has to apply: By the end of the month following the month in which the qualifying event occurred.

Special situations: Surviving spouse who is 50 or older may have coverage until remarriage or eligibility for Medicare or other insurance.

Maine

Me. Rev. Stat. tit. 24-A, § 2809-A

Employers affected: All employers that offer group health insurance and are not subject to COBRA.

Eligible employees: Employees employed for at least six months.

Length of coverage for employee: 12 months.

Length of coverage for dependents: 12 months.

Qualifying event: Temporary layoff; permanent layoff if employee is eligible for federal premium assistance for laid-off employees who continue coverage; loss of employment because of a work-related injury or disease.

Time employee has to apply: 31 days from termination of coverage.

Maryland

Md. Code Ins. §§ 15-407-15-409

Employers affected: All employers that offer group health insurance.

Eligible employees: Employees continuously insured for previous three months.

Length of coverage for employee: 18 months.

Length of coverage for dependents: 18 months.

Qualifying event: Termination of employment; death of employee; change in marital status.

Time employer has to notify employee: Must notify insurer within 14 days of receiving employee's continuation request.

Time employee has to apply: 45 days from termination of coverage. Employee begins application process by requesting an election of continuation notification form from employer.

Massachusetts

Mass. Gen. Laws ch. 175, §§ 110G, 110I; ch. 176J, § 9

Employers affected: All employers that offer group health insurance and have fewer than 20 employees.

Eligible employees: All covered employees are eligible.

Length of coverage for employee: 18 months; 29 months if disabled.

Length of coverage for dependents: 18 months upon termination or reduction in hours; 29 months if disabled; 36 months on divorce, death of employee, employee's eligibility for Medicare, or employer's bankruptcy.

State Health Insurance Continuation Laws (continued)

Qualifying event: Involuntary layoff; death of insured employee; change in marital status.

Time employer has to notify employee: Carrier must notify beneficiary within 14 days of learning of qualifying event.

Time employee has to apply: 60 days.

Special situations: Termination due to plant closing: 90 days' coverage for employee and dependents, at the same payment terms as before closing.

Minnesota
Minn. Stat. §§ 62A.17, 62A.20, 62A.21, 62A.148

Employers affected: All employers that offer group health insurance and have two or more employees.

Eligible employees: All covered employees are eligible.

Length of coverage for employee: 18 months; indefinitely if employee becomes totally disabled while employed.

Length of coverage for dependents: 18 months for current spouse or child after termination of employment; divorced or widowed spouse can continue until eligible for Medicare or other group health insurance. Upon divorce or death of employee, dependent children can continue until they no longer qualify as dependents under plan.

Qualifying event: Termination of employment; reduction in hours.

Time employer has to notify employee: Within 14 days of termination of coverage.

Time employee has to apply: 60 days from termination of coverage or receipt of employer's notice, whichever is later.

Mississippi
Miss. Code § 83-9-51

Employers affected: All employers that offer group health insurance and have fewer than 20 employees.

Eligible employees: Employees continuously insured for previous three months.

Length of coverage for employee: 12 months.

Length of coverage for dependents: 12 months.

Qualifying event: Termination of employment; divorce; employee's death; employee's eligibility for Medicare; loss of dependent status.

Time employer has to notify employee: Insurer must notify former or deceased employee's dependent child or divorced spouse of option to continue insurance within 14 days of their becoming ineligible for coverage on employee's policy.

Time employee has to apply: Employee must apply and submit payment before group coverage ends; dependents or former spouse must elect continuation coverage within 30 days of receiving insurer's notice.

Missouri
Mo. Rev. Stat. § 376.428

Employers affected: All employers that offer group health insurance and are not subject to COBRA.

Eligible employees: All employees.

Length of coverage for employee: 18 months.

State Health Insurance Continuation Laws (continued)

Length of coverage for dependents:
18 months if eligible due to termination or reduction in hours; 36 months if eligible due to death or divorce.

Qualifying event: Termination of employment; death of employee; divorce; reduction in hours; employee's eligibility for Medicare; loss of dependent status.

Time employer has to notify employee: Same rules as COBRA.

Time employee has to apply: Same rules as COBRA.

Montana

Mont. Code §§ 33-22-506-33-22-507

Employers affected: All employers that offer group disability insurance.

Eligible employees: All employees.

Length of coverage for employee: One year (with employer's consent).

Qualifying event: Reduction in hours.

Special situations: Insurer may not discontinue benefits to child with a disability after child exceeds age limit for dependent status.

Nebraska

Neb. Rev. Stat. §§ 44-1640 and following, 44-7406

Employers affected: Employers not subject to federal COBRA laws.

Eligible employees: All covered employees.

Length of coverage for employee: Six months.

Length of coverage for dependents: One year upon death of insured employee. Subjects of domestic abuse who have lost coverage under abuser's plan and who do not qualify for COBRA may have 18 months' coverage (applies to all employers).

Qualifying event: Involuntary termination of employment (layoff due to labor dispute not considered involuntary).

Time employer has to notify employee: Within ten days of termination of employment must send notice by certified mail.

Time employee has to apply: Ten days from receipt of employer's notice.

Nevada

Nev. Rev. Stat. § 689B.0345

Employers affected: All employers that offer group health insurance.

Eligible employees: Employees who are on unpaid leave due to total disability.

Length of coverage for employee: 12 months.

Length of coverage for dependents: 12 months.

New Hampshire

N.H. Rev. Stat. § 415:18

Employers affected: All employers that offer group health insurance.

Eligible employees: All insured employees are eligible.

Length of coverage for employee: 18 months; 29 months if disabled at termination or during first 60 days of continuation coverage.

Length of coverage for dependents: 18 months; 29 months if disabled at termination or during first 60 days of continuation coverage; 36 months upon death of employee, divorce or legal separation, loss of dependent status, or employee's eligibility for Medicare.

State Health Insurance Continuation Laws (continued)

Qualifying event: Any reason employee or dependent becomes ineligible for coverage.

Time employer has to notify employee: Carrier must notify beneficiary within 30 days of receiving notice of loss of coverage.

Time employee has to apply: Within 45 days of receipt of notice.

Special situations: Layoff or termination due to strike: six months' coverage with option to extend for an additional 12 months. Surviving, divorced, or legally separated spouse who is 55 or older may continue benefits available until eligible for Medicare or other employer-based group insurance.

New Jersey

N.J. Stat. §§ 17B:27-51.12, 17B:27A-27

Employers affected: Employers with two to 50 employees.

Eligible employees: Employed full time (25 or more hours).

Length of coverage for employee: 18 months; 29 months if disabled at termination or during first 60 days of continuation coverage.

Length of coverage for dependents: 18 months; 36 months upon death of employee, divorce or legal separation, loss of dependent status, or employee's eligibility for Medicare.

Qualifying event: Termination of employment; reduction in hours; change in marital status; death.

Time employer has to notify employee: At time of qualifying event.

Time employee has to apply: Within 30 days of qualifying event.

Special benefits: Coverage must be identical to that offered to current employees.

Special situations: Total disability: Employee who has been insured for previous three months and employee's dependents entitled to continuation coverage that includes all benefits offered by group policy (applies to all employers).

New Mexico

N.M. Stat. § 59A-18-16

Employers affected: All employers that offer group health insurance.

Eligible employees: All insured employees are eligible.

Length of coverage for employee: Six months.

Length of coverage for dependents: Six months for termination of employment. May continue group coverage or convert to individual policies upon death of covered employee or divorce or legal separation.

Qualifying event: Termination of employment.

Time employer has to notify employee: Insurer or employer must give written notice at time of termination.

Time employee has to apply: 30 days after receiving notice.

New York

N.Y. Ins. Law § 3221(m)

Employers affected: All employers that offer group health insurance.

Eligible employees: All covered employees are eligible.

State Health Insurance Continuation Laws (continued)

Length of coverage for employee:
36 months.

Length of coverage for dependents:
36 months.

Qualifying event: Termination of employment; death of employee; divorce or legal separation; loss of dependent status; employee's eligibility for Medicare.

Time employee has to apply: 60 days after termination or receipt of notice, whichever is later.

North Carolina

N.C. Gen. Stat. §§ 58-53-5-58-53-40

Employers affected: All employers that offer group health insurance.

Eligible employees: Employees continuously insured for previous three months.

Length of coverage for employee:
18 months.

Length of coverage for dependents:
18 months.

Qualifying event: Termination of employment.

Time employer has to notify employee: Employer has option of notifying employee as part of the exit process.

Time employee has to apply: 60 days.

North Dakota

N.D. Cent. Code §§ 26.1-36-23, 26.1-36-23.1

Employers affected: All employers that offer group health insurance.

Eligible employees: Employees continuously insured for previous three months.

Length of coverage for employee:
39 weeks.

Length of coverage for dependents:
39 weeks; 36 months if required by divorce or annulment decree.

Qualifying event: Termination of employment; change in marital status, if divorce or annulment decree requires employee to continue coverage.

Time employee has to apply: Within ten days of termination or of receiving notice of continuation rights, whichever is later, but not more than 31 days from termination.

Ohio

Ohio Rev. Code §§ 1751.53, 3923.38

Employers affected: All employers that offer group health insurance.

Eligible employees: Employees continuously insured for previous three months who were involuntarily terminated for reasons other than gross misconduct on the part of the employee.

Length of coverage for employee:
12 months.

Length of coverage for dependents:
12 months.

Qualifying event: Involuntary termination of employment.

Time employer has to notify employee: At termination of employment.

Time employee has to apply: Whichever is earlier: 31 days after coverage terminates; ten days after coverage terminates if employer notified employee of continuation rights prior to termination; ten days after employer notified employee of continuation rights, if notice was given after coverage terminated.

State Health Insurance Continuation Laws (continued)

Oklahoma

Okla. Stat. tit. 36, § 4509

Employers affected: All employers that offer group health insurance.

Eligible employees: Employees insured for at least six months. (All other employees and their dependents entitled to 30 days' continuation coverage.)

Length of coverage for employee: 63 days for basic coverage; six months for major medical at the same premium rate prior to termination of coverage (only for losses or conditions that began while group policy in effect).

Length of coverage for dependents: 63 days for basic coverage; six months for major medical at the same premium rate prior to termination of coverage (only for losses or conditions that began while group policy in effect).

Qualifying event: Any reason coverage terminates (except employment termination for gross misconduct).

Time employer has to notify employee: Carrier must notify employee in writing within 30 days of receiving notice of termination of employee's coverage.

Time employee has to apply: 31 days after receipt of notice.

Special benefits: Includes maternity care for pregnancy begun while group policy was in effect.

Oregon

Or. Rev. Stat. §§ 743B.343-743B.347

Employers affected: Employers not subject to federal COBRA laws.

Eligible employees: Employees continuously insured for previous three months.

Length of coverage for employee: Nine months.

Length of coverage for dependents: Nine months.

Qualifying event: Termination of employment; reduction in hours; employee's eligibility for Medicare; loss of dependent status; termination of membership in group covered by policy; death of employee.

Time employer has to notify employee: Ten days after qualifying event.

Time employee has to apply: Within the time limit determined by the insurer, which must be at least ten days after the qualifying event or employee's receipt of notice, whichever is later.

Special situations: Surviving, divorced, or legally separated spouse who is 55 or older and dependent children entitled to continuation coverage until spouse remarries or is eligible for other coverage; must include dental, vision, or prescription drug benefits, if they were offered in original plan (applies to employers with 20 or more employees).

Pennsylvania

40 Pa. Stat. § 764j

Employers affected: Employers that offer group health insurance and have two to 19 employees.

Eligible employees: Employees continuously insured for at least three months.

Length of coverage for employee: Nine months.

State Health Insurance Continuation Laws (continued)

Length of coverage for dependents: Nine months.

Qualifying event: Termination of employment; reduction in hours; death of employee; change in marital status; employees eligibility for Medicare; loss of dependent status; employer's bankruptcy.

Time employer has to notify employee: 30 days after qualifying event.

Time employee has to apply: 30 days after receiving notice.

Rhode Island

R.I. Gen. Laws §§ 27-19.1-1, 27-20.4-1-27-20.4-2

Employers affected: All employers that offer group health insurance.

Eligible employees: All insured employees are eligible.

Length of coverage for employee: 18 months (but not longer than continuous employment); cannot be required to pay more than one month premium at a time.

Length of coverage for dependents: 18 months (but not longer than continuous employment); cannot be required to pay more than one month premium at a time.

Qualifying event: Involuntary termination of employment; death of employee; change in marital status; permanent reduction in workforce; employer's going out of business.

Time employer has to notify employee: Employers must post a conspicuous notice of employee continuation rights.

Time employee has to apply: 30 days from termination of coverage.

Special situations: If right to receiving continuing health insurance is stated in the divorce judgment, divorced spouse has right to continue coverage as long as employee remains covered or until divorced spouse remarries or becomes eligible for other group insurance.

South Carolina

S.C. Code § 38-71-770

Employers affected: All employers that offer group health insurance.

Eligible employees: Employees continuously insured for previous six months.

Length of coverage for employee: Six months (in addition to part of month remaining at termination).

Length of coverage for dependents: Six months (in addition to part of month remaining at termination).

Qualifying event: Any reason employee or dependent becomes ineligible for coverage.

Time employer has to notify employee: At time of termination, employer must clearly and meaningfully advise employee of continuation rights.

South Dakota

S.D. Codified Laws §§ 58-18-7.5, 58-18-7.12, 58-18C-1

Employers affected: All employers that offer group health insurance.

Eligible employees: All covered employees.

Length of coverage for employee: 18 months; 29 months if disabled at termination or during first 60 days of continuation coverage.

State Health Insurance Continuation Laws (continued)

Length of coverage for dependents: 18 months; 29 months if disabled at termination or during first 60 days of continuation coverage; 36 months upon death of employee, divorce or legal separation, loss of dependent status, or employee's eligibility for Medicare.

Qualifying event: Termination of employment; death of employee; divorce or legal separation; loss of dependent status; employee's eligibility for Medicare.

Special situations: When employer goes out of business: 12 months' continuation coverage available to all employees. Employer must notify employees within ten days of termination of benefits; employees must apply within 60 days of receipt of employer's notice or within 90 days of termination of benefits if no notice given.

Tennessee
Tenn. Code § 56-7-2312

Employers affected: All employers that offer group health insurance.

Eligible employees: Employees continuously insured for previous three months.

Length of coverage for employee: Three months (in addition to part of month remaining at termination).

Length of coverage for dependents: Three months (in addition to part of month remaining at termination); 15 months upon death of employee or divorce (in addition to part of month remaining at termination).

Qualifying event: Termination of employment; death of employee; change in marital status.

Special situations: Employee or dependent who is pregnant at time of termination entitled to continuation benefits for six months following the end of pregnancy.

Texas
Tex. Ins. Code §§ 1251.252-1251.255; 1251.301-1251.310

Employers affected: All employers that offer group health insurance.

Eligible employees: Employees continuously insured for previous three months.

Length of coverage for employee: Nine months; for employees eligible for COBRA, six months after COBRA coverage ends.

Length of coverage for dependents: Nine months; for employees eligible for COBRA, six months after COBRA coverage ends. Three years for dependents with coverage due to the death or retirement of employee or severance of the family relationship.

Qualifying event: Termination of employment (except for cause); employee leaves for health reasons; severance of family relationship; retirement or death of employee.

Time employee has to apply: 60 days from termination of coverage or receiving notice of continuation rights from employer or insurer, whichever is later. Must give notice within 15 days of severance of family relationship. Within 60 days of death or retirement of family member or severance of family relationship, dependent must give notice of intent to continue coverage.

State Health Insurance Continuation Laws (continued)

Utah

Utah Code § 31A-22-722

Employers affected: All employers that offer group health insurance.

Eligible employees: Employees continuously insured for previous three months.

Length of coverage for employee: 12 months.

Length of coverage for dependents: 12 months.

Qualifying event: Termination of employment; retirement; death; divorce or legal separation; reduction in hours; sabbatical; leave of absence; disability; loss of dependent status.

Time employer has to notify employee: In writing within 30 days of termination of coverage.

Time employee has to apply: Within 60 days of qualifying event.

Vermont

Vt. Stat. tit. 8, §§ 4090a-4090c

Employers affected: All employers that offer group health insurance.

Eligible employees: All covered employees are eligible.

Length of coverage for employee: 18 months.

Length of coverage for dependents: 18 months.

Qualifying event: Termination of employment; reduction in hours; death of employee; change of marital status; loss of dependent status.

Time employer has to notify employee: Within 30 days of qualifying event.

Time employee has to apply: Within 60 days of receiving notice following the occurrence of a qualifying event.

Virginia

Va. Code §§ 38.2-3541-38.2-3542

Employers affected: Employers not subject to federal COBRA laws.

Eligible employees: Employees continuously insured for previous three months.

Length of coverage for employee: 12 months.

Length of coverage for dependents: 12 months.

Qualifying event: Any reason employee or dependent becomes ineligible for coverage, except employee's termination for gross misconduct.

Time employer has to notify employee: 14 days from termination of coverage.

Time employee has to apply: Within 31 days of receiving notice of eligibility, but no more than 60 days following termination.

Special situations: Employee may convert to an individual policy instead of applying for continuation coverage (must apply within 31 days of termination of coverage).

Washington

Wash. Rev. Code § 48.21.075

Employers affected: All employers that offer disability insurance.

State Health Insurance Continuation Laws (continued)

Eligible employees: Insured employees on strike.

Length of coverage for employee: Six months if employee goes on strike.

Length of coverage for dependents: Six months if employee goes on strike.

Qualifying event: If employee goes on strike.

Special situations: All employers have option of offering continued group health benefits.

West Virginia
W. Va. Code §§ 33-16-2, 33-16-3(e); W. Va. Code R. § 114-93-3

Employers affected: Employers providing insurance for between two and 20 employees.

Eligible employees: All employees are eligible.

Length of coverage for employee: 18 months in case of involuntary layoff.

Qualifying event: Involuntary layoff.

Time employer has to notify employee: Carrier must notify beneficiaries within 15 days of receiving notice from beneficiary of intent to apply.

Time employee has to apply: 20 days to send notice of intention to apply; 30 days to apply after receiving election and premium notice.

Wisconsin
Wis. Stat. § 632.897

Employers affected: All employers that offer group health insurance.

Eligible employees: Employees continuously insured for previous three months.

Length of coverage for employee: 18 months (or longer at insurer's option).

Length of coverage for dependents: 18 months (or longer at insurer's option).

Qualifying event: Any reason employee or dependent becomes ineligible for coverage (except employment termination due to misconduct).

Time employer has to notify employee: Five days from termination of coverage.

Time employee has to apply: 30 days after receiving employer's notice.

Wyoming
Wyo. Stat. § 26-19-113

Employers affected: Employers not subject to federal COBRA laws.

Eligible employees: Employees continuously insured for previous three months.

Length of coverage for employee: 12 months.

Length of coverage for dependents: 12 months.

Time employee has to apply: 31 days from termination of coverage.

State Family and Medical Leave Laws

Arizona

Ariz. Rev. Stat. §§ 13-4439, 23-371 and following

Domestic Violence: Paid sick leave may also be used to allow employee to obtain (for self or family member) or do any of the following when needed: (1) medical care (including counseling) to recover from physical or psychological injury or disability caused by domestic violence, sexual violence, abuse, or stalking; (2) services from domestic violence, sexual violence, or victim services organization; (3) legal services; or (4) relocate or take steps to secure home. Employers with 50 or more employees must give unpaid leave to all crime victims to attend certain legal proceedings.

Paid Sick Leave: All employers must provide one hour paid sick time for every 30 hours worked. Employers with 15 or more employees may cap accrual and use at 40 hours per year; employers with fewer than 15 employees may cap accrual and use at 24 hours per year. Sick leave may be used for the employee's illness, to care for an ill family member, to seek assistance relating to domestic violence, or due to the closure of the employee's work or a child's school due to a public health emergency.

Arkansas

Ark. Code §§ 9-9-105, 11-3-205

Family and Medical Leave: Employers that allow employees to take leave for the birth of a child must give the same leave to employees adopting a child no older than 18 (does not apply to stepparent or foster parent adoptions).

Organ and Bone Marrow Donation: Private employers must provide up to 90 days of unpaid leave for organ or bone marrow donation to employees who are not eligible for FMLA leave.

California

Cal. Gov't. Code §§ 1508-1513, 12945, 12945.2; Cal. Lab. Code §§ 230 and following, 245.5, 246, 246.5; Cal. Unemp. Ins. Code §§ 2601 and following, 3300 and following

Family and Medical Leave: Employers with five or more employees must provide up to 12 weeks of leave each year to care for child, parent, grandparent, grandchild, sibling, spouse, or domestic partner with serious health condition; for employee's own serious illness; to bond with new child; or for qualifying exigency related to active military duty of employee or spouse, domestic partner, child, or parent. Employees are eligible if they have worked for the employer for more than 12 months and have worked 1,250 hours in the previous year (or meet special eligibility requirements for certain employees of air carriers).

Pregnancy Disability Leave: Employers with five or more employees must provide up to four months of pregnancy disability leave to employees who are unable to work due to pregnancy or childbirth. This time is in addition to 12 weeks of bonding leave under state family leave law.

School Activities: Employers with 25 or more employees must provide up to 40 hours per year, but not more than eight hours per calendar month, to enroll a child in a school or a licensed child care provider

State Family and Medical Leave Laws (continued)

or to participate in activities related to the school or licensed child care provider.

Domestic Violence: Employers with 25 or more employees must provide employees who are victims of domestic violence, stalking, sexual assault, or certain other crimes with a reasonable amount of time off to obtain medical treatment, counseling, or mental health services; take safety measures; or deal with other issues related to the crime.

Organ and Bone Marrow Donation: Employers with 15 or more employees must provide paid leave for organ donation (up to 30 days in one-year period) or bone marrow donation (up to five days within one-year period), plus additional unpaid leave for organ donation (up to 30 days). As condition of initial leave, employer may require employee to use accrued sick leave, vacation time, or paid time off (up to two weeks for organ donation or five days for bone marrow donation).

Paid Sick Leave: All employers must provide employees with one hour of sick leave for every 30 hours worked. Employers may cap sick leave at 24 hours per year. Employees are eligible if they have worked at least 30 days for the employer. Employees may use sick leave for their own illnesses, to care for an ill family member, or to deal with the effects of domestic violence.

Paid Family Leave: Employees may receive up to eight weeks of paid family leave benefits from the state disability insurance program when taking leave to bond with a new child; to care for a seriously ill family member; or for qualifying exigencies related to covered active military duty or the employee or the employee's spouse, domestic partner, child, or parent.

Temporary Disability Insurance: Employees may receive up to 52 weeks of short-term disability from the state when unable to work due to disability (including pregnancy).

Colorado

Colo. Rev. Stat. §§ 8-13.3-203, 8-13.3-401-8-13.3-418, 19-5-211, 24-34-402.7

Family and Medical Leave: Employers that offer leave for the birth of a child must give the same leave for adoption (doesn't apply to stepparent adoption).

Colorado employees are entitled to FMLA leave to care for seriously ill domestic partner or partner in civil union.

School Activities: Colorado's previous law requiring employers to provide time off to employees for a child's school activities expired in 2015.

Domestic Violence: Employees who are victims of domestic violence, sexual assault, or harassment (or have family members who are victims) may use accrued paid sick leave to seek medical attention, obtain victim services or counseling, relocate, or seek legal services related to such violence or harassment. In addition, employers with 50 or more employees must provide up to three days paid or unpaid leave per year to seek restraining order, obtain medical care or counseling, relocate, or seek legal assistance relating to domestic violence, sexual assault, or stalking. Employees are eligible for this leave if they have worked for the employer for one year.

State Family and Medical Leave Laws (continued)

Paid Sick Leave: Private and state/local public employers with 15 or more employees must provide at least one hour paid sick for every 30 hours worked, beginning on first day of employment. (Effective January 1, 2022, requirement applies regardless of number of employees.) Employees may use sick leave for their own illnesses, to care for ill family member, when public health emergency closes place of business (or closes schools, and employees need to care for children), or to deal with effects of domestic violence. Employees may roll over up to 48 hours accrued sick leave to next year. During public health emergencies, employers must also supplement accrued paid sick leave as necessary to ensure that full-time employees may take at least 80 hours of leave for certain reasons related to emergency.

Connecticut

Conn. Gen. Stat. §§ 31-49e-31-49t; 31-51kk-31-51qq; 31-51ss; 31-57r-31-57t; 46a-60

Family and Medical Leave: Through 12/31/2021, employers with 75 or more employees must provide total of 16 weeks of leave during any 24-month period for childbirth, adoption, the employee's serious health condition, a family member's serious health condition, or a qualifying exigency arising out of a family member's active duty in the military. As of 1/1/2022, employers with at least one employee must provide total of 12 weeks' leave during any 12-month period for same reasons; employee may take additional two weeks for serious, incapacitating health condition during pregnancy.

Employee may take up to 26 weeks in a 12-month period for a family member who is a current member of the armed forces and is undergoing medical treatment for a serious illness or injury. Through 12/31/2021, eligible employees must have worked for the employer for one year and for at least 1,000 hours in the previous year; as of 1/1/2022, employees are eligible if they worked for the employer at least three months immediately before request for leave.

Pregnancy Disability Leave: Employers with three or more employees must provide a reasonable amount of leave to employees who are unable to work due to pregnancy.

Domestic Violence: Employers with three or more employees must allow employee who is victim of family violence to take paid or unpaid leave when necessary to seek medical treatment/counseling, obtain victim services, relocate, or participate in legal proceeding related to the violence. Employers may limit unpaid leave to 12 days in calendar year.

Organ and Bone Marrow Donation: Employees may also take leave to serve as organ or bone marrow donor, subject to same eligibility requirements and time limits as any other family and medical leave.

Paid Sick Leave: Employers in the service industry with 50 or more employees must provide employees with one hour of paid sick leave for every 40 hours worked, but may cap accrual at 40 hours per year. Employees may use leave for their own illness or to care for an ill family member.

State Family and Medical Leave Laws (continued)

Paid Family and Medical Leave: Beginning in January 2022, covered employees will receive compensation for up to 12 weeks of leave in any 12-month period from the state Paid Family and Medical Leave Insurance Program, plus two additional weeks for serious, incapacitating health condition during pregnancy.

District of Columbia

D.C. Code §§ 32-501 and following; 32-521.01 and following; 32-531.01 and following; 32-541.01 and following

Family and Medical Leave: Employers with 20 or more employees must provide up to 16 weeks in a 24-month period for the birth of a child, adoption, foster care, placement of a child with the employee for whom the employee permanently assumes and discharges parental responsibility, or to care for family member with a serious health condition. Employees may take an additional 16 weeks in a 24-month period for their own serious health conditions. Employees must have worked for the employer for at least one year and worked at least 1,000 hours in the year before the start of leave.

School Activities: All employers must provide up to 24 hours of unpaid leave per year for an employee to attend a child's school activities.

Domestic Violence: Paid sick leave may also be used for employee or family member who is a victim of stalking, domestic violence, or abuse to get medical attention, get services, seek counseling, relocate, take legal action, or take steps to enhance health and safety.

Paid Sick Leave: All employers must provide paid sick leave for employees to use for their own illness or to care for a family member. Amount of paid leave ranges from three days to seven days per year, depending on size of the employer. Sick leave may be used for the employee's illness, to care for an ill family member, or to deal with the effects of stalking, domestic violence, or abuse against the employee or a family member.

Paid Family Leave: Employees may receive paid family leave benefits from the district when taking leave for their own serious health conditions (two weeks), to care for a family member with a serious health condition (six weeks), or to bond with a new child (eight weeks).

Florida

Fla. Stat. § 741.313

Domestic Violence: Employers with at least 50 employees must provide up to three days of unpaid leave each year to employees who are the victims of domestic violence or sexual abuse or whose family members are victims. Employees are eligible if they have worked for the employer for at least three months.

Georgia

Ga. Code § 34-1-10

Family and Medical Leave: No requirement to provide sick leave, but employers with 25 or more employees that choose to do so must allow up to five days each year to be used to care for a sick immediate family member.

State Family and Medical Leave Laws (continued)

Hawaii

Haw. Rev. Stat. §§ 378-1; 378-71-378-74; 392-23; 398-1-398-11; 398A-3; Haw. Code R. 12-46-108

Family and Medical Leave: Employers with 100 or more employees must provide up to four weeks of unpaid leave each year for the birth of a child or adoption, or to care for family member with a serious health condition. (If employer provides paid sick leave, up to 10 days may be used for these purposes.) Employees are eligible if they have worked for the employer for six months.

Pregnancy Disability Leave: All employers must provide a reasonable period of time off for disability resulting from pregnancy, childbirth, or a related condition.

Domestic Violence: All employers must provide domestic violence leave. Employers with 50 or more employees must allow up to 30 days' unpaid leave per year for employee who is a victim of domestic or sexual violence or if employee's minor child is a victim. Employer with 49 or fewer employees must allow up to five days' leave.

Organ and Bone Marrow Donation: Employers with 50 or more employees must provide up to seven days of unpaid leave for bone marrow donation and 30 days' unpaid leave for organ donation.

Temporary Disability Insurance: Eligible employees who are temporarily unable to work because of illness or injury (including pregnancy) may collect up to 26 weeks of benefits through the state disability insurance program.

Illinois

820 Ill. Comp. Stat. §§ 147/1 and following; 154/1 and following; 180/1 and following

School Activities: Employers with 50 or more employees must allow eligible employees to take up to two weeks of unpaid child bereavement leave, or up to total of six weeks leave within 12-month period if more than one of employee's children dies. Law does not give employee right to take total unpaid leave exceeding amount allowed under federal Family and Medical Leave Act (12 weeks per year).

School Activities: Employers with 50 or more employees must provide eight hours per year, but not more than four hours in a day, for employees to participate in a child's school activities. Employees are eligible if they have worked for the employer at least half time for six months and have no paid leave available.

Domestic Violence: All employers must provide unpaid leave each year to an employee who is a victim of domestic violence, sexual violence, or gender violence, or whose family or household member is a victim. Employers with 50 or more employees must provide 12 weeks of leave; employers with 15 to 49 employees must provide eight weeks of leave; and employers with 14 or fewer employees must provide four weeks of leave.

Iowa

Iowa Code § 216.6

Pregnancy Disability Leave: Employers with four or more employees must provide eight weeks of leave for disability due to pregnancy, childbirth, or related conditions.

State Family and Medical Leave Laws (continued)

Kentucky

Ky. Rev. Stat. § 337.015

Family and Medical Leave: All employers must provide six weeks of leave to employees adopting a child under seven years old.

Louisiana

La. Rev. Stat. §§ 23:341 to 23:342; 23:1015 and following; 40:1263.4

Pregnancy Disability Leave: Employers with 25 or more employees must provide a reasonable period of time off for disability due to pregnancy and childbirth, not to exceed six weeks for normal pregnancies or four months for more disabling pregnancies.

School Activities: All employers must provide 16 hours of leave each year to attend a child's school or day care activities.

Organ and Bone Marrow Donation: Employers with 20 or more employees must provide 40 hours of paid leave each year for employees to donate bone marrow. Employees are eligible if they work at least 20 hours per week.

Maine

Me. Rev. Stat. tit. 26, §§ 637, 843 and following, 850

Family and Medical Leave: Employers with 15 or more employees at one location must provide ten weeks of leave in a two-year period for the birth of a child, adoption (for child 16 or younger), the employee's serious health condition, a family member's serious health condition, organ donation, or the death or serious health condition of a family member incurred while on active military duty. Employees are eligible if they have worked for the employer for at least one year.

Domestic Violence: All employers must provide reasonable and necessary leave to an employee who is the victim of domestic violence, sexual assault, or stalking, or whose parent, spouse, or child is a victim. Leave may be used to prepare for and attend court, for medical treatment, and for other necessary services

Paid Leave: Employers with more than 10 employees must allow employees to earn up to 40 hours paid leave annually; paid leave accrues at one hour for every 40 hours worked.

Maryland

Md. Code, Lab. & Empl. §§ 3-1301-3-1311, 3-801, 3-803

Family and Medical Leave: Employers with 15 or more employees must provide the same leave for adoption as allowed for the birth of a child. Employers with 50 or more employees must give employees a day off when an immediate family member leaves for or returns from active military duty outside the United States. Employees are eligible if they have worked for the employer for at least 12 months and worked at least 1,250 hours in the last year.

State Family and Medical Leave Laws (continued)

Paid Sick Leave: Employers with 15 or more employees must provide sick leave; smaller employers must provide unpaid sick leave. Employees accrue one hour of sick leave for every 30 hours worked. However, employers may cap accrual at 40 hours per year and use at 64 hours per year. Employees may use sick leave for their own illnesses, to care for an ill family member, for preventative medical care for the employee or a family member, for maternity or paternity leave, or to deal with the effects of domestic violence.

Massachusetts

Mass. Gen. Laws ch. 149, §§ 52D, 52E, 105D, 148C; ch. 151B, § 1(5); ch. 175M, §§ 1-11

Family and Medical Leave: Employers with six or more employees must provide eight weeks of unpaid leave to employees for the birth of a child or the adoption of a minor. Employees are eligible once they have completed their initial probationary period of employment, as long as it doesn't exceed three months.

Employers with 50 or more employees must provide 24 hours of leave each year to take a minor child or relative who is 60 or older to medical or dental appointment (combined with school activities leave). Employees must meet the same eligibility requirements of the FMLA.

School Activities: Employers with 50 or more employees must provide 24 hours of leave each year for an employee to attend a child's school activities (combined with family and medical leave for medical appointments). Employees must meet the same eligibility requirements of the FMLA.

Domestic Violence: Employers with 50 or more employees must provide 15 days of unpaid leave in a 12-month period if the employee, or the employee's family member, is a victim of abusive behavior. Leave may be used to seek medical attention or counseling, obtain a protective order from a court, attend child custody proceedings, and other related purposes. Employees must meet the same eligibility requirements of the FMLA.

Paid Sick Leave: All employers must provide one hour of sick leave for every 30 hours worked, although employers may cap annual accrual at 40 hours. Employers with 11 or more employees must provide paid time off; employers with ten or fewer employees may provide unpaid time off. Employees may use leave for their own illnesses, to care for an ill family member, or domestic violence reasons.

Paid Family and Medical Leave: Eligible employees, former employees (within 26 weeks from separation), and some self-employed individuals are eligible to receive paid benefits when taking up to 20 weeks of medical leave for their own serious health condition; up to 12 weeks of family leave to care for a family member with a serious health condition, to bond with a new child, or because of an emergency related to a family member's active duty in the military; or up to 26 weeks to care for a family member who is a covered servicemember. Benefits are not paid during first seven days of leave, but individuals may use accrued sick/vacation pay during that time.

State Family and Medical Leave Laws (continued)

Michigan

Mich. Comp. Laws §§ 408.961 and following

Paid Sick Leave: Employers with 50 or more employees must provide paid medical leave. Employees accrue one hour of paid leave for every 35 hours worked, but not more than one hour of paid leave per workweek. Employers may cap accrual and use at 40 hours per year. Employees may use sick leave for their own illnesses or preventative care; a family member's illness or preventative care; to deal with the effects of domestic violence or sexual assault; or due to the closure of the employee's workplace or a child's school due to a public health emergency.

Minnesota

Minn. Stat. §§ 181.940 and following

Family and Medical Leave: Employers with 21 or more employees at one site must provide 12 weeks of leave for the birth of a child or adoption. Employees may also use accrued sick leave to care for an ill family member. Employees are eligible if they have worked at least half time for one year.

School Activities: All employers must provide 16 hours in a 12-month period to attend a child's activities related to child care, preschool, or special education. Employees are eligible if they have worked half time for at least one year.

Domestic Violence: Employers with 21 or more employees must allow accrued sick leave to be used to seek assistance due to sexual assault, domestic violence, harassment, or stalking

Organ and Bone Marrow Donation: Employers with 20 or more employees must provide 40 hours of paid leave each year to donate bone marrow. Employees are eligible if they work at least 20 hours per week.

Montana

Mont. Code §§ 49-2-310, 49-2-311

Pregnancy Disability Leave: All employers must provide a reasonable leave of absence for pregnancy disability and childbirth.

Nebraska

Neb. Rev. Stat. § 48-234

Family and Medical Leave: Employers that allow employees to take leave for the birth of a child must give the same leave for adoption of a child no older than eight, or a child no older than 18 if the child has special needs (does not apply to stepparent or foster parent adoptions).

Nevada

Nev. Rev. Stat. §§ 392.920, 392.4577, 608.0197, 608.0198, 613.4383

Pregnancy Disability Leave: Employers that provide sick or disability leave to employees with other medical conditions must provide the same leave for pregnancy, miscarriage, childbirth and related medical conditions.

School Activities: Employers with 50 or more employees must provide employees with a child in public school four hours of leave per school year to attend parent-teacher conferences, school-related activities during regular school hours, school-sponsored events, or to volunteer or be involved at the school. All employers may not fire or threaten to fire a parent,

State Family and Medical Leave Laws (continued)

guardian, or custodian for attending a school conference or responding to a child's emergency.

Domestic Violence: All employers must provide 160 hours of unpaid leave within one year of an incident of domestic violence for the following purposes: to seek medical treatment, to obtain counseling, to participate in court proceedings, or to create a safety plan. Employees are eligible if they have worked for at least 90 days and if they are victims of domestic violence or have a family member who is a victim.

Paid Leave: Employers with at least 50 employees must provide employees with at least .01923 hours of paid leave for each hour worked; employers may limit use or carryover of accrued paid leave to 40 hours per year.

New Hampshire

N.H. Rev. § 354-A:7(VI)

Pregnancy Disability Leave: Employers with six or more employees must provide temporary disability leave for pregnancy, childbirth, or a related medical condition.

New Jersey

N.J. Stat. §§ 34:11B-1 and following, 34:11C-1 and following, 34:11D-1 and following, 43:21-25 and following

Family and Medical Leave: Employers with 30 or more employees must provide 12 weeks of leave (or 24 weeks reduced leave schedule) in any 24-month period to care for a family member with a serious health condition; to care for a new child; to care for a child at home because a school or child care center has closed

during a public health emergency; or to quarantine or care for a family member in quarantine during an epidemic. Employees are eligible if they have worked for at least one year and at least 1,000 hours in the previous 12 months.

Domestic Violence: Employers with 25 or more employees must provide 20 unpaid days in one 12-month period for employee who is (or whose family member is) a victim of domestic violence or a sexually violent offense. Employees are eligible if they have worked for at least one year and worked at least 1,000 hours in the last 12 months.

Paid Sick Leave: All employers must provide paid sick leave to their employees. Employees accrue one hour of paid sick leave for every 30 hours worked. However, employers may cap accrual and use at 40 hours per year. Employees may use sick leave for their own illnesses, to care for an ill family member, or for preventative medical care for themselves or a family member; to attend a child's school meeting or other events; to deal with the effects of domestic violence; or, due to a public health emergency, when the employee is unable to work because the workplace or a child's school or care center has closed, the employee is in quarantine, or the employee must care for a family member in quarantine.

Paid Individual Temporary Disability Leave: Employees may receive temporary disability benefits from the state for up to 26 weeks when they are unable to work because of their own disability (including disability resulting from bone/organ

State Family and Medical Leave Laws (continued)

donation or exposure to a communicable disease during a public health emergency) or because they are victims of domestic or sexual violence.

Paid Family Temporary Disability Leave: Employees may receive temporary disability benefits from the state to care for a seriously ill family member, assist a family member who has been a victim of domestic or sexual violence, bond with a new child, or care for a family member in quarantine due to exposure to a communicable disease during a public health emergency. Family temporary disability leave limited to six weeks (or 42 days for intermittent leave) if leave started before July 1, 2020, or 12 weeks (or 56 days if intermittent) if leave started on or after that date.

New Mexico

N.M. Stat. §§ 50-4A-1 and following.

Domestic Violence: All employers must provide intermittent leave for up to 14 days each calendar year, but no more than eight hours in one day, to obtain an order of protection or other judicial relief from domestic abuse, to meet with law enforcement officials, to consult with attorneys or district attorneys' victim advocates, or to attend court proceedings related to the domestic abuse of an employee or an employee's family member.

New York

N.Y. Lab. Law §§ 196-b, 201-c, 202-a; N.Y. Workers' Comp. Law §§ 200 and following; 2020 N.Y. Laws Ch. 25

Family and Medical Leave: Employers that allow employees to take leave for the birth of a child must provide the same leave to employees adopting a child of preschool age or younger (or no older than 18 if disabled).

Organ and Bone Marrow Donation: Employers with 20 or more employees at one site must provide 24 hours' leave to donate bone marrow. Employees are eligible if they work at least 20 hours per week.

Paid Sick Leave: Employers with five or more employees (or net income over $1 million) must provide employees with paid sick leave: up to 40 hours per year for employers with five to 99 employees, or up to 56 hours per year for employers with at least 100 employees. Employers with more than 10 employees must provide five days of paid sick leave (or 14 days if employer has at least 100 employees) during quarantine due to COVID-19.

Paid Temporary Disability Leave: Employees who have worked for a covered employer for at least four consecutive weeks may receive benefits from the state for up to 26 weeks while unable to work due to disability (including pregnancy).

Paid Family Leave: Employees may receive benefits from the state when taking leave to care for a family member with a serious health condition, to bond with a new child, or for qualifying exigency arising out of a family member's call to active duty in the military. Paid family leave is limited to 12 weeks within any 52-week period.

State Family and Medical Leave Laws (continued)

North Carolina

N.C. Gen. Stat. §§ 50B-5.5, 95-28.3

School Activities: All employers must give employees four hours of leave per year to parents or guardians of school-aged children to participate in school activities.

Domestic Violence: All employers must provide reasonable time off to obtain or attempt to obtain relief from domestic violence and sexual assault.

Oregon

Or. Rev. Stat. §§ 657B.005 and following, 659A.029, 659A.150 and following, 659A.270 and following, 659A.312, 653.601 and following

Family and Medical Leave: Employers with 25 or more employees must provide 12 weeks off per year for the birth or adoption of a child (parental leave), the employee's serious health condition, to care for a family member with a serious health condition, to care for a child with an illness or injury that requires home care (sick child leave), or to deal with the death of a family member (bereavement leave). Bereavement leave is capped at two weeks. Employees can take 12 weeks of parental leave and an additional 12 weeks for sick child leave. Employees are eligible if they have worked 25 or more hours per week for at least 180 days (except parental leave, which only requires that the employee has worked 180 days).

Pregnancy Disability Leave: Employers with 25 or more employees must provide 12 weeks off per year for pregnancy disability. This is in addition to 12 weeks for parental leave and 12 weeks for sick child

leave. Employees are eligible if they have worked 25 or more hours per week for at least 180 days.

Domestic Violence: Employers with six or more employees must provide reasonable leave to employee who is victim of, or whose minor child is a victim of, domestic violence, harassment, sexual assault, or stalking. Leave may be used to seek legal treatment, medical services, counseling, or to relocate or secure existing home.

Organ and Bone Marrow Donation: All employers must allow the employee to use accrued leave or must provide the employee with 40 hours of unpaid leave, whichever is less, to donate bone marrow. Employees are eligible if they work at least 20 hours per week. Also, for purposes of family leave, a serious health condition includes a period required for donation of a body part, organ, or tissue.

Paid Sick Leave: All employers must provide one hour of sick leave for every 30 hours worked, although employers may cap accrual and use at 40 hours per year. Up to 40 hours of accrued leave must carry over to the next year. Employers with ten or more employees must provide paid time off; employers with nine or fewer employees may provide unpaid time off. Employees may use leave for their own illnesses, to care for an ill family member, to deal with domestic violence issues, or for any purpose described under the "Family and Medical Leave" section.

Paid Family and Medical Leave: Beginning January 1, 2023, eligible employees (as well as self-employed workers who have

State Family and Medical Leave Laws (continued)

elected coverage and contributed to the insurance fund) will be entitled to benefits from a state insurance fund for leave due to employee's own serious health condition, to care for family member with serious health condition, or to care for and bond with new child. All employers and eligible employees must contribute to the insurance fund beginning January 1, 2022.

Rhode Island

R.I. Gen. Laws §§ 28-48-1 and following; 28-41-34-28-41-42; 28-57-1 and following

Family and Medical Leave: Employers with 50 or more employees must provide 13 weeks of leave in a two-year period for the birth of a child, adoption of child up to 16 years old, the employee's serious health condition, or to care for family member with serious health condition. Employees must have worked an average of 30 or more hours a week for at least 12 consecutive months.

School Activities: Employers with 50 or more employees must provide up to ten hours a year to attend a child's school conferences or other activities.

Paid Sick Leave: Employers with 18 or more employees must provide one hour of paid sick leave for every 35 hours worked, up to a maximum of 40 hours. Employers with fewer than 18 employees must provide the same amount of unpaid sick leave. Sick leave may be used for the employee's own illness, to care for an ill family member, for reasons relating to domestic violence, or due to the closure of the employee's work

or a child's school due to a public health emergency.

Paid Family Leave: Employees who take time off to bond with a new child or care for a family member with a serious health condition may receive four weeks of temporary caregiver benefits from the state.

Temporary Disability Insurance: Employees who are unable to work due to illness, injury, or pregnancy may collect up to 30 weeks of benefits from the state through its short-term disability insurance program (temporary caregiver benefits are counted against the 30 weeks).

South Carolina

S.C. Code § 44-43-80

Organ and Bone Marrow Donation: Employers with 20 or more employees in the state at one site may—but are not required to—allow employees to take up to 40 hours' paid leave per year to donate bone marrow. Employees are eligible if they work at least 20 hours per week.

Tennessee

Tenn. Code § 4-21-408

Family and Medical Leave: Employers with 100 or more employees must provide up to four months of unpaid leave for pregnancy, childbirth, nursing, and adoption. Employees must give three months' notice unless a medical emergency requires the leave to begin sooner. Employees are eligible if they have worked full-time for the employer for 12 consecutive months.

State Family and Medical Leave Laws (continued)

Texas

Tex. Lab. Code § 21.0595

Family and Medical Leave: Employers with 15 or more employees that provide leave to care for a sick child must also allow leave to care for a sick foster child.

Vermont

Vt. Stat. tit. 21, §§ 471 and following, 481 and following

Family and Medical Leave: Employers with ten or more employees must provide unpaid leave for pregnancy, childbirth, or parental leave for the birth of a child or adoption of a child 16 or younger. Employers with 15 or more employees must also provide unpaid leave for the employee's serious health conditions or to care for family member with a serious health condition. Employees may take up to 12 weeks each year for any of these purposes. Employers with 15 employees must provide an additional four hours of leave in a 30-day period, but not more than 24 hours per year, to take a family member to a medical, dental, or professional well-care appointment or respond to a family member's medical emergency (combined with school activities leave). Employees are eligible if they have worked an average of 30 hours per week for one year.

School Activities: Employers with 15 or more employees must provide employees with four hours of leave in a 30-day period, but not more than 24 hours per year, to participate in a child's school activities (combined with leave to take a family member to medical appointments).

Employees are eligible if they have worked an average of 30 hours per week for one year.

Domestic Violence: Unpaid leave for victims of crime, including domestic violence and sexual assault, to attend certain legal proceedings.

Paid Sick Leave: All employers must provide at least one hour of paid sick leave for every 52 hours worked. Employers may cap accrual at 40 hours per year. Employees are eligible if they have worked for a covered employer for an average of 18 hours per week for at least 20 weeks. Employees may use sick leave for their own illnesses, to care for an ill family member, for preventative medical care for themselves or a family member, to arrange long-term care for a family member, to deal with the effects of domestic violence on themselves or a family member, or to care for a family member when a school or business is closed due to a public health emergency.

Washington

Wash. Rev. Code §§ 49.12.265 and following; 49.12.350 and following; 49.46.200 and following; 49.76.010 and following; 50A.05.005 and following; Wash. Admin. Code 162-30-020

Pregnancy Disability Leave: Employers with eight or more employees must provide leave for the period of time when an employee is temporarily disabled due to pregnancy or childbirth. This is in addition to any leave available under federal FMLA and state family and medical leave laws.

State Family and Medical Leave Laws (continued)

Domestic Violence: All employers must provide reasonable leave from work to employees who are victims of domestic violence, sexual assault, or stalking—or whose family member is a victim—to prepare for and attend court, for medical treatment, and for other necessary services.

Paid Sick Leave: All employers must provide one hour of paid sick leave for every 40 hours worked. No annual cap on accrual, but employees may only carry over 40 hours of accrued leave from year to year. Employees may use sick leave for their own illness, the illness of a family member, the closure of a child's school or day care due to a public health emergency, and to seek services relating to domestic violence.

Paid Family and Medical Leave: Eligible employees (who have worked at least 820 hours during previous 12 months for any Washington employers) are entitled to benefits from state insurance program when taking medical leave due to employee's own serious health condition or family leave to care for family member with serious health condition, to bond with new child, or to deal with urgent need due to family member's active military duty. Paid family or medical leave is limited to 12 weeks in 52-week period, plus two additional weeks for employee's pregnancy-related incapacitating health condition. Combined family and medical leave may not exceed total of 16 weeks in 52-week period (or 18 weeks if it includes employee's pregnancy-related condition)..

Wisconsin

Wis. Stat. § 103.10

Family and Medical Leave: Employers with 50 or more employees must provide six weeks of leave per 12-month period for pregnancy, childbirth, and to bond with a baby arriving by birth or adoption. These employers must provide an additional two weeks off each year for the employee's own serious health condition and an additional two weeks each year to care for a family member with a serious health condition. Employees are eligible if they have worked for at least one year and have worked 1,000 hours in the preceding 12 months.

State Laws Prohibiting Discrimination in Employment

Alabama

Ala. Code §§ 25-1-20, 25-1-21

Law applies to employers with: 20 or more employees

Private employers may not make employment decisions based on:
- Age (40 and older)
- Refusal to provide pay history

Alaska

Alaska Stat. §§ 18.80.220, 18.80.300, 39.20.520 , 47.30.865

Law applies to employers with: One or more employees

Private employers may not make employment decisions based on:
- Age
- Ancestry or national origin
- Physical or mental disability
- Gender
- Marital status, including changes in status
- Pregnancy, childbirth, and related medical conditions, including parenthood and breast-feeding (accommodations required)
- Race or color
- Religion or creed
- Mental illness

Arizona

Ariz. Rev. Stat. §§ 41-1461, 41-1463, 41-1465

Law applies to employers with: 15 or more employees

Private employers may not make employment decisions based on:
- Age (40 and older)
- Ancestry or national origin

- Physical or mental disability
- AIDS/HIV
- Gender
- Race or color
- Religion or creed
- Genetic testing information

Arkansas

Ark. Code §§ 11-4-601, 11-5-116, 11-5-403, 16-123-102, 16-123-107

Law applies to employers with: Nine or more employees

Private employers may not make employment decisions based on:
- Ancestry or national origin
- Physical, mental, or sensory disability
- Gender
- Pregnancy, childbirth, and related medical conditions (accommodations required)
- Race or color
- Religion or creed
- Genetic testing information

California

Cal. Gov't. Code §§ 12920, 12926, 12926.1, 12940, 12941, 12945; Cal. Lab. Code § 1101, 432.3

Law applies to employers with: Five or more employees

Private employers may not make employment decisions based on:
- Age (40 and older)
- Ancestry or national origin
- Physical or mental disability
- AIDS/HIV
- Gender
- Marital status

State Laws Prohibiting Discrimination in Employment (continued)

- Pregnancy, childbirth, and related medical conditions (including breast-feeding and other accommodations)
- Race or color (including hairstyles)
- Religion or creed
- Sexual orientation
- Genetic testing information
- Gender identity, gender expression
- Medical condition
- Political activities or affiliations
- Status as victim of domestic violence, sexual assault, or stalking
- Military and veteran status
- Salary history, unless voluntarily disclosed

Colorado

Colo. Rev. Stat. §§ 24-34-301, 24-34-401, 24-34-402, 24-34-402.3, 24-34-402.5, 27-65-115; 3 Colo. Code Regs. §§ 708-1:60.1, 708-1:80.8

Law applies to employers with: One or more employees; 25 or more employees (marital status only)

Private employers may not make employment decisions based on:

- Age (40 and older)
- Ancestry or national origin
- Physical, mental, or learning disability
- AIDS/HIV
- Gender
- Marital status (only applies to marriage to a coworker or plans to marry a coworker)
- Pregnancy, childbirth, and related medical conditions (accommodations required)
- Race or color (including hairstyles)
- Religion or creed

- Sexual orientation, including perceived sexual orientation
- Lawful conduct outside of work
- Mental illness
- Transgender status
- Wage differential based on sex, or salary history

Connecticut

Conn. Gen. Stat. §§ 31-40z, 31-51ss, 46a-51, 46a-60, 46a-81a, 46a-81c

Law applies to employers with: Three or more employees

Private employers may not make employment decisions based on:

- Age
- Ancestry or national origin
- Present or past physical, mental, learning, or intellectual disability
- Gender
- Marital status, including civil unions
- Pregnancy, childbirth, and related medical conditions (accommodations required)
- Race or color
- Religion or creed
- Sexual orientation, including having a history of such a preference or being identified with such a preference
- Genetic testing information
- Gender identity or expression
- Arrests or convictions that have been erased, pardoned, or rehabilitated
- Status as a veteran
- Salary history, unless voluntarily disclose
- Status as victim of domestic violence or stalking

State Laws Prohibiting Discrimination in Employment (continued)

Delaware

Del. Code tit. 19, §§ 710, 711, 724

Law applies to employers with: Four or more employees

Private employers may not make employment decisions based on:

- Age (40 and older)
- Ancestry or national origin
- Physical or mental disability
- AIDS/HIV
- Gender
- Marital status
- Pregnancy, childbirth, and related medical conditions including breast-feeding (accommodations required)
- Race or color
- Religion or creed
- Sexual orientation
- Genetic testing information
- Gender identity
- Family responsibilities
- Status as victim of domestic violence, sexual offense, or stalking
- Family responsibilities, or "reproductive health decisions"
- Salary history

District of Columbia

D.C. Code §§ 2-1401.02, 2-1401.05, 2-1402.11, 2-1402.82, 7-1703.03, 32-531.08

Law applies to employers with: One or more employees

Private employers may not make employment decisions based on:

- Age (18 and older)
- Ancestry or national origin
- Physical or mental disability
- Gender (includes reproductive health decisions)

- Marital status, including domestic partnership
- Pregnancy, childbirth, and related medical conditions, including parenthood and breast-feeding (accommodations required)
- Race or color
- Religion or creed
- Sexual orientation
- Genetic testing information
- Enrollment in vocational, professional, or college education
- Family duties
- Personal appearance
- Political affiliation
- Gender identity or expression
- Status as unemployed
- Tobacco use
- Credit information
- Victim of domestic violence, sexual offense, or stalking

Florida

Fla. Stat. §§ 448.075, 760.01, 760.02, 760.10, 760.50

Law applies to employers with: 15 or more employees

Private employers may not make employment decisions based on:

- Age
- Ancestry or national origin
- "Handicap"
- AIDS/HIV
- Gender
- Marital status
- Pregnancy, childbirth, and related medical conditions
- Race or color
- Religion or creed
- Sickle cell trait

State Laws Prohibiting Discrimination in Employment (continued)

Georgia

Ga. Code §§ 34-1-2, 34-5-1, 34-5-2, 34-6A-1 and following

Law applies to employers with: 15 or more employees (disability); ten or more employees (gender) (domestic and agricultural employees not protected); one or more employees (age).

Private employers may not make employment decisions based on:
- Age (40 to 70)
- Physical, mental, or learning disability
- Gender (wage discrimination only)
- Pregnancy, childbirth, and related medical conditions including breastfeeding (accommodations required)

Hawaii

Haw. Rev. Stat. §§ 378-1 and following; Haw. Admin. Rules §§ 12-46-107, 12-46-182

Law applies to employers with: One or more employees

Private employers may not make employment decisions based on:
- Age
- Ancestry or national origin
- Physical or mental disability
- AIDS/HIV
- Gender
- Marital status
- Pregnancy, childbirth, and related medical conditions, including breastfeeding (accommodations required)
- Race or color
- Religion or creed
- Sexual orientation
- Genetic testing information
- Arrest and court record (unless there is a conviction directly related to job)
- Salary history, unless voluntarily disclosed
- Credit history or credit report, unless the information in the individual's credit history or credit report directly relates to a bona fide occupational qualification
- Gender identity and gender expression
- Status as a victim of domestic or sexual violence (if employer has knowledge or is notified of this status)

Idaho

Idaho Code §§ 39-8303, 67-5902, 67-5909, 67-5910

Law applies to employers with: Five or more employees

Private employers may not make employment decisions based on:
- Age (40 and older)
- Ancestry or national origin
- Physical or mental disability
- Gender
- Pregnancy, childbirth, and related medical conditions
- Race or color
- Religion or creed
- Genetic testing information

Illinois

410 Ill. Comp. Stat. § 513/25; 775 Ill. Comp. Stat. §§ 5/1-102, 5/1-103, 5/2-101, 5/2-102, 5/2-103; 820 Ill. Comp. Stat. §§ 105/4, 180/30; Ill. Admin. Code tit. 56, § 5210.110

Law applies to employers with: One or more employees.

Private employers may not make employment decisions based on:
- Age (40 and older)

State Laws Prohibiting Discrimination in Employment (continued)

- Ancestry or national origin
- Physical or mental disability
- Gender
- Marital status
- Pregnancy, childbirth, and related medical conditions (accommodations required)
- Race or color
- Religion or creed
- Sexual orientation
- Genetic testing information
- Citizenship status
- Military status
- Unfavorable military discharge
- Gender identity
- Arrest record
- Genetic information
- Victims of domestic violence
- Order of protection status
- Lack of permanent mailing address or having a mailing address of a shelter or social service provider
- Salary history

Indiana

Ind. Code §§ 22-2-14-2, 22-9-1-2, 22-9-2-1, 22-9-2-2, 22-9-5-1 and following

Law applies to employers with: six or more employees; One or more employees (age only); 15 or more employees (disability only)

Private employers may not make employment decisions based on:

- Age (40 to 75—applies to employers with one or more employees)
- Ancestry or national origin
- Physical or mental disability (15 or more employees)
- Gender

- Pregnancy, childbirth, and related medical conditions (accommodations required)
- Race or color
- Religion or creed
- Status as a veteran
- Off-duty tobacco use
- Sealed or expunged arrest or conviction record

Iowa

Iowa Code §§ 216.2, 216.6, 216.6A, 729.6

Law applies to employers with: Four or more employees

Private employers may not make employment decisions based on:

- Age (18 or older)
- Ancestry or national origin
- Physical or mental disability
- AIDS/HIV
- Gender
- Pregnancy, childbirth, and related medical conditions (accommodations required)
- Race or color
- Religion or creed
- Sexual orientation
- Genetic testing information
- Gender identity
- Wage discrimination

Kansas

Kan. Stat. §§ 44-1002, 44-1009, 44-1112, 44-1113, 44-1125, 44-1126, 65-6002(e)

Law applies to employers with: Four or more employees

Private employers may not make employment decisions based on:

- Age (40 or older)

State Laws Prohibiting Discrimination in Employment (continued)

- Ancestry or national origin
- Physical or mental disability
- AIDS/HIV
- Gender
- Race or color
- Pregnancy, childbirth, and related medical conditions (accommodations required)
- Religion or creed
- Genetic testing information
- Military service or status

Kentucky

Ky. Rev. Stat. §§ 207.130, 207.135, 207.150, 342.197, 344.010, 344.030, 344.040

Law applies to employers with: Eight or more employees

Private employers may not make employment decisions based on:
- Age (40 or older)
- Ancestry or national origin
- Physical or mental disability
- AIDS/HIV
- Gender
- Pregnancy, childbirth, and related medical conditions (accommodations required)
- Race or color
- Religion or creed
- Occupational pneumoconiosis with no respiratory impairment resulting from exposure to coal dust
- Off-duty tobacco use

Louisiana

La. Rev. Stat. §§ 23:301 to 23:368

Law applies to employers with: 20 or more employees

Private employers may not make employment decisions based on:
- Age (40 or older)
- Ancestry or national origin
- Physical or mental disability
- Gender
- Pregnancy, childbirth, and related medical conditions (accommodations may be required) (applies to employers with 25 or more employees)
- Race or color
- Religion or creed
- Genetic testing information
- Sickle cell trait
- Being a smoker or nonsmoker

Maine

Me. Rev. Stat. tit. 5, §§ 19302, 4552, 4553, 4571 to 4577; tit. 26, § 833; tit. 39-A, § 353

Law applies to employers with: One or more employees

Private employers may not make employment decisions based on:
- Age
- Ancestry or national origin
- Physical or mental disability
- AIDS/HIV
- Gender
- Pregnancy, childbirth, and related medical conditions (accommodations may be required)
- Race or color
- Religion or creed
- Sexual orientation, including perceived sexual orientation
- Genetic testing information
- Gender identity or expression
- Past workers' compensation claim
- Past whistle-blowing

State Laws Prohibiting Discrimination in Employment (continued)

- Medical support notice for child
- Salary history, unless voluntarily disclosed

Maryland

Md. Code (State Government) §§ 20-101, 20-601–20-608; Md. Code (Lab. & Empl.) § 3-1407; Md. Code Regs. § 14.03.02.02

Law applies to employers with: 15 or more employees/contractors; one or more employees/contractors (harassment only).

Private employers may not make employment decisions based on:

- Age
- Ancestry or national origin
- Physical or mental disability
- AIDS/HIV
- Gender
- Marital status
- Pregnancy, childbirth, and related medical conditions (accommodations required)
- Race or color (including hairstyles)
- Religion or creed
- Sexual orientation
- Genetic testing information
- Civil Air Patrol membership
- Gender identity
- Organ donation
- Wage history

Massachusetts

Mass. Gen. Laws ch. 149, §§ 24A, 105A; ch. 151B, §§ 1, 4; 804 Code Mass. Regs 3.01

Law applies to employers with: Six or more employees

Private employers may not make employment decisions based on:

- Age (40 or older)

- Ancestry or national origin
- Physical or mental disability
- Gender
- Marital status
- Pregnancy, childbirth, and related medical conditions, including breast-feeding (accommodations required)
- Race or color
- Religion or creed
- Sexual orientation
- Genetic testing information
- Military service
- Arrest record
- Status as a veteran
- Salary history
- Sealed or expunged criminal record

Michigan

Mich. Comp. Laws §§ 37.1103, 37.1201, 37.1202, 37.2201, 37.2202, 37.2205a, 750.556

Law applies to employers with: One or more employees

Private employers may not make employment decisions based on:

- Age
- Ancestry or national origin
- Physical or mental disability
- AIDS/HIV
- Gender
- Marital status
- Pregnancy, childbirth, and related medical conditions
- Race or color
- Religion or creed
- Genetic testing information
- Height or weight
- Misdemeanor arrest record
- Civil Air Patrol membership

State Laws Prohibiting Discrimination in Employment (continued)

Minnesota

Minn. Stat. §§ 144.417, 181.81, 181.9414, 181.974, 363A.03, 363A.08

Law applies to employers with: One or more employees; 21 or more employees (pregnancy and childbirth accommodations)

Private employers may not make employment decisions based on:

- Age (18 to 70)
- Ancestry or national origin
- Physical, sensory, or mental disability
- Gender
- Marital status
- Pregnancy, childbirth, and related medical conditions (accommodations required)
- Race or color
- Religion or creed
- Sexual orientation, including perceived sexual orientation
- Genetic testing information
- Gender identity
- Member of local commission
- Receiving public assistance
- Familial status (protects parents or guardians living with a minor child)

Mississippi

Miss. Code § 33-1-15

Law applies to employers with: One or more employees

Private employers may not make employment decisions based on:

- Military status
- No other protected categories unless employer receives public funding

Missouri

Mo. Rev. Stat. §§ 191.665, 213.010, 213.055, 375.1306

Law applies to employers with: Six or more employees

Private employers may not make employment decisions based on:

- Age (40 to 70)
- Ancestry or national origin
- Physical or mental disability
- AIDS/HIV
- Gender
- Race or color
- Religion or creed
- Genetic testing information
- Off-duty use of alcohol or tobacco

Montana

Mont. Code. §§ 49-2-101, 49-2-303, 49-2-310

Law applies to employers with: One or more employees

Private employers may not make employment decisions based on:

- Age
- Ancestry or national origin
- Physical or mental disability
- Gender
- Marital status
- Pregnancy, childbirth, and related medical conditions
- Race or color
- Religion or creed

Nebraska

Neb. Rev. Stat. §§ 20-168, 48-236, 48-1001–48-1010, 48-1102, 48-1104

Law applies to employers with: 15 or more employees; 20 or more employees (age only).

State Laws Prohibiting Discrimination in Employment (continued)

Private employers may not make employment decisions based on:

- Age (40 or older—applies to employers with 20 or more employees)
- Ancestry or national origin
- Physical or mental disability
- AIDS/HIV
- Gender
- Marital status
- Pregnancy, childbirth, and related medical conditions (accommodations required)
- Race or color
- Religion or creed
- Genetic testing information (applies to all employers)

Nevada

Nev. Rev. Stat. §§ 608.0193, 608.0198, 613.310 and following, 613.4353

Law applies to employers with: 15 or more employees

Private employers may not make employment decisions based on:

- Age (40 or older)
- Ancestry or national origin
- Physical or mental disability
- AIDS/HIV
- Gender
- Pregnancy, childbirth, and related medical conditions, including breast-feeding (accommodations required)
- Race or color
- Religion or creed
- Sexual orientation, including perceived sexual orientation
- Genetic testing information
- Use of service animal

- Gender identity or expression
- Opposing unlawful employment practices
- Credit report or credit information (with some exceptions)
- Requesting leave or reasonable accommodation due to status as victim of domestic violence (applies to all employers)

New Hampshire

N.H. Rev. Stat. §§ 141-H:3, 354-A:2, 354-A:6, 354-A:7

Law applies to employers with: Six or more employees

Private employers may not make employment decisions based on:

- Age
- Ancestry or national origin
- Physical or mental disability
- Gender
- Marital status
- Pregnancy, childbirth, and related medical conditions
- Race or color
- Religion or creed
- Sexual orientation
- Genetic testing information
- Victims of domestic violence, harassment, sexual assault, or stalking
- Gender identity
- Off-duty use of tobacco products

New Jersey

N.J. Stat. §§ 10:5-1, 10:5-4, 10:5-4.1, 10:5-5, 10:5-12, 10:5-29.1, 34:6B-1 43:21-49

Law applies to employers with: One or more employees

State Laws Prohibiting Discrimination in Employment (continued)

Private employers may not make employment decisions based on:

- Age (18 to 70)
- Ancestry or national origin
- Past or present physical or mental disability
- AIDS/HIV
- Gender
- Marital status, including civil union or domestic partnership status
- Pregnancy, childbirth, and related medical conditions, including breast-feeding (accommodations required)
- Race or color
- Religion or creed
- Sexual orientation, including affectional orientation and perceived sexual orientation
- Genetic testing information
- Atypical hereditary cellular or blood trait
- Accompanied by service or guide dog
- Military service
- Gender identity
- Unemployed status
- Liability for service in the U.S. Armed Forces
- Familial status
- Salary history (job applicants).

New Mexico

N.M. Stat. §§ 24-21-4, 28-1-2, 28-1-7, 50-4A-4; N.M. Admin. Code 9.1.1

Law applies to employers with: Four or more employees; 50 or more employees (marital status only).

Private employers may not make employment decisions based on:

- Age (40 or older)
- Ancestry or national origin
- Physical or mental disability
- Gender
- Marital status (applies to employers with 50 or more employees)
- Pregnancy, childbirth, and related medical conditions
- Race or color
- Religion or creed
- Sexual orientation, including perceived sexual orientation
- Genetic testing information
- Gender identity
- Serious medical condition
- Domestic abuse leave

New York

N.Y. Exec. Law §§ 292, 296; N.Y. Lab. Law § 201-d

Law applies to employers with: One or more employees.

Private employers may not make employment decisions based on:

- Age (18 or older)
- Ancestry or national origin
- Physical or mental disability
- Gender
- Marital status
- Pregnancy, childbirth, and related medical conditions (accommodations required)
- Race or color
- Religion or creed
- Sexual orientation, including perceived sexual orientation
- Genetic testing information
- Lawful recreational activities when not at work
- Military status or service

State Laws Prohibiting Discrimination in Employment (continued)

- Observance of Sabbath
- Political activities
- Use of service dog
- Arrest or criminal accusation
- Domestic violence victim status
- Familial status
- Gender identity and transgender status
- Reproductive health decision-making

North Carolina

N.C. Gen. Stat. §§ 95-28.1, 95-28.1A, 127B-11, 130A-148, 143-422.2, 168A-5

Law applies to employers with: 15 or more employees

Private employers may not make employment decisions based on:
- Age
- Ancestry or national origin
- Physical or mental disability
- AIDS/HIV
- Gender
- Race or color
- Religion or creed
- Genetic testing information
- Military status or service
- Sickle cell or hemoglobin C trait
- Lawful use of lawful products off site and off duty

North Dakota

N.D. Cent. Code §§ 14-02.4-02, 14-02.4-03, 34-01-17

Law applies to employers with: One or more employees

Private employers may not make employment decisions based on:
- Age (40 or older)

- Ancestry or national origin
- Physical or mental disability
- Gender
- Marital status
- Pregnancy, childbirth, and related medical conditions (accommodations required)
- Race or color
- Religion or creed
- Lawful conduct outside of work
- Receiving public assistance
- Keeping and bearing arms (as long as firearm is never exhibited on company property except for lawful defensive purposes)
- Status as a volunteer emergency responder

Ohio

Ohio Rev. Code §§ 4111.17, 4112.01, 4112.02

Law applies to employers with: Four or more employees

Private employers may not make employment decisions based on:
- Age (40 or older)
- Ancestry or national origin
- Physical, mental, or learning disability
- AIDS/HIV
- Gender
- Pregnancy, childbirth, and related medical conditions
- Race or color
- Religion or creed
- Military status
- Caring for a sibling, child, parent, or spouse injured while in the armed services

State Laws Prohibiting Discrimination in Employment (continued)

Oklahoma

Okla. Stat. tit. 10A tit. § 1-2-101; 25, §§ 1301, 1302; tit. 36, § 3614.2; tit. 40, § 500; tit. 44, § 208

Law applies to employers with: One or more employees

Private employers may not make employment decisions based on:

- Age (40 or older)
- Ancestry or national origin
- Physical or mental disability
- Gender
- Pregnancy, childbirth, and related medical conditions (except abortions where the woman is not in "imminent danger of death")
- Race or color
- Religion or creed
- Genetic testing information
- Military service
- Being a smoker or nonsmoker or using tobacco off duty
- Reporting child abuse or neglect

Oregon

Or. Rev. Stat. §§ 659A.030, 659A.122 and following, 659A.303, 659A.357; 2019 Oregon Laws Ch. 139

Law applies to employers with: One or more employees;

Private employers may not make employment decisions based on:

- Age (18 or older)
- Ancestry or national origin
- Physical or mental disability (applies to employers with six or more employees)
- Gender

- Marital status
- Pregnancy, childbirth, and related medical conditions (accommodations required) (applies to employers with six or more employees)
- Race or color
- Religion or creed
- Sexual orientation
- Genetic testing information
- Parent who has medical support order imposed by court
- Domestic violence victim status
- Refusal to attend an employer-sponsored meeting with the primary purpose of communicating the employer's opinion on religious or political matters
- Credit history
- Whistle-blowers
- Off-duty use of tobacco products
- Salary history, unless voluntarily disclosed

Pennsylvania

43 Pa. Cons. Stat. §§ 954 to 955

Law applies to employers with: Four or more employees

Private employers may not make employment decisions based on:

- Age (40 to 70)
- Ancestry or national origin
- Physical or mental disability
- Gender
- Pregnancy, childbirth, and related medical conditions
- Race or color
- Religion or creed

State Laws Prohibiting Discrimination in Employment (continued)

- Relationship or association with a person with a disability
- GED rather than high school diploma
- Use of service animal

Rhode Island

R.I. Gen. Laws §§ 12-28-10, 23-6.3-11, 28-5-6, 28-5-7, 28-6-18, 28-6.7-1

Law applies to employers with: Four or more employees; one or more employees (gender-based wage discrimination only)

Private employers may not make employment decisions based on:
- Age (40 or older)
- Ancestry or national origin
- Physical or mental disability
- AIDS/HIV
- Gender
- Pregnancy, childbirth, and related medical conditions, including breast-feeding (accommodations required)
- Race or color
- Religion or creed
- Sexual orientation, including perceived sexual orientation
- Genetic testing information
- Domestic abuse victim
- Gender identity or expression
- Homelessness

South Carolina

S.C. Code §§ 1-13-30, 1-13-80

Law applies to employers with: 15 or more employees

Private employers may not make employment decisions based on:
- Age (40 or older)
- Ancestry or national origin

- Physical or mental disability
- AIDS/HIV
- Gender
- Pregnancy, childbirth, and related medical conditions (accommodations required)
- Race or color
- Religion or creed

South Dakota

S.D. Codified Laws §§ 20-13-1, 20-13-10, 60-12-15, 60-2-20, 62-1-17

Law applies to employers with: One or more employees

Private employers may not make employment decisions based on:
- Ancestry or national origin
- Physical or mental disability
- Gender
- Race or color
- Religion or creed
- Genetic testing information
- Preexisting injury
- Off-duty use of tobacco products

Tennessee

Tenn. Code §§ 4-21-102, 4-21-401 and following, 8-50-103, 50-2-201, 50-2-202

Law applies to employers with: Eight or more employees; one or more employees (gender-based wage discrimination only)

Private employers may not make employment decisions based on:
- Age (40 or older)
- Ancestry or national origin
- Physical, mental, or visual disability
- Gender

State Laws Prohibiting Discrimination in Employment (continued)

- Pregnancy, childbirth, and related medical conditions (accommodations required)
- Race or color
- Religion or creed
- Use of guide dog
- Volunteer rescue squad worker responding to an emergency

Texas

Tex. Lab. Code §§ 21.002, 21.051, 21.101, 21.106, 21.402; Tex. Fam. Code § 261.110

Law applies to employers with: 15 or more employees

Private employers may not make employment decisions based on:

- Age (40 or older)
- Ancestry or national origin
- Physical or mental disability
- Gender
- Pregnancy, childbirth, and related medical conditions (accommodations required)
- Race or color
- Religion or creed
- Genetic testing information
- Reporting child abuse or neglect

Utah

Utah Code §§ 26-45-103, 34A-5-102, 34A-5-106

Law applies to employers with: 15 or more employees

Private employers may not make employment decisions based on:

- Age (40 or older)
- Ancestry or national origin
- Physical or mental disability

- AIDS/HIV
- Gender
- Pregnancy, childbirth, and related medical conditions, including breast-feeding (accommodations required)
- Race or color
- Religion or creed
- Sexual orientation
- Gender identity
- Genetic testing information

Vermont

Vt. Stat. tit. 18, § 9333; tit. 21, §§ 305, 495, 495d, 495m

Law applies to employers with: One or more employees

Private employers may not make employment decisions based on:

- Age (18 or older)
- Ancestry or national origin
- Physical, mental, or emotional disability
- AIDS/HIV
- Gender
- Pregnancy, childbirth, and related medical conditions (accommodations required)
- Race or color
- Religion or creed
- Sexual orientation
- Genetic testing information
- Gender identity
- Place of birth
- Credit report or credit history
- Status as crime victim
- Salary history

State Laws Prohibiting Discrimination in Employment (continued)

Virginia

Va. Code §§ 2.2-3900, 2.2-3901, 2.2-3905, 40.1-28.6, 40.1-28.7:1, 51.5-41

Law applies to employers with: 15 or more employees; six or more for unlawful discharge; and six or more but fewer than 20 for unlawful discharge based on age.

Private employers may not make employment decisions based on:

- Age (40 and older)
- Ancestry or national origin
- Physical or mental disability
- AIDS/HIV
- Gender
- Marital status
- Pregnancy, childbirth, and related medical conditions (accommodations required)
- Race or color (including hairstyles)
- Religion or creed
- Genetic testing information
- Veteran status
- Sexual orientation
- Arrest or conviction for marijuana possession.

Washington

Wash. Rev. Code §§ 38.40.110, 49.002.011, 49.44.090, 49.44.180, 49.58.020, 49.58.040, 49.60.030, 49.60.040, 49.60.172, 49.60.180, 49.76.120; Wash. Admin. Code § 162-30-020

Law applies to employers with: Eight or more employees; one or more employees (gender-based wage discrimination only); 15 or more employees (pregnancy and childbirth accommodations)

Private employers may not make employment decisions based on:

- Age (40 or older)

- Ancestry or national origin
- Physical, mental, or sensory disability
- AIDS/HIV
- Gender
- Marital status
- Pregnancy, childbirth, and related medical conditions, including breast-feeding (accommodations required)
- Race or color (including hairstyles)
- Religion or creed
- Sexual orientation
- Genetic testing information
- Hepatitis C infection
- Member of state militia
- Use of service animal by a person with a disability
- Gender identity
- Domestic violence victim
- Salary history
- Immigration.

West Virginia

W. Va. Code §§ 5-11-3, 5-11-9, 15-1K-4, 16-3C-3, 21-5B-1, 21-5B-3

Law applies to employers with: 12 or more employees; one or more employees (gender-based wage discrimination only)

Private employers may not make employment decisions based on:

- Age (40 or older)
- Ancestry or national origin
- Physical or mental disability, or blindness
- AIDS/HIV
- Gender
- Pregnancy, childbirth, and related medical conditions (accommodations required)
- Race or color

State Laws Prohibiting Discrimination in Employment (continued)

- Religion or creed
- Off-duty use of tobacco products
- Membership in the Civil Air Patrol (for employers with 16 or more employees)

Wisconsin

Wis. Stat. §§ 111.32 and following

Law applies to employers with: One or more employees

Private employers may not make employment decisions based on:

- Age (40 or older)
- Ancestry or national origin
- Physical or mental disability
- Gender
- Marital status
- Pregnancy, childbirth, and related medical conditions
- Race or color
- Religion or creed
- Sexual orientation, including having a history of or being identified with a preference
- Genetic testing information

- Arrest or conviction record
- Military service
- Declining to attend a meeting or to participate in any communication about religious matters or political matters
- Use or nonuse of lawful products off duty and off site

Wyoming

Wyo. Stat. §§ 19-11-104, 27-9-102, 27-9-105

Law applies to employers with: Two or more employees

Private employers may not make employment decisions based on:

- Age (40 or older)
- Ancestry or national origin
- Disability
- Gender
- Pregnancy, childbirth, and related medical conditions
- Race or color
- Religion or creed
- Military service or status

State Laws That Control Final Paychecks

Note: The states of Alabama, Florida, Georgia, and Mississippi are not included in this chart because they do not have laws specifically controlling final paychecks. Contact your state department of labor for more information.

Alaska

Alaska Stat. § 23.05.140(b)

Paycheck due when employee is fired: Within three working days after termination.

Paycheck due when employee quits: Next regular payday at least three days after employee gives notice.

Unused vacation pay due: Only if agreed to by employer or required by company policy or practice.

Arizona

Ariz. Rev. Stat. §§ 23-350, 23-353

Paycheck due when employee is fired: Next payday or within seven working days, whichever is sooner.

Paycheck due when employee quits: Next regular payday or by mail at employee's request.

Unused vacation pay due: No provision.

Arkansas

Ark. Code § 11-4-405

Paycheck due when employee is fired: Next regular payday.

Paycheck due when employee quits: No provision.

Unused vacation pay due: No provision.

Special employment situations: Railroad or railroad construction: day of discharge.

California

Cal. Lab. Code §§ 201 - 202, 227.3

Paycheck due when employee is fired: Immediately.

Paycheck due when employee quits: Immediately if employee has given 72 hours' notice; otherwise, within 72 hours.

Unused vacation pay due: Yes.

Special employment situations: Motion picture business: next payday.

Oil drilling industry: within 24 hours (excluding weekends and holidays) of termination.

Seasonal agricultural workers: within 72 hours of termination.

Colorado

Colo. Rev. Stat. § 8-4-109

Paycheck due when employee is fired: Immediately. (Within six hours of start of next workday, if payroll unit is closed; 24 hours if unit is offsite.) When paycheck is not due immediately, employer may make the check available at the work site, the employer's local office, or the employee's last-known mailing address.

Paycheck due when employee quits: Next payday.

Unused vacation pay due: Yes.

Connecticut

Conn. Gen. Stat. §§ 31-71c, 31-76k

Paycheck due when employee is fired: Next business day after discharge.

Paycheck due when employee quits: Next payday.

State Laws That Control Final Paychecks (continued)

Unused vacation pay due: Only if policy or collective bargaining agreement requires payment on termination.

Delaware

Del. Code tit. 19, § 1103

Paycheck due when employee is fired: Next payday.

Paycheck due when employee quits: Next payday.

Unused vacation pay due: Only if required by employer policy or agreement, in which case vacation must be paid within 30 days after it becomes due.

District of Columbia

D.C. Code §§ 32-1301, 32-1303

Paycheck due when employee is fired: Next business day unless employee handles money, in which case employer has four days.

Paycheck due when employee quits: Next payday or seven days after quitting, whichever is sooner.

Unused vacation pay due: Yes, unless there is an agreement to the contrary.

Hawaii

Haw. Rev. Stat. § 388-3

Paycheck due when employee is fired: Immediately or next business day, if timing or conditions prevent immediate payment.

Paycheck due when employee quits: Next payday or immediately, if employee gives one pay period's notice.

Unused vacation pay due: No.

Idaho

Idaho Code §§ 45-606, 45-617

Paycheck due when employee is fired: Next payday or within ten days (excluding weekends & holidays), whichever is sooner. If employee makes written request for earlier payment, within 48 hours of receipt of request (excluding weekends & holidays).

Paycheck due when employee quits: Next payday or within ten days (excluding weekends & holidays), whichever is sooner. If employee makes written request for earlier payment, within 48 hours of receipt of request (excluding weekends & holidays).

Unused vacation pay due: No provision.

Illinois

820 Ill. Comp. Stat. § 115/5

Paycheck due when employee is fired: At time of separation if possible, but no later than next payday. Employer must comply with employee's written request to mail final paycheck.

Paycheck due when employee quits: At time of separation if possible, but no later than next payday. Employer must comply with employee's written request to mail final paycheck.

Unused vacation pay due: Yes.

Indiana

Ind. Code §§ 22-2-5-1, 22-2-9-1, 22-2-9-2

Paycheck due when employee is fired: Next payday.

Paycheck due when employee quits: Next payday. (If employee has not left address, (1) ten business days after employee

State Laws That Control Final Paychecks (continued)

demands wages or (2) when employee provides address where check may be mailed.)

Unused vacation pay due: If employer agrees to vacation pay, absent an agreement to the contrary, employer must pay out accrued unused vacation upon termination.

Special employment situations: Does not apply to railroad employees.

Iowa

Iowa Code §§ 91A.2(7)(b), 91A.4

Paycheck due when employee is fired: Next payday.

Paycheck due when employee quits: Next payday.

Unused vacation pay due: Yes.

Special employment situations: If employee is owed commission, employer has 30 days to pay.

Kansas

Kan. Stat. § 44-315

Paycheck due when employee is fired: Next payday.

Paycheck due when employee quits: Next payday.

Unused vacation pay due: Only if required by employer's policies or practice.

Kentucky

Ky. Rev. Stat. §§ 337.010, 337.055

Paycheck due when employee is fired: Next payday or within 14 days, whichever is later.

Paycheck due when employee quits: Next payday or within 14 days, whichever is later.

Unused vacation pay due: Yes.

Louisiana

La. Rev. Stat. § 23:631

Paycheck due when employee is fired: Next payday or within 15 days, whichever is earlier.

Paycheck due when employee quits: Next payday or within 15 days, whichever is earlier.

Unused vacation pay due: Yes.

Maine

Me. Rev. Stat. tit. 26, § 626

Paycheck due when employee is fired: Next payday or within 14 days, whichever is earlier.

Paycheck due when employee quits: Next payday or within 14 days, whichever is earlier.

Unused vacation pay due: Only if required by employer's policies or practice.

Special employment situations: Employer must pay employees all wages due within two weeks of the sale of a business.

Maryland

Md. Code (Lab. & Empl.) § 3-505

Paycheck due when employee is fired: Next scheduled payday.

Paycheck due when employee quits: Next scheduled payday.

Unused vacation pay due: Yes.

Massachusetts

Mass. Gen. Laws ch. 149, § 148

Paycheck due when employee is fired: Day of discharge.

State Laws That Control Final Paychecks (continued)

Paycheck due when employee quits:
Next payday. If no scheduled payday, then following Saturday.

Unused vacation pay due: Yes.

Michigan
Mich. Comp. Laws §§ 408.471–408.475; Mich. Admin. Code § 408.9007

Paycheck due when employee is fired: Next payday.

Paycheck due when employee quits: Next payday.

Unused vacation pay due: Only if required by written policy or contract.

Special employment situations: Hand-harvesters of crops: within one working day of termination.

Minnesota
Minn. Stat. §§ 181.13, 181.14, 181.74

Paycheck due when employee is fired: Within 24 hours.

Paycheck due when employee quits: Next regular payday. If next payday is less than five days after employee's last day, employer may delay payment until payday after that. But in no event may payment exceed 20 days from employee's last day.

Unused vacation pay due: Only if required by written policy or contract.

Special employment situations: If employee was responsible for collecting or handling money or property, employer has ten days after termination or resignation to audit and adjust employee accounts before making payment.

Commissions must be paid to sales employees within three days if employee is fired or quits with at least five days' notice. Otherwise, commissions must be paid within six days.

Migrant agricultural workers who resign: within five days.

Missouri
Mo. Rev. Stat. § 290.110

Paycheck due when employee is fired: Day of discharge.

Paycheck due when employee quits: No provision.

Unused vacation pay due: Only if required by agreement.

Special employment situations: Requirements do not apply if employee is paid primarily based on commission and an audit is necessary or customary to determine the amount due.

Montana
Mont. Code § 39-3-205; Mont. Admin.R. § 24.16.7521

Paycheck due when employee is fired: Immediately if fired for cause or laid off (unless there is a written policy extending time to earlier of next payday or 15 days).

Paycheck due when employee quits: Next payday or within 15 days, whichever comes first.

Unused vacation pay due: Only if required by policy.

Nebraska
Neb. Rev. Stat. §§ 48-1229 - 48-1230

Paycheck due when employee is fired: Next payday or within two weeks, whichever is earlier.

State Laws That Control Final Paychecks (continued)

Paycheck due when employee quits: Next payday or within two weeks, whichever is earlier.

Unused vacation pay due: Only if required by agreement.

Special employment situations: Commissions due on next payday following receipt.

Nevada

Nev. Rev. Stat. §§ 608.020, 608.030

Paycheck due when employee is fired: Immediately.

Paycheck due when employee quits: Next payday or within seven days, whichever is earlier.

Unused vacation pay due: Only if required by policy.

New Hampshire

N.H. Rev. Stat. §§ 275:43(v), 275:44

Paycheck due when employee is fired: Within 72 hours. If laid off, next payday.

Paycheck due when employee quits: Next payday, or within 72 hours if employee gives one pay period's notice.

Unused vacation pay due: Only if required by policy.

New Jersey

N.J. Stat. § 34:11-4.3

Paycheck due when employee is fired: Next payday.

Paycheck due when employee quits: Next payday.

Unused vacation pay due: Only if required by policy.

New Mexico

N.M. Stat. §§ 50-4-4, § 50-4-4(A), 50-4-5

Paycheck due when employee is fired: Within five days; ten days for commission or piece-based workers.

Paycheck due when employee quits: Next payday.

Unused vacation pay due: Only if required by policy.

Special employment situations: If paid by task or commission, ten days after discharge.

New York

N.Y. Lab. Law §§ 191(3), 198-c(2)

Paycheck due when employee is fired: Next payday.

Paycheck due when employee quits: Next payday.

Unused vacation pay due: Only if required by policy.

North Carolina

N.C. Gen. Stat. §§ 95-25.7, 95-25.12

Paycheck due when employee is fired: Next payday.

Paycheck due when employee quits: Next payday.

Unused vacation pay due: Only if required by policy.

Special employment situations: If paid by commission or bonus, on next payday after amount calculated.

North Dakota

N.D. Cent. Code § 34-14-03; N.D. Admin. Code 46-02-07-02(12)

Paycheck due when employee is fired: Next payday.

State Laws That Control Final Paychecks (continued)

Paycheck due when employee quits: Next payday.

Unused vacation pay due: Yes. However, if an employer provides written notice at the time of hire, employer need not pay out vacation that has been awarded, but not yet earned. And, if an employee quits with less than five days' notice, employer may withhold accrued vacation, as long as the employer gave written notice of the limitation at the time of hire and the employee was employed for less than one year.

Ohio

Ohio Rev. Code § 4113.15

Paycheck due when employee is fired: First of month for wages earned in first half of prior month; 15th of month for wages earned in second half of prior month.

Paycheck due when employee quits: First of month for wages earned in first half of prior month; 15th of month for wages earned in second half of prior month.

Unused vacation pay due: Yes, if company has policy or practice of making such payments.

Oklahoma

Okla. Stat. tit. 40, §§ 165.1(4), 165.3

Paycheck due when employee is fired: Next payday.

Paycheck due when employee quits: Next payday.

Unused vacation pay due: Yes.

Oregon

Or. Rev. Stat. §§ 652.140, 652.145

Paycheck due when employee is fired: End of first business day after termination.

Paycheck due when employee quits: Immediately, with 48 hours' notice (excluding weekends & holidays); without notice, within five business days or next payday, whichever comes first (must be within five days if employee submits time records to determine wages due).

Unused vacation pay due: Only if required by policy.

Special employment situations: Seasonal farmworkers: fired or quitting with 48 hours' notice, immediately; quitting without notice, within 48 hours or next payday, whichever comes first. If the termination occurs at the end of harvest season, the employer is a farmworker camp operator, and the farmworker is provided housing at no cost until wages are paid, employer must pay by noon on the day after termination.

Pennsylvania

43 Pa. Stat. §§ 260.2a, 260.5

Paycheck due when employee is fired: Next payday.

Paycheck due when employee quits: Next payday.

Unused vacation pay due: Only if required by policy or contract.

Rhode Island

R.I. Gen. Laws § 28-14-4

Paycheck due when employee is fired: Next payday. Paycheck is due within 24 hours if employer liquidates, merges, or disposes of the business, or moves it out of state.

Paycheck due when employee quits: Next payday.

State Laws That Control Final Paychecks (continued)

Unused vacation pay due: Yes, if employee has worked for one full year and the company has verbally or in writing awarded vacation.

South Carolina

S.C. Code §§ 41-10-10(2), 41-10-50

Paycheck due when employee is fired: Within 48 hours or next payday, but not more than 30 days.

Paycheck due when employee quits: No provision.

Unused vacation pay due: Only if required by policy or contract.

South Dakota

S.D. Codified Laws §§ 60-11-10, 60-11-11, 60-11-14

Paycheck due when employee is fired: Next payday (or until employee returns employer's property).

Paycheck due when employee quits: Next payday (or until employee returns employer's property).

Unused vacation pay due: No.

Tennessee

Tenn. Code § 50-2-103

Paycheck due when employee is fired: Next payday or within 21 days, whichever is later.

Paycheck due when employee quits: Next payday or within 21 days, whichever is later.

Unused vacation pay due: Only if required by policy or contract.

Special employment situations: Applies to employers with five or more employees.

Texas

Tex. Lab. Code §§ 61.001, 61.014

Paycheck due when employee is fired: Within six days.

Paycheck due when employee quits: Next payday.

Unused vacation pay due: Only if required by policy or contract.

Utah

Utah Code § 34-28-5; Utah Admin. Code § 610-3

Paycheck due when employee is fired: Within 24 hours.

Paycheck due when employee quits: Next payday.

Unused vacation pay due: Only if required by policy or contract.

Special employment situations: Requirements do not apply to commission-based portion of sales employees' earnings if audit is necessary to determine the amount due.

Vermont

Vt. Stat. tit. 21, § 342(c)

Paycheck due when employee is fired: Within 72 hours.

Paycheck due when employee quits: Next regular payday or next Friday, if there is no regular payday.

Unused vacation pay due: No provision.

State Laws That Control Final Paychecks (continued)

Virginia

Va. Code § 40.1-29(A.1)

Paycheck due when employee is fired: Next payday.

Paycheck due when employee quits: Next payday.

Unused vacation pay due: Only if agreed to in a written statement.

Washington

Wash. Rev. Code § 49.48.010

Paycheck due when employee is fired: End of pay period.

Paycheck due when employee quits: End of pay period.

Unused vacation pay due: No provision.

West Virginia

W. Va. Code §§ 21-5-1, 21-5-4

Paycheck due when employee is fired: Next regular payday (minus withheld amount for replacement cost of employer's unreturned property).

Paycheck due when employee quits: Next regular payday (minus withheld amount for replacement cost of employer's unreturned property).

Unused vacation pay due: Only if required by policy or contract.

Wisconsin

Wis. Stat. §§ 109.01(3), 109.03

Paycheck due when employee is fired: Next payday or within one month, whichever is earlier. If termination is due to merger, relocation, or liquidation of business, within 24 hours.

Paycheck due when employee quits: Next payday.

Unused vacation pay due: Yes.

Special employment situations: Does not apply to managers, executives, or sales agents working on commission basis.

Wyoming

Wyo. Stat. §§ 27-4-104, 27-4-501, 27-4-507(c)

Paycheck due when employee is fired: Next regular payday.

Paycheck due when employee quits: Next regular payday.

Unused vacation pay due: No, if employer's policies state that vacation is forfeited upon termination of employment and the employee acknowledged the policy in writing.

Special employment situations: Requirements do not apply to commissioned sales employees if audit is necessary to determine the amount due.

Index

A

ABC test, 324, 325

Accent of employee, 226

Accidents
drug testing and, 199
drug testing of employee involved in, 33
prevention of, 190
workers' compensation and, 190, 191–192

Accommodations. *See* Reasonable
accommodations

Accountants, for tax help, 132, 134

ADA. *See* Americans with Disabilities Act
(ADA)

ADA Amendments Act (ADAAA), 234,
237–238

ADEA. *See* Age Discrimination in
Employment Act (ADEA)

Administrative employees
Equal Pay Act, applicability of, 95
exempt status of, 84–85

Adoption, and FMLA leave, 154–155

Adoption assistance programs, 130

Advertisements, for jobs. *See* Job
advertisements

Affordable Care Act, 112, 113, 114, 117

Age discrimination, 204, 221–224
avoiding claims, 224
waiver of claims in early retirement
programs, 222–223
See also Age Discrimination in
Employment Act (ADEA); Older
Workers Benefit Protection Act

Age Discrimination in Employment Act
(ADEA), 204, 221–222
businesses covered, 221
employees covered, 221
release of claims by terminated employee
and, 277

Agricultural work. *See* Farm workers

Airline pilots, drug testing of, 198

Alcohol abuse, 197, 201
ADA protections and, 34, 201
assistance program, offering, 197
employee handbook provisions, 61

Alcohol testing, state laws on, 355–369

Americans with Disabilities Act (ADA),
204, 234–258
alcoholism and, 34, 201
broad coverage of, 240
business covered by, 237
conditions and behaviors not qualifying as
"disability," 242
COVID-19, 235–236
drug abuse problems and, 34, 242
EEOC enforcement of, 257–258
emotional impairments and, 251–254
exceptions to coverage, 242–244
Family and Medical Leave Act (FMLA)
and, 167, 168–169
health and safety standards and, 255–256
impairments limiting life activity,
237–238
job descriptions and, 16, 240, 241
medical information, rules for handling, 55

Q